The Origins of the English Gentry

The gentry played a central role in medieval England, yet this is the first sustained attempt to explore the origins of the gentry and to account for its contours and peculiarities as a social formation. The book offers definition and conceptual vigour, and argues that the gentry, a kind of lesser nobility, was formed between the mid-thirteenth and the mid-fourteenth century.

The book deals with the deep roots of the gentry, but argues against views which see the gentry as formed or created earlier. It investigates the relationship between lesser landowners and the Angevin state, the transformation of knighthood, and the role of knights in the rebellion of mid-thirteenth-century England. The role of lesser landowners in the society and politics of Edwardian England is then put under close scrutiny. The book moves on to explore the effects of the explosion of commissions which took place from the 1290s onwards, the rise of the House of Commons and the emergence of justices of the peace – which produced a veritable partnership in government between the crown and the gentry. Finally it emphasises changes in social terminology and the rise of social gradation, the emergence of the county as an important focus of identity, the gentry's control over the populace, and its openness to the upward mobility of professionals.

PETER COSS is Professor of Medieval History, School of History and Archaeology, Cardiff University. His previous books include *Lordship, Knighthood and Locality: A Study in English Society c. 1180–c. 1280* (1991), *The Knight in Medieval England* (1993) and *The Lady in Medieval England* (1998).

Past and Present Publications

General Editors: LYNDAL ROPER, *University of Oxford*, and
CHRIS WICKHAM, *University of Birmingham*

Past and Present Publications comprise books similar in character to the articles
in the journal *Past and Present*. Whether the volumes in the series are collections
of essays – some previously published, others new studies – or monographs, they
encompass a wide variety of scholarly and original works primarily concerned with
social, economic and cultural changes, and their causes and consequences. They will
appeal to both specialists and non-specialists and will endeavour to communicate
the results of historical and allied research in the most readable and lively form.

For a list of titles in Past and Present Publications, see end of book.

The Origins of the English Gentry

PETER COSS
Cardiff University

CAMBRIDGE
UNIVERSITY PRESS

PUBLISHED BY THE PRESS SYNDICATE OF THE UNIVERSITY OF CAMBRIDGE
The Pitt Building, Trumpington Street, Cambridge CB2 1RP, United Kingdom

CAMBRIDGE UNIVERSITY PRESS
The Edinburgh Building, Cambridge, CB2 2RU, UK
40 West 20th Street, New York, NY 10011–4211, USA
477 Williamstown Road, Port Melbourne, VIC 3207, Australia
Ruiz de Alarcón 13, 28014 Madrid, Spain
Dock House, The Waterfront, Cape Town 8001, South Africa

http://www.cambridge.org

First published 2003
Reprinted 2004

Printed in the United Kingdom at the University Press, Cambridge

Typefaces Times 10/12 pt. and Plantin   *System* LaTeX 2$_\varepsilon$ [TB]

A catalogue record for this book is available from the British Library

ISBN 0 521 82673 X hardback

In memory of Rodney Hilton (1916–2002),
great scholar and friend

Contents

Illustrations

x

Preface

The Origins of the English Gentry stems directly from an essay published in *Past and Present* 147 (May 1995), entitled 'The Formation of the English Gentry'. In this essay I lamented the lack of conceptual rigour in the use of the term 'gentry' and offered a six-point definition. I argued, further, that the gentry was formed in 'an accelerating process' between the mid-thirteenth and the mid-fourteenth century. What follows is essentially an amplification of that study. The amplification is required because some of the issues were dealt with rather cursorily there and require a more extended treatment than I was able to give them at that time. I have been especially conscious that the process of gentry formation has not only to be described but to be fully explained. This could only be done in an extended study. In developing and refining my argument, moreover, I have also been able to take account of some important work that has been published during the intervening years.

My principal concern throughout the book has been to understand the origins of the gentry. It is intended, therefore, not as a history of the gentry *per se*, but as a contribution to that history. Of necessity, I have restricted my chronology and concentrated on the issues I consider central. I have approached the subject historiographically so that the reader can appreciate where my interpretation diverges from other, often more traditional, expositions. In doing so I have drawn on the work of a great many scholars and I have engaged constructively and, I hope, amicably with their views. I wish to acknowledge my debt to them, not only where I have concurred but also where I have disagreed. History, it should never be forgotten, is a collective enterprise and our understanding is forwarded by debate and the testing of hypotheses as much as by the accumulation of evidence.

The immediate research for this book was undertaken during the academic year 1999–2000, and I am most grateful to Cardiff University for the sabbatical leave which made it possible. It is underpinned, however, by earlier research, much of which is published elsewhere. Three of my essays, being especially germane, are republished here. In addition to 'The formation of the English gentry', which constitutes the greater part of chapter 1, these are 'Identity and the gentry *c*.1200–*c*.1340', published in P.R. Coss and S.D. Lloyd (eds.), *Thirteenth Century England II* (Woodbridge, 1988) and 'Knights, esquires and the origins of social gradation in England', published in *Transactions of the Royal Historical Society*, 6th series, vol. 5 (1995), which, with a small amount of readjustment, constitute chapters 8 and 9 respectively. I am most grateful to the Council of the Royal Historical Society for permission to reproduce the essay from its *Transactions*.

During the preparation of the book I have accumulated numerous other, more personal, debts. I would like to thank the following for their kindness in allowing me to draw directly on their unpublished theses: M.J. Fernandes, R.C. Gorski, J.S. Illsley, C.H. Knowles, T.E. MacIver, J.D. Mullan, and J.A. Quick. I owe very special thanks to Dr Richard Gorski for his great generosity in allowing me to study his lists of fourteenth-century office-holders and commissioners, and indeed for allowing me to print his Warwickshire list covering the years 1290–1348 as my Appendix V. Without this access chapter 7, in particular, would have taken a great deal longer to produce. I am most grateful, too, to David Crook of the Public Record Office, Kew, who very kindly drew my attention to the three volumes of unpublished transcriptions by C.A.F. Meekings from the dorse of the patent rolls covering the years 1232–46, and to Paul Brand who similarly drew my attention to the obsolete manuscript calendars and indexes from the Patent Rolls, still extant in the Public Record Office, covering the years 31–57 Henry III and 10–16 Edward I. These sources greatly eased the research for chapters 3 and 6. I would also like to thank Maurice Keen and Anthony Musson for allowing me to read work of theirs in advance of publication, and Ann Williams and Rosamond Faith for their close reading of an early version of chapter 2 and for saving me from error. Andrew Ayton, Clive Knowles, John Maddicott and Chris Wickham not only read the whole typescript but made innumerable suggestions and invaluable observations. I have also greatly profited from a series of stimulating conversations with Maurice Keen over a range of issues discussed in the book. Whatever its merits or demerits may prove to be, it is a much better book for the intervention of these scholars. Needless to say, they are responsible neither for its errors nor for interpretations with which they may disagree. I would also like to thank the staff of Cambridge University Press, and in particular my copy-editor, Frances Brown, for her patience in ironing out inconsistencies. And, finally, as always, I owe colossal thanks to my wife, Angela Coss, who has commented on numerous drafts of the text, perfected the footnotes, typed the index and offered liberal advice at every stage of the work.

1. *The formation of the English gentry*

In his first foray into the question as to whether there had ever been a peasant society in England Alan Macfarlane distinguished between on the one hand the common-sense or dictionary definition of peasant ('countryman, rustic, worker on the land') and on the other the technical meaning of the term.[1] In order to facilitate comparative study and in particular to answer the question whether England was in fact a peasant society, Macfarlane attempted to construct an 'ideal-type' model in the Weberian sense. In his defence of his methodology he repeats Weber's advice: 'Hundreds of words in the historian's vocabulary are ambiguous constructs created to meet the unconsciously felt need for adequate expression and the meaning of which is only concretely felt but not clearly thought-out.' And again, 'If the historian ... rejects an attempt to construct such ideal types as a "theoretical construction", i.e. as useless or dispensable for his concrete heuristic purposes, the inevitable consequence is either that he consciously or unconsciously uses other similar concepts, without formulating them verbally and elaborating them logically or that he remains stuck in the realm of the vaguely "felt".'[2] Despite such warnings, historians are often suspicious of model-building, suspecting that it may fail to locate the dynamics of a specific society and that it may cause the observer to distort his analysis in order to remain within his given framework. Nevertheless there are great gains to be had from close definition, as long as any definition or model is reformulated, even abandoned, if it fails substantially against empirical research. Not only does historical study gain in rigour, and debate become more meaningful and comprehensible, but definition also allows for more effective comparative study. The study of peasantries is a case in point.

There could hardly be a greater contrast with how the question of the 'gentry' has been handled. Indeed, the plain fact is that the study of the gentry has been

---

[1] Alan Macfarlane, *The Culture of Capitalism* (Oxford, 1987), p. 3; reprinted from David Green *et al.*, *Social Organisation and Settlement*, BAR International Series (Supplementary) 47 (ii), (Oxford, 1978).
[2] *The Culture of Capitalism*, Postscript, p. 207.

1

conducted very largely within the realms of dictionary or common-sense study. As G.E. Mingay has written:

> despite the lack of an agreed definition, 'the gentry' remains an indispensable term; it is one of those vastly convenient portmanteau expressions which historians are obliged to employ in formulating the broad generalisations that make up the main strands of the historical fabric. It is the more indispensable since it was so widely used by statesmen and writers of the past. 'The gentry' was a convenient symbol for them, too, and was evidently meaningful to their audiences.

But, as he goes on to say, in its broad usage 'the gentry' is a term more vague than helpful.[3] For no period is this truer than for the later middle ages.

One major reason for the continuance of common-sense usage of 'gentry' is undoubtedly its persistence as a living social term. It came to be used, of course, to cover the lower strata of landed society once nobility became restricted to the peerage; and, in this sense, its usage continues to the present day. However, this happened only slowly. Later sixteenth- and seventeenth-century commentators preferred to write of the peerage as the *nobilitas major* and the knights, esquires and gentlemen (to be joined after 1611 by the baronets) as the *nobilitas minor*. In common parlance, however, 'gentry', once synonymous with nobility, came to be used of the lesser nobility. Once interchangeable, these terms became complementary: 'nobility' and 'gentry'.[4] As J.V. Becket has written, 'The dissolution of the seamless noble robe, and its replacement by a distinctive nobility . . . took place gradually, until the early nineteenth-century writers were able to emphasize the loss of position.'[5] The nobility of the English gentry then became a matter of some debate. It is this narrow meaning of gentry which has been taken over into English historiography. Perhaps we should see this as one more result of the elite's success in maintaining a stable social and political system, to which the Stones have recently drawn our attention.[6]

Historians have by no means confined their use of the term gentry to England or to the age when it was a living social term. On the contrary, it has been readily exported. We read of American, Russian and Chinese gentry; we read of medieval gentry, of Anglo-Saxon gentry, and even of the gentry of the ancient world. It is used transhistorically and transculturally on the assumption that it will be readily understood. But is this not an illusion? As far as later medieval England is concerned, to look no further, it was not in fact a living social term, at least not in any way which resembles modern usage. The word gentry stems

---

[3] G.E. Mingay, *The Gentry: The Rise and Fall of a Ruling Class* (London, 1976), p. 1.
[4] See, in particular, M.J. Sayer, *English Nobility: The Gentry, the Heralds and the Continental Context* (Norwich, 1979), pp. 3–5, and J.C. Becket, *The Aristocracy in England 1660–1914* (Oxford, 1986), pp. 18–20.
[5] Becket, *Aristocracy in England*, p. 19.
[6] Lawrence Stone and Jeanne C. Fawtier Stone, *An Open Elite? England 1540–1880* (Oxford, 1984), pp. 303–6.

from 'gentrice' and its commonest usage was to indicate gentle birth and high rank or to describe the qualities shared by the gentle. For example:[7]

> He wole han pris of his gentrye ffor he was boren of a gentil hous
> > (Chaucer, *Wife of Bath's Tale*)
>
> For thy genterye, thus cowardly let me nat dye
> > (*Sir Beves of Hamtoun*)
>
> And the gentry of wymmen thare es to hafe smal fete
> > (*Travels of Sir John Mandeville*)

It was occasionally used, by extension, as a synonym for the nobility but this seems to have been comparatively rare, at least before the sixteenth century.[8]

One might have expected, therefore, that medievalists would have given some thought to definition, not least because questions of origin and questions of definition are intimately related. Their failure to do so stems partly from the factors already mentioned. But there may also be an historiographical explanation. The three great formative influences upon how medieval society has been perceived in England in recent times have been McFarlane, Postan and Hilton. Now all three, in their different ways, have advocated a broad approach to the subject and all of them have inspired studies of the gentry; but for none of the three was the gentry the central interest and the lack of rigour in matters of definition may well stem partly from this plain fact. There are no Ford lectures devoted to the origins of the gentry. Meanwhile, there has been much conceptual leaning upon early modern studies, where the problem of definition appears to be somewhat less acute.

The common-sense approach implies that the meaning of gentry is obvious. In practice, however, this is not the case, as reading the introductory chapters to studies of the medieval gentry of specific counties at specific points in time immediately makes clear. Most often scholars begin with the disarmingly simple question: Who were the gentry? One basic approach is simply to equate gentry with gentility; the gentry are all those who are accepted as, or who lay claim to being, gentle. Often this involves taking legislation or instances of recognition of the gentility of status groups at face value. After the sumptuary legislation of 1363 we can speak confidently of esquires as well as knights as gentle. The evolution of the esquire is a complex phenomenon which is as yet imperfectly understood. However, there can be little doubt that many of those so distinguished had been regarded as gentle for some time. Moreover, the same legislative act makes it clear that gentility extended beyond the esquires for it speaks of 'esquires and all manner of gentle men below the estate of knight'. And, when we look closely at thirteenth-century evidence, we become aware that gentility was by no means confined to the knights. Texts relating to household

---

[7] *OED*, 1st edn, vol. VI (1901), pp. 121–2; 2nd edn, vol. VI (1989), p. 455.

[8] The author of *Cleanness*, for example, refers to the *gentryse* of the Jews and of Jerusalem – *Middle English Dictionary*, ed. H. Kurath *et al.* (Ann Arbor, 1954–), vol. IV (1963), pp. 77–8.

or retinue make this clear enough. The *Rules* of Bishop Robert Grosseteste of 1240–2, for example, spoke not only of knights but also of gentle men (*gentis hommes*) who wore livery. Gentility is often associated with service, and most particularly with household service. But it also existed in society at large. In a famous instance in the Somerset county court in 1204, Richard Revel informed the sheriff that he and his male kin were natives and gentle men (*naturales homines et gentiles*) within their locality (*patria*).[9] The sheriff replied that so, too, was he within his. It seems certain that gentility was widely felt and articulated within society long before legislation was in place to tell us so. The notorious Statute of Additions of 1413, by which the mere gentleman appears to come of age, is equally problematic. This act offers a clear line of demarcation between gentleman and yeoman. As an idea it was to prove enduring. As Shakespeare has Somerset say to Richard Plantagenet in *Henry VI, Part One*:

> Was not thy father, Richard Earl of Cambridge,
> For treason executed in our late king's days?
> And by his treason stand'st thou not attainted,
> Corrupted, & exempt from ancient gentry?
> His trespass yet lives guilty in thy blood;
> And till thou be restor'd thou art a yeoman.

In reality, however, the line remained blurred, and in the law courts, which the act was basically designed to cover, men could be variously described as gentlemen or yeomen.[10] Moreover, the full social acceptance of the mere gentleman took some time yet to achieve, as the thorough study of esquires and gentlemen of fifteenth-century Warwickshire by Christine Carpenter makes clear.[11]

The problem of delineating the gentry, moreover, is not a problem manifested only at the lower end of the social scale. Where is the line between gentry and higher nobility? Admittedly, we appear to be on relatively safe ground once we have a stable peerage from which to differentiate the gentry. However, the restricted peerage crystallised relatively slowly. Personal summons to parliament was a flexible instrument in the time of Edward I, and some flexibility remained

---

[9] *Curia Regis Rolls*, vol. III, p. 129; for a recent discussion of this case and its implications see my *Lordship, Knighthood and Locality: A Study in English Society c.1180–c.1280* (Cambridge, 1991), p. 10.

[10] See, for example, Susan M. Wright, *The Derbyshire Gentry in the Fifteenth Century* (Chesterfield, 1983), p. 6, and Eric Acheson, *A Gentry Community: Leicestershire in the Fifteenth Century, c.1422–c.1485* (Cambridge, 1992), p. 34. Acheson writes: ' "gentleman" was adopted haltingly and with some confusion, as the omission of status and the procession of *aliases* in the Pardon Rolls reveal'.

[11] Christine Carpenter, *Lordship and Polity: A Study of Warwickshire Landed Society, 1401–1499* (Cambridge, 1992), ch. 3: 'Who Were the Gentry?'
For a wide-ranging discussion of gentility in the fifteenth century, see D.A.L. Morgan, 'The Individual Style of the English Gentleman', in Michael Jones (ed.), *Gentry and Lesser Nobility in Late Medieval Europe* (Gloucester, 1986), pp. 15–35.

throughout the greater part of the fourteenth century.[12] For earlier periods there is even more difficulty. If we are determined to stand on contemporary terminology, we have to negotiate the fluctuating and unclear concept of the baronage.[13] Some thirteenth-century barons were certainly rather insignificant figures, to mention only the least of the problems.

A second approach is to move from gentility to land. The gentry are the lesser landowners, or 'the lesser landowners with a claim to gentility'. Not only does the problem of demarcation with the higher nobility appear again – even in the fifteenth century there were some knights, like Sir John Fastolf, who were richer than some of the peers[14] – but at the lower end severe difficulties emerge. Once again, fourteenth- and fifteenth-century legislation appears to come to our aid in offering various property qualifications for holding local office – most often £20 – but in practice this is far from satisfactory.[15] It is quite restrictive, as no doubt it was intended to be. What, then, should be the cut-off point? One view, based on the income tax of 1436, defines the gentry 'very loosely' as 'all lay, non-baronial landowners with an income of £5 per annum or more from freehold property'.[16] There are advantages in adopting an all-inclusive approach; but there are also some problems. How inclusive should one be? Sources which give income levels are often unreliable, while the source of income may be as important in contemporary perceptions of status as its level. Is a rural estate the true prerequisite for gentry status? Not only do we come up against the problem of the upwardly mobile professionals, whose source of income is various, but there is also the problem of the towns. In a famous essay Rosemary Horrox argued eloquently for the existence of an urban gentry in fifteenth-century England and against the simple equation of land equals gentility. On the contrary, she points to a strong interconnection of urban and rural gentry at this time. Moreover, she suggests that although the terminology to describe the situation may have been lacking, these basic facts had long existed.[17]

---

[12] For a recent discussion of the issues see C. Given-Wilson, *The English Nobility in the Later Middle Ages* (London and New York, 1987), ch. 2.

[13] See, for example, David Crouch, *The Image of Aristocracy in Britain 1000–1300* (London and New York, 1992), pp. 106–19.

[14] See T.B. Pugh, 'The Magnates, Knights and Gentry', in S.B. Chrimes, C.D. Ross and R.A. Griffiths (eds.), *Fifteenth-Century England* (Manchester, 1972), pp. 99–100.

[15] J.M.W. Bean employs the £20 unit of assessment in the income tax of 1412 as a means of structural analysis, whilst, however, stressing its limitations (J.M.W. Bean, 'Landlords', in E. Miller (ed.), *The Agrarian History of England and Wales*, III: *1348–1500* (Cambridge, 1991), pp. 526–42.

[16] See S.J. Payling, *Political Society in Lancastrian England: The Greater Gentry of Nottinghamshire* (Oxford, 1991), p. 3.

[17] Rosemary Horrox, 'The Urban Gentry in the Fifteenth Century', in J.A.F. Thomson (ed.), *Towns and Townspeople in the Fifteenth Century* (Gloucester, 1988), pp. 22–44. See also R.L. Storey, 'Gentlemen Bureaucrats', in C.H. Clough (ed.), *Profession, Vocation and Culture in Later Medieval England* (Liverpool, 1982), pp. 90–114.

Over and above all of this we have the association of gentry with office-holding under the crown. But, naturally, the desire and capacity of men to hold office were extremely variable and some offices were more prestigious than others. Office-holding, too, has to be rejected as a sole criterion for gentry status.[18] In order to overcome these problems, scholars examining particular localities have tended to go for an amalgam of factors. Susan Wright, for example, in her study of the gentry of fifteenth-century Derbyshire, includes 'all who in the period 1430–1509 provided a knight or were distrained, served as knight of the shire, sheriff, justice of the peace, commissioner of array, escheator or tax collector, together with those who were recorded in inquisitions post mortem or in five tax returns from 1412 to 1524–7 as having an income of £5 or over or as a tenant-in-chief'.[19]

In the matter of definition, medievalists have received no clear lead from their early modern counterparts. Some have looked for a property qualification (£10 of freehold land), but most have acknowledged the obvious pitfalls in this.[20] There has been much reliance on the tripartite structure of knight, esquire, gentleman, which by the sixteenth century was certainly more entrenched. Some scholars have emphasised the role of heraldry: 'The official badge of gentility was the coat of arms and for the purposes of this study the term "gentry" has been taken to cover all families beneath the peerage which had a specific right to bear such arms.'[21] Of course, the heraldic visitations operated under the crown, from 1530 to 1688, as a means of regulating the gentry, and the kings of arms were empowered, under their commissions, to deface or remove bogus arms. In practice, however, possession of arms cannot be used quite so easily in this way. Heraldic visitations were intermittent, and not all gentry were armigerous.[22] Coats of arms may have expressed gentle status, but they did not define it. Sir Thomas Smith makes it clear in *De Republica Anglorum* (1583) that the reputation of being a gentleman came first, with the confirmation by a king of arms following, if necessary, thereafter. Moreover, such reputation was achieved by various means, including prowess at the law or study in a university. Or, as the same author puts it most famously, 'who can live idly and without manual labour and will bear the port, charge and countenance of a gentleman ... shall be taken for a gentleman'.[23] The same view was expressed by William

---

[18] And see below note 41.

[19] Wright, *The Derbyshire Gentry*, p. 4. A similar analysis opens Eric Acheson's study of the Leicestershire gentry in the fifteenth century: 'the family names gleaned from the 1428 and the 1436 subsidies, along with those who accepted the burdens of local government, provide us with our starting point of 249 families of either gentry or potential gentry status' (Acheson, *A Gentry Community*, p. 38).

[20] For a summary of views on this see Acheson, *A Gentry Community*, pp. 29–30.

[21] J.T. Cliffe, *The Yorkshire Gentry from the Reformation to the Civil War* (London, 1969), pp. 2–3.

[22] For criticism of this approach see Becket, *Aristocracy in England*, pp. 34–5, and works cited there.

[23] Sir Thomas Smith, *De Republica Anglorum: A Discourse on the Commonwealth of England*, ed. L. Alston (Cambridge, 1906), pp. 39–40. See also Sayer, *English Nobility*, pp. 3–7.

Harrison.[24] Others spoke of the gentry as being those who were exempt from labour. In practice, however, the line between gentleman and yeoman remained blurred, and contemporaries confessed to difficulties in distinguishing between them.[25] It is possible, therefore, for a historian to speak of families who were 'occasional gentry', acting only as gentry in intermittent contacts with the wider world.[26] Early modernists have difficulty, too, with professionals and with urban residents with claims to gentility.[27] In reality, neither heraldry nor the tripartite schema helps the historian very much towards a definition. If the meaning of gentry is obvious, it is certainly not obvious from our sources.

Historians have subdivided the early modern gentry in other ways, differentiating county elite from parish gentry for example, or distinguishing between upper, middling and inferior gentry.[28] Later medievalists have tended to follow suit. Wright, for example, sees an enormous gulf – in economic, political and social terms – between the knights and esquires on the one hand, the 'gentry proper' as she calls them, and the ephemeral and ambiguous category of gentlemen on the other.[29] Acheson, too, speaks of the 'economic chasm' separating esquires from gentlemen.[30] Recently, Simon Payling has added a further dimension. He concentrates upon those he calls the 'greater gentry', the dozen or so wealthy families which, as he shows, dominated in fifteenth-century Nottinghamshire.[31] These are similar, both in numbers and in activities, to the 'county governors' whom Peter Clark sees operating in sixteenth-century Kent.[32] These approaches are perfectly valid in terms of analysis, of course, and they have paid great dividends. But what has to be stressed is that they are driven by external observation and not upon contemporary perception. And what is true of the parts is true of the whole. The plain truth is that 'gentry' as employed by historians is a construct.

In this respect it may be compared with 'aristocracy', which came to be widely used in England, it has been argued, precisely because of the confusion over the concept of nobility.[33] It is often used by historians as though it were synonymous with nobility, in the wider sense of the term. However, the terms are not strictly interchangeable as aristocracy may contain stronger connotations

---

[24] See Mingay, *The Gentry*, p. 2 and Acheson, *A Gentry Community*, p. 35.

[25] David Cressy, 'Describing the Social Order of Elizabethan and Stuart England', *Literature and History* 3 (1976), pp. 29–44.

[26] P. Clark, *English Provincial Society from the Reformation to the Revolution: Religion, Politics and Society in Kent, 1500–1640* (Hassocks, 1977), p. 126.

[27] See Cressy, 'Describing the Social Order', for example, for debate around these issues. For the content of gentility in this period see, in particular, J.P. Cooper, 'Ideas of Gentility in Early Modern England', in G.E. Aylmer and J.S. Morrill (eds.), *Land, Men and Beliefs: Studies in Early Modern History* (London, 1983), pp. 43–77.

[28] See, for example, Lawrence Stone, 'Social Mobility in England', *Past and Present* 33 (1966), p. 18; Cliffe, *The Yorkshire Gentry*, p. 29.

[29] Wright, *The Derbyshire Gentry*, p. 6.   [30] Acheson, *A Gentry Community*, p. 43.

[31] Payling, *Political Society in Lancastrian England*, ch. 1, and *passim*.

[32] Clark, *English Provincial Society*, part 2.   [33] Becket, *Aristocracy in England*, pp. 20–2.

of leadership and authority, betraying its classical origins when it referred to a system of government.[34] There are no absolutes in the use of such terms.

The 'gentry', then, is a construct. The way it is used, however, leaves us open to Weber's strictures about the 'vaguely felt'. Arguably, this does have its virtues. Despite the lack of definition, historians of the English gentry have a remarkably consistent view about the parameters of their studies. A recent book on the society of Angevin Yorkshire, by Hugh M. Thomas, shows this clearly.[35] The author asserts that his book is about the gentry, and in the same mould as studies in later periods. This is shown not by conceptualisation, however, but by content. We find discussions of office-holding, of collective action, of relations with the crown and higher nobility, of crime, of manipulation of the law and arbitration, as well as of estates and improving landlords, of family, household and inheritance, and of religious sentiment. In other words, the common-sense approach to the study of the gentry is based upon a series of shared assumptions. It also allows historians to borrow fairly freely from one another in conveying a sense of, or a feel for, the society under scrutiny. When we look more closely, Thomas's recognition of gentry seems to be founded on his observation of increasing horizontal ties and of a sense of community among lesser landowners. Similarly, John Blair invokes 'the English country gentry' to describe the late Anglo-Saxon thegnage as a means of comprehending the evolution of the manor and the rise of the local parish church.[36]

But on the other hand, how can we be sure we are comparing like with like? Admittedly, there are many continuities; but, equally, there is hardly an area of life in which the fifteenth-century world, for example, was not radically different in some respects from that of the eleventh or twelfth. There is another reason why, at the present time, medievalists should concern themselves with the question of definition. Alongside the recent burgeoning of studies in the medieval gentry, what we might call the second wave, there are the beginnings of a discernible tendency to take a more evolutionary approach.[37] This is a positive development, although there are dangers. One is that the history of the gentry may be conceived as wholly linear, a question even of progress. In seeking understanding across time we need to look for breaks as well as continuities. The history of knighthood, for example, ought not to be seen as a straightforward and gradual shift from military and chivalric values to civilian duty.[38]

---

[34] See Jonathan Powys, *Aristocracy* (Oxford, 1984), esp. ch. 1.

[35] Hugh M. Thomas, *Vassals, Heiresses, Crusaders and Thugs: The Gentry of Angevin Yorkshire, 1154–1216* (Philadelphia, 1993).

[36] John Blair, *Early Medieval Surrey: Landholding, Church and Settlement before 1300* (Stroud, 1991), pp. 160–1: 'the appearance of a broad, locally-based class of minor aristocracy: the proliferation between 900 and 1066 of the English country gentry'.

[37] See, for example, Colin Richmond, 'The Rise of the English Gentry 1150–1350', *The Historian* 26 (1990), pp. 14–18, and also Carpenter, *Lordship and Polity*, pp. 39–49.

[38] As implied in Carpenter, *Lordship and Polity*, pp. 55–65. The comparative strength of fifteenth-century studies in this area carries the danger of contrasting a fifteenth-century present with a relatively undifferentiated pre-fifteenth-century past.

Another is that we may be tempted to gloss over major differences in favour of superficial similarity, side-stepping serious shifts. More rigorous definition of the gentry is, therefore, long overdue.

Perhaps too much attention has been given to the problem of delineation of the gentry. Should we not ask, rather, what distinguishes a gentry as a social formation? What are its essential characteristics? When can we speak of the existence of a gentry, and when can we not?

Some characteristics are so obvious as to require little comment. Land was an important constituent. Members of the gentry are most often local seigneurs or landowners. However, as we have observed of both later medieval and early modern society, gentility was experienced more widely than this. Which observation brings us to the second characteristic. Gentry share with greater lords a nobility or gentility which is designed to express an essential social difference between them and the rest of the population. In other words, a fairly well-developed sense of social difference must exist; or, to put it another way, the gentry is predicated upon the existence of a nobility. Whether we think in terms of nobility or aristocracy does not seriously affect the issue.[39] Neither does the less developed sense of noble privilege in England compared to continental nobilities.[40] Nor, indeed, the peculiar separation of nobility and gentry which was to develop in England. The existence, and the persistence, of gentility is sufficient. But, if preferred, we can use magnates or greater aristocracy in place of higher nobility.

The remaining characteristics of the gentry, it seems to me, can be encapsulated in a single word – territoriality. Immanent rather than declared in most studies in the subject, territoriality is crucial to the understanding of the gentry as a social formation. All landownership is, in the most basic sense, territorial; but what distinguishes the territoriality of the gentry is its collective nature. This territoriality has four essential components: collective identity, status gradation, local public office and authority over the populace.

Collective identity can be expressed in various ways. There is a natural tendency for landowners and other locally significant men to develop ties of association with others of similar station, notwithstanding any vertical relationship they may have with territorial magnates or with a distant authority. However,

---

[39] European scholars have been much exercised as to when it becomes legitimate to talk in terms of a nobility and as to whether or not it is better to envisage a vaguer, less clearly defined aristocracy giving way to a more sharply perceived and increasingly juridically defined nobility. The best introduction to these problems is probably still L. Génicot, 'Recent Research on the Medieval Nobility', in T. Reuter (ed. and trans.), *The Medieval Nobility: Studies on the Ruling Class of France and Germany from the Sixth to the Twelfth Century* (Amsterdam, 1979), pp. 17–35. Because of the difficulties in perception stemming from the use of nobility in the middle ages, David Crouch has recently argued for the adoption of aristocracy in its place: *Image of Aristocracy*, pp. 2–9.

[40] On this point see, in particular, M.L. Bush, *Noble Privilege* (Manchester, 1983), and his précis of the English situation in *The English Aristocracy: A Comparative Synthesis* (Manchester, 1984), ch. 2.

there is a qualitative difference between associations of this kind and the type of group identity which requires clear articulation of shared interests and concerns. Such interests can only be expressed through formal assemblies, whether of a local or a national kind. This is undoubtedly why historians have been so concerned about the existence or not of county communities, and why there has been so much interest in factors working for and against cohesion within local societies. Despite disagreements over the level of coherence of county societies, there can be no doubt that a capacity for collective self-expression is a vital ingredient of the gentry.

The significance of status gradations is that they express status in terms of horizontal bands, rather than in terms of service or vertical association. They result, therefore, from a type of abstract thinking which equates individuals in status terms across a given area. The major determinant of these perceived differences in grade tends to be wealth. True, other derivations of status may co-exist with the territorial one, but they are accommodated within its dominant framework.

The holding of local public office has to be understood in relation to the needs of the state or central authority. All such authority has to function by means of agents and agencies. In many cases, it works through salaried officials. In other cases, a bureaucratic solution is not feasible. It requires a high level of resource and a high degree of acceptance, especially given that revenue may have to be drawn from society in order to finance it. The alternative is to work through local society itself. This may be done, to some extent, via ties of dependency, such as vassalage. But, for the most part, it means drawing on the services of members of the local elite. From the point of view of the latter, the existence of an effective, but relatively distant, public authority is to be welcomed, as long as it remains within bounds. Between centre and locality, therefore, there is a mutual acceptance which is real but qualified. The centre may wish to define status in relation to government service; in some societies it succeeds in doing this. In others, however, it is forced to draw upon the services of men whose status and whose stake in society are anterior to the holding of office. This is the case with the gentry. Of course, there is status in unsalaried, public office; men would hardly seek it otherwise. But, to a great extent, the status acquired through office is incremental.[41]

And, finally, there is the matter of authority over the population as a whole. Naturally, the exercise of justice is the key to this. There can be no doubt that collective responsibility for the administration of justice is an important facet of the gentry. Justices of the peace figure prominently in all studies of the English gentry from the fourteenth century on. Their numbers and their duties

---

[41] It is important not to be beguiled, in this respect, by the aspirations of the crown. For an exaggerated sense of service to the crown in defining status within the emerging gentry see Carpenter, *Lordship and Polity*, ch. 3.ii.

increased significantly under the Tudors.[42] None the less, they were already a prominent feature of English society during the later medieval period. It is easy to see why they should figure so prominently in gentry studies. They became the cornerstone of English local government. Their authority extended beyond the individual, private interests of the local seigneurial courts, and eventually it superseded them. Most significantly, it was authority over a defined area, whether one is talking of the county as a whole through quarter sessions or locally over the parishes where as individuals they resided. Athough they were not formally elected by them, the justices represented the collective social power of the members of the gentry.

I would suggest, then, that the defining characteristics of the gentry as a social formation are as follows:

1 A gentry is a type of lesser nobility.
2 Although based on land and landownership, it is able to encompass other types of property, including urban property, and to accommodate a steady influx of professionals.
3 It is a territorial elite. It transcends status derived from service or personal association, on the one hand, and the authority derived from mere landlordship, on the other. Given that levels of wealth vary, there is a natural tendency towards the development of social gradation.
4 It relates to a public authority which is both active and relatively distant; that is to say, a public authority which requires the services of a local elite but which is unable to support a paid bureaucracy in the localities.
5 It seeks to exercise collective social control over the populace on a territorial basis, reinforcing individual status and power.
6 It has a collective identity, and collective interests which necessitate the existence of some forum, or interlocking fora, for their articulation.

When, then, can we speak of the existence of a gentry and when can we not? The argument of this book is that the English gentry was formed in an accelerating process from the middle decades of the thirteenth century to the mid-fourteenth. By the middle decades of the fourteenth century a recognisable gentry was in existence.

I am conscious at the outset that my view on the origins of the gentry is in contention with two others: one that regards the gentry as already present in the late Anglo-Saxon state, and one that sees the gentry as the direct and

---

[42] Among other studies, see M.L. Zell, 'Early Tudor JPs at Work', *Archaeologia Cantiana* 93 (1977), pp. 125–43; A. Hassell Smith, *County and Court: Government and Politics in Norfolk, 1558–1603* (Oxford, 1974), part 2: 'Office-Holding: Its Significance in County Politics, 1572–1603'; Clark, *English Provincial Society*, esp. ch. 4: 'The Structure of Politics: The Growth of Stability'; Cliffe, *The Yorkshire Gentry*, ch. 11: 'The Government of the County'.

immediate product of the Angevin legal reforms. It seems to me, however, that a nobility, a sufficiently broad landowning class, a central authority (in practice, kingship) and public courts are all in the nature of preconditions. They were certainly present in tenth- to twelfth-century England, but they do not in themselves signal the presence of a gentry, except perhaps under the very broadest of definitions. A more traditional argument is that it was the Angevin polity, with its institutional growth, its substantially increased liaison between localities and central government, and the sharp increase in its deployment of local men – the famous 'self-government at the king's command' – which provided the seed-bed from which the gentry grew; or, as Jean Scammell has recently put it, Henry II was the 'midwife' of the English gentry.[43] However, whilst it is undeniable that Angevin England witnessed momentous legal and governmental changes, not least the birth of the English common law, and that these changes were of significance in terms of the genesis of the gentry, it is quite another matter to envisage the gentry arising directly out of them. Moreover, such a view tends to mask the continuities that undoubtedly existed between late Anglo-Saxon and Angevin England.

Chapter 2 deals explicitly with these matters and examines the deep roots of the gentry. It takes cognisance of the challenge from late Anglo-Saxon history and reflects on the current reassessment of the Angevin legal reforms, most particularly their genesis and historical significance. However, athough I argue against the two positions outlined above, my primary purpose in the chapter is not a negative but a positive one. It is to trace the development and maturation of a lesser nobility from late Anglo-Saxon times through to Angevin England – the lesser nobility upon which the evolution of the gentry is predicated.

Chapter 3 deals more fully with the Angevin legacy by examining the role of the lesser landowners as jurors and the like and as agents of the state during the reign of Henry III. That legacy, I argue, has been seriously misunderstood through the failure to distinguish between its different dimensions, principally between the ubiquitous public obligations of knights and free men on the one hand and the receipt of high-status commissions from the crown on the other. Such commissions were enjoyed by a much narrower body of knights and others who functioned as trusted agents of the state. This failure to distinguish between distinct phenomena has created in the minds of historians a monolithic and cohesive knightly class which did not exist in this period.

The resulting distortions will be seen when we come to discuss the political relations between landowners and the state in chapter 5. In the meantime, in chapter 4, I turn to a matter which is equally significant but in large measure

---

[43] 'The Formation of the English Social Structure: Freedom, Knights, and Gentry, 1066–1300', *Speculum* 68, no. 3 (1993), p. 618.

internal to the history of the nobility itself, the transformation of knighthood from the rather all-embracing Angevin variety to the more exclusive and fully chivalric knighthood that had triumphed in England by the middle decades of the thirteenth century. The result was a stronger and better-defined elite mentality. As is well known, this phenomenon was accompanied by a serious fall in the number of knights. It is a phenomenon which needs to be explained if we are to understand the origins of the gentry correctly. This necessarily involves reviewing the debate on the crisis of the knightly class. In 1975 I published an essay entitled 'Sir Geoffrey de Langley and the Crisis of the Knightly Class in Thirteenth-Century England'.[44] This essay was wrongly formulated in certain key respects, chiefly in its chronology and in its failure to distinguish clearly between two different hypotheses, viz. Hilton's crisis hypothesis and Postan's hypothesis of decline. In chapter 5 I conduct a thorough review of the debate and its ramifications. I conclude by stressing the importance of resource issues and by reaffirming that there is a connection between instances of seigneurial failure and the more widespread phenomenon of retreat from knighthood. Both are explicable within the broad social and economic climate of the late twelfth and early thirteenth centuries, although not solely in terms of external factors acting upon the economy of lesser landowners as I had previously suggested. The discussion highlights some of the tensions which existed within landed society. The net result, however, was a more exclusive knightly class, even if the full consequences of this tended to be medium rather than short term.

Chapter 5 completes a triad of chapters that centre on the first half of the thirteenth century, by looking at the role of knights in contemporary politics. This role has tended to be distorted by historians. Many years ago R.F. Treharne wrote, famously, that the role played by the knights in the period of reform and rebellion, 1258–67, constituted a critical phase in the rise of a new class, 'a new class produced largely by the operation of the Angevin administrative machine'.[45] For him the knights were 'a small well-knit class of men, substantial in wealth, secure and authoritative in local position, expert in the art of local government, and possessing a sound knowledge of both the strength and the defects of the system which they worked'.[46] In reality, the idea that there was a wide and spontaneous involvement in a movement of reform by a cohesive knightly class schooled in collective responsibility by 'self-government at the

---

[44] *Past and Present* 68 (1975), pp. 3–37; reprinted in T.H. Aston (ed.), *Landlords, Peasants and Politics in Medieval England* (Cambridge, 1987).

[45] R.F. Treharne, 'The Knights in the Period of Reform and Rebellion, 1258–67: A Critical Phase in the Rise of a New Social Class', *Bulletin of the Institute of Historical Research* 21 (1946–8), pp. 1–12.

[46] *Ibid.*, p. 10.

king's command' is impossible to sustain. Given that knightly society was less cohesive and knightly involvement in the judicial and administrative structures of post-Angevin England more variegated than portrayed by Treharne, it is not surprising that things did not quite happen in that way. In chapter 5 I examine the political relationship between lesser landowners and the state, by means of a close study of the turbulent years 1225–7 before turning to the events of 1258–67. Much centres on the nature and functions of the county court. It is true enough that counties communicated collectively from time to time with the central government, receiving charters and addressing petitions.[47] Two features are particularly striking, however, in the relationship between the crown and the counties. One is the socially inclusive nature of the representations made at county level. The other is its prevailing negativity. The objective was to keep the government at bay. When we examine the operation of the county court more generally it hardly appears as a forum for political debate, and still less as an organ for the expression of specifically knightly interests. There are important lessons here for how we should approach the essentially baronial revolt of the year 1258.

Notwithstanding these correctives, however, the period of reform inaugurated in 1258 was something of a watershed. A relatively broad political community was asked to participate in the process of reform. In particular, a central authority now called upon county knights to act as agents channelling criticism and complaints to the government in parliament. Consequently the county was to become, in the course of time, a genuine forum to express the views of local elites. Highly significant here was the linking of local complaint with parliament and with the machinery for redress. One of the characteristic features of the English polity in the time of Edward I was precisely this integration.

The stage was being set, as it were, for the transformation of the lesser nobility into the gentry. Chapter 6 puts that stage under scrutiny. In the England of Edward I we can observe how the more exclusive knighthood which was a product of the early to mid-thirteenth century coalesced to provide a strikingly powerful vehicle for expressing the social and cultural hegemony of the higher reaches of secular society. We can also observe the role played by the knights within the Edwardian polity, a political system which both consolidated the innovations of the period of reform and at the same time preserved the function of county knights as members of judicial commissions. The motives which inspired their participation begin to be clearly observable. As is well known, the drawing of representatives to Westminster became an increasingly regular feature of this polity. The growth in regular petitioning to parliament was bound

---

[47] J.C. Holt, 'The Prehistory of Parliament', in R.G. Davies and J.H. Denton (eds.), *The English Parliament in the Middle Ages* (Manchester, 1981), pp. 1–28, and J.R. Maddicott, 'Magna Carta and the Local Community, 1215–1259', *Past and Present* 102 (1984), pp. 25–65.

to have the effect of strengthening the representative nature of the county, as the meeting of the Commons provided a regular channel for communication between government and local interests.[48]

It is likely that a stronger sense of collective identity was starting to emerge among the lesser nobility at this time. It is tempting to speak of a proto-gentry operating within the Edwardian polity. To do so, however, risks exaggerating the speed of developments, and the term might be better preserved for the early decades of the fourteenth century when several elements in what I have called the territoriality of the gentry were spectacularly enhanced. A sea change occurred, in fact, during the last two decades of the reign of Edward I, in what I call an explosion of commissions. This explosion and its consequences are the subject of chapter 7. My contention is that the gentry stems in large measure from the needs of an expanding royal government, chiefly – though by no means exclusively – owing to the increasing demands of war. A growing percentage of county knights was called upon to participate in high-level commissions of one sort or another. They functioned as tax collectors, as commissioners of array, and in various judicial capacities, including that of keeper of the peace. At the same time they were being called upon increasingly to represent their counties at parliament, a development that was itself by no means unconnected with the needs of war. By the 1320s, if not before, at least 75–80 per cent of county knights were functioning in various capacities as agents of the state.[49] What was achieved was effectively a partnership in government.

It was in the 1320s that the Commons emerged as a political force. Separated institutionally from the Lords and dominated by county knights, the Commons became the mouthpiece, one might say, of an emergent gentry. Although continuous Parliament Rolls survive only from 1339, sufficient can be pieced together from the 1320s and 1330s to show continuous pressure on the government being applied by the Commons and a strong concern with the abuse of power by the great lords.[50] A particular concern was with law and order. In short, the expression of Commons policy, fluctuating and inconsistent though it may have been, can be discerned. The three-cornered polity of the later middle ages, comprising crown, magnates and Commons, was now in place. It would be wrong, however, to concentrate solely upon events at the centre. Although we should

---

[48] The seminal work here is by J.R. Maddicott: 'The County Community and the Making of Public Opinion in Fourtenth-Century England', *Transactions of the Royal Historical Society*, 5th series, 28 (1978), pp. 27–43; 'Edward I and the Lessons of Baronial Reform: Local Government, 1258–80', in P.R. Coss and S.D. Lloyd (eds.), *Thirteenth-Century England I* (Woodbridge, 1986), pp. 1–30; and 'Parliament and the Constituencies, 1272–1377', in Davies and Denton (eds.), *English Parliament in the Middle Ages*, p. 62.

[49] To judge, that is, from a very detailed analysis of the knights of Warwickshire. See below, pp. 168–79.

[50] For a recent review of the evidence here see W.M. Ormrod, 'Agenda for Legislation 1322–c.1340', *English Historical Review* 105 (1990), pp. 1–33.

be careful not to glamorise the county court or to dismiss its shortcomings, local articulation of interests and grievances must have been greatly aided by the existence of a national body in which collective concerns could be voiced.

What partnership in government meant to local lords is best seen on the ground. The first half of the fourteenth century was crucial in terms of the development of collective control over the populace. By the middle of the fourteenth century a large measure of devolved justice had been achieved, the most significant and enduring feature of which was the transformation of the keeper into the justice of the peace.[51] To understand how this occurred we need to consider not only governmental need but also the needs of the landowners themselves, and most especially their need to participate increasingly in the exercise of royal justice. If we focus solely on the relationship between the lord and the state we can, at best, only partially comprehend. No lord could afford to neglect his material base. This meant not only the protection of one's interests through the courts, the running of estates by means of officials and the marketing of produce. It also meant dealing with peasants. Judicial authority was a matter of vital importance to lords, of whatever level. Courts were important in terms of income, of course, but they were also essential in terms of social control without which income and status, that is to say lordship, could not be assured. It is important, therefore, to consider the effect of the development of the central courts during the thirteenth century upon their judicial power. In general, the greater the growth in the jurisdiction of the central courts, the more the horizons of tenants widened. Consequently it was far better, from the landlord's point of view, that he, rather than justices coming in from outside, should handle the operation of royal courts.

To be sure, private courts had a lot of mileage in them yet; and it is important not to exaggerate the speed of change. As yet, it is a question not of a shift away from manorial control but, rather, of the emergence of an additional plane of authority. Royal jurisdiction had grown to such an extent that there was no going back, and everyone knew that. Since the landlord could not operate individually in this respect, as he could in his own court, the only recourse was for the landowners to operate collectively as justices of the peace, hearing and determining cases that came before them. Their status, collectively, would be ensured.

What the government and the professional justices preferred, no doubt, was that local men should keep the peace by receiving indictments but that justice should be done by the professionals. Equally, the higher lords stood to lose a great deal if they failed to involve themselves in the commissions and if they

---

[51] The early history of the justices of the peace has been subject to serious revision recently. This is taken on board below, pp. 181–7.

failed to influence the choice of justices. The end result was a compromise, or rather a series of compromises. The government bowed before gentry aspirations, but the justices were appointed by the crown, and their appointment generally took account of the realities of both local and central power. The JPs were drawn, therefore, from three groups: from the gentry predominantly, but also from the magnates and from the professional lawyers.

Up to the 1320s high-status commissions, of the various kinds, were predominantly the preserve of knights. From then on, however, the commission-holding elite widened to include landowners who were sub-knightly as well as administrators and lawyers. From the same decade the social groups from which the county MPs were drawn similarly widened, signalling the absorption both of successful professionals and of sub-knightly landowners into the social elite. When we study the careers of individuals it is particularly striking that professionals tend to be called upon as commissioners predominantly after their acquisition of a major stake in the land.

Two contemporary and complementary developments of major significance are dealt with in chapters 8 and 9. One is the stronger sense of identity between lesser landowners and the shire which appears to have developed during the early fourteenth century. Once again it looks as though the 1320s may be especially significant. The question of identity, however, is a difficult one, and chapter 8 takes a deliberately broad sweep across the thirteenth and early fourteenth centuries. Social identity has many dimensions and they are not mutually exclusive. Looking across the period one can detect a series of interlocking identities among provincial landowners. These include what might be described as the immediate neighbourhood, the broader locality, the lordship or component of a lordship (whether this be the vestiges of an old honour or a magnate affinity), the sub-county in some instances, and, of course, the county itself. How far county sentiment existed in the thirteenth century is a difficult question, but there are grounds for supposing it was present in at least a limited form. There are also gounds for supposing that this sentiment heightened in Edwardian England. Petitioning to parliament and interaction with the central assembly were now added to the traditional roles of the county in terms of administration and of communication with the crown. The effects of all of this became stronger over time. It is notable that during the 1320s the sheriffs were returning writs with endorsements which spoke of *milites residentes* and of knights who were *commorantes* within their counties. The evidence is fragile but it is surely indicative. Furthermore, the appearance of this terminology coincides with the time when the Commons was becoming assertive politically.

It was during this same period that the status gradations which were to be such a longstanding feature of the English gentry began to emerge. This is the subject of chapter 9. There are some indications that status was already beginning to be understood territorially during the thirteenth century. The distinctions, however, were rather inchoate. What happened in the fourteenth century was of a different order, and it became permanent. The esquire now emerged as a clear gradation below the more prestigious chivalric knight. However, this did not happen overnight. On the contrary, it was long delayed, and when it finally occurred esquire was more than just a residual category for those families who had ceased to produce knights. Notwithstanding its lingering service and military connotations, esquire now came to designate membership of a particular social rung. This was the time when esquire replaced valet as the term used to describe non-knightly retainers in indentures. It was also the time when the heads of families of local substance who had never been knightly joined the collaterals and the once-knightly in sealing heraldically. What was happening in the localities was reflected in the sumptuary legislation of 1363, when parliament attempted to regulate apparel by statute. The rung of esquire, as it finally took shape, was a fairly inclusive one, and was achieved, no doubt, at the expense of subtler, and more local, distinctions. Nevertheless there was room for considerable future development. The esquire did not subsume all of the *gentiles*, and the arrival of the gentleman in the fifteenth century produced some realignment. But the decades immediately prior to the sumptuary legislation had been crucial. The gradual working out of the territorial idea of status produced a nation-wide system of social gradation within the emergent gentry. It can hardly be coincidental that this occurred at the very time when the emergent gentry was becoming increasingly conscious of itself politically. With the appearance of definite social gradation the gentry finally came of age.

The various manifestations of the 'territoriality' of the gentry coalesced during the first half of the fourteenth century: the development of horizontal banding, the enhanced capacity for collective self-expression, the emergence of collective power over the populace and the development of a true partnership with the crown in government as opposed to mere agency of the state. By the middle of the century the gentry had been formed.

The process of gentry formation has been fully described. However, it also needs to be explained. Much of the explanation is, of course, inherent in what has gone before. The manpower needs of the state and the self-interested response to those needs take us a long way towards an understanding. The rise of the Commons and the impact of that rise upon the counties were vital ingredients. Nevertheless, there are additional social factors to be addressed, factors which help to explain the appearance of social gradation and to determine the future contours of the gentry. These are discussed in the final chapter. Why was it, I ask, that England ultimately failed to develop a caste nobility around the phenomenon of knighthood? Why was it that the future lay with a restricted nobility and a gentry which embraced the knightly, the sub-knightly and a steady influx of lawyers and other professionals? How and why did the several social groups which came to constitute the gentry combine in the manner they did? In answering these questions we are taken deep into the social structure: into the demarcation between higher and lesser nobility, into increasing professionalisation, and, most importantly, into the coincidence of interests and similarity of life-style between the knights and their fellow landowners who were directly below them.

2. The roots of the English gentry

It is the argument of this book that the social formation known as the gentry grew out of thirteenth-century conditions and that it reached fruition in the early decades of the fourteenth. Nevertheless, and especially in so far as the gentry was a form of lesser nobility, it had deep roots which stretched back to late Anglo-Saxon England. The purpose of this chapter is to examine those roots and to show how they underpinned the later gentry. At the same time I will explain why I think it is inappropriate to talk of a gentry, as yet, in either late Anglo-Saxon or Angevin England.

Close attention has been given recently to the middle strata of late Anglo-Saxon society, to the thegns and to the variety of other men who acted as intermediaries between the state and the magnates on the one hand and the mass of peasantry and townsmen on the other. A number of scholars – among them Henry Loyn, James Campbell and Richard Abels – have been struck by the similarities between the lesser landowners of the pre-Conquest state and the gentry of later times.[1] Others have been less circumspect. John Blair, in particular, has long been suggesting that the lesser landowners of late Anglo-Saxon England constituted a gentry.[2] He has recently been joined in this by Rosamond Faith.[3] Drawing on the breadth of this scholarship, and most particularly on the work of John Blair and James Campbell, John Gillingham has offered a direct

---

[1] R.P. Abels, 'An Introduction to the Bedfordshire Domesday', in *The Bedfordshire Domesday* (Alecto Historical Editions, London, 1991), p. 34: 'In 1066 the greater part of the shire belonged to a handful of wealthy king's thegns and a host of lesser landowners who *much resemble* [my italics] the country gentry and yeomanry of later times'; Henry Loyn, 'Thegns', in P.E. Szarmach, M.T. Tavormina & J.T. Rosenthal (eds.), *Medieval England: An Encyclopedia* (New York and London, 1998), pp. 731–2; James Campbell, 'England *c.* 991', in Janet Cooper (ed.), *The Battle of Maldon: Fact and Fiction* (London, 1983); reprinted in J. Campbell, *The Anglo-Saxon State* (London, 1998), p. 168.

[2] See, for example, *Early Medieval Surrey*, pp. 160–1: 'the appearance of a broad, locally based class of minor aristocracy: the proliferation between 900 and 1066 of the English country gentry'.

[3] Rosamond Faith, *The English Peasantry and the Growth of Lordship* (Leicester, 1997), e.g. p. 126: 'well before the Conquest smaller landowners with bookland . . . came to be a self-conscious class, whom there is no reason not to regard as a gentry, however anachronistic the term'.

and forthright challenge to historians of the medieval gentry. It is a challenge which we would be foolish to ignore, not least because it forces us to confront our own conceptualisation.[4]

Gillingham focuses upon what he calls 'the long eleventh century', from the battle of Maldon and Byrhtferth of Ramsay's 'Life of Oswald' in the 990s to the world of Geoffrey Gaimar in the 1130s. His lines of reasoning are as follows: First, there already existed in Anglo-Saxon England a code of honour that was at least quasi-chivalric and which contained elements that were also appropriate to what we might call civilian life. This elite mentality was shared by the men who served the king and the great lords, and many of these men were both knights and landlords in their own right. Secondly, following John Blair, he argues that the economic base from which these lesser landowners operated was essentially the same as that pertaining in later centuries, i.e. it focused upon manor and church. The emergence of this 'country gentry' was part and parcel of the drastic changes in the economy and society of the tenth and eleventh centuries which also produced nucleated villages, common field systems and the estate churches around which the modern parish system was later to crystallise. The rapid economic growth during this period not only allowed many of these men to be equipped as knights but also, most probably, resulted in a new concern over the issue of upward social mobility.

But John Gillingham is perfectly well aware that more than landholding and a code of honour is involved in the identification of a gentry. His third line of reasoning, therefore, is that, just as in later centuries, local landowners in late Anglo-Saxon England related directly to a powerful monarchy, enjoying local public office and even participating in national assemblies. Moreover, the important place occupied by shire and hundred courts in late Anglo-Saxon society, he argues, gave rise to essentially the same 'county solidarities' as were to be found in the thirteenth century and after. It is these last characteristics above all, he suggests, which distinguished 'the peculiarly English brand of the lesser nobility' which historians refer to as the gentry.[5]

The late Anglo-Saxon England depicted by Gillingham is avowedly 'Campbell's kingdom'.[6] In a series of powerful essays James Campbell has presented a compelling picture of the late Anglo-Saxon state. England was a place where strong public authority persisted, and where there was a close connection between the strength of the state, peace and prosperity.[7] It was a highly centralised

---

[4] J. Gillingham, 'Thegns and Knights in Eleventh-Century England: Who Was Then the Gentleman?', *Transactions of the Royal Historical Society*, 6th series, 5 (1995).

[5] *Ibid.*, p. 131.   [6] *Ibid.*, p. 130.

[7] See, especially, 'Was It Infancy in England? Some Questions of Comparison', in M. Jones and M. Vale (eds), *England and Her Neighbours, 1066–1453: Essays in Honour of Pierre Chaplais* (1989), pp. 1–17; 'Some Agents and Agencies of the Late Anglo-Saxon State', in J.C. Holt (ed.), *Domesday Studies* (Woodbridge, 1987), pp. 201–18; and 'The Late Anglo-Saxon State: A Maximum View', *Proceedings of the British Academy* 87 (1994), pp. 39–65. These are reprinted in Campbell, *The Anglo-Saxon State*.

state in which relations between the central authority and the localities were extremely important, and where many men, thegns and others, functioned as agents of the state.[8] Campbell, with much justice, argues that many of the institutions of tenth- and eleventh-century England resemble those of the Carolingian Empire of the eighth and ninth. English counties and hundreds with their courts recall their Carolingian counterparts. Other parallels include the general oath for the maintenance of peace imposed on all free men, the national taxation system and the system used for military service. In short, 'late Anglo-Saxon England was a state of what might be called a Carolingian type'.[9]

For Gillingham, then, Hastings was fought on the English side by nobles and gentry: 'in the continuing network of shires and hundreds we have an institutional framework which allows us to see the "lesser nobility" as a gentry – both before and after 1066'. He thus takes issue with the 'scholars who regard themselves as historians of the gentry' but who 'seem reluctant to admit that the phenomenon they are studying can have existed much before 1200, if then'. He picks out as immediate targets Jean Scammell, for whom the gentry was effectively created by Henry II's legal reforms,[10] those reforms which have long been seen as crucial in the formation of the English common law, and Hugh M. Thomas, who has argued for the Angevin period as the 'time when the gentry in some ways were first beginning to emerge as an independent force in English history'.[11]

What Gillingham fails to make clear, however, is that Thomas is himself a revisionist. Like Gillingham, he is much concerned with continuity. But, in his case, it is continuity with the future rather than the past. The Pastons, he argues, would have felt 'very much at home in Angevin Yorkshire', while the reader 'familiar with the gentry in the later Middle Ages or even of the Early Modern period may get a sense of déjà vu ... for the Yorkshire gentry, particularly by the end of the Angevin period, resembled their successors in a remarkable number of ways'.[12]

Thomas makes a strong case for continuity in social organisation and social relations between Angevin England and the fifteenth century. He shows lesser landowners involved in many of the same activities as they were to be later. We see their participation in interpersonal violence and in the manipulation of legal procedures as well as in the operation of the law courts. We hear of improving landlords. We are told of ties between gentry and magnates which were 'marked by the same fluidity that characterised bastard feudalism and subsequent patronage systems'. Moreover, 'nuclear families, family closeness,

---

[8] Campbell, 'Some Agents', p. 205.
[9] James Campbell (ed.), *The Anglo-Saxons* (Oxford, 1982), p. 241.
[10] 'Henry II', as she puts it, 'was the gentry's midwife': Scammell, 'The Formation of the English Social Structure', p. 618.
[11] Thomas, *Vassals, Heiresses, Crusaders and Thugs*.   [12] *Ibid.*, p. 193.

a sense of lineage, and lay religiosity, all characteristics of later gentry society, can also be found in the late twelfth and early thirteenth centuries'.[13]

Two characteristics, however, appear to be defining. First, with one eye on the idea of county community, traditionally seen as an important constituent of the gentry, Thomas stresses the significance of horizontal ties, especially those cutting across honorial and intracounty boundaries. He notes, in particular, marriage alliances and the lists of pledges that members of the gentry gathered to guarantee payment of proffers or other sums owed to the government, both occurring across honorial boundaries, and cites with approval the work of C.J. Wales to the same effect, i.e. 'that knights began creating such horizontal networks with little reference to honors as feudal ties declined'.[14]

The second defining characteristic is the utilisation of knights for many routine tasks of royal government in the localities:

> The use of local figures for the purposes of royal government was a practice that dated back at least to the Carolingian style government of the late Anglo-Saxon kings, if not before, but the ability of the Angevin kings to adapt this for the new and increasing tasks of their government allowed them to have a direct and growing influence on local areas at the same time as their indirect influence through the honors was decreasing.[15]

Linking through to the work of J.C. Holt and J.R. Maddicott, Thomas sees important political consequences of these developments. In 1215 'gentry support allowed the rebel barons to achieve their important if incomplete successes in reforming and limiting royal government' and 'the precedent for gentry involvement and influence in politics had been set and this precedent lay behind the growing activism of gentry that Maddicott describes for the reign of Henry III'.[16] The historiographical position which Thomas is effectively seeking to revise is more often implicit rather than explicit in later medievalists' work.[17] However, Colin Richmond has spoken of the gentry as 'the class which was to dominate England from the fourteenth to the nineteenth century' and considers the century or so after 1200 as being the era of the proto-gentry.[18] I have argued myself that the gentry was formed in an accelerating process from the mid-thirteenth century to the mid-fourteenth and have offered a definition.[19]

---

[13] *Ibid.*, p. 193.

[14] *Ibid.*, p. 185, fn. 58, citing C. Wales, 'The Knight in Twelfth Century Lincolnshire' (Cambridge PhD thesis, 1983), pp. xxxiii–xxxv, 89–91, 93–4, 213–60, 283–5.

[15] Thomas, *Vassals, Heiresses, Crusaders and Thugs*, pp. 174–5.   [16] *Ibid.*, pp. 190, 191n.

[17] It should be noted, however, that Thomas is somewhat hesitant in employing the term gentry, as it has no contemporary resonance. He chooses it as 'the least unsatisfactory' term to describe the 225 families who are the subject of his inquiry and because of its 'historiographical connotations' (*ibid.*, pp. 10–11).

[18] Richmond, 'The Rise of the English Gentry', pp. 14–18. The quotation comes from p. 14.

[19] See above, pp. 9–11.

Thus there are not two perspectives on the origins of the gentry but three.[20] In concentrating his fire against Thomas and Scammell, one cannot help feeling that Gillingham has limited his target. His evidence and his arguments need to be set not only against those for Angevin England but also against a model derived from the fourteenth century, where it is universally agreed that a fully fledged gentry was in existence. There is, moreover, a particular difficulty with the Gillingham position. He wishes to argue for the Anglo-Saxon origins of the gentry whilst, at the same time, maintaining its peculiarity as a type of lesser nobility. This thesis is, I think, essentially untenable. There is clearly a great deal to be said for regarding late Anglo-Saxon and Angevin England as societies of the Carolingian type. It is possible to argue that they contained a weak, or embryonic, gentry which became the strong, or mature, gentry of later times. However, to do so implies the likely existence of gentries elsewhere within the Carolingian Empire.[21] If we go down this road, the specificity of the English gentry would soon begin to dissolve.

What I want to suggest here, however, is a rather different perspective: an evolutionary one. In this perspective, the institutions of Anglo-Saxon England constituted part of the raw material from which the gentry was ultimately derived. Late Anglo-Saxon history is a minefield, especially for the non-specialist, and the role of the lesser landowners impinges on some of its most difficult and contentious aspects. However, recent advances in scholarship make it feasible to attempt a comparative history of lesser landowners at different points in time.

Gillingham centres his analysis around the 4,000–5,000 'middling landowners' in 1066 revealed by Domesday Book. On close inspection, however, the society of Anglo-Saxon England was considerably more complex than this simple revelation might imply. Anglo-Saxon law codes distinguished between those men of high status who enjoyed a higher *wergeld*, or bloodprice, than the ordinary free men and whose rights and obligations were generally calculated differently. From the seventh century such men were generally described as gesiths (the king's companions), but this term gradually gave way before thegn.[22] The eleventh-century thegns, however, were far from being undifferentiated. The laws of Cnut (II Cnut 71) make the very important distinction between king's thegns and mean or median thegns when it comes to the heriot

---

[20] Perhaps four if we include Robert Palmer's suggestion that the gentry was effectively brought into existence by the state's need to implement labour legislation after the Black Death (Robert Palmer, *English Law in the Age of the Black Death, 1348–1381: A Transformation of Government and Law* (Chapel Hill and London, 1993), pp. 14–27).

[21] The Breton machtiern comes first to mind. See Wendy Davies, *Small Worlds: The Village Community in Early Medieval Brittany* (London, 1988), esp. pp. 138–42 and ch. 7.

[22] See, specifically H.R. Loyn, 'Gesiths and Thegns in Anglo-Saxon England from the Seventh to the Tenth Century', *English Historical Review* 70 (1955), pp. 529–49, and for an excellent general discussion the same author's *Anglo-Saxon England and the Norman Conquest* (London, 1962), ch. 5, 'Kingship and Nobility', and *The Governance of Anglo-Saxon England 500–1087* (London, 1984), ch. 2, 'Kingship and the Ranks of Men'.

they owed the king.[23] Amongst laymen it was principally, perhaps exclusively, the king's thegns who enjoyed the judicial privileges involved in sake and soke, privileges that certainly rendered profits of justice and may have involved the convening of private courts.[24]

However, the differentiation between king's thegns and median thegns was only part of the story. There was undoubtedly an upper layer of king's thegns, many of them of old ealdormanic families, who with the few great earls constituted the nobility of Anglo-Saxon England. These are the men described as *proceres* (chief men), *optimates* (best men), *magnates* (great men) and the like in the sources; magnates in modern usage. There were probably not more than about a hundred landholders in this category, although to be sure there is no clear line of demarcation. Peter A. Clarke's ninety men who held £40 worth of land or more in Edward the Confessor's England constitute perhaps the closest modern approximation.[25] The *Liber Eliensis* differentiates the *proceres* from other thegns on the basis of holding forty hides of land and suggests that endogamous marriage was the norm for at least the daughters within this restricted group.[26] In other words, in Anglo-Saxon England there was very definitely a narrow nobility, just as there was in contemporary societies on the continent.[27] It was men from this group, figures like Ealdorman Byrhtnoth, who lost his life at the battle of Maldon, and great thegns like Wulfric Spot, the founder of Burton Abbey – regional magnates and nobility under any definition[28] – who, together with the eleventh-century earls, were the men most likely to have

---

[23] *Die Gesetze der Angelsachsen*, 3 vols., ed. F. Liebermann (Halle, 1903–16), vol. I, pp. 358–9.

[24] For the argument that sake and soke was restricted to king's thegns see David Roffe, 'From Thegnage to Barony: Sake and Soke, Title, and Tenants-in-Chief', in Marjorie Chibnall (ed.), *Anglo-Norman Studies*, XII: *Proceedings of the Battle Conference 1989* (Woodbridge, 1990), pp. 157–76. See also R.R. Reid, 'Barony and Thanage', *English Historical Review* 35 (1920), pp. 161–99. For some cautionary remarks, however, see Peter A. Clarke, *The English Nobility under Edward the Confessor* (Oxford, 1994), pp. 130–2.

[25] *The English Nobility*, ch. 2, 'The Largest Non-Earlish Estates'. K. Mack lists seventy thegns with £60 land or more: see Robin Fleming, *Kings and Lords in Conquest England* (Cambridge, 1991), p. 65, note 47.

[26] *Ibid.*, pp. 31–4.

[27] See Crouch, *Image of Aristocracy*, esp. pp. 2–3 and references given there. For a recent discussion of nobility in Old English see Jane Roberts, 'The Old English Vocabulary of Nobility', in Anne J. Duggan (ed.), *Nobles and Nobility in Medieval Europe: Concepts, Origins, Transformations* (Woodbridge, 2000), pp. 69–84.

[28] For Wulfric Spot and for a general discussion of such figures see Pauline Stafford, *Unification and Conquest: A Political and Social History of England in the Tenth and Eleventh Centuries* (London and New York, 1989), ch. 9. For some more recent studies of other regional magnates and their families see the following essays by Ann Williams: '*Princeps Merciorum Gentis*: The Family, Career and Connections of Ælfhere, Ealdorman of Mercia', *Anglo-Saxon England* 10 (1981), pp. 143–72; 'Land, Power and Politics: The Family and Career of Odda of Deerhurst' (published by The Friends of Deerhurst Church, 1997); and 'A West-Country Magnate of the Eleventh Century: The Family, Estates and Patronage of Beorhtric Son of Ælfgar', in K.S.B. Keats-Rohan (ed.), *Family Trees and the Roots of Politics* (Woodbridge, 1997), pp. 41–68. See also Fleming, *Kings and Lords in Conquest England*, part 1, 'Cnut's Conquest'.

adopted the courtly manners to which John Gillingham, following Stephen Jaeger, has referred.[29]

When we look at the thegnage more broadly, however, we begin to appreciate that late Anglo-Saxon England was not a static society but a dynamic one. Much emphasis has been placed in recent years upon the fragmentation of the great or 'multiple estates' and its consequences, including the growth of myriad small estates, the forerunners of the manors that are so familiar to students of medieval England.[30] To take just one example, the break-up of the old and large estate at Fawsley, Northamptonshire, created four small manors between 944 and 1023, and two of these had been split up into eight by the time of Domesday Book.[31] These small estates arose in a variety of ways, and the reality was probably more complex than the fragmentation model implies,[32] but there can be no doubt that at the heart of the process lay reward for service, the rewarding of members of private bureaucracies and of agents of the state, and the provision of warriors with land. In addition, there appears, in some areas at least, to have been an active land market. The result was a diverse and dynamic landowning sector. At the top end of this were the king's thegns with their bookland (land held by charter). Others held leased land (or loanland), especially from the great religious houses. On this land, howsoever derived, the thegns built their residences and often perhaps reorganised the settlement to suit the new arrangement, creating nucleated villages and associated field systems.[33] Many of these residences, situated within defensible enclosures and increasingly, no doubt, including both a hall and a private bower, are revealed by place-names ending in -burh or tun.

In an eleventh-century tract known as the 'promotion law' we are told that 'if a ceorl prospered so that he had fully five hides of his own land, church and kitchen, bell house and burh-geat, seat and special office in the king's hall, then was he thenceforward entitled to the rank of thegn'. It has been convincingly

---

[29] 'Thegns and Knights', pp. 147–9. C. Stephen Jaeger, The Origins of Courtliness: Civilizing Trends and the Formation of Courtly Ideals 939–1210 (Philadelphia, 1985).

[30] For a recent overview of the evidence see Faith, English Peasantry and the Growth of Lordship, ch. 6, 'The Growth of Small Estates and the Beginnings of the Seigneurial Life'.

[31] This example is taken from P. Stafford, The East Midlands in the Early Middle Ages (Leicester, 1985), pp. 34–9; Faith, English Peasantry and the Growth of Lordship, p. 155.

[32] The 'multiple estate' model has been brought into question, while some of the small estates were undoubtedly created 'from below'. For a recent review of the literature and the arguments see D.M. Hadley, The Northern Danelaw: Its Social Structure, c.800–1100 (London, 2000), pp. 24–6, 85–8. Hadley writes: 'In addition to the breaking up of large early territories "from above", the creation of small estates also went on "from below". Together these processes gave rise to the complex and varied pattern of estate structure recorded by Domesday Book' (ibid., p. 163).

[33] The agency by which villages were nucleated and field systems reorganised is a matter of some debate. For a recent study, which reviews the arguments and dismisses mono-causal explanations – and indeed agents – see C. Lewis, P. Mitchell-Fox and C. Dyer, Village, Hamlet and Field: Changing Medieval Settlements in Central England (Manchester, 1997).

argued that this tract conveys the principal marks of thegnly status.[34] Its most significant item, arguably, is the *burh-geat*. *Burh* means fortification and the *burh-geat* (the gate of the *burh*), therefore, indicates a fortified manor house. The gatehouse would be the most important feature of a fortified enclosure surrounding the manor house. The bell-tower may also suggest a church tower forming part of a lord's enclosure or *burh*. These features fit well with the excavations of the manor houses at Goltho in Lincolnshire and Sulgrave in Northamptonshire. Both show a large hall with bank and ditch. At Sulgrave, which belongs to the early eleventh century, there are associated buildings including what appears to have been a kitchen as well as a church.[35]

A thegnly residence of this type is indicated in a writ of Edward the Confessor dated between 1042 and 1046 by which he confirmed to Westminster Abbey the estate granted by Azur Swart (the Black) and his wife Ælfgyth. This was the *burh* of Wennington in Essex, with its four hides of land, church and churchsoke, together with land called 'At the Lea'.[36] The reference to churches in all of this is of great significance. Estate churches were constructed to serve both the lord and his family and the peasant tenants where nucleation had occurred. The church would often be in close proximity to the manor house. No doubt it afforded greater control over an increasingly subject peasantry.[37] In the early twelfth century the legal work known as the *Leges Henrici Primi* brings the manor court, or hall-moot, clearly into view.

It was by this complex process that the seigneurial class of medieval England came into existence: 'Certainly on the firm foundations of the security of tenure

---

[34] For what follows see Ann Williams, 'A Bell-House and a Burh-Geat: Lordly Residences in England before the Norman Conquest', in C. Harper-Bill and Ruth Harvey (eds.), *Medieval Knighthood IV* (Woodbridge, 1992), pp. 221–40. For the text, known as the *Gethynctho*, and now attributed to Archbishop Wulfstan, see *Die Gesetze*, ed. Liebermann, vol. I, pp. 456–8, *English Historical Documents*, vol. I, ed. D. Whitelock (London, 1955), pp. 468–9, and P. Wormald, *The Making of English Law: King Alfred to the Twelfth Century*, vol. I: *Legislation and Its Limits* (London, 1999), pp. 391–4. See also F. M. Stenton, 'The Thriving of the Anglo-Saxon Ceorl', in D.M. Stenton (ed.), *Preparatory to Anglo-Saxon England: Being the Collected Papers of Frank Merry Stenton* (Oxford, 1970).

[35] For the excavations at Goltho see Guy Beresford, *Goltho: The Development of an Early Medieval Manor c.850–1150* (Historical Buildings and Manuscript Commission for England, 1987). For Sulgrave see B. Davidson, 'Excavations at Sulgrave, Northamptonshire, 1960–76' (*Archaeological Journal* 125 (1968), pp. 105–14). See also G. Cadman and G. Foard, 'Raunds, Manorial and Village Origins', in M.L. Faull (ed.), *Studies in Anglo-Saxon Settlement* (Oxford, 1984), pp. 81–100, and John Blair, 'Hall and Chamber: English Domestic Planning 1000–1250', in G. Meirion-Jones and M. Jones (eds.), *Manorial Domestic Building in England and Northern France*, Society of Antiquaries of London, Occasional Papers 15 (London, 1993), pp. 1–21.

[36] See F.E. Harmer, *Anglo-Saxon Writs* (Manchester, 1952), no. 73.

[37] As Rosamond Faith writes, 'The close links that were evolving in late Anglo-Saxon England between seigneurial curia and seigneurial church provided a setting in which a much closer degree of social control could be exercised by landowners over peasants who were also the congregations of "their" churches' (*English Peasantry and the Growth of Lordship*, p. 167). Not all churches owed their origins to lords, however. Some were built by collective action on the part of prosperous peasantry.

given by bookland, a long lease from a local monastic house, or part of their family's inherited land, the lesser landlords of later Anglo-Saxon England were able to build their "magnate farmsteads" and strike the roots of the seigneurial life.'[38]

There can be no doubt that by the eleventh century England was sustaining a larger number of landowners than ever before.[39] However, these landowners were very far from homogeneous. In the countryside the considerable differences in the wealth of landowners must have been obvious. And not only in the countryside. Robin Fleming has shown just how involved the late Anglo-Saxon landholders were with towns and with town life.[40] Even below the level of king's thegn the thegnage covered a spectrum of wealth and status. The wealthier and more prestigious thegns, in particular, had thegns of their own.[41] Moreover, some of the men who were rewarded with major holdings as the multiple estates split were not thegns at all. In the west midlands we hear, for example, of radknights and radmen (riding-men), who were effectively mounted retainers or servitors, and of geneats whose services were essentially honourable, though they were not thegns. In the Danelaw the upper reaches of free men (sokemen and *liberi homines*) overlapped with thegns, while in parts of the north there were figures such as drengs whose services seem to have conferred honourable status.

This was a society undergoing change: change that was gathering speed across the eleventh and twelfth centuries. The very elaborate fortified manor houses, revealed by excavations at Goltho, Raunds and Sulgrave, and described in the 'promotion law', must in reality have pertained more to the upper strata of king's thegns and the like. The construction of manor houses was very probably a long drawn out process across the tenth to the twelfth centuries. And the same will have been true of estate churches.[42] The period from *c*.1050 to *c*.1150, in particular, has been described as a time of a 'Great Rebuilding' of ordinary churches.[43] In fact, many extant churches which had once been thought to be architecturally 'Anglo-Saxon' were probably built by English-trained masons in the half-century following the Conquest.[44] In short, what we are witnessing

---

[38] Faith, *English Peasantry and the Growth of Lordship*, p. 176.

[39] 'The aristocracy in the eleventh century was almost certainly more numerous, absolutely and relatively, than it had been in the seventh century': Loyn, *Anglo-Saxon England*, p. 223.

[40] See Robin Fleming, 'Rural Elites and Urban Communities in Late-Saxon England', *Past and Present* 141 (1993), pp. 3–37.

[41] As indicated by the *Gethynctho*; see above note 34.

[42] See, especially, John Blair (ed.), *Minsters and Parish Churches: The Local Church in Transition 950–1200* (Oxford, 1988), pp. 1–19. See also the same author's *Early Medieval Surrey*, chs. 4–6.

[43] See Richard Gem, 'The English Parish Church in the Eleventh and Early Twelfth Centuries: A Great Rebuilding?', in Blair, (ed.), *Minsters and Parish Churches*, pp. 21–30.

[44] Moreover, 'from *c*.1050 onwards new churches were built, and old ones rebuilt, in a more permanent and imposing form, a change which reflected a gradual progress of local churches at all levels towards greater permanence and stability': John Blair, 'Local Churches in Domesday Book and Before' in Holt (ed.), *Domesday Studies*, pp. 265–78. The quotation is from p. 275.

in all of this is the formation of a broad seigneurial class. With it came the realisation of a lesser nobility.[45] This was a protracted process but one whose foundations were undoubtedly laid in Anglo-Saxon England.

It has become fashionable recently to prefer the use of the term aristocracy rather than nobility when analysing the upper reaches of society in the high middle ages.[46] Aristocracy is not, of course, a contemporary term and its use allows historians to describe a broad elite of landholders without having to trouble over who was regarded as noble or not, given that the ascription of noble was subject to change, even fluctuations.[47] But its advantage is also its disadvantage, that is to say it masks contemporary distinctions at the same time as it obviates the need for precise delineation. Contemporary perceptions *are* important. Given the clear differentiation in the sources between the *proceres* and the rest, it would be better perhaps to describe the thegns of late Anglo-Saxon England as part of a broad aristocracy whilst restricting the term nobility to those to whom contemporary society accorded the higher status. This would allow the historian, witnessing the stronger articulation of gentility and the increasingly wide adoption of its attributes, to perceive the formation and extension of a true lesser nobility out of that broad aristocracy during the eleventh and twelfth centuries.[48]

How did this Anglo-Saxon aristocracy function? What were its essential characteristics? The first point to make is that it was a service aristocracy. In the words of Ann Williams, 'the English aristocracy as a whole was a service aristocracy, in which status was defined not only by birth and wealth, but by the status of the lord to whom service was due: thus the laws of Cnut distinguish between the king's thegn, who served the king, and the median thegn, who served some other lord'.[49] The word thegn itself has strong service connotations.

---

[45] It is appropriate that Rosamond Faith should speak of the lesser king's thegns in precisely those terms. See *English Peasantry and the Growth of Lordship*, p. 157.

[46] See the arguments of Crouch in *Image of Aristocracy*, Introduction.

[47] Thus, Judith Green, for example, employs the term aristocracy 'to reflect the peculiar combination of birth, wealth and power' found in that land of opportunity which was Anglo-Norman England. The chronicler Orderic Vitalis, by contrast, tends to restrict the attribute noble to those families who had been great in pre-Conquest Normandy: Judith Green, *The Aristocracy of Norman England* (Cambridge, 1997), Introduction, esp. pp. 7–9. Nevertheless, Judith Green uses aristocracy in a more restricted sense than I am suggesting here.

[48] In practice some historians use both terms simultaneously but distinctively, which is what I am suggesting, perhaps more self-consciously, here. See, for example, Paul Dalton, *Conquest, Anarchy and Lordship: Yorkshire 1066–1154* (Cambridge, 1994).

[49] Williams, 'Land, Power and Politics', p. 8. It is indicative that *taini* are listed together with *ministri* and *servientes* at the end of the surveys for some of the counties in Domesday Book. It seems likely that most if not all of those described as *taini* in Domesday Book were in royal service, which is precisely how they came to survive as landholders. However, many of these were relatively lowly men, and are not to be confused with the king's thegns (*cyninges thegnas*) of pre-Conquest days. See Ann Williams, *The English and the Norman Conquest* (Woodbridge, 1995), ch. 5: 'The Service of the King'. For David Roffe they are, in effect, the king's own median thegns who did not have bookland or soke ('From Thegnage to Barony', p. 170).

It is present in the derivation of the term: 'one who serves', later 'a powerful one who serves'.[50] When thegn is translated into Latin the equivalent term is most usually *minister*.

Thegns occupied an important place within a strongly service-orientated society. But service was by no means peculiar to them. James Campbell has shown that 'the number of men, below the level of sheriff, who were in some sense agents of the government, was very large'.[51] However, it was not just a matter of service to the state. Lords with large scattered estates to control needed riding-men, for example, to help in holding them together, hence the radmen and geneats of the sources. It is in the context of service that we should understand the Anglo-Saxon cniht. In function the cniht was very similar if not identical to the Norman *miles*. He was essentially a retainer in the service of his lord. He would fight when called upon to do so. But he also provided escort, hunting and similar duties.[52]

Lordship was an overwhelmingly powerful ingredient in the society of Anglo-Saxon England. Even if Maitland's vision of a country increasingly dominated by private franchises is no longer secure and the older view that the judicial rights of great lords were restricted to a share in the profits of justice rather than the direction of justice itself is back in fashion,[53] the greater lords certainly manipulated the public law courts. The 'trustworthy persons', for example, whom Bishop Wulfstan of Worcester was able to call on in support of his jurisdictional claims before the Domesday commissioners are yet another indication of where power actually lay, and how power actually operated, in the Anglo-Saxon localities.[54] Wherever we look we see vertical lines of association. The *hlaford* (lord) was central to the system of law enforcement. Domesday Book shows us that commendation, whether to lord or to landlord, was a vital element in late Saxon society.[55] The military side to aristocratic life tells the same story. Lordship played a vital role in military organisation and in military action. Loyalty to one's lord as well as to one's king is the dominant message of *The Battle of Maldon*.[56] The up-to-the-mark war-gear enjoyed by an increasing number of

---

[50] Loyn, 'Gesiths and Thegns', p. 529.   [51] 'Some Agents', p. 205.

[52] Peter Coss, *The Knight in Medieval England 1000–1400* (Stroud, 1993), pp. 12–13.

[53] For this view and for the history of the debate on the question of 'immunities' in Anglo-Saxon England see Patrick Wormald, 'Lordship and Justice in the Early English Kingdom: Oswaldslow Revisited', in Wendy Davies and Paul Fouracre (eds.), *Property and Power in the Early Middle Ages* (Cambridge, 1995), pp. 114–36.

[54] *Ibid.*, pp. 123–5.

[55] For a recent discussion of the implications of commendation on the ground see Abels, 'An Introduction to the Bedfordshire Domesday', pp. 32–40.

[56] On the military role of lordship see, especially, Richard P. Abels, *Lordship and Military Obligation in Anglo-Saxon England* (London, 1988). For the most recent work on the battle of Maldon see Donald Scragg (ed.), *The Battle of Maldon AD 991* (Oxford, 1991) and Cooper (ed.), *Battle of Maldon*.

thegns was largely supplied by their lords, as the continuing importance of heriots (the obligatory return of war-gear from man to lord upon death) signifies.[57]

In short, this society was dominated by vertical lines of association, even if the pattern was not a neat one and the lord a man commended himself to was not necessarily the lord of his land. Even the relationship between the thegnage and the king is in one sense merely a form of vertical relationship, heavily imbued with the notion of lordship. By contrast, it is the preponderance of horizontal over vertical ties, it will be recalled, which underlies the view of Hugh Thomas that the lesser landowners of Angevin England constituted a gentry.

On the other hand, it could be argued that the heavy preponderance of vertical over horizontal ties is to some degree a product of the sources upon which the historian of Anglo-Saxon England has to rely. Moreover, if horizontal ties cannot easily be shown they can be surmised. John Blair has pointed to one local scenario from which horizontal ties, based upon neighbourhood, can be deduced. Of the thirteen thegns who witnessed the lease of Great Tew by the abbey of St Albans to Tova, widow of Wihtric in 1050–2, five are linked by the preposition *aet* to Oxfordshire place-names. They were, suggests Blair, 'a group of gentlemen-farmers: Tova's friends and neighbours'. 'We cannot know if these people normally used toponymic surnames, but their names as stated in the lease are strikingly like those adopted by minor manorial lords in the twelfth and thirteenth centuries. The impression is of a gentry firmly rooted in the land.'[58] Such ties logically persisted during the Anglo-Norman period, where they underlay the honour. They are a natural consequence of neighbouring lordship.

There must surely have been horizontal ties, too, between members of county-based elites. Ann Williams has recently pointed to the existence of 'a coherent group of neighbours who dominated the local society of Kent',[59] while Richard Abels has identified 'a coterie of thegns whose wealth and influence set them above their neighbours' in the Bedfordshire of 1066. Below these lay 'a host of lesser landowners who much resemble the country gentry and yeomanry of later times'.[60] This structure, with a group of landholders operating below the level of the truly national figures and the magnates of broader, regional interests is one which the historians of later medieval gentry would easily appreciate and recognise. That there existed horizontal ties between at least some of their number is hardly to be doubted. It is likely, too, that ties existed between men

---

[57] See, in particular, N.P. Brooks, 'Arms, Status and Warfare in Late Saxon England', in David Hill (ed.), *Ethelred the Unready*, BAR British Series 59 (Oxford, 1978), pp. 81–103.

[58] John Blair, *Anglo-Saxon Oxfordshire* (Stroud, 1994), pp. 138–40.

[59] Ann Williams, 'Lost Worlds: Kentish Society in the Eleventh Century', *Medieval Prosopography* 20 (1999), pp. 51–74.

[60] Abels, 'An Introduction to the Bedfordshire Domesday', p. 34.

commended to the same lord, which, at the lower levels in particular, will have reinforced ties of neighbourhood. We generally lack the sources that would give us details of marriage alliances and of people acting as surety for one another in civil matters.[61] Nevertheless, though subordinate to lordship, horizontal ties must have co-existed with it, and sometimes even reinforced it.

Whether such horizontal ties could result in the articulation of sectional interests on the part of the late Anglo-Saxon thegnage, however, is quite another matter. This brings us to the assemblies, national and local, in which John Gillingham envisages his Anglo-Saxon 'gentry' playing a major role. He makes much of the Anglo-Saxon Chronicle's report of thrice-yearly crown wearings attended by 'all the powerful men over all England, archbishops and bishops, abbots and earls, thegns and knights (cnihtas)'.[62] What is being envisaged here, however, is far from clear. Are we dealing perhaps with an amalgam of important king's thegns and the like on the one hand and the magnates' companions and followers on the other? It seems unlikely that the chronicler was envisaging a mass of petty landholders. But even if he were, we are a long way indeed from the representation, petitions, public opinion and legislation of the fourteenth-century parliaments, and from the articulation between county and parliament which was to be such an important ingredient of the English gentry.

What, then, of the shire? John Gillingham has pointed to the counties oper-ating as military and political entities. After the monarchy the shire court was, arguably, 'the most important institution in Anglo-Saxon England'. It was 'a folk-court, the shire or the comitatus in action'. Although it met only twice a year, its meetings were 'public events, social as well as legal occasions'.[63] Attendance at the shire court was wide, but they were presided over by ealdor-men and bishops and dominated by magnates. The extant evidence overwhelm-ingly suggests this. The lease of Great Tew in Oxfordshire which dates from 1050–2, for example, indicates immediately where power lay at the Oxfordshire county court. The witness list comprises Bishop Ulf of Dorchester, Earl Leofric of Mercia, the abbots and communities of Abingdon and Eynsham, 'Vagn and all the earl's housecarls', thirteen thegns, the portreeve of Oxford, the earl's reeve and 'all the townsmen'. As John Blair points out, 'What emerges clearly from all this is the prominence of Earl Leofric, turning up to the shire court in

---

[61] For a marriage agreement between two Kentish thegns see *Anglo-Saxon Charters*, ed. A.J. Robertson (Cambridge, 1956), no. 77, and Williams, 'Lost Worlds', pp. 10, 24. For a list of sureties, for the estates of Peterborough Abbey, see *Anglo-Saxon Charters*, ed. Robertson, no. 40. See also Fleming, *Kings and Lords*, ch. 2: 'Cnut's Conquest and the Destruction of the Royal Kindred'.

[62] 'Thegns and Knights in Eleventh-Century England', p. 133.

[63] Loyn, *Governance of Anglo-Saxon England*, pp. 138–40. See also Patrick Wormald, 'Char-ters, Law and the Settlement of Disputes in Anglo-Saxon England', in W. Davies and P. Fouracre (eds.), *The Settlement of Disputes in Early Medieval Europe* (Cambridge, 1986), pp. 149–68.

the doubtless forbidding company of his Danish household troops.'[64] Patrick Wormald writes similarly of the famous Herefordshire case in the reign of Cnut when a lady effectively disinherited her son in favour of her kinswoman: 'given that the winning party was the wife of the most powerful local magnate, the loser stood no chance'.[65] Certainly thegns, including median thegns, participated in the shire court, and one can see them as forerunners of the later knights of the shire if one wishes,[66] but what comes across loud and clear is the dominant presence and the power of a fairly restricted nobility. Whatever else they were, these were not county courts operating as the mouthpiece of a lesser nobility.

The humbler hundred court with its monthly meetings must undoubtedly have impinged more on the lives of most median thegns and the like.[67] In the Wantage Code, providing for public security in the Danelaw, Æthelred stipulated that the twelve leading thegns in each wapentake should swear on holy relics that they would not accuse any innocent man or shield any guilty one, and allowed for majority verdicts from them. The thegns' oath-helping duties that figure elsewhere in Æthelred's laws were also most probably exercised very largely in the hundred and wapentake courts.[68] Even in these courts, however, there is every reason to suppose that magnate influence will have been strong, whether they were under private control or not.

Magnate influence must also have been important when it came to the dissemination of a code of honour. This is the area to which Gillingham pays most attention, and he has no difficulty in showing that a code of honour that one might describe as, at least, quasi-chivalric did indeed exist in Anglo-Saxon England, although he also shows that it developed in important ways in subsequent decades.[69] Here he is in good company. The work of Karl Leyser and Janet Nelson, in particular, has suggested that an earlier generation of historians has

[64] Blair, *Anglo-Saxon Oxfordshire*, p. 107. He goes on to suggest that the earl's reeve was exercising the shrieval functions as no royal sheriff is named.

[65] 'Charters, Law and the Settlement of Disputes', p. 167. For the details of this case see *Anglo-Saxon Charters*, ed. Robertson, no. 78. See also the record of Bishop Æthelwold's acquisition of an estate at Downham in Cambridgeshire reported in the *Liber Eliensis*: Stafford, *Unification and Conquest*, pp. 131–3.

[66] Loyn, *Governance of Anglo-Saxon England*, p. 148: 'Many thegns in the tenth and eleventh centuries exercised functions that would not have been utterly strange to the knights of the shire in the central medieval period.'

[67] For the hundred court see, in particular, H. Loyn, 'The Hundred in England during the Tenth and Early Eleventh Centuries', in H. Hearder and H.R. Loyn (eds.), *British Government and Administration: Studies Presented to S.B. Chrimes* (Cardiff, 1974); reprinted in H. Loyn, *Society and Peoples: Studies in the History of England and Wales, c.600–1200* (London, 1992), pp. 111–34.

[68] I Æthelred 1 (2), (8), (12); III Æthelred 3 (1), 13; Loyn, *Governance of Anglo-Saxon England*, pp. 144–5.

[69] On this latter see John Gillingham, '1066 and the Introduction of Chivalry into England', in G. Garnett and J. Hudson (eds.), *Law and Government in Medieval England and Normandy* (Cambridge, 1994), pp. 31–55. See also Matthew Strickland, *War and Chivalry: The Conduct and Perception of War in England and Normandy, 1066–1217* (Cambridge, 1996).

postdated the development of basic chivalry in European society.[70] This early chivalry was directly related to the concept of nobility in the Carolingian world. Two important issues, however, are by no means clear cut: namely, the extent to which this code of honour was shared with subordinates such as functioning knights and the extent to which it passed into what we might call civilian life, i.e. the extent to which the code contributed towards the development of an elite mentality within the expanding aristocracy as a whole.

On the first issue Gillingham may be right to point to the greater availability of arms in the early eleventh century as indicating a point of significant change, not only in the wealth of England but also in the sense that the growth in the number of highly equipped soldiers must have aided the transmission of a code of honour from the lords to their now wealthier men; this is perhaps so even though the still high cost of the equipment must have meant that in practice it was supplied by lords, a fact indicated by the continuing importance of heriots in Anglo-Danish society. On the other hand he makes light of the contempt for the rustic knights which is reported so much in chronicles of the early to mid-twelfth century and which would seem to suggest that there was as yet something less than a uniform *esprit de corps*.[71] It is certainly true that the military classes become more integrated, but this integration is better seen as a process which took place across the eleventh and twelfth centuries as a whole.

On the second issue – the presence of a code of honour in civilian life – Gillingham points in particular to the writer Geoffrey Gaimar, whose work, the *Estoire des Engleis*, was commissioned by a local Lincolnshire family between 1135 and 1140, and whose evidence, he argues, is 'decisive'.[72] The story of the commissioning is well known. Constance, wife of a lesser Lincolnshire landowner, Ralf fitz Gilbert, sent to Walter Espec, lord of Helmsley in Yorkshire, for his copy of Geoffrey of Monmouth's *History of the Kings of Britain*, itself commissioned by Earl Robert of Gloucester.[73] John Gillingham has shown, very clearly, that this work exhibits a very strong sense of gentility.[74] Moreover, it shows a minor landowning family of the early to mid-twelfth century with pretensions to gentility. A certain degree of caution is needed in that the

[70] Karl Leyser, 'Early Medieval Canon Law and the Beginnings of Knighthood', in L. Fenske, W. Rösener and T. Zotz (eds.), *Institutionen, Kultur und Gesellschaft im Mittelalter: Festschrift für J. Fleckenstein* (Sigmaringen, 1984), pp. 549–66; reprinted in his *Communications and Power in Medieval Europe: The Carolingian and Ottonian Centuries*, ed. T. Reuter (London, 1994); Janet L. Nelson, 'Ninth-Century Knighthood: The Evidence of Nithard', in her *The Frankish World 750–900* (London, 1996), pp. 75–87.
[71] On this see Coss, *The Knight*, pp. 27–9, 43.   [72] Gillingham, 'Thegns and Knights', p. 136.
[73] For a discussion of the context see Ian Short, 'Gaimar's Epilogue and Geoffrey of Monmouth's *Liber Vetustissimus'*, *Speculum* 69 (1994), pp. 323–43. For Walter Espec see also Crouch, *Image of Aristocracy*, p. 328.
[74] John Gillingham, 'Kingship, Chivalry and Love. Political and Cultural Values in the Earliest History Written in French: Gaimar's *Estoire des Engleis'*, in W. Warren Hollister (ed.), *Anglo-Norman Political Culture and the Twelfth Century Renaissance* (Woodbridge, 1997), pp. 33–58.

family concerned had some very high-powered connections. Walter Espec was a favoured royal justice and *curialis*, the founder of Rievaulx and two other Cistercian monasteries. Moreover, Ralf and Constance were related by marriage to the Clares. Gentility was probably as much a matter of connections as of intrinsic merit. Nevertheless, and despite the qualification, Gaimar's evidence shows that a developed concept of gentility had spread into at least some reaches of local society. It is little wonder that the pretensions of lesser knights and their families provoked reactive comments against rustic knights by some high-born aristocrats.

Such pretensions must have been reinforced, if not actually fired, by the higher standards of seigneurial consumption which followed in the wake of the Norman Conquest and which were paid for by the increased burdens which were imposed upon the peasantry.[75] Anglo-Saxon thegns had hunted on their estates, but we now see the spread of deer parks, as well as gardens, vineyards, dovecotes, moats and fishponds. Much of the rebuilding was now in stone. The various stages in the growth of the manor house at Goltho are again indicative. Sometime during the Anglo-Norman period a defensive ringwork was built, within which were a motte, a hall and a tower. This was later followed by the sweeping away of the old buildings and the ringwork in favour of an imposing fortified house. Later still, this was moved to a new site where a moat was added.[76]

There can be no doubt whatsoever that the concept of nobility was widening and deepening in twelfth-century England, in what Paul Dalton calls 'a process of aristocratic cultural popularisation, involving the gradual devolution through the social hierarchy of the cultural patterns of those in the upper ranks'.[77] As he points out, at the heart of this culture and 'basic to the concept of *nobilitas*' lay 'family dynastic feeling, the veneration of ancestors, a sense of lineage'. During the twelfth century the adjective noble is increasingly widely diffused, as is its vernacular equivalent, *gentil*, a word which, as David Crouch has reminded us, is derived from the Latin *gens*, meaning 'family' or 'stock'.[78] During the second and third generations after the Norman Conquest attributes of nobility were increasingly diffused: primogeniture and the practical heritability of land, independent jurisdiction, toponymic surnames, the use of seals and the advocacy

---

[75] For a recent and very strong statement in favour of increased seigneurial pressure see Faith, *English Peasantry and the Growth of Lordship*, esp. ch. 8.

[76] Beresford, *Goltho*, pp. 85–122; Faith, *English Peasantry and the Growth of Lordship*, pp. 194–5. Paul Everson has argued vigorously for a redating of these later sequences, and has postulated a post-Conquest break in continuity. This would produce a castle dating from the reign of Stephen, a late twelfth-century hall and an early thirteenth-century moated site, all associated with the substantial knightly family of Kyme: P. Everson, 'What's in a Name? Goltho, "Goltho" and Bullington', *Lincolnshire History and Archaeology* 23 (1988), pp. 93–9. However, this redating does not materially affect the argument offered here.

[77] *Conquest, Anarchy and Lordship*, pp. 293–4.   [78] Crouch, *Image of Aristocracy*, p. 4.

of monasteries.[79] It was around the 1140s that lesser men began to imitate the great tenants-in-chief in their use of equestrian seals.[80] Seal usage spread swiftly downwards during the mid to late twelfth century, famously causing Richard de Lucy, Henry II's justiciar, to thunder to Gilbert de Balliol that 'it was not formerly the custom for every petty knight to have a seal, which befits kings and great personages'.[81] But this was like trying to stem the tide. As Dalton puts it, 'Seals were a symbol of lordship, and their proliferation in the mid- and late twelfth century may be an indication that many tenants viewed themselves as their own men, as lords in their own right.'[82] It was at this same point in time that men who are often described as honorial barons, the greatest of the under-tenants, were aping their superiors in founding monastic houses. Recent studies have shown this most clearly for Yorkshire, where the sparseness of monasteries at the Conquest offered a *tabula rasa* for the aspiring aristocrat in this respect, but there is every reason to believe that it is a general phenomenon.[83]

These features are broadly contemporary with the development of toponymic surnames, with men describing themselves as *x de* (of) *y*. At the time of Domesday Book many, although not all, tenants-in-chief either already possessed hereditary surnames, or held names that were to become hereditary thereafter. During the first half of the twelfth century other families of baronial or substantial knightly rank can be shown to have developed their own hereditary surnames, the majority of them toponymic, and a substantial proportion of knightly sub-tenants followed suit.[84] There is a strong contrast here with Anglo-Saxon England, where the development of toponymic surnames seems to have made a rather halting start. Bynames were used, and these included toponymic ones, but it looks as though hereditary surnames had not developed very far.[85] Examples can certainly be found – Sired of Chilham in Kent was probably descended from the Kentish magnate Siward of Chilham[86] – but they are relatively rare.

[79]   Dalton, *Conquest, Anarchy and Lordship*, pp. 293–4.
[80]   Crouch, *Image of Aristocracy*, p. 243.
[81]   See Eleanor Searle, *Lordship and Community: Battle Abbey and Its Banlieu 1066–1538* (Toronto, 1974), p. 42.
[82]   Dalton, *Conquest, Anarchy and Lordship*, p. 272.
[83]   For Yorkshire see Dalton, *Conquest, Anarchy and Lordship*, pp. 293–4 and Janet Burton, *The Monastic Order in Yorkshire 1069–1215* (Cambridge, 1999), esp. pp. 190–3. As Dalton says, 'A very large majority of the religious foundations made by men of second rank in Yorkshire occurred in the period 1140–65.' See also Crouch, *Image of Aristocracy*, pp. 331–2, and Janet Burton, *Monastic and Religious Orders in Britain 1000–1300* (Cambridge, 1994), ch. 10.
[84]   For a brief summary of knowledge on this subject see Peter Coss, *The Lady in Medieval England 1000–1500* (Stroud, 1998), pp. 11–12. To the works cited there one should now add D. Postles, *The Surnames of Leicestershire and Rutland* (Leicester, 1998).
[85]   Forenames may have been used to some extent to distinguish people on status grounds. The sort of Englishmen who provided the Domesday jurors, thegns and greater freeholders, tended to have names that can be distinguished from those of peasants and slaves: C.P. Lewis, 'The Domesday Jurors', *Haskins Society Journal* 5 (1993), pp. 22–3.
[86]   Williams, 'A West Country Magnate', p. 46. The question is reviewed by Ann Williams in *The English and the Norman Conquest*, pp. 206–10.

The development of toponymic surnames is generally connected by historians of the European continent with the concept of lineage, with its accent upon patrilineal descent and primogeniture. Their slow penetration of pre-Conquest England suggests that here the shift away from the broader kin, traditionally so important in terms of protection and social cement, had not yet gone very far.[87]

In short, wherever we look it seems as though the manifestations of nobility appear to grow stronger and wider as the twelfth century moves on. Seen from the perspective of the diffusion of noble attributes it might be better to regard the evidence of Gaimar's *Estoire des Engleis* as marking not so much the end of one stage in the development of an elite mentality as the beginnings of another.

Moreover, despite the recent work on early chivalry, there is still a great deal to be said for the diffusion of a stronger sense of nobility during the latter part of the twelfth century, in England as in France, around the concept of knighthood. At the heart of this social change lay the refinement of chivalry and its adoption as an ideology of exclusion.[88] Romance literature points to the development of a clearer class consciousness within aristocratic circles towards the end of the twelfth century, investing knighthood with strong and exclusive moral and social values. The works of Chrétien de Troyes, produced around the 1170s and early 1180s, are especially significant here. Among the manifestations of this change were the increased significance attached to knighthood by the greater men, with particular emphasis upon the ceremony of dubbing, the development of heraldry, and on the part of lesser men the use of the hitherto reserved title *dominus* in their charters. Heraldry belongs to a highly aristocratic world. Prompted initially perhaps by the tournament, heraldry began to take on an hereditary form from the 1140s and was disseminated downwards from the highest families during the later twelfth and into the thirteenth century through associations of land tenure and service. A fully chivalric knighthood was born.[89]

During the course of the twelfth century, then, a much stronger elite mentality was forged than ever before. One clear expression of status consciousness which is seen in twelfth-century sources is the language of deference.[90] The French writer on love Andrew the Chaplain tells us of a certain air (*natura*) which

---

[87] For a recent discussion of how kinship functioned among the landowners of late Anglo-Saxon England see Fleming, *Kings and Lords*, pp. 3–11.

[88] The classic statement is by Georges Duby: 'It seems that the years before and after 1200 were a period in French society when the aristocracy was gradually transformed into a genuine nobility' ('The Transformation of the Aristocracy'; reprinted in *The Chivalrous Society*, trans. Cynthia Postan (London, 1977), pp. 171–85). A different view is taken by John Gillingham, who appears to see chivalry as a fully developed elite mentality by the time of Gaimar if not before. See his '1066 and the Introduction of Chivalry into England', pp. 31–55.

[89] For an extended discussion of these changes and their consequences see Coss, *The Knight in Medieval England*, chs. 3–4.

[90] See the fascinating discussion in Crouch, *Image of Aristocracy*, pp. 150–1, drawing on L. Foulet, 'Sir, messire', *Romania* 71 (1950), pp. 1–48.

great men possessed and which lesser men tried to copy or acquire.[91] But, notwithstanding a powerful spirit of exclusion among the great, an increasing number of men and women perceived themselves to be, or indeed were perceived by others to be, noble or gentle. Two examples will suffice, one from the reign of Henry II and the other from the reign of John. In the first, the chronicler Roger of Howden, reporting on the abduction of an heiress and its consequences for one Gilbert de Plumpton, younger brother of a powerful Yorkshire knight, calls him a knight born of noble stock (*miles nobili prosapia ortus*).[92] In the second and more famous case Richard Revel, who at the county court in 1204 wanted to impress the sheriff of Somerset with the social position and local standing of himself, his father and brothers, told him roundly that they were *naturales homines et gentiles* of the *patria*, that is to say that they were natives and gentle men within their locality. The sheriff replied that so, too, was he within his.[93]

What we see as we look across John Gillingham's long eleventh century, through the twelfth and into the early thirteenth century is a lesser nobility steadily being formed. In summary, late Anglo-Saxon England reveals an incipient lesser nobility which already possessed some of the characteristics which historians of later periods normally associate with a gentry: rural estates, seigneurial authority, an elite status, horizontal ties, participation in judicial procedures and local government. But a sense of proportion is required. When placed in their contemporary setting, these attributes seem relatively underdeveloped compared with later times. Moreover, that setting with its heavy emphasis upon service and subordination reveals little or no opportunity for collective self-awareness or sectional articulation.

Nevertheless, there seems to have been a growing self-confidence and assertiveness among the lesser nobility during the twelfth century and this has a direct bearing on how the Angevin legal reforms should be understood. Those reforms are no longer seen by scholars as *deus ex machina*. Among a new generation of legal historians, John Hudson, in particular, has been arguing for continuity with what went before. Under Henry I there was already considerable security of tenure and royal intervention in land cases, lay as well as ecclesiastical.[94] Royal writs were already becoming a key feature of justice in England and

[91] Crouch, *Image of Aristocracy*, p. 12.
[92] Cited and discussed by Thomas, *Vassals, Heiresses, Crusaders and Thugs*, pp. 8, 65, 74 and 83–4.
[93] See Coss, *Lordship, Knighthood and Locality*, p. 10, and the references given there.
[94] For what follows see John Hudson, *Land, Law, and Lordship in Anglo-Norman England* (Oxford, 1994), esp. pp. 250–81. For an excellent introduction to the Angevin reforms as a whole see the same author's *The Formation of the English Common Law: Law and Society in England from the Norman Conquest to Magna Carta* (London, 1996). For two other important recent treatments see J. Biancalana, 'For Want of Justice: Legal Reforms of Henry II', *Columbia Law*

landowners were becoming used to invoking the crown. Hudson stresses the importance of the early years of the reign of Henry II, as royal authority was being reconstructed during the 1150s and early 1160s after the civil war of Stephen's reign: 'The developments of the land law from *c.*1166 are of course striking, but they were most notably an acceleration of administrative change, not an unprecedented leap forward.'[95] Royal assertiveness was a key factor, but Hudson sees the operation of consumer demand as significant. The immediate popularity of Henry II's assizes in itself suggests this. And, as Paul Hyams has pointed out, a large number of those who sought confirmation of their lands from Henry II at the outset of his reign had been sub-tenants;[96] thereafter, they were likely to be enthusiastic supporters of royal justice as they could call upon the crown in support of their tenure. Paul Dalton has recently pointed to defiance of greater lords by lesser during the reign of Stephen,[97] suggesting the likelihood that pressure from local seigneurs lay behind the reforms: 'the Angevin reforms which are supposed to have initiated social change appear on close analysis to reflect a society that was already changing'.[98]

But these seigneurs were not yet a gentry in any meaningful sense. Gillingham and others are surely right to point to elements of continuity between Anglo-Saxon and Angevin England. The social structure was not dissimilar. If the king's barons, and in some respects the honorial barons too, are equatable with king's thegns, the parallel between knighthood and thegnage is, arguably, even stronger. Knights encompassed a wide spectrum in Angevin England, as thegns had done in the Anglo-Saxon state. Moreover, the Angevin legal reforms had reinforced, even extended, the service component in knighthood.[99] Old ideas of knighthood based on service – service to great lords as well as to the state – took a long time to pass away.[100] Although knights were in many ways a mainstay of Angevin legal procedures, freeholders were similarly drawn into judicial and administrative procedures, just as their forebears had been in Anglo-Saxon

---

Review 88 (1988), pp. 433–536, and P.A. Brand, ' "Multis Vigiliis Excogitatam et Inventam", Henry II and the Creation of the English Common Law', in his *The Making of the Common Law* (London, 1992), pp. 77–102.

[95] Hudson, *Land, Law, and Lordship*, p. 281. See also Graeme J. White, *Restoration and Reform 1153–1165: Recovery from Civil War in England* (Cambridge, 2000), ch. 5: 'The Administration of Justice'. Meanwhile Patrick Wormald, taking a much broader view, has argued for pre-Conquest foundations for the Angevin 'leap forward': 'English law is distinctive because it is as old as the English kingdom ... Henry II made law like no other twelfth-century king, because he inherited a system of royal justice that was already uniquely old and active' (Wormald, *The Making of English Law*, vol. I, p. xi).

[96] See P.R. Hyams, 'Warranty and Good Lordship in Twelfth-Century England', *Law and History Review* 5 (1987), pp. 46–7.

[97] Dalton, *Conquest, Anarchy and Lordship*, pp. 185–92.   [98] *Ibid.*, p. 295.

[99] For a recent discussion of Angevin knighthood see Coss, *The Knight in Medieval England*, ch. 3: 'Angevin Knighthood and Its Transformation, *c.*1150–*c.*1250'.

[100] See, for example, P.R. Coss, 'Knighthood and the Early Thirteenth-Century County Court', in P.R. Coss and S.D. Lloyd (eds.), *Thirteenth Century England II* (Woodbridge, 1988).

England. Knights, like thegns, participated in the public obligations incumbent upon all free men, with certain obligations peculiar to them.

The public courts of shire and hundred had done more than persist through Anglo-Norman England; indeed, when we glimpse the county court in the mid-twelfth century it does not seem unlike those of the later Anglo-Saxon period. The Wigmore Chronicle describes a session at the Herefordshire county court, between 1141 and 1143, which was attended by the bishop and the magnate Hugh de Mortemer, together with their retinues, as well as many knights, free men and clerks of the shire.[101] When proffers were made for disafforestation during the early years of Henry III's reign they were made by a wide spectrum of county society, and often with elevated leadership. For instance, in 1225 a proffer was made for the disafforestation of Cornwall by the bishop of Exeter, barons, knights and all of the county.[102] In terms of the administration of justice, the county court was a vital institution within the Angevin polity but, despite the changes, it had many features in common with the courts of Anglo-Saxon England.

Horizontal ties may be more in evidence in Angevin England than in earlier times, but the power of lordship remained extremely strong. Indeed, in some respects it was even stronger than it had been in Anglo-Saxon England, despite the steady weakening of the honour courts. The strength of the honour court in twelfth-century England is a contentious issue. It is true that the post-Conquest honour has taken something of a bashing in recent years, in reaction against Stenton's conception of the honour as 'a feudal kingdom in miniature' and Milsom's world of autonomous seigneurial justice. For Hugh Thomas, by the close of the Angevin period, the honour was in 'an advanced state of senescence as an institution governing the loyalty of both lords and vassals', and he speaks repeatedly of lords and tenants breaking out of what he calls 'the honorial straightjacket'.[103] Paul Dalton offers a quite devastating list of factors which were undermining the honour and its court in the twelfth century, and concludes that 'When viewed against the background of the political enfeoffment in progress in the reign of Stephen, and the cross-honorial tenurial, religious and family ties which were developing throughout the Anglo-Norman period, some honours look more like artificial constructs than functioning self-contained communities around which society and government were principally organised.'[104] For Crouch, similarly, the honour was

---

[101] David Crouch, 'From Stenton to McFarlane: Models of Societies of the Twelfth and Thirteenth Centuries', *Transactions of the Royal Historical Society*, 6th series, 5 (1995), p. 191.

[102] This is among the examples given by J.R. Maddicott, 'Magna Carta and the Local Community', *Past and Present* 102 (1984), pp. 48–9.

[103] Thomas, *Vassals, Heiresses, Crusaders and Thugs*, p. 47. For the 'honorial straightjacket' see, for example, pp. 27, 44.

[104] Dalton, *Conquest, Anarchy and Lordship*, pp. 249–72. The quotation comes from p. 254.

in essence no more than an accumulation of acts of patronage between a lord and those who had consented to become his men; frozen by custom and obligation. Initially, it would be flexible and even lively, capable of growth while free lands were available for further distribution. Then in two, three or four generations that flexibility would in the end stiffen, and the honor would become a fossilised shell of a community of interests long departed.[105]

Some would argue, however, that this reaction against the honour has gone too far,[106] and, indeed, David Carpenter has mounted a rearguard action, stressing its importance throughout the second century of English feudalism.[107] He points, *inter alia*, to the language of Magna Carta, which assumes the contemporary significance of honours and fees, and indeed of tenure, to the 1235 aid which was still collected through feudal structures, and to the continuing importance of feudal rights of relief, wardship, marriage and escheat (reversion of land to its overlord) which he aptly terms not 'feudal incidents' but 'feudal essentials'.

These 'feudal essentials', like the honour court itself, and indeed the private hundreds and liberties which so abounded in post-Conquest England, played an important part in institutionalising, and therefore strengthening, lordship. But the honour, as David Crouch has repeatedly emphasised, is only one component in magnate power. A powerful man could draw men who were not his tenants into his courts. A magnate without a strong or inherited regional base, like William the Marshal, earl of Pembroke, could intrude his power in other ways, by means of what would later be called an affinity. It is arguable that the most significant form of political organisation in England in the twelfth and thirteenth centuries was 'a form of power focused on a discrete region and a dominant personality who sought to control it'.[108] Magnates were always trying to make their power truly territorial. Generally speaking – the reign of King Stephen being an exception – kings tried to stop them.[109] When it came to rebellion, as in

---

[105] Crouch, 'From Stenton to McFarlane', p. 198.

[106] In reviewing the situation for the Anglo-Norman period, Judith Green has recently written: 'It may be that recent writers such as Dalton and Hudson have taken an overly pessimistic view of the effectiveness of the honorial court and the related issue of the lord's discipline over his tenants. Honorial justice did not exist in a vacuum, but honorial courts were not necessarily less effective than the alternatives. Lords could offer an arbitration service, publicity and ratification for family arrangements, and a regional forum for the expression of solidarity' (*Aristocracy of Norman England*, p. 273). As far as the early thirteenth century is concerned I have argued that an honour could still be a vibrant organism if it corresponded with other features and gave institutional focus to local society, e.g. the honour and locality of Coventry (Coss, *Lordship, Knighthood and Locality*, pp. 8, 55–7).

[107] David Carpenter, 'The Second Century of English Feudalism', *Past and Present* 168 (2000), pp. 30–71.

[108] Crouch, 'From Stenton to McFarlane', p. 194. See also his contribution to the debate 'Bastard Feudalism Revised', *Past and Present* 131 (1991), pp. 165–77.

[109] See C. Warren Hollister, 'The Aristocracy', in Edmund King (ed.), *The Anarchy of Stephen's Reign* (Oxford, 1994).

the civil war of 1215–17, magnates often took both tenants and other members of their affinity with them.[110] Although it is hard to deny lesser landowners their own grievances against the king, the influence which they brought to bear and which found its expression in Magna Carta was derived from their membership of retinues – that is to say through vertical ties of association.

Even in Angevin England the cohesion of lesser landowners can easily be overstated. Horizontal ties are certainly significant but in themselves constitute a rather blunt instrument for detecting the existence or not of a gentry. After all, it is hard to find a time when either vertical or horizontal ties were insignificant. And how would one decide how far the scales needed to tip on one side or the other to make a substantial difference? Horizontal ties do not, in themselves, provide a means of articulation. It is true that knights were occasionally brought to Westminster during the early thirteenth century for consultation. However, it is difficult to see where they could have discussed and expressed a sectional interest. Too much can be invested in the county court in this respect. Despite the fact that in most counties it was now held every four weeks and that its routine business increased in the wake of judicial reforms, the shire court was in many ways a sorry affair compared to its predecessor in Anglo-Saxon England. Arguably, the fact that it had ceased to be the full microcosm of provincial society – with magnate attendance – was a necessary precondition for the role it was later to play in gentry society. But there is too much negativity surrounding the county court during the first half of the thirteenth century for us to see it easily as a forum for debate among the lesser landowners. Not only was it for the most part poorly attended, but men also sought to limit its duration.[111] As David Crouch aptly puts it: 'By the thirteenth century the real importance of the shire court lay in its providing a theatre for touring royal justices, rather than acting as a village hall to air local concerns and house local ambitions.'[112]

If it is difficult to accept the view that the gentry goes back to late Anglo-Saxon England, it is equally difficult to sustain the argument that it was created at a stroke by the Angevin monarchy. The short-term effects of the Angevin legal reforms were less revolutionary than has sometimes been supposed, though of course their longer-term effects – in bringing the lesser landowners, and of course other free men, increasingly into direct relationship with the state – can hardly be overstated.[113] In Angevin England the reach of public authority was

---

[110] The extent to which the great lords were followed by their tenants is a contentious issue. In J.C. Holt's view, King John's great northern rebels 'were followed by the men whom they might reasonably regard as their particular tenants almost to a man' (*The Northerners: A Study in the Reign of King John* (Oxford, 1961), pp. 43–5.) This view is criticised, however, by Thomas, *Vassals, Heiresses, Crusaders and Thugs*, pp. 44–7. For further discussion of this matter see below, pp. 119–20.

[111] See below, pp. 112–14, 121.   [112] Crouch, 'From Stenton to McFarlane', p. 192.

[113] For the consequences of this see P.R. Coss, 'Bastard Feudalism Revised', *Past and Present* 25 (1989), pp. 27–64.

extended and the employment of knights, and others, for judicial and administrative tasks greatly expanded. However, the emphasis which some historians put on the public obligations placed upon the free man – the so-called self-government at the king's command – is something of a red herring as far as the evolution of the gentry is concerned. Much more significant, as I shall argue below, were the direct commissions which lesser landowners received from the crown. By the fourteenth century, the role of local seigneurs in the operation of public justice had gone beyond mere agency of the state. The collective authority over the populace which came to be invested in them as local justices, pre-eminently in their capacity as justices of the peace, brought them effectively into partnership with the state. Similarly, it is not until the fourteenth century that we see horizontal banding, properly speaking. These gradations were not some icing on the gentry cake. On the contrary, they betokened a fundamentally different way of perceiving status from those derived from service and vertical association.[114] It was a shift in perception whose significance went way beyond the appearance, and increasing prevalence, of horizontal ties. The gradations were closely bound up with the gentry's collective identity. And finally, the parliamentary Commons, with whose history that of the gentry was so intertwined, has no equivalent in those earlier times.

In any case, my concern in this book is not with institutional continuities but with the evolution of the gentry.[115] Some of the basic building blocks are traceable to Anglo-Saxon England: a primitive code of honour and other aspects of elite mentality, for example; the beginnings of seigneurialism; and a public authority which drew upon local landowners, among others, as its agents. By the time of the Angevins a maturing lesser nobility was making its presence felt. The behavioural traits which Hugh Thomas witnesses among the lesser landowners of Angevin England, however, are essentially the characteristics of any nobility; they do not in themselves denote the existence of a gentry. The gentry, then, evolved out of a lesser nobility which had its roots in the society of late Anglo-Saxon England. How precisely this happened is the subject of the chapters that follow.

---

[114] For this argument see above, ch. 1, pp. 9–11. Of the twelfth century David Crouch writes: 'We are trapped . . . in hierarchical thinking. I would suggest that in the twelfth and thirteenth centuries people did not think in those terms, and . . . I would venture to suggest that we should not either' ('From Stenton to McFarlane', p. 200).

[115] In my view it is better to remain within the context of the society one is studying and to avoid the teleology of the Stubbsian framework which seeks the origins of English liberty, if not the peculiarities of the English character, in the remote past. See Campbell, *The Anglo-Saxon State*, pp. xxviii–xxix, and 247–68.

3. The Angevin legacy: knights as jurors and as agents of the state in the reign of Henry III

It is one thing to see the Angevin polity as the seed-bed out of which the English gentry was to grow. It is quite another to regard the gentry as already formed in Angevin England. Why some historians should do so has much to do with the existence of a knightly class. Knights, after all, were later to form the highest gradation within the gentry. However, it is not so much knighthood itself which is held to be significant in this context, but the tasks which Angevin and post-Angevin knights were called upon to perform, both within the judicial system and within local administration. This, for example, is where Hugh Thomas, a major recent proponent of an Angevin gentry, lays his greatest stress.[1] I will argue in this chapter, however, that two distinct phenomena have been confused. There was a major difference between participating in judicial procedures – which was expected of a knight as a matter of course – and the employment of a much smaller body of selected landowners and others as trusted agents of the state. The confounding of the two has much to do with the idea of self-government at the king's command, the notion that English kings, and the Angevins in particular, called forth the people to govern themselves on the king's behalf. This idea, although in essence much older, was popularised by A.B. White in 1933.[2] It may be said to have influenced unduly the study of the gentry ever since. The tendency to combine two distinct dimensions of governance has created in the minds of historians a more monolithic and cohesive knightly class than is warranted. The result has been to distort reality. Furthermore, these two phenomena have been combined with three others – the expression of collective grievances against the state, the representation of local communities by knights in national assemblies and the election of such knights at the county court – to create an anachronistic picture. The result is that an embryo has been mistaken for a mature organism, that is to say the gentry.

[1] See above, p. 23.
[2] A.B. White, *Self-Government at the King's Command* (Minneapolis, 1933; reprinted Westport, CT, 1974).

The political relationship between lesser landowners and the state is a matter for chapter 5. What we need to do here is to conduct a thorough examination of the role of knights within the Angevin legal system. In particular, we must clarify the distinction between lesser landowners as participants within the judicial system and as agents of the state, in essence between knights as jurors and knights as justices. Having done so we will then note the stresses that had appeared within the 'Angevin system' by the middle of the thirteenth century. Let us begin with the knights as 'jurors'.

ANGEVIN LEGAL PROCESSES: THE GRAND ASSIZE

As is well known, knights were specifically called upon within the Angevin legal system for a variety of purposes, including the viewing of parties to legal actions who were offering the excuse of bed-sickness (the essoin *de malo lecti*) for their non-attendance at court, the receiving of names of attorneys, conveying the record of the county court on occasions to Westminster, and as electors and jurors of the grand assize. Whilst ordinary free men were deemed sufficient as jurors in the petty assizes, the added status of knights was considered essential for the operation of the grand assize.[3] This procedure has yielded valuable evidence for historians of knighthood seeking to calculate the number of knights active within a county for civilian business at any one moment in time. Here, however, we shall turn to it as an aid to understanding the role of lesser landowners within the Angevin legal processes themselves. What was expected of them, and how did they respond to those expectations?

Introduced in 1179, the grand assize gave the defendant in an action concerning the right to land the opportunity of opting for a jury in place of trial by battle. In order to do this, the defendant replied to a writ of right, which was normally brought to the county court, with a writ of peace. This suspended the action, allowing the grand assize to take over. It was conducted not at the county court, however, but either at the central courts or before the central court justices in eyre. Glanville's treatise gives the writ to the sheriff, ordering him to summon four knights from the neighbourhood in question who were to choose 'twelve law-worthy knights from the same neighbourhood who best know the truth of the matter'.[4] This effectively opened the process. The writ, however, tells us only the bare bones of the procedure. We know that the sheriff chooses four knights but we do not actually know how or where. As the so-called Justiciar's Writs of 1199 indicate, this writ subsequently underwent some development.

---

[3] For an exploration of the actual status of Angevin knights see Coss, *The Knight in Medieval England*, ch. 3: 'Angevin Knighthood and Its Transformation'.

[4] *The Treatise on the Laws and Customs of the Realm of England Commonly called Glanvill*, ed. G.D.G. Hall (Oxford, 1965), p. 30.

The four knights are now to be of the county rather than of the neighbourhood or locality, the *visnetum*, and the twelve knights of the *visnetum* are now to be chosen from among the *more* law-worthy.[5] It is possible that in shifting from the *visnetum* to the county the writ was encouraging the sheriff to choose the electors in the county court, but there is nothing which shows that this was so. Similarly, we know that the four were expected to choose twelve knights from the locality in question and that their choice was brought to Westminster on a specified return day or at the first session of the eyre in the county, but we know nothing of how that choice was made. What we do know, in fact, is that commonly not twelve but sixteen or seventeen knights were named. Sometimes the rolls tell us which twelve of the potential jurors were sworn. How were they whittled down? We know that the defendant was present at the election, presumably to ensure fair play. Does this mean that the defendant could object to some of the knights as jurors, on the grounds that they may prove to be partial or inadequate in some way? Is this why in practice more than twelve knights are named? Alternatively, it might be suggested that more than twelve were elected in case one or more of the knights should die or become unavailable. Perhaps this was a secondary factor.

The court rolls themselves are generally spartan in the information they impart. However, they do contain hints as to the precise procedures involved. The following snippets come from various midland counties during the time of King John. Let us begin with the role of the sheriff in the choice of the four electors. Nowhere is there any suggestion that they were nominated by the county court. On the contrary, the choice is clearly the sheriff's responsibility, although it is possible that he may have made or announced his choice there. What the rolls do tell us is that when a replacement was ordered for one of the four by the courts it was the sheriff's responsibility to nominate him. This was so in an Oxfordshire case in 1206, for example, when the sheriff was ordered to find a suitable replacement for Ralf fitz Roger who had died.[6] In a Bedfordshire case in 1203 the sheriff was ordered to put another knight in place of Ralf de Tivill, who was overseas.[7]

A little more can be gleaned over the final choice of jurors. A Staffordshire case of 1205 tells us that both parties are present to hear the election. A further day was given for this because of the non-appearance of two of the electors.[8] From this we may legitimately infer that both parties were routinely present at the election, and not just the defendant who is specifically summoned by the writ. A Leicestershire case from 1200 names eleven recognitors (jurors) who had come to court followed by a knight who was to be summoned to make

---

[5] For a discussion of these changes and their possible significance see Coss, *Lordship, Knighthood and Locality*, pp. 211–12.
[6] *Curia Regis Rolls*, vol. IV, pp. 316–17.   [7] *Curia Regis Rolls*, vol. III, p. 71.
[8] *Curia Regis Rolls*, vol. III, p. 285.

the assize with those eleven. The important statement is the one which comes next: 'And it is to be known that both parties hold themselves content with the aforesaid knights.'[9] It is likely that there had been some procedural irregularity here, which is why we have the additional information. However, the important point is that both parties have a right to be satisfied with the jury which is to give a verdict. In an extreme case the court might order the election of further knights. In a Northamptonshire case of 1203 the four knights were summoned again to elect a further six in place of those who 'by the consideration of the court should be removed'. This is difficult to interpret with any certainty but it looks as though too many knights may have been the subject of objections for a jury to emerge. It is to be presumed that there had to be legitimate grounds for exception. The most likely was that one or more potential jurors belonged to the affinity of either party.[10]

It is clear from the cases on the central court rolls that the twelve jurors did not emerge on the day of election but were to be subsequently chosen from those elected when a case next came to court. All those elected were expected to appear for this session, during these early decades of the grand assize at least. An Oxfordshire case of 1208, to take one example, shows an assize being respited (i.e. postponed) for default of recognitors. In fact, eleven had turned up, two others had essoined – that is to say they had excused themselves – and three were to be attached (i.e. compelled to provide guarantees) for their failure either to appear or essoin.[11] In other words, the entire sixteen who had originally been elected must have been expected in court.

In sum, the procedure laid down in the writ appears to have been carried out to the letter and the jury emerges in the following way: First, the sheriff arranges for four electors. This was his responsibility and there is no evidence that they were chosen in the county court. The sheriff found replacements if such were required by the court. Secondly, these four elected a number of knights, most often sixteen, and in the presence of the parties to the case.[12] These were the knights from whom the twelve later emerged. Thirdly, the elected knights subsequently came to court where the jury of twelve was chosen. The parties probably considered the names and prepared any objections to present to the

[9] *Et sciendum quod utraque pars tenuit se pacatum de predictis militibus* (*Curia Regis Rolls*, vol. I, pp. 306–7). It is not clear which variety of assize this is. It refers in the first instance to *legales homines*, which suggests one of the possessory assizes, but the twelve are subsequently called knights.

[10] See, for example, a case in 1223 when a view of two manors was to be conducted by knights who were not of either affinity (*Curia Regis Rolls*, vol. XI, no. 640). See also N. Denholm-Young, *Seignorial Administration in England* (Oxford, 1937), pp. 116–18, and Coss, *Lordship, Knighthood and Locality*, pp. 325–6.

[11] *Curia Regis Rolls*, vol. V, p. 177.

[12] Both Glanville and Bracton refer to the knights being elected on oath. In a Staffordshire case of 1210 a further day was given for the election because no oath could be taken at Advent (*Curia Regis Rolls*, vol. VI, p. 109).

justices.[13] In short, the procedure of the grand assize was a time-consuming one. An examination of the actual cases that were resolved by means of the assize during the reign of King John shows it working reasonably well at the county end but – not surprisingly, and like the possessory assizes, those concerned with possession rather than right – subject to delays at the central courts. A plea which came to the Common Bench at the Michaelmas term, 1201, over a knight's fee at Maidford, in Green's Norton Hundred, in south-west Northamptonshire, shows just how long drawn out the procedure could be. The plaintiff was described as Henry de Alneto of Cornwall, and the defendant Henry de Alneto of Maidford. The defendant had put himself on the grand assize. The four electors who had been chosen for the task of electing the jurors were Richard de Grimscote, Richard de Lyons, Richard de Hinton and William de Nonancurt. Although the writs no longer specified that they should be of the relevant *visnetum*, all four would appear to have held land in the south-west of the county. None of them appears to have been from the hundred of Green's Norton, but they were landowners in the surrounding hundreds.[14] Although the writ merely specifies that the sheriff should choose four knights of the county it looks as though it remained important to the spirit of the assize to choose men from at least the broad area in which the disputed property lay.

The Plea Roll gives the names not only of the electors but also of the sixteen knights they elected. Most of these can be readily shown to have belonged to the immediate locality. Some held property in vills that were contiguous with Maidford or in the same hundred: Robert de Salcey at Plumpton, Henry de Armenters at Stowe, Geoffrey de Norton at Blakesley, William Gulafre at Blakesley, Gilbert de Wandevill at Seawell and Bradden. Others held land in Nobottle Grove Hundred immediately to the east or Fawsley Hundred immediately to the north: Geoffrey de Insula at Barby and Richard de Heyford at Heyford, while Richard de Holdenby presumably held in Holdenby and Philip de Staverton in Staverton. The property of William le Brun and Robert fitz Alan

---

[13] It is difficult to see the process of narrowing down to twelve as primarily a means of dealing with possible absences when the jury came to court, as the same procedure was followed not only at Westminster but also at the eyre, when a much shorter time scale was involved between the election of the jury and the hearing of the case.

[14] Richard de Grimscote held a knight's fee at Floore in Nobottle Grove, while Richard de Hinton most probably came from Hinton in the hundred of Chipping Warden. (There is another Hinton, viz. Hinton in the Hedges, but this too is in a neighbouring hundred, that of King's Sutton.) William de Nonancurt seems to have held land at Braunston in another contiguous hundred, that of Fawsley. I have seen no contemporary evidence of the Northamptonshire property of the Lyons family at this date, but by the late thirteenth century they were well entrenched at Warkworth in the southern tip of the county in King's Sutton Hundred, once again contiguous with Green's Norton, and there is every reason to believe therefore that they were established in the locality earlier. It should be noted that the hundreds do not appear to have played any formal part in the procedure of the grand assize. I have used them here simply to locate landowners' local interests in relation to the property in dispute.

has not been traced but most likely they, too, were local knights. William and Peter Mautravers held a little further away at Collingtree in Wymersley Hundred, and Roger de Blukevill at Winwick in Guilsborough Hundred. The final two men were important mid-county knights: Simon de Maidwell at Maidwell in Rothwell Hundred and Herlewin de Raunds at Raunds in Higham Ferrers Hundred. It is quite possible, of course, and even likely that these men held additional interests closer to Maidford.

In terms of carrying out the terms of the writ, therefore, everything seems to have worked efficiently within the county. It was when the case came to the central courts, however, that problems began. A day was given to the parties and potential jurors. But the next we hear of the case in the rolls is Easter 1203. Clearly it was not progressing well. The names of twelve knights are recorded, but only five actually appeared in court. The others essoined, that is to say they gave excuses for non-attendance. As a result, as the roll says, the assize was respited for default of recognitors. A further day was given at the Trinity term following. It was not until the Michaelmas term, however, that we have a further account of the case. The situation was worse than before. Only two of the knights arrived, Herlewin de Raunds and Roger de Blukevill. As Roger was not one of the twelve named at the previous session it seems clear that the parties had not yet got their final jury. Moreover, only three knights had given excuses. At the next session only four came and two essoined. Six others, including Richard de Heyford whose name had not figured since the very first naming of the sixteen, were ordered to be attached. The same thing happened at the Michaelmas term 1204. At the Hilary term 1205 as many as ten managed to attend. Even so, three were named as defaulters. As the roll says, they had made many defaults, and the sheriff was ordered to have their bodies, i.e. to arrest them to ensure their appearance. It did little good, for when the case came up again at Easter, five knights were named once more as defaulters. It is not surprising, perhaps, that the case was deferred to the travelling justices, to be held at Northampton, the Sunday after the Ascension (22 May) 1205.[15] The frustration not only for the litigants but also for those recognitors who did turn up can be imagined. Altogether, when it came to making the necessary journey to Westminster it can hardly be said that the knights had got their act together. This case may be towards the extreme end in terms of the delays encountered, but the problem was all too typical. Men may have been more than ready to take advantage of the Angevin procedures, but when it came to implementing them, especially if this involved inconvenient journeys to Westminster or wherever, they could be considerably less enthusiastic.

None the less, at the beginning of the thirteenth century the grand assize and the other procedures which officially required knights drew in a considerable

---

[15] *Curia Regis Rolls*, vol. II, pp. 27, 199; vol. III, pp. 13, 67, 179, 254–5, 307.

number of men. The Plea Rolls reveal the names of at least 215 Northampton-shire men who were called upon between 1194 and 1214.[16] These tasks were clearly not the monopoly of a few. At least sixty-one of the 215 functioned on four or more occasions. The Northamptonshire assize roll of 1202–3 shows the situation even more clearly. Eighty-three knights figure in this roll, indicating incidentally the minimum of landed knights in Northamptonshire that could be gathered together in one place at one time during the first decade of the thirteenth century, excluding all barons, major or minor, *curiales* (courtiers) with land in the county, landless knights attached to households, any who were absent from the county on other business, and any potential knights who were currently under age. Of these eighty-three, no less than forty appear on two or three occasions. However, no one man occurs more than three times.[17] There was decidedly no small elite who crowded out the others in such matters, at least not at this date.

This remains very largely true during the next generation, despite the fact that the number of knights was falling. The rolls of the central courts from 1219 to 1237 reveal the names of at least 106 Northamptonshire knights[18] who functioned in one or more judicial tasks which were deemed to require the status of knight: grand assize, essoin *de malo lecti*, receiving the names of attorneys, and so on. Naturally, some men occur more frequently than others. In fact, twenty-one men occur twice, eight men occur three times, and nineteen men occur in relation to four or more cases. Of these nineteen, Richard de Besevill occurs nine times, Henry de Isham eight times, and Simon le Beaud and Ralf Ridel seven times each. William Buttevilain, Geoffrey Mautravers and Godfrey Quatremar figure six times. The others are: Robert de Acle, Ralf Barre, Richard Gubiun, David de Hackleton, Richard de Hinton, William de Houghton, Alan

---

[16] For the knights see *Rotuli Curiae Regis*, vol. I, pp. 27, 145–6, 287, 401; vol. II, pp. 34, 152, 159, 186–7, 193; *Curia Regis Rolls*, vol. I, pp. 16, 75, 120, 233, 288, 341, 402, 450, 456, 474; vol. II, pp. 18, 27, 28, 72, 138, 157, 199, 207, 214, 222, 252–3; vol. III, pp. 13, 67, 149, 179, 195, 206, 227–8, 229, 254–5, 266, 286, 290, 307, 328, 341, 342; vol. IV, pp. 56–7, 68, 145, 159, 183, 202, 277, 298; vol. V, pp. 3, 31, 36, 43, 70, 110, 136–7, 247, 275; vol. VI, 1210–12, pp. 31–2, 58–9, 94, 142, 200, 253; vol. VII, pp. 140, 203.

[17] Always assuming that Robert de Stokes and Robert de Stokes of Bradden, who each appear twice, are in fact two different men. For the names see *The Earliest Northamptonshire Assize Rolls, A.D. 1202 and 1203*, ed. Doris M. Stenton, Northamptonshire Record Society 5 (1930), nos. 107, 111, 121, 159, 283, 317, 320, 406, 439, 451, 461, 463–7, 503, 544, 598, 635–6, 667, 801.

[18] The knights are derived from the following entries: *Curia Regis Rolls*, vol. VIII, 1219–20, pp. 9, 13–14, 22–3, 82–3, 97, 102, 149, 153, 197, 239, 252, 290, 366; vol. IX, pp. 91–2, 141, 215–16, 251–2, 351–2; vol. X, pp. 11, 64, 70, 190, 202; vol. XI, nos. 115, 146, 217, 246, 640, 1084, 1192, 1211, 1346, 2007, 2040, 2085, 2575; vol. XII, nos. 349, 553, 776, 1055, 1381, 1588, 2517; vol. XIII, 1227–30, nos. 734, 1303, 1909, 2187; vol. XIV, nos. 1297, 1491, 1769; vol. XV, nos. 817, 1118, 1159, 1566, 1710, 1984. There are ninety-four separate surnames, some of which must represent more than one generation. There are occasional problems where similar names may denote the same man.

de Maidwell, John Mautravers, Nicholas de Noers, Richard fitz Osbert, Henry de Raunds and William de Whiston.

It is sometimes assumed that the men who occur most prominently in these judicial matters constituted an upper group of county knights, perhaps with an aptitude for such work. There may be some truth in this, but a cautionary note is necessary. As we have seen, the grand assize, which necessarily supplies the greatest quantity of names, required knights of the locality in question so that the uneven geographical spread in the incidence of the grand assize is always likely to bring some men into the frame more often than others. The same is true, broadly speaking, of the electors. The smattering of cases reported on the central court rolls reveals no particular concentration of men figuring as electors. Nine full panels are reported, and the names of one or two electors from four others. A total of twelve men appear twice. If some men were called upon more often here, and in other capacities such as checking on litigants who were essoining through bed-sickness, it may have been because they were more amenable or, perhaps, less resistant to being called upon by the sheriff. In these post Magna Carta years, however, the knights were no more enthusiastic about travelling to Westminster than they had been before. The rolls continue to show as many respites through essoins and unexplained absences as they had done before. Few grand assizes went through to a conclusion in only two terms. In short, the records suggest a high participation rate of knights within the Angevin legal procedures, whilst at the same time indicating a level of inconvenience involved. Many men did their judicial duty, although in very few cases can this duty have constituted a major part of their lives.

Having looked in detail at the knights as jurors and the like, let us now turn to their role as justices.

OFFICE-HOLDING UNDER THE CROWN: THE JUSTICES OF ASSIZE

Many landowners participated intermittently as jurors in the assizes. Some of them functioned as justices. It was Magna Carta in 1215 which introduced the idea of county knights as justices. After the famous clause 17, which fixed common pleas effectively at Westminster, came two clauses concerned with the possessory assizes. Clause 18 stipulated that:

Recognizances of novel disseisin, mort d'ancestor and darrein presentment shall not be held elsewhere than in the county [court] in which they occur, and in this manner: we, or if we are out of the realm our chief justiciar, shall send two justices through each county four times a year who, with four knights of each county chosen by the county, shall hold the said assizes in the county [court] on the day and in the place of meeting of the county [court].

Clause 19 followed with:

> And if the said assizes cannot all be held on the day of the county [court,] so many knights and freeholders of those present in the county [court] on that day shall remain behind as will suffice to make judgements, according to the amount of business done.[19]

Where the inspiration lay for these clauses is unknown. It is certainly possible to regard clause 18, in particular, as emanating from the county knights themselves, as a demand for greater local participation. However, clause 19 might equally well suggest that the motive was to make the county itself run more efficiently when it came to the operations of the assizes. Whatever is the case, these provisions were altered in the 1217 reissue and the alterations confirmed in Magna Carta 1225:

> we will send justices into each county once a year who will take the aforesaid assizes with knights of the counties in the counties. And those that are unable to be terminated by the aforesaid justices sent for taking the said assizes on their arrival in the county, shall be terminated by them elsewhere on their eyre. And those that are unable to be terminated by them on account of the difficulty of any article shall be referred to our justices of the bench and terminated there.

Furthermore:

> assizes of darrein presentment shall always be taken before our justices of the bench and terminated there.[20]

These changes increased the freedom of action of the central court justices. However, there is nothing to suggest that they were a bone of contention in the localities, or that this was a cause of resentment among county knights.[21] It seems unlikely that the original 1215 provision for the choosing of knight justices at the county court was ever carried out. Indeed, evidence for the panels holding multiple assizes at all is hard to come by. From 1220 to 1241, however, it was common for four men from each county (usually knights) to be commissioned to hear *individual* possessory assizes.[22] Similarly, from the 1220s onwards either four knights or one or two justices of the central courts received commissions for the delivery of gaols.[23] After 1241 there was a change, with

---

[19] J.C. Holt, *Magna Carta* (2nd edn, Cambridge, 1992), pp. 456–7. The assizes of novel disseisin, mort d'ancestor and darrein presentment were concerned, respectively, with recent and unjust dispossession, the claim to succeed to an inheritance, and the right to nominate a cleric to a church living, most often a parish.

[20] 1217 clauses 13–15 (*Select Charters*, ed. W. Stubbs (9th edn, Oxford, 1913), p. 342); 1225 clauses 12–13 (Holt, *Magna Carta*, pp. 504–5).

[21] For the political issues in the counties in these years see below, pp. 110–21.

[22] As noted by P.A. Brand, 'The Origins of the English Legal Profession', *Law and History Review* 5, no. 1 (1987); reprinted in his *The Making of the Common Law* (London, 1992), p. 26. These commissions appear on the dorse of the Patent Rolls.

[23] *Crown Pleas of the Wiltshire Eyre*, ed C.A.F. Meekings (Devizes, 1961), p. 5. Meekings points out that gaol delivery was often done by justices taking possessory assizes at the same time as

the possessory assizes being taken by one or sometimes two central court justices (or royal servants with judicial experience)[24] who were to associate local men of their own choosing with them. However, local knights continued to be commissioned for gaol delivery beyond that date.

Who were these justices? Taking Northamptonshire once again as an example, we find thirty-five men appearing on the Patent Rolls under commission to take individual assizes or to deliver gaols in the county during the years 1221 to 1241.[25] However, the body of local men is rather less extensive than this implies. For one thing, the central court justices were themselves employed in this capacity. The system by which a justice was specially commissioned to take an individual assize did not begin in 1242, but was in use intermittently from 1216. The earliest example appears to have been King John's great justice, Simon de Pattishall, who received such a commission to take an assize at Northampton in March 1216, during the civil war.[26] Another great justice, William de Raleigh, was given two such commissions, to take an assize and to appoint his own associate justices, one an assize d'utrum (to determine whether land was held in lay fee or alms) in 1233 and the second, an assize of novel disseisin, in 1234. Robert de Lexington was similarly commissioned in 1241. On other occasions central court justices were appointed as members of panels. Stephen de Segrave, for example, was appointed on four occasions: in 1221, 1228, 1229 and 1231. On the first occasion he was joined by another justice, the clerk Thomas de Heydon, who was employed again in this capacity in 1223. Yet another central court justice who figures is Ralf Hareng, in 1222. William de Insula was commissioned in this way no less than eleven times, right across the period when he was a central court justice, from 1227 to 1237. William de Culworth, another Westminster justice, was employed on five occasions in Northamptonshire between 1238 and 1241, and yet again in 1242. Gilbert de Preston was perhaps a different case, in that he was employed as a local justice before he became a central court justice in 1240. We shall return to his case shortly.

Ralf Turner has pointed out that central court justices tended to be employed – as justices of gaol delivery for example – in the areas where they enjoyed their own residences, often during vacation time. On one occasion, 'William de Raleigh saved his neighbours the inconvenience of making payments of a composition ending a lawsuit at Westminster in 1225. Instead, they could pay at his house at Blatherwycke, Northamptonshire, while he was spending his summer vacation there.'[27] This is a matter of some significance. Despite the fact that his

their assize sessions. He also says that the early history of gaol delivery is obscure, and that in the early thirteenth century gaols were delivered by means which have not been recorded.

[24] Brand, 'Origins of the English Legal Profession', p. 26.

[25] For a list of the panels see below, Appendix I.

[26] Ralf V. Turner, *The English Judiciary in the Age of Glanvill and Bracton c.1176–1239* (Cambridge, 1985), pp. 198–9.

[27] *Ibid.*, p. 199.

family originated in Devon, William de Raleigh had strong Northamptonshire interests. He had begun his professional life as clerk to another Northamptonshire man, the chief justice Martin de Pattishall. He had been presented to the Blatherwycke living by a member of the Engayne family in 1220, and in 1228 had acquired the wardship and marriage of the heir of William Engayne. He received gifts of venison and licence to hunt in Rockingham Forest and was made keeper of Rockingham Castle for life by the regime of Peter de Rivallis in 1231.[28] Among the livings held by the justice Thomas de Heydon were the Northamptonshire churches of Cold Higham and Raunds.[29] Ralf Hareng and Stephen de Segrave were both midlanders.[30] Originating in Leicestershire, Stephen was a powerful figure locally even before he became chief justiciar. He was actually sheriff of Northamptonshire in 1228–9. In the 1242–3 inquest his son, Gilbert de Segrave, was returned as the holder of estates at Chalcombe and Raunds. William de Insula was a Northamptonshire knight whose chief estates were at Brampton Ash and Harringworth.[31] So, too, was William de Culworth, whose interests centred on Culworth, Sulgrave and Thorpe.

The government, or the central court justices, also called on relatives of the judges and on other men who were otherwise known to them. Walter de Pattishall was called upon three times for Northamptonshire assizes between 1221 and 1224. Son of Simon de Pattishall, he was himself a justice in eyre of 1218–19 and sheriff of Bedfordshire and Buckinghamshire in 1224–8.[32] Peter de Raleigh, who figures twice in 1241, was very likely a relative of William de Raleigh, although his own Northamptonshire interests are unclear. Other men must have been well known at the centre before they were called upon as justices in the localities. William de Insula, as we have seen, was much used for Northamptonshire assizes during the time he was a central court justice. A royalist in the time of King John, he had already served the government of the minority as keeper of one or more Northamptonshire forests and as constable of Rockingham Castle. Moreover, he had been one of the knights associated with Simon de Pattishall in a Northamptonshire assize in March 1216 and had served with Martin de Pattishall in the limited eyre for possessory assizes

---

[28] For these details see C.A.F. Meekings, 'Martin Pateshull and William Raleigh', *Bulletin of the Institute of Historical Research* 26 (1953); reprinted in his *Studies in 13th Century Justice and Administration* (London, 1981), p. 165.

[29] Turner, *English Judiciary*, pp. 249–50.

[30] Ralf Hareng's interests were centred on Buckinghamshire and Oxfordshire. He had begun his professional life as steward of the honour of St Valery and later acted as its custodian: Turner, *English Judiciary*, pp. 221–2, 248.

[31] For the career of William de Insula see C.A.F. Meekings, *The 1235 Surrey Eyre*, Surrey Record Society 31 (Guildford, 1979), vol. I, pp. 212–13. He held other estates at Floore, Maidwell, Sibthorpe and Stoke Doyle. Cited by Turner, *English Judiciary*, pp. 207, 217–18. He was one of the knights associated with Simon de Pateshull in the assize of March 1216.

[32] Turner, *English Judiciary*, p. 189. He was described as 'man and knight' of William de Beauchamp: David Carpenter, *The Minority of Henry III* (London, 1990), p. 353.

and gaol delivery that was held in September 1225.[33] Everything suggests that Gilbert de Preston, who became a royal justice in 1240 and whose career as a judge was to span thirty years, must also have been highly thought of before he was used on assizes on three occasions between 1235 and 1241. He was later much employed to take Northamptonshire assizes with his own associates. It is highly likely that the centre was also well acquainted with Walter de Preston, who functioned on four occasions between 1222 and 1240.[34] Indeed, the evidence suggests that he had been a trusted servant of King John, from whom he had received the manor of Gretton as half a knight's fee.[35] He had been sheriff of Northamptonshire in 1206 and 1207. Like William de Insula and William de Culworth, the Prestons were well rooted in the county. The inquest of 1242–3 reveals interests in Preston itself and eight other Northamptonshire vills. On other occasions men must have come in as associates of others known at the centre. Some who figure on only one occasion may thus have had no connection with Northamptonshire. Thomas de Haddon, for example, featured once as a substitute for Thomas de Heydon.

Were any of these assize justices employed solely in their capacity as county knights? Already we can subtract eleven of the thirty-five men who figure between 1221 and 1241 in that they either were central court justices or were probably employed largely because they were known at the centre. We might want to tackle the matter in a different, and more traditional, way and look for the existence of an elite who were called upon most often. Of the thirty-five men who figure between 1221 and 1241, eleven were called upon only once, while another ten functioned two or three times. This leaves fourteen men who participated as assize justices or justices of gaol delivery on four or more occasions. Three men figure pre-eminently: John de Hulcote who features eighteen times, and Geoffrey de Armenters and Henry de Raunds who each figure seventeen times. A middle group comprises William de Insula, Robert de Salcey and Simon de Thorpe, each of whom figures between ten and twelve times, and Maurice de Aundely who features on nine occasions. A final group are found between four and seven times, viz. David de Esseby (seven times), William de Whiston, William de Culworth and Robert de Pavely (six times), Walter de Preston (five times), and Ralf fitz Reginald and Stephen de Segrave, who appear four times each.[36] Culworth, Insula and Preston

[33] Meekings, *Surrey Eyre*, p. 212.

[34] Additionally, he was appointed with three associates, on 16 January 1228, to hear complaints against Hasculf de Allexton for his misdeeds at Northampton (*Calendar of Patent Rolls, 1225–32*, p. 209).

[35] *Book of Fees*, vol. II, p. 931.

[36] It should be noted that there is some overlap between Northamptonshire and Rutland. Those who figure in both counties are among the most prominent, viz. Geoffrey de Armenters, William de Culworth, John de Hulcote, William de Insula, Henry de Raunds, Ralf fitz Reginald, Stephen de Segrave and Simon de Thorpe.

we have already encountered. John de Hulcote had accounted as under-sheriff for Walter de Preston in 1206. More recently he had been under-sheriff for Falkes de Bréauté for Cambridgeshire–Huntingdonshire, 1219. He was under-sheriff again, in Bedfordshire–Buckinghamshire in 1233, for Stephen de Segrave, and was later to become sheriff in his own right for Oxfordshire, in 1232, and Norfolk–Suffolk, in 1239.[37] Ralf fitz Reginald was under-sheriff for Essex–Hertfordshire in 1220, and sheriff of Lincolnshire in 1226 and of Bedfordshire–Buckinghamshire in 1234. Robert de Salcey had been sheriff of Northamptonshire in 1204.

Why others should figure so prominently is less clear. In one case, at least, one can envisage why the centre should have become aware of him. Henry de Raunds was indeed lord of Raunds in north Northamptonshire. The rector of its church, as we have seen, was none other than Thomas de Heydon, central court justice. Medieval government tended to recruit men on the basis of foreknowledge and word of mouth recommendation, and this is what seems to have been happening here.[38] Although some men figure regularly across periods of time there do not appear to have been standing panels, and there is nothing whatsoever to suggest that these men were elected in the county. The prominence of the central court justices Insula and Culworth suggests otherwise. Moreover, the letters of appointment are issued alongside mandates to the sheriffs ordering them to set up the necessary local machinery. This seems to have been the point at which the sheriff was first aware of the panel's existence. For a Rutland assize in 1236 Henry de Boyvill was substituted for William de Gunthorp 'because there is no such William in that county'. It was an error which could hardly have been made had these men been chosen in the county.

Property-wise the leading participants were solidly if variably based. Geoffrey de Armenters was a man of some importance with four knights' fees of the honour of Gant, two at Kislingbury and Heyford and two at Stowe Nine Churches. Henry de Raunds, on the other hand, held two fractional fees, of one eighth and one quarter, at Raunds. Robert de Salcey held a fee of the honour of Peverel, three parts of which were in Northamptonshire. Simon de Thorpe held half a knight's fee at Thorpe near Daventry. John de Hulcote was lord of Hulcote and Maurice de Aundely was lord of Addington. David de Esseby held a fee at Ashby and Grendon.

Everything seems to suggest that these men were called upon because they were trusted at the centre, even if in some cases the relationship with the government is not clear.[39] There is no particular correlation between these men

---

[37] For the staff by which Falkes de Bréauté ran his four shrievalties see Carpenter, *The Minority*, p. 17.

[38] See, for example, the recruitment of King John's household knights: S.D. Church, *The Household Knights of King John* (Cambridge, 1999), ch. 2.

[39] Some may have been involved in forest administration. Maurice de Aundeley was a verderer of Rockingham Forest during the early 1250s, for example.

and those who were nominated as electors and jurors of the grand assize. Only two of them – Henry de Raunds and William de Whiston – figure four times as Northamptonshire knights in the grand assize or in similar judicial capacities on the rolls of the central courts for 1219–37. Moreover, the total overlap between the justices and the 106 knights who figure in those procedures is no more than seventeen.[40] Where there is a clear correlation, however, is between these local justices, if we may call them that, and the men appointed centrally to other sensitive tasks. Thus the men appointed to assess and collect the tax of a fifteenth from Northamptonshire in 1225 were Robert de Salcey, David de Esseby and Maurice de Aundely, with Thomas de Haddon acting as the clerk.[41] The two men appointed escheators for the county in 1232, important officers who looked after royal rights in wardships and escheated lands, were Robert de Salcey and David de Esseby.[42] The commissioners initially assigned to assess and collect the fortieth of 1232 were Robert de Salcey, John de Hulcote and Henry de Raunds, together with Richard de Bernack whom we have not previously encountered. John de Hulcote was later replaced by Robert Grimbaud, by letter from the king.[43] Robert figures as a justice in Northamptonshire on three occasions in 1235–6, and should probably be regarded as another member of this inner group of commissioned justices. Similarly the thirtieth of 1237 was to be assessed and collected by Geoffrey de Armenters, John de Hulcote, Henry de Raunds and Gilbert de Preston, together with a clerk. However, John and Gilbert were soon replaced by Simon de Thorpe and, once again, Richard de Bernack.[44] In 1227 Walter de Preston had been appointed to conduct the taxation known as tallage in Northamptonshire, Bedfordshire and Buckinghamshire, together with Thomas de Cirencester and the respective sheriffs.[45] Geoffrey de Armenters and Gilbert de Preston were the collectors of the aid of 1235–6 in Northamptonshire.[46]

When we turn to inquiries involving the royal forests in the counties we find the same phenomenon. In 1225 John de Hulcote was appointed with Roger de Torpel as the local justices who joined the chief justice of the forest and his colleagues for perambulating the forest in Northamptonshire.[47] Back in 1219 the commission of inquiry into assarts in the forest had included Maurice de Aundely and Ralf fitz Reginald as clerk, as well as Henry de Braibroc, sheriff of

---

[40] Of these seventeen, the following (nine) appear only once: Maurice de Aundely, Richard de Blukevill, William de Culworth, David de Esseby (replacing Robert de Salcey), Robert de Pavily, Walter de Preston, Robert de Salcey (although he did not function), Eustace de Watford and Roger de Whelton. Robert Grimbaud, John de Hulcote, Ascelinus de Sidenham and Geoffrey de Wandevill appear twice. Saer de Wollaston apears three times, Henry de Raunds four times, Robert Gubiun and William de Whiston five times. On the other hand, of the nineteen knights who figure four or more times in the grand assize and other judicial procedures only three – Richard Gubiun, Henry de Raunds and William de Whiston – occur as justices.

[41] *Patent Rolls, 1216–25*, p. 565.   [42] *Close Rolls, 1231–4*, p. 131.   [43] *Ibid.*, p. 158.

[44] *Close Rolls, 1234–7*, p. 552.   [45] *Rotuli Litterarum Clausarum*, vol. II, p. 208b.

[46] *Close Rolls, 1234–7*, p. 191.   [47] *Pat. Rolls, 1216–25*, pp. 567–8.

the county from 1211 to 1215 and formerly under-sheriff to Robert de Braibroc his father.[48] In 1223 the Northamptonshire branches of the nation-wide commission for the sale of windfall wood had comprised Walter de Preston, David de Esseby and Henry Gubiun, with Thomas de Heydon as clerk, for 'this side of Northampton', and Maurice de Aundely, together with Ascelinus de Sidenham and Nicholas de Bassingbourne (both of whom figure once as assize justices), for 'beyond Northampton'.[49] On the one occasion when the Patent Rolls record a panel appointed for assizes of novel disseisin in general as opposed to a single case, in 1235, the panel comprised William de Insula, no doubt as central court justice, John de Hulcote, Robert Grimbaud and Henry de Raunds.

Perhaps these men are the elusive *buzones* whom 'Bracton' refers to as playing a prominent role at the opening of the eyre, and whom historians have found it difficult to locate precisely:

> These [preliminary] remarks having been made, the justices ought to betake themselves to some private place and call before them four or six or more of the greater men of the county, who are called 'buzones' of the county and on whose nod the views of the others depend, and let them consult with these men in turn.[50]

In Warwickshire, to take another county, the situation was substantially the same, although there are some differences. Here, rather more men were appointed as justices of assize and/or gaol delivery than in Northamptonshire. Perhaps as many as fifty-two men figure on the Patent Rolls in those capacities between 1220 and 1241.[51] Of these, however, seventeen appear only once and a further fifteen only two or three times. This leaves twenty men who occur on four or more occasions, of whom twelve appeared ten or more times. Bardolf de Chesterton was particularly prominent (being on twelve panels) in 1241. The remainder stand out not only for the number of panels on which they sat but also for the length of time during which they figured. They are: John de Ladbroke, twenty-five times (1228–41); John Durvassal, twenty times (1227–38); William de Luddington, twenty times (1227–41); William de Curli, eighteen times (1220–41); Robert de Grendon, seventeen times (1235–41); Maurice le Butler, thirteen times (1229–41); Philip de Esseby, twelve times (1227–41); William

---

[48] *Ibid.*, p. 214. The others were Peter Fletcher and Ralf de Flore.   [49] *Ibid.*, pp. 309–401.

[50] G.E. Woodbine (ed.), trans. (with revision and notes) Samuel E. Thorne, 'Bracton' (*Bracton de legibus et consuetudinibus Angliae: Bracton on the Laws and Customs of England*), 4 vols. (Oxford, 1968–77), vol. II, p. 327. See also G.T. Lapsley, 'Buzones', *English Historical Review* 47 (1932).

[51] It is possible, however, that Walter de Boyvill is Walter d'Eyville, that William de Curn is William de Curli, and that Robert and Roger Foliot are one and the same. This would reduce the number to forty-nine. A further complication is that some gaol delivery panels include gaols in both Warwickshire and Leicestershire. Hence they include men from both counties. I have excluded Reginald Basset, William Basset, William Picot and Henry de Nafford as representing Leicestershire. I have also excluded the members of the panel held at Northampton in 1229. For the list of panels see below, Appendix II.

de Bishopton, twelve times (1227–37); William de Wilmcote, twelve times (1227–36); and Walter d'Eyvill ten times (1227–35). These eleven men would seem to constitute an inner core of men employed as justices in Warwickshire during this twenty-one-year period. Central court justices seem to figure less here than in Northamptonshire. Only Robert de Lexington figures among the twenty who occur four times or more. Others do occur, but with no great frequency. We find Stephen de Segrave on three occasions, and William de Insula and William de Culworth on two occasions each.[52] The most likely explanation for their less prominent role in Warwickshire is that the central court justices lacked the personal stake in the county which the central authority seemed to value in assize justices.

In place of the resident justices is another factor. Of the twelve men who occur most often, no less than five figure also as stewards to the earls of Warwick or to Ranulf III, earl of Chester, who held an important base at Coventry in the north of the county. Walter d'Eyvill was Ranulf's last steward in the area; the earl died in 1232. John de Ladbroke, William de Wilmcote and John Durvassal were stewards of Henry, earl of Warwick (d. 1229), while John Durvassal and Robert de Grendon were both stewards to his son, Earl Thomas (d. 1242).[53] It was not merely as functioning stewards that they occur, however, for they continue to be called upon as justices after their terms of office as stewards had expired. It was rather that these men functioned for magnates who were largely loyal to the regime and that this brought them to the notice and into the trust of the central authority. In this sense their functioning is more than a simple reflection of magnate power. In fact, Earl Thomas of Warwick cut a rather mean figure in comparison with his predecessors,[54] while the earl of Chester's successors as lords of the honour of Coventry had relatively little direct stake in the county.

At least two other men were known to the centre in another capacity that can be discerned. William de Luddington accounted as under-sheriff of the county in 1221,[55] while William de Lucy was keeper of Kenilworth Castle and sheriff of Warwickshire in 1236. The son of Walter de Charlecote, usher of the king's chamber in the time of Henry II, William de Lucy was a man whose family had a long history of royal service and who himself had strong court connections.[56] These men were trusted justices. William de Luddington

[52] Stephen de Segrave also occurs twice heading gaol delivery commissions across the two counties.
[53] For the stewards of the earls of Warwick see David Crouch, 'The Local Influence of the Earls of Warwick, 1088–1242: A Study in Decline and Resourcefulness', *Midland History* 21 (1996), pp. 1–22, esp. Appendix B, and see P.R. Coss, 'Knighthood and the Early Thirteenth-Century County Court', in P.R. Coss and S.D. Lloyd (eds.), *Thirteenth Century England II* (Woodbridge, 1988). For Walter d'Eyvill see Coss, *Lordship, Knighthood and Locality*, pp. 35, 37, 50, 181.
[54] Crouch, 'Local Influence of the Earls of Warwick', pp. 13–14.
[55] *Lists and Indexes, PRO*, no. IX, p. 144.
[56] For William de Lucy see Nicholas Vincent, *The Lucys of Charlecote: The Invention of a Warwickshire Family, 1170–1302*, Dugdale Society Occasional Papers 42 (Stratford-upon-Avon, 2002).

was appointed to join the third stage of Robert de Lexington's eyre in 1236, and functioned in Warwickshire and Leicestershire. John Durvassal's name had also been included in this commission on the Patent Roll, although it was subsequently deleted and he did not function. Another man who did, however, was John de Hulcote of Northamptonshire.[57] The one general panel for assizes of novel disseisin in Warwickshire, as authorised by Magna Carta, comprised the royal justice, Robert de Lexington, with Walter d'Eyvill, William de Bishopton and John de Ladbroke (1228). As with Northamptonshire, the assessors of the subsidies tended to be taken from this small group. In 1232 they comprised John de Ladbroke, John Durvassal and Maurice le Butler, together with Adam de Napton who, surprisingly, does not figure as an assize justice.[58] In 1237 they consisted of William de Bishopton, John de Ladbroke, Robert de Grendon and Richard de Amundevill, the latter figuring as justice seven times between 1236 and 1238.[59] In 1225 the assessors for Warwickshire had been William de Hartshill – four times justice, under-sheriff of Warwickshire for Walter de Cantilupe back in 1201 and an important tenant, familiar and charter-witness of Earl Ranulf of Chester – and Ralf le Butler, who occurs once as a justice in 1225 and who was the father of Maurice le Butler.[60] William de Luddington was responsible for collecting Warwickshire's contribution to the aid of 1235–6 with Richard Peche.[61] The escheators appointed for Warwickshire in 1232 were John de Ladbroke and William de Bishopton.[62]

There is more overlap between the justices and men prominent in the grand assize than in Northamptonshire. William de Wilmcote, William de Bishopton and William de Luddington were among the twelve most prominent grand assize knights in the Warwickshire eyre of 1221–2, and were the three most prominent electors. These three together with Maurice le Butler were among the fourteen most prominent knightly jurors in the eyre of 1232, although none was among the five electors functioning more than twice.[63] Of the ninety-seven men who are recorded as knights in judicial procedures in Warwickshire between 1220 and 1232, thirty-one also figure as justices.[64] Only half of these, however, played a substantial role: eight appear only once as justices, and a further seven only two or three times. Moreover, seven of the twelve most prominent jurors in the 1221–2 eyre did not figure at all as justices, and nor did six of the fourteen

[57] *Cal. Pat. Rolls, 1232–47*, p. 164.   [58] *Close Rolls, 1231–4*, p. 158.
[59] *Close Rolls, 1234–7*, p. 552.
[60] Assuming the justice and tax assessor to be Maurice le Butler of Oversley not Maurice le Butler of Exhall. They worked alongside William de Martivast and Henry de Segrave, no doubt representing Leicestershire, and were accompanied by Walter de Preston and Master William le Tornor, added to the commission through letters from the king: *Cal. Pat. Rolls, 1216–25*, p. 562.
[61] *Book of Fees*, vol. I, pp. 506, 511.   [62] *Close Rolls, 1231–4*, p. 130.
[63] For details of the Warwickshire knights see Coss, *Lordship, Knighthood and Locality*, ch. 7: 'Knighthood in Society'. A list of the knights will be found there as Appendix 7.1.
[64] Reginald Basset and William Picot, who seem to represent Leicestershire in joint gaol delivery commissions, also figure as knights of the grand assize in Warwickshire.

most prominent in 1232. If the centre called on a somewhat wider range of men from time to time as justices than it did in Northamptonshire, it was probably because they did not have central court justices with local interests to draw upon.[65] As with Northamptonshire, however, the landed stake in the county of the most relied upon justices was variable. William de Wilmcote was a man of small estate, as was Philip de Esseby. It is not clear at all what factor or factors had brought Philip to the centre's attention. The important points are that the range of men functioning as justices compared to jurors is more restricted and that within this more restricted group a relatively small number of men predominated. The tasks were simply of a different order.

After 1241 there may have been rather less for such men to do, with the professional justices taking the assizes and the lack of extraordinary taxation between 1237 and 1269. However, they continued to be employed as justices of gaol delivery. Sixteen men figure on the Patent Rolls as gaol delivery justices in Northamptonshire between 1242 and 1246. Apart from the justices, Gilbert de Preston and William de Culworth, these included Henry de Raunds, Simon de Thorpe, Ralf fitz Reginald, John de Hulcote, Robert de Pavely and Geoffrey de Armenters (on no less than three occasions). Moreover, three others had previously functioned as assize justices (Geoffrey de Wandevill, Roger de Whelton and Eustace de Watford). In Warwickshire fourteen men occur as gaol delivery justices between 1242 and 1247. All of them except Henry de Ladbroke, son of John and himself a steward of the earl of Warwick, had already occurred as justices before 1242. They include: Robert de Grendon, Philip de Esseby, John Durvassal, Richard de Amundevill, William de Curli, William de Luddington and Maurice le Butler. Others like William Trussell, Henry Pipard and Hugh de Mancetter were just coming into prominence.[66] In 1242 the Assize of Arms (ensuring that men possessed the weapons appropriate to their rank) was taken in Warwickshire by John Durvassal and Robert de Amundevill, and in Northamptonshire by Geoffrey de Armenters and Robert de Pavely.[67] In 1255 commissioners were sent out to organise the sale of part of the king's woods. The knights appointed to assist them in Northamptonshire were William de Insula and Simon de Thorpe.[68]

From 1236 onwards, moreover, men of this type were employed more frequently as sheriffs in place of the old *curiales*. Sheriffs generally became custodians rather than farmers of the office who had paid over fixed sums to the crown, and the royal manors were progressively taken out of their hands.

---

[65] They seem to have drawn more on men with administrative experience, men like Philip de Kineton, under-sheriff for Warwickshire in 1213 and 1217 and for Ranulf, earl of Chester in Shropshire in 1220. The prior of Coventry also figures on one occasion. It is surprising that Stephen de Segrave was employed only once as an assize justice.

[66] Gaol delivery panels continued to be recorded on the Patent Rolls up to the early 1250s but only sporadically thereafter. They continue to show considerable overlap with earlier panels. Details can be found in PRO OBS 1/465–6. Substantial recording began again in the late 1260s.

[67] *Close Rolls, 1237–42*, p. 484.   [68] *Cal. Pat. Rolls, 1247–58*, pp. 432–4.

Farming returned from 1241 but with higher and higher increments.[69] Sheriffs of Northamptonshire, for example, included William de Culworth, with his son acting as under-sheriff, in 1240, Simon de Thorpe in 1248, and William de Insula in 1252 and 1255, with Eustace de Watford appointed by the baronial regime in 1258. Another sheriff, Nicholas de Hotton, seems to have been appointed by William de Insula, presumably as under-sheriff around 1254. In Warwickshire, William Trussell, assize justice in 1241 and justice of gaol delivery in 1242 and 1243, was sheriff in 1246.[70] Thus the notion that the sheriff should be a vavasour, that is to say a substantial landowner, of the county he administered, a prominent feature of the reform programme of 1258, was not exactly a novel one.[71]

It is no coincidence that there was a strong correlation between the local men who functioned as justices of assize and the tax assessors. S.K. Mitchell, the historian of taxation, made a study of the royal agents, county commissioners or *missi* as he preferred to call them, from the reign of Richard I to that of Henry III. Of the relatively few panels of royal taxers that are extant for the assessment of the thirteenth of 1207, he had this to say:

> almost without exception the commissioners were landholders in the shire to which they were appointed justices and in general their chief lands lay in that county. This cannot be chance; it must have been deliberate. Thus the direction of the levy of these taxes lay in the hands of the lesser landholders and primarily of the rear vassals of each shire. But there is another characteristic of these commissioners that must be noted: many, perhaps all, of these county commissioners had held other office under John in the county to which they were now appointed as assessors of the thirteenth. They had acted as wardens of castles, custodians of lands in hand, tallagers and the like. The justices were therefore chosen from among the ranks of the king's local administrative officials. They had already a certain experience as executives: they had demonstrated their loyalty to the king; they had broadened their knowledge of local conditions – all these things gave them qualities essential to their success in the new office.[72]

---

[69] On this see David Carpenter, 'The Decline of the Curial Sheriff in England, 1194–1258', *English Historical Review* 101 (1976); reprinted in his *The Reign of Henry III* (London, 1996), pp. 151–82.

[70] William Trussell was returned as lord of Billesley in 1235 and 1242. According to Dugdale's pedigree he was the younger brother of Richard Trussell, lord of Billesley, and finally succeeded him there after the latter's death at Evesham (*VCH Warwickshire*, vol. III, p. 60). This William married Rohese, daughter and heiress of William Pantulf of Cublesdon, Staffordshire, suggesting a younger son who had established himself independently. (See G. Templeman, *The Sheriffs of Warwickshire in the Thirteenth Century*, Dugdale Society Occasional Papers 7 (Oxford, 1948), p. 46.) However, the fact that William, the sheriff, held Billesley at an earlier date might suggest that he was of an earlier generation, anterior to Richard and William.

[71] See below, pp. 128, 162–3.

[72] S.K. Mitchell, *Taxation in Medieval England* (New Haven and London, 1951), p. 70. Chapter 2 of this work is a full and valuable discussion of the development of the local machinery of taxation.

Mitchell found the same characteristics in the fuller record for Henry III, verifying his findings, in particular, through a study of the commissioners operating in Lincolnshire in 1225. Many were 'considerable landholders and prominent in the local administrative system of the monarchy, acting as wardens of lands in hand, as tallagers, as itinerant justices, justices of assize, forest justices and the like. These were the men whom the Angevin monarchy employed to carry on the work of government.'[73]

A close look at the machinery employed for the assessment and collection of the fifteenth of 1225 brings out graphically the difference between those knights who were the crown's trusted agents, its justices in the broad sense, and the great majority of the county knights *per se*. On 15 February 1225 the king wrote to the taxers for each of the counties – literally 'our justices for assessing and collecting the fifteenth of all movables' – giving them very precise instructions on how they were to operate.[74] First, the sheriff would assemble all the knights of the county to be before the justices at the county town on the Sunday before mid-Lent (presumably 2 March). On that day they were to have four knights chosen for every hundred (or wapentake, in the counties of 'Danish' England); more or less than four if the size of the hundred warranted it. It was these knights who were to go to the hundreds and conduct the actual assessment. They were forbidden to deal with hundreds in which they were resident, but were to be responsible for neighbouring hundreds. The letters detailed precisely what was to be taxed and what was not. Everyone, with the exception of earls, barons and knights, was to swear to the quantity and value of his own movables and those of his two nearest neighbours. Where there was any dispute the knights would investigate the truth through the oath of twelve upright and lawful neighbours, or of as many as would suffice for the purpose. Stewards (here *servientes*), or reeves if the stewards were not available, were to swear as to the movables of their lords – earls, barons and knights – in every vill. Half of the money was to be paid on the feast of Holy Trinity (25 May), and the other half at Michaelmas (29 September). The manner of collection was to be as follows: in each hundred the four knights were to receive the money from the hands of four men and the reeve of each vill, using tallies as receipts, and then carry it to the justices who were to store it in a safe place, cathedral, abbey or priory in the county, under their seals and the seals of the knights, until arrangements were made for it to be sent on. The knights were also to hand over to them immediately all writings and rolls produced during the assessment and keep copies. The justices were to deal directly in person with any part of the county where they considered there might be difficulty. The knights were to swear on oath, in the presence of the justices and touching sacred objects, that they would carry out the assessment and taxation faithfully and diligently and would do nothing amiss out of love,

---

[73] *Ibid.*, p. 72.   [74] *Pat. Rolls, 1216–25*, pp. 560–1.

hatred or anything else in the world. The justices themselves were also to swear to carry it through faithfully and diligently in the presence of the sheriff and all the knights gathered on the initial day. If any of the justices, cleric or layman, should prove unable to carry this through for manifest and reasonable cause, the others were to have power to co-opt a colleague, providing that he, too, had taken the appropriate oath. Finally, they were given instructions on how to deal with the lands of archbishops, bishops, abbots, priors and all other religious, and the letter ends with a formal injunction to carry the whole matter through faithfully according to their fealty.

It was by no means unusual that the panels were called justices in the records of 1225. Their forebears had been so called in 1207, as indeed had the commissioners who had been in charge of the Assize of Arms back in 1181.[75] As royal justices these men received remuneration, initially in the form of expenses but after 1232 in the form of a regular fee.[76] The same was true of other important offices, such as escheator.[77] When it came to employing knights, the crown's view seems to have been precisely that articulated in the *Dialogue of the Exchequer* back in the 1180s: 'It is the king's prerogative as chief of the executive that any man in the kingdom, if the King need him, may be freely taken and assigned to the King's service, whose man soever he be, and whomsoever he serves in war or in peace.'[78] There was a major difference then between exercising such office and merely participating in judicial procedures, which was expected of a knight as a matter of course. It is very odd that some historians should persist in referring to participants in the grand assize as administrator knights. They were, of course, nothing of the sort. The public duty involved in jury service and the like can hardly be said to constitute administration. The idea is damaging precisely because it elides the crucial distinction between the majority of knights who fulfilled their duty when called upon – whether this be in an enthusiastic or in a dilatory manner – and those more active men who were in receipt of prestigious commissions from the central government.

It is worth noting in passing that there is also a distinction to be made in general between operating as a royal justice in the broader sense and exercising the lesser offices in the shire, such as coroner and verderer, which were elective and unpaid. There was some overlap in personnel, but the status and power involved was of a different order. Coroners, for example, tended on the whole to be drawn from the lesser knights, although there was a smattering of more elevated men. In Northamptonshire, for example, they included William de

---

[75] *Ibid.*, pp. 83–4.   [76] Mitchell, *Taxation in Medieval England*, pp. 85–7.

[77] See E.R. Stevenson, 'The Escheator', in J.F. Willard, W.A. Morris *et al.* (eds.), *The English Government at Work 1327–1336* (Cambridge, MA, 1947), vol. II, pt iii, p. 158.

[78] *Dialogus de Scaccario, The Course of the Exchequer*, ed. Charles Johnson (Oxford, 1983), pp. 83–4.

Houghton and William de Deneford,[79] and in the early 1250s men like Luke de Culun, William de Trayly, Robert de Hotot and Robert de Plumpton, as well as Roger de Whelton who had figured as a justice of assize.[80] In Warwickshire the coroners at the 1232 eyre were Peter de Wolverton, Gerard de Alspath and Robert de Morton, together with no less a figure than John de Ladbroke.[81] In 1247, they included Gerard de Alspath and William de Edstone as well as Philip de Esseby.[82]

ON THE EVE OF 1258

The system bequeathed by the Angevins can be said to have worked tolerably well during the early decades of the reign of Henry III. As we approach the débâcle of 1258, however, there are increasing signs of strain. Much depended, at the lower levels, on the routine obligations of a broad range of knights and freeholders in the shires. We cannot simply assume that men prized these roles and that they participated in them willingly, although some may well have done. Increasingly, the government could not assume it either. The purchase of exemptions from the crown, which has a great deal to tell us about attitudes towards unpaid work in the shires, rose to a crescendo during the 1250s.[83] About 5 per cent of these were for exemption from suit to public courts such as the county and the hundred. The king granted quittance of common summons to favoured men, including influential landowners. In Northamptonshire, for example, twenty-three men were excused attendance at the 1252 eyre.[84] The majority of the grants, however, were exemptions for life from serving on 'assizes, juries and recognitions' and from local offices, such as coroner. Between 1233 and 1272, Henry III issued over 1,200 charters of exemption from these civil obligations, the great majority of them during the 1250s. At this point exemptions often involved the office of sheriff too. No wonder John Maddicott refers to 'a retreat from office-holding on a massive scale'.[85] Moreover, there is further evidence of reluctance to serve. Such exemptions were available only to those willing and able to pay for the privilege and/or having access to powerful patronage. We have ample evidence of sheriffs and bailiffs taking bribes

---

[79] The sheriff of Northampton was ordered to have Houghton replaced on 7 October 1236 and Deneford on 3 March 1241: *Close Rolls, 1234–7*, p. 321; *Close Rolls, 1237–42*, p. 278.

[80] PRO Just 1/615 (Northamptonshire Eyre Roll for 1253), m. 1, listing the coroners since the last eyre.

[81] PRO Just 1/951A m. 7d.

[82] PRO Just 1/954 m. 48. The name of the fourth coroner is incomplete owing to damage to the roll: *Robert L. . . .*

[83] For what follows see, in particular, the important essay by Scott L. Waugh, 'Reluctant Knights and Jurors: Respites, Exemptions, and Public Obligations in the Reign of Henry III', *Speculum* 58 (1983).

[84] *Ibid.*, p. 963.   [85] Maddicott, 'Magna Carta and the Local Community', p. 45.

to release men from serving on juries and recognitions. This evidence, taken as a whole, speaks reams about how thirteenth-century men actually viewed 'self-government at the king's command'.

As Scott L. Waugh has emphasised, however, exemption *per se* is not the whole of the story. As he points out, although some men certainly used exemptions to avoid public service altogether, others used them in a discriminating way, 'to avoid only unremunerative, routine service so that they could pursue work which they considered more profitable or prestigious'.[86] Local landowners, and others, sought the privilege of doing what they wanted, when they wanted, and it may well be true that this behaviour pattern meant the crown's policy of selling respites from knighthood and exemptions from civil obligations may have disrupted the running of local administration less than might appear at first sight and less than the reformers of 1258–9 claimed.[87] However, some disruption there certainly was. It added to the confusion in Northamptonshire in 1257, for example, when its team of four coroners came to the end of its life. In March 1257, with Luke de Culun dead and William de Trayly now languid and weakened by old age, the king sought to replace them by direct substitution rather than election, appointing Hugh Fauvel and Henry de Osevyle. However, this seems not to have worked, for in January 1258 the sheriff was ordered to proceed with the normal election to replace them. In fact, the sheriff was ordered to replace not two coroners but three, for Robert de Hotot had thrown in the towel, producing his charter of exemption.[88] Robert had been the man chosen in the county to replace Robert de Plumpton in 1252.[89] It was the medieval equivalent of presenting your 'get out of gaol free card', i.e. Robert was choosing to leave office at a moment suitable to him. The result must have been a serious rupture in office-holding at the local level, even if each coroner was generally operating his own fairly discrete district.[90] Within three months, moreover, a fourth coroner, Geoffrey de Cundy, was dead, and in September 1258 Hugh de Messenden stepped down on the grounds that he held no land in the county.[91]

Resistance to local office, together with the steady fall in the number of knights – the subject of the following chapter – may help to explain why a few of the more influential figures within the counties are found as coroners. The sale of exemptions may also have lessened the crown's grip on more significant local positions. Let us take the sub-escheators of Warwickshire as an example.

[86] Waugh, 'Reluctant Knights and Jurors', p. 971.
[87] *Ibid.*, pp. 968–71.   [88] *Close Rolls, 1256–9*, pp. 40, 183.
[89] *Close Rolls, 1247–51*, p. 48; PRO Just 1/615 m. 1. The team had been in office for some years. The coroners at the 1253 eyre were Roger de Whelton, Luke de Culun, William de Trayly and Robert de Hotot.
[90] See R.F. Hunnisett, *The Medieval Coroner* (Cambridge, 1961), ch. 8.
[91] *Close Rolls, 1256–9*, pp. 209, 270.

The sub-escheator was an important office from the king's point of view, being directly concerned with royal rights. As a result the two occupants of the office were generally appointed by the crown. It was not an office elected in the localities. In 1232, for example, in a nation-wide appointment of escheators, Warwickshire was to be served by the much-trusted John de Ladbroke and William de Bishopton. In 1249 the holders of the office were Hugh de Arden and Henry de Wingham. At the end of that year, however, Hugh de Arden was allowed to step down. Henry de Wingham was asked to nominate a substitute and to let the king know his name. Notwithstanding this, in April 1250 the king substituted Henry Pipard. The following year he substituted Thomas de Clinton for Henry Pipard. In June 1253 Thomas de Clinton was absolved from office and Thomas le Irreys put in his place. There then follows something of a pantomime. In August 1253 Thomas le Irreys substituted Hugh de Mancetter. On 9 October the king substituted Walter d'Eyville, Hugh de Mancetter being dead. On 18 October, however, he removed Walter d'Eyville in favour of Adam de Napton. This was not a good choice, however. In July 1254 the king turned to William de Waver because Adam was too weak to exercise the office. William de Waver, however, had a charter of exemption. On this being pointed out, the king proceeded to choose Robert de Harcourt, in March 1255. When the abbot of Pershore, the escheator south of the Trent, pointed out that Robert was unsuitable, Alexander Bacon was substituted. It looks as though he was not suitable either, for on 1 August 1255 the king appointed Henry de Ladbroke on the advice of the abbot of Pershore.[92]

Although it was still there in outline, the Angevin system – of ruling the shires through a relatively small group of trusted men with pre-existing strong roots in the localities who operated as a medium between shire and centre – may well have been breaking down. For one thing, there was the rise of the truly professional local administrators, exemplified by a particular type of sheriff who was beginning to emerge in contradistinction not only to the old *curialis* but also to the true vavasour of the shire. As we move towards 1258, the government seems to have been turning increasingly to professional administrators of obscure origin with no base or standing in the particular counties to which they were assigned.[93] One of these was Hugh de Manby, an unpopular clerk who was sheriff of Northamptonshire in 1253 and 1256 and who was later to be brought before Hugh Bigod, the baronial justiciar, to answer for his crimes.[94] There can be little doubt that networks of administrators were developing at this time, men who enjoyed vertical ties with the crown and the magnates and

---

[92] *Close Rolls, 1231–4*, p. 130; *Close Rolls, 1247–51*, pp. 248, 277, 474; *Close Rolls, 1251–3*, pp. 409, 420, 422; *Close Rolls, 1253–4*, p. 81; *Close Rolls, 1254–6*, pp. 58, 95–6, 121.

[93] Carpenter, 'The Decline of the Curial Sheriff', pp. 178–9.

[94] See also E.F. Jacob, *Studies in the Period of Baronial Reform and Rebellion, 1258–67* (Oxford, 1925), pp. 48–9.

horizontal ties among themselves.[95] At the same time, with a more prominent role being taken by the central court justices and the lack of extraordinary taxation, there was rather less for the old style *missi dominici* to do. One has the impression that by the 1250s there was less discrimination in the system, with the tasks at the several levels devolving increasingly upon whoever was willing and available.

A profound change occurred during the 1240s and 1250s with the development of a more elitist and exclusive knighthood. This, too, in lessening the distinctions within knightly ranks, may have made the old system difficult to maintain. It is to this matter that we must now give consideration.

---

[95] Scott Waugh sees them as a 'ministerial gentry' emerging during the course of the thirteenth century ('Reluctant Knights and Jurors', p. 976).

4. *The crisis of the knightly class revisited*

As is well known, the first half of the thirteenth century saw a thinning of knightly ranks and the development of a more exclusive knighthood in England. By the 1240s the powerful force exerted by a fully fledged chivalric knighthood was forcing earlier connotations firmly into the background. The rather inclusive Angevin conception of knighthood, with its heavy service component, was fast giving way before a new and rather narrow elitism.[1] Among the expressions of this was the separation of knights from others in charter witness lists so that the knights and the greater lords, and only they, were designated *dominus* or sir.[2] Another was the knightly effigy, now making its first serious inroads into the churches.[3] A third was heraldry, manifested not only in the appearance of rolls of arms but increasingly as a visual expression of status within the public sphere.[4]

It is important to emphasise that this new, exclusive knighthood was no surface matter, a mere shift of emphasis. On the contrary, it was a development of momentous importance in the history of gentility. A fundamental social divide was emerging between the knights, including the great lords who were also of course knights, and the rest, including the erstwhile knight-bearing families below them. It is one thing, however, to observe such phenomena; it is quite another to explain them and to address their historical significance. And yet it is vital that we make the attempt if we are to appreciate the role of knighthood in the evolution of the gentry. I will do so here by reviewing the debate on 'the crisis of the knightly class'.

---

[1] For a more detailed discussion of these issues see my *The Knight in Medieval England*, chs. 3–4.

[2] On this point see Coss, *Lordship, Knighthood and Locality*, pp. 214–17, 251, and D.F. Fleming, 'Milites as Attestors to Charters in England, 1000–1300', *Albion* 22 (1990), pp. 185–98.

[3] For effigies see H.A. Tummers, *Early Secular Effigies in England in the Thirteenth Century* (Leiden, 1980).

[4] For the use of heraldry in the various media see J. Cherry, 'Heraldry as Decoration in the Thirteenth Century', in W.M. Ormrod (ed.), *England in the Thirteenth Century* (Stamford, 1991), pp. 123–34 and references given there. See also, more generally, Crouch, *Image of Aristocracy* and Maurice Keen, *Chivalry* (Yale, 1984), pp. 123–34, and references given there.

In 1975 I published an essay entitled 'Sir Geoffrey de Langley and the Crisis of the Knightly Class in Thirteenth-Century England'.[5] In it I argued that, in and around the reign of Henry III, 'the knightly class was passing through a period of economic crisis, a crisis that was both extensive and prolonged'. It was not an entirely new idea. In the mid-1960s Michael Postan had suggested that the thirteenth century was a time of great difficulty for smaller landowners, when considerable quantities of land passed out of their possession into the hands of religious houses. At the same time, Rodney Hilton was arguing that the rise of chivalric knighthood had been accompanied by a severe social and economic crisis for the knightly class as a whole. There was much to point scholars in that direction. The earlier researches of Denholm-Young had indicated that the number of knights severely declined during the course of the thirteenth century, while H.G. Richardson, in particular, had shown the extent to which ecclesiastical landowners were involved in the redemption of land indebted to the Jews. In 1973 Paul Harvey argued that the period from *c*.1180 to *c*.1220 had constituted the first great inflation in English history and outlined a range of economic, social and political consequences. None the less, as far as the land market and the fortunes of lesser landowners were concerned there were warning voices. Edmund King in a perceptive essay analysing the acquisitions of Peterborough Abbey from knightly landowners advised against a too-ready assumption that this constituted the dominant trend on the land market. With the bulk of surviving evidence coming from the great ecclesiastical corporations there was a serious danger of distortion, a point also made by J.Z. Titow. In preference, King would envisage 'a world . . . in which the rise and fall of landed families was a thing taken for granted'.[6]

I decided not to heed these warnings, but to push the crisis argument as far as it would go. Armed with evidence from the Langley Cartulary, which detailed the investments of the royal servant, Geoffrey de Langley, I indicated that the crisis hypothesis could accommodate a range of known phenomena including the decline in the incidence of knighthood, inflationary pressures in the economy, the uneven capacity to adjust to such pressures, the widely observable phenomenon of alienation through economic necessity, the fairly widespread trafficking in encumbered estates by royal servants as well as by religious houses, the political repercussions of this traffic which was clearly regarded, in some quarters at least, as scandalous, and the partisan relief of Jewish debtors by the Montfortian government of 1264–5. In this context I wrote approvingly of Postan's suggestion that 'if what Simon de Montfort and Edward I tried to do was to win the support of the knightly class, they did so not by bowing to its new strength

---

[5] *Past and Present* 68 (1975), pp. 3–37; reprinted in T.H. Aston (ed.), *Landlords, Peasants and Politics in Medieval England* (Cambridge, 1987).

[6] E. King, 'Large and Small Landowners in Thirteenth-Century England', *Past and Present* 47 (1970), p. 48.

but by coming to its relief'.[7] Looking across the history of indebted estates and the fact that difficulties were often cumulative, I concluded that the height of the crisis was not the period of heaviest inflation but the period of continuous but slower inflation which followed (from *c.*1220 to *c.*1260), or in other words the reign of Henry III.

Retribution followed in 1980 when David Carpenter countered with his seminal essay, 'Was There a Crisis of the Knightly Class in the Thirteenth Century? The Oxfordshire Evidence'.[8] Carpenter based himself not on the views of Postan and Hilton but on those of Treharne and Holt. In his study of the knights during the period of reform and rebellion R.F. Treharne had spoken of 'the greatly enhanced wealth of the mid thirteenth-century knight, and the much higher standard of living and civilization which he enjoyed' upon which their participation in those heroic events was predicated; precisely the view that Postan had been seeking to revise.[9] For J.C. Holt, the political independence of men of knightly rank that had been expressed during the reign of King John 'had a secure basis in wealth and administrative experience'.[10] Carpenter compiled a list of Oxfordshire knights from the 1220s and subjected the fortunes of them and their descendants up to the early fourteenth century to rigorous analysis. Omitting fourteen knights whose property could not be traced, he divided the remainder into four groups. Group one consisted of five knights, each with four or more manors. Group two comprised twenty knights with two or three manors. Group three contained twenty-five knights with one manor containing three or more hides of land. Group four comprised only seven knights with less than three hides of land each. In practice, however, he discounted four of the latter as not being lords of manors. His analysis is based, therefore, on fifty-three knights who constituted 'a reasonably representative sample of the middle and upper sections of the knightly class'.[11]

Carpenter's results are clearly presented and unequivocal. As far as Oxfordshire is concerned there was no crisis of the knightly class during the reign of Henry III. His results are as follows. Dealing with the three knightly families with only one small manor from group four separately, he found that one sold out, one disappeared for lack of heirs and one survived. Of the fifty knights who comprised groups one to three, nine failed during the course of the century for default of male heirs. Only six sold out through economic weakness. Two others seem to have passed their property to religious houses for reasons of genuine piety, and two disappeared without trace. As Carpenter says, even if these four are added to the six, only ten out of fifty can be said to have submitted

[7] M.M. Postan, *The Medieval Economy and Society* (London, 1972), p. 165.
[8] *English Historical Review* 377 (1980), pp. 721–52.
[9] Treharne, 'The Knights in the Period of Reform and Rebellion', p. 8.
[10] Holt, *The Northerners*, p. 55.
[11] Carpenter, 'Was There a Crisis of the Knightly Class?', p. 725.

during the course of the century. The traffic in manors was not great and the number of gentry families who sold out can hardly be said to have been 'large', as had been suggested by my formulation. Moreover, of the thirty families who survived the century only five suffered an overall loss of lands. By contrast, seventeen families maintained their lands intact and a further nine increased their holdings. Of the families who disappeared for lack of male heirs, three had previously suffered some loss of land while two others had increased their landed wealth. In short, 'In Oxfordshire, the underlying material position of many middling and upper knightly families seems secure.'[12] If there was a crisis during the thirteenth century it was 'a crisis less of a class than of some individuals within it'.[13]

As far as the middling and upper reaches of Oxfordshire's knightly families during the 1220s are concerned at least, Carpenter argues convincingly that there was no crisis. An economic failure rate of somewhere between 12 and 20 per cent across three quarters of a century hardly constitutes a revolution in landholding. In addition to the bald statistics, moreover, David Carpenter brought some powerful arguments to bear against the crisis hypothesis, showing it to have been wrongly formulated in some crucial respects. My first reaction when reading his essay, however, was one of surprise. Although he, like me, was writing in terms of crisis, he seemed to be addressing a rather different hypothesis, viz. was there a *decline* of the knightly class in the thirteenth century? The Oxford English Dictionary defines crisis as follows: 'A vitally important or decisive stage in the progress of anything; a turning point; also a state of affairs in which a decisive change for better or worse is imminent; now applied especially to times of difficulty, insecurity, and suspense in politics or commerce.'[14] It was essentially the last of these propositions that I had in mind. The validity of the crisis hypothesis, when used in this sense, is by no means dependent upon a wholesale revolution in landholding. It is significant that Carpenter turns the phrase 'crisis of the class as a whole', which I borrowed from Hilton, into 'crisis of the whole class', implying I think a crisis involving all or most of its members. The distinction is a subtle but important one. Hilton, after all, was talking about a crisis which he saw as accompanying the very rise in social standing of the chivalric knight.[15]

However, it was not David Carpenter who invented the confusion between crisis and decline. It was present in my original formulation. It was present, arguably, in the rhetoric which tended, cumulatively, to overstate the case:[16] 'it

---

[12] *Ibid.*, p. 750.   [13] *Ibid.*, p. 751.

[14] *Oxford English Dictionary* (2nd edn, Oxford, 1989), vol. IV, p. 27.

[15] 'This increase in social standing, as is so often the case, accompanied a severe social and economic crisis for the class as a whole': R.H. Hilton, *A Medieval Society: The West Midlands at the End of the Thirteenth Century* (London, 1966), pp. 49–55.

[16] The quotations that follow come from Coss, 'The Crisis of the Knightly Class', pp. 23, 24, 27, 34.

can hardly be doubted that, for some areas of the country at least, the quantity of land passing from smaller landowners to the church was considerable'; 'for the market to have been so buoyant and its participants so confident there can have been no dearth of desperate debtors'; 'the large numbers who from the late twelfth century onwards became indebted, primarily to the Jews, and were ultimately forced to sell out'; 'financial strain and the horrors of debt take us a long way towards explaining why the reformist earls received such widespread support from the knightly class in thirteenth-century England'. More fundamentally, it was present in my failure to distinguish between the Hilton and the Postan hypotheses, the second of which bordered at least on a full-scale thesis of decline: 'the contention that land transactions were reducing the smaller man's share in England's land'.[17]

That Carpenter's essay nailed the Postan thesis is, I think, clear. It is true, as Carpenter admits, that Oxfordshire is an ideal county from which to launch an optimistic view of the fortunes of England's lesser landowners. A rich and highly manorialised county of ancient cultivation, it lacked the great religious houses whose aggrandisement in some regions put pressure on the land market. Kosminsky's study of the Hundred Rolls of 1279 reveals that Oxfordshire had relatively few small manors. The average-sized lay manor was 575 acres, compared with 368 acres in Cambridgeshire, for example.[18] Furthermore, as Carpenter points out, the families who sold out were to some extent at least replaced by newcomers. The *curialis*, Geoffrey de Langley, one of the arch profiteers from encumbered estates, founded not one solid knightly family but two. In addition to those who had the advantage of royal service, men like the king's serjeant, Lawrence de Broke, there were others who rose from freeholding ranks, largely through seigneurial service; families like the Louches and the Abberburys.[19] He is surely right, too, to suggest that the extent to which the great religious houses could actually distort the land market is liable to be exaggerated. Moreover, solidly based knightly families, in particular, had in-built advantages which bolstered their position, including the marriage market and the prospects of local office. There is evidence, too, of the 'higher standard of living and civilization' of which Treharne wrote. In short, the majority do not appear to have been seriously under pressure and many can be said to have been thriving. Oxfordshire presents a best-case scenario for the middling and upper ranks of the knightly class. Nevertheless, the results of Carpenter's analysis are such as to strongly suggest that a thesis which posits the economic decline of the knightly class is never likely to be a serious contender.

[17] Postan, *The Medieval Economy and Society*, appendix I, p. 247.
[18] Carpenter, 'Was There a Crisis of the Knightly Class?', p. 749.
[19] For Lawrence de Broke see also Brand, *The Origins of the English Legal Profession*, pp. 64–5, and *Select Cases in the Court of King's Bench*, ed. G.O. Sayles, Selden Society (London, 1957), vol. V, pp. xxxii–xxxv.

It is a tribute to the thoroughness of Carpenter's Oxfordshire study that it set the parameters of debate from then on. My attempt to clarify matters in a postscript to the reprinting of my essay in 1987 failed to make any real impact.[20] Indeed, so resilient is the prime debate that my later efforts to move the discussion on – in a book centring on north Warwickshire, published in 1991 – did not succeed in knocking the original exchange from centre stage.[21] Even as late as 1999 Nicholas Vincent contributed to the debate very much in anti-Postan terms.[22] However, when such arguments are set against the Hilton thesis of a longer-term social and economic crisis accompanying the rise of chivalric knighthood, the results are less clear cut. Carpenter's essay suggested a polarisation between one-manor families and those possessing two or more. All of the Oxfordshire families which collapsed came from the former group. Moreover, all of the one-manor families had jettisoned knighthood by the end of the century, making the knights a wealthier and more exclusive group. When we add to these families the eighteen of the original seventy-one knights who were omitted from consideration, either because they were poorly endowed or because their property could not be traced, the possibility of a rather different interpretation is opened up. Carpenter, anchored in the reign of Henry III, has a wholly optimistic interpretation of knightly debt, seeing it as often strategic and/or determined by short-term need, such as financing litigation. On his reasoning, severe difficulties, when they did occur, were more likely the result of bad management than of an adverse economic climate. It is possible to view knightly indebtedness during the reign of Henry III, however, as the last and most visible episode in a much longer story.

In the wake of the Coss–Carpenter debate studies of the knightly class have gone in two directions. One has looked forward from the 1220s, seeking further illumination of developments during the reign of Henry III and keeping one eye on the heroic events of the years 1258–67. The other has looked backwards from the 1220s and has been primarily concerned with interpreting the observable decline in the number of knights. The time has come to review these findings. I shall follow both lines of inquiry in turn, indicating where they have enriched our understanding since the debate of 1975–80, before suggesting how we should best interpret the broader fortunes of knighthood and the knightly class.

FORWARD PROJECTION: THE POSTAN THESIS AND THE REIGN OF HENRY III

David Carpenter's view of the fortunes of the knightly class received unqualified support from a doctoral thesis on the knights of Kent between the years 1232

---

[20] Aston (ed.), *Landlords, Peasants and Politics in Medieval England*, p. 201.

[21] *Lordship, Knighthood and Locality.*

[22] Nicholas Vincent, 'The Earliest Nottinghamshire Will (1257): Robert of Wichford Counts His Debts', *Transactions of the Thoroton Society of Nottinghamshire* 102 (1998), pp. 43–56.

and 1280.[23] Of eighty or so knightly families which he saw operating in Kent across this period, Jeremy Quick could find only half a dozen which sold estates. The most prominent purchaser here was the priory of Christ Church Canterbury which acquired estates from Sir Reginald Cornhill, Sir Stephen Haringod and Peter Bending, the latter in consequence of Jewish debts. As he says, in words that directly echo David Carpenter, these are 'hardly enough to constitute a crisis of a whole class in Kent'.[24] Looking at knightly fortunes as a whole, Quick placed himself firmly in the Carpenter camp: 'Like all landowners in this period, the knightly class were in a position to enjoy the benefits of a growing agrarian economy which was especially suited to demesne production.'[25] This is not to say, however, that the Kentish knights as a group were especially rich. Quick finds a tendency to demesnes of less than 300 acres, and a dependence upon wage labour. The inquisitions into rebel lands after the battle of Evesham indicate that average knightly wealth was £22 per annum, hardly above the minimum level of distraint to knighthood.[26] The most he will allow, however, is that 'smaller landlords, when compared to greater landlords, improved their financial positions at a slower pace and to a lesser degree'.[27] Moreover, as he points out, some men were able to improve their position by service as estate stewards. Such service to Christ Church Canterbury earned them a salary of £10 per annum in 1272 and 1273. Furthermore, this type of administrative experience could open the way to government service.[28]

Carpenter's position received additional support from K.J. Stringer in his study of Earl David of Huntingdon. Whilst primarily concerned with this earl's tenure of the honour, that is to say from 1185 to 1219, Stringer had some more general points to make across a broader timespan. Producing what was, in effect, a reconsideration of the Braybrooke material, he recited the acute financial hardships and progressive alienations experienced by the families of Rushton, Foxton, Foliot and Leidet (the latter, in fact, successors to the Foliots), and the opportunities for investment afforded for the rising shrieval family of Braybrooke.[29] Stringer suggests that these were not the only casualties within the honour of Huntingdon, and that in all probability the families of Audri, Boughton and Lisures should be added to them. Interestingly, he argues that the period of Earl David's tenure was not the prelude to a period of greater difficulty for minor landowners, but was itself 'the age of greatest economic hardship for the Huntingdon knights and minor gentry'.[30] However, he

---

[23] J.A. Quick, 'Government and Society in Kent 1232–1280' (Oxford DPhil thesis, 1986). Chapter 2 (pp. 111–45) deals explicitly with the knights and their fortunes.

[24] *Ibid.*, p. 125.   [25] *Ibid.*, p. 120.

[26] Although he acknowledges that these inquisitions are of questionable accuracy and that they exclude lands outside Kent.

[27] *Ibid.*, p. 122.   [28] On this subject see Denholm-Young, *Seignorial Administration*, ch. 2.

[29] K.J. Stringer, *Earl David of Huntingdon 1152–1219: A Study in Anglo-Scottish History* (Edinburgh, 1985).

[30] *Ibid.*, p. 140.

specifically targets the Postan thesis of decline, regarding my own formulation as one expression of it. His major points are ones that are, by now, well known. First, the cases of decline among the Huntingdon gentry 'simply seem to indicate the possible extremes of personal fortune rather than any crisis of the whole class'.[31] Secondly, while some families fell, others rose. Here he cites not only the Braybrookes, but also the case of Ralf Morin of Harrold, Bedfordshire, who accompanied Prince John to Ireland and acquired property there, but who subsequently, by offices and investments, laid the foundations of an important family in the English shires.[32] One of his relatives, Robert Morin, managed to elope with the daughter of John Mauduit of Easton Mauduit in Northamptonshire, thereby securing her inheritance. That this was done against the wishes of the royal chamberlain, Robert Mauduit of Hanslope, may well reflect the new influence of Ralf Morin. Thirdly, 'most knightly *lignages* do not in fact occur as either ruinously in debt nor vigorously emphasising their social superiority'. In consequence, they appear less often in the records:

> Solicitous conservation of the patrimonial estate was more than a matter of family instinct or legal restraints; sustained over the years it could guarantee financial security. A tenant might limit his expenses by checking the claims of piety, scaling down his contractual obligations, or deliberately avoiding the costs of knighthood. The Huntingdon gentry also added to their property by judicious marriages into land, by success in litigation, by taking on beneficial leases as *firmarii* [farmers], by assarting, and by small purchases. All these were ways of procuring the extra substance to maintain one generation and support the next without dissipating the main family property.[33]

In short, 'no-one analysing the whole body of Huntingdon evidence would be likely to support the concept of a declining thirteenth-century gentry and a rising aristocracy'.[34]

My own further studies into the society of thirteenth-century Warwickshire encompassed both honour and county. The honour of Coventry, scene of some of Geoffrey de Langley's most spectacular investment in the land market, would seem to have experienced a higher than normal incidence of indebted landowners. Of families with interests confined to the immediate vicinity of the city of Coventry, both the Nerbones of Stivichall and the Keresleys of Keresley succumbed, while several others were in serious decline. The manor of Shortley was alienated by the d'Aubignys of Great Wishford who, by marriage, imported their troubles into the area. The decline and fall of the d'Eyvilles, once a ministerial family serving both the earl of Warwick and the earl of Chester,

---

[31] *Ibid.*, p. 138.

[32] Ironically, Ralf's grandson, John, avoided knighthood, despite it being said that he was worth over £30 per annum in 1255, and died insolvent in 1263. Meanwhile his sister had married the clerk to her father's kitchen: *ibid.*, pp. 139–40.

[33] *Ibid.*, p. 139.   [34] *Ibid.*, p. 141.

and the even more illustrious Ardens of Ratley, the elder line of the family that stemmed from Turchil of Warwick, 'indicate that it was not only lesser brethren within the broad seigniorial class who could face severe problems in early and mid-thirteenth-century conditions'.[35]

My study of Warwickshire knights in general, however, produced results consistent with those obtained by Carpenter for Oxfordshire. Of ninety-seven knights who participated in the grand assize between 1221 and 1232, thirty-one or almost a third held either minor interests or interests which are no longer discernible. If we exclude these petty knights or *milituli*, we are left with sixty-six knights representing sixty-two families.[36] Only thirty-three of these sixty-two, however, survived into the fourteenth century. Of those which did not survive, sixteen can be shown to have become extinct in the male line. There are seven clear examples of total or near total alienation,[37] and six other cases where there is no clear descent of their estates. In other words, the number of families failing via alienation lies somewhere between seven and thirteen, that is between 11 and 21 per cent of the sample. However, this is by no means the whole of the story. Some of the families who survived into the fourteenth century did so with reduced status or even in reduced circumstances. These include the Ardens of Radbourne, the Pascis, the Semillys and the Wandards. Many of the single-manor families, in particular, often show signs of alienation and other difficulties. These include the Chetwoods, the Foliots, the Bassets and the Luddingtons. Others families, often of more consequence, can be shown to have passed through periods of difficulty yet remained intact. Some were avoiding knighthood. Altogether, seventeen Warwickshire knights fined for distraint of knighthood in 1256. Of these, no less than eleven were from the sixty-two families constituting the sample of established county knights drawn from the period 1221–32.

None the less, when all of this has been said, the majority of the thirty-three surviving families from the reduced sample of sixty-two were to constitute the hard core of Warwickshire's future gentry. Some of these were certainly aided by advantageous marriages, often to the heiresses of families which failed to survive. A few families – the Peches, the Clintons of Coleshill and the Butlers of Oversley – gained fairly spectacularly. In short,

> when we take a sizeable sample of knightly families from the reign of Henry III we find, as indeed we would expect to find, that it is only a minority who forcibly alienate land on any scale, that there are others who show a net gain particularly through marriage, and that the haemorrhaging of estates, as

---

[35] Coss, *Lordship, Knighthood and Locality*, p. 204.
[36] For what follows see, especially, pp. 294–304.
[37] Arden of Ratley, Parles of Handsworth, Bagot of Morton Bagot, Frankton of Frankton, Barton of Barton-on-the-Heath, Fitz Odo of Harbury and Chesterton, and Bagot of Preston Bagot. The Parles family managed to hang on through an additional interest that had descended to them.

Edmund King so aptly puts it, is to some degree compensated for by the rise of new families, or scions of old ones, through the mechanism of service. What we do not find is the wholesale revolution of landholding which some of the critics of the crisis hypothesis would seem to expect.[38]

More recently, Anne Polden has surveyed the knights of thirteenth-century Buckinghamshire along the same lines as David Carpenter's study of Oxfordshire and with similar results. She begins with a sample of eighty-eight knightly jurors from grand assize juries and forest inquisitions during the 1220s.[39] Of these, fourteen are omitted 'because no coherent picture of their lands or histories could be constructed from the evidence'.[40] The remaining seventy-four knights come from seventy-two families, of which ten are group one families with four or more manors, thirty-four are group two families with two or three manors, nineteen are group three families with one manor of three hides or more or one knight's fee, and nine are group four families with less than this. Polden found that as many as thirty-six families, or almost half of the sample, had disappeared by the early fourteenth century; however, at least two-thirds of them had disappeared through lack of heirs. But she also found that twelve families had alienated lands with fatal consequences, that five others disappear from view unaccountably (one of which was in serious difficulties), and that eight others had sustained serious loss. In other words, somewhere between twelve and seventeen families failed economically, while somewhere between twenty and twenty-five experienced serious difficulties. To put this in percentage terms, if we take the maximum figures, 35 per cent of the sample experienced serious difficulties while 24 per cent succumbed to them. Taking the minimum figures, more than 28 per cent experienced difficulties and 17 per cent succumbed.

Interestingly, she found that of the twelve families which definitely succumbed, only six were in the lowest groups (groups three and four). Of the others, five were in group two and one in group one. Not surprisingly, those in the higher groups which alienated had a stronger chance of survival: three out of four in group one, five out of five in group two, none out of six in groups three and four. She concludes that sales forced on indebted families constituted a phenomenon by no means unique to the poorer families, but that 'families holding single manors were far more liable to disappear from the landed class entirely as a result of such sales'.[41] Another finding is equally important. Knighthood followed wealth. Of the thirty-nine families from the sample who survived into

---

[38] Coss, *Lordship, Knighthood and Locality*, p. 303.

[39] Anne Polden, 'A Crisis of the Knightly Class? Inheritance and Office among the Gentry of Thirteenth-Century Buckinghamshire', in P. Fleming, A. Gross and J.R. Lander (eds.), *Regionalism and Revision: The Crown and Its Provinces in England 1200–1650* (London, 1998), pp. 29–58. Her original sample was reduced from eighty-nine because one of its number was essentially a Northumbrian knight.

[40] *Ibid.*, p. 30.   [41] *Ibid.*, p. 45.

the early fourteenth century, only sixteen, it seems, were still knight bearing. It was largely the holders of single manors who had dropped out.[42]

All of this, of course, is only one side of the story. To set against those who lost land or went under are at least sixteen families who gained land. Eight families made significant gains through marrying heiresses. Eight made substantial purchases. The most important statistic, perhaps, is the 50 per cent of families who 'simply held on to what they had', suggesting that 'continuity and stability within the gentry class were at least as marked a feature of their collective thirteenth-century experience as mobility'.[43]

Detailed research, then, has failed to find an economic decline of the knightly class. Moreover, it has shown why such a decline was never likely to have occurred. The knightly class, as a whole, possessed too many advantages. However adverse their material circumstances may have been, minor landowners enjoyed additional resources over and above their actual estates which, barring something utterly cataclysmic, would always have ensured their continued survival as a sector. In a recent essay, Nicholas Vincent has highlighted two of these. One is access to patronage, and the other is marriage.[44] The indebted family he is concerned with is that of Whichford of Warwickshire whose principal interests centred, initially, on Whichford itself and on Dunton in Curdworth. Nicholas de Whichford, who succeeded his brother Thierry in or after 1221, was the well-known knight who sought licence from the king in 1233 to take an aid from his tenants to help discharge the debts incurred by his knighthood.[45] He had been in debt to the Jews of Nottingham, however, from as early as October 1221. In 1239 he quitclaimed his manor of Whichford to his overlord, Reginald de Mohun, for the sum of seventy marks. The estate comprised a manor house and three carucates of land. An active knight who had fought in the Brittany campaign of 1230, Nicholas faced several difficulties. At Dunton, his brother Thierry had been forced to acknowledge a rent charge of 30s. per annum, and Nicholas had had no choice but to follow suit. From 1226 until 1231 he faced a rival claimant to the family's newly acquired manor at Flintham in Nottinghamshire and the ensuing litigation resulted in further annual outgoings of four marks per annum and the recognition of a new overlord whose presence weakened his relationship with his tenants. Meanwhile, in 1233, he had sought

---

[42] *Ibid.*, pp. 52–3. The figures here are rather vague because the wrong table seems to have been printed at this point.

[43] *Ibid.*, p. 56. Unfortunately, the figures do not quite tally. The text tells of twenty families which lost land, seventeen which gained and thirty-nine (of which twenty-two were surviving ones) staying still. This makes a total of seventy-six families, i.e. four more than the sample. It is likely that some families figure twice. The Dairels, for example, lost the land they had acquired through marriage. Table 2 gives slightly different figures from those in the text, viz. eighteen families losing land, sixteen gaining and thirty-nine staying still, i.e. a total of seventy-three.

[44] For what follows see Vincent, 'The Earliest Nottinghamshire Will'.

[45] *Calendar of Patent Rolls, 1232–47*, p. 16. Vincent's suggestion that he was forced to take up knighthood by the distraint seems to me unlikely. He could easily have fined.

to reacquire the advowson at Flintham from the abbot of Welbeck, but without success.

Nicholas de Whichford had many of the hallmarks of the seriously indebted knight, parting with a substantial part of his patrimony after some years of strain. The family may not have been helped by its own fecundity. Nicholas himself was one of four brothers, to one of whom, Matthew, he gave substantial holdings in Dunton, while he himself had at least five sons and one daughter. That Nicholas did not go under was due in large measure to the family's newly acquired estate at Flintham. The origins of this property are instructive. It had been acquired from the crown by the courtier Philip d'Aubigny, and bestowed on Thierry de Whichford. Thierry had been in the Holy Land, most probably on the Fifth Crusade, as had Philip d'Aubigny and very likely Nicholas de Whichford too. An association between d'Aubigny and the Whichfords clearly stems from this time and resulted in Thierry's enfeoffment at Flintham. It was an association which continued after Thierry's death, for Nicholas joined the Brittany campaign as part of Philip d'Aubigny's contingent. The situation is to be explained by the twin needs for patronage and for service. Moreover, as Nicholas Vincent says, there was a further dimension to this: 'it was the patronage of the royal court, filtered down through the courtier Philip d'Aubigné to Thierry and Nicholas de Whichford'.[46] Through this patronage, the family was relocated in Nottinghamshire. This being so, their Warwickshire property was no doubt considered the more expendable. Not that any landowning family let their estates go lightly. What the new property had done was to cushion Nicholas in his difficulties, and it almost certainly saved him and his family.

If patronage, or at least the fruits of patronage, saved Nicholas, his son's prospects were greatly enhanced by marriage. Robert de Whichford, who had succeeded his father by 1252, was married to the heiress Petronilla, daughter of William de Trumpington. She brought him lands in Cambridgeshire, Suffolk and Leicestershire. Robert died in 1257, leaving his daughter Agnes as his heir. She was later married to the Nottinghamshire knight Sir John Hose. In the meantime, Robert had consolidated somewhat at Flintham, acquired some new land there, and had secured freedom from suit of court from two Leicestershire overlords. He and Petronilla had divested themselves of some Cambridgeshire property, probably as part of a rationalisation of their interests. By 1254, as a result of family arrangements, Robert had lost control of the family land at Dunton, although the continuing family interest in the area resulted in property at Dosthill passing to his descendants. When he died, however, Robert owed almost four times the amount of money he bequeathed. His will indicates a series of bequests to family, friends and servants, to the value of £12, and debts to a variety of creditors totalling no less than £49. One of these creditors was

46 *Ibid.*, p. 46.

Sir Andrew Luttrell, the ancestor of Sir Geoffrey Luttrell of the famous psalter. Interestingly, not only Robert's iron hauberk and armour but also two of the rings he bequeathed, one a sapphire and the other an amethyst, were said to be in Luttrell's hands, opening the possibility that they were there as security for debt.[47] Nevertheless, Vincent sees Robert as a flourishing landowner and the debts as symptomatic of 'a flourishing credit economy'. Given the scale of his property, much enhanced by marriage, this level of indebtedness does not seem to have been problematic. In Vincent's view Robert de Whichford's will is 'a warning against the temptation to assume that debts such as Robert's are necessarily a portent of impending disaster', and he concludes that, 'As David Carpenter has argued, in opposition to Coss and the other prophets of doom, it is resilience and the careful management of resources, rather than crisis and bankruptcy, that best characterise the 13th century gentry. Robert de Whichford, a debtor who survived, is thus typical of his time and class.'[48]

Access to the marriage market and the possibility of patronage, then, were two of the most obvious assets that landowners possessed, even if they did not possess them in anything like equal measure. In addition to aristocratic patronage, there was of course royal patronage. Its potential benefits have been shown clearly by Peter Michel in his study of the career of Sir Philip d'Arcy, a minor Lincolnshire baron.[49] Apart from the £20 annual pension he was granted in 1253, the benefits this knight received from royal service included intervention in litigation, the cancellation of debts at the Exchequer, and finally in 1261 the pardon of his Jewish debts, viz. bonds totalling some £200. Meanwhile, in 1255 the king had requested that Philip's free tenants should grant him an aid because 'he has fallen into great debt on account of his probity and his service to the king'. Philip died in 1264. His son Norman d'Arcy compounded his family's problems by joining the Montfortians and having to redeem his lands under the terms of the Dictum of Kenilworth. Norman, however, followed ultimately in his father's footsteps and became a household knight of Edward I, serving in both the Welsh and the Scottish wars. His baronial relief was pardoned, his Jewish debts and debts to the Exchequer cancelled. Surprisingly, neither these actions nor the annuities he received from the king ultimately succeeded in alleviating his financial difficulties. In 1291 his main seat at Stallingborough, Lincolnshire, was mortgaged, and it was eventually lost to the family.

Royal intervention to alleviate debt was by no means unusual. Anne Polden cites two interesting examples. In 1245, much moved by the poverty of Thomas de Doynton, Henry III ordered that the lands mortgaged to Jewish creditors should be returned to him and that reasonable terms for the repayment of the

---

[47] Alternatively, as Vincent suggests, this could have been another service association.
[48] *Ibid.*, pp. 50–1.
[49] 'Sir Philip d'Arcy and the Financial Plight of the Military Knight in 13th-Century England', *Lincolnshire History and Archaeology* 19 (1984), pp. 49–56.

debts should be arranged. In 1268 John Neirenuit was pardoned the £20 per annum which his father had owed to the Jews, while he or a later John was given a custody in 1300 to pay off a debt of 100 marks. 'The Doyntons ended up alienating estates, despite royal assistance, but the Neirenuits, who survived and flourished, may have owed this in part at least to royal favour.'[50]

These instances are perhaps at the extreme end of royal help. Royal favour was important when it came to coping with the normal run of Exchequer debts. Michel and Polden both see favour at court as a significant factor within the lesser landowning community. Michel gives a number of instances where royal intervention in the operation of the courts helped Philip d'Arcy out of difficulties. For Anne Polden, the exercise of local office was particularly important in ensuring financial viability: 'Along with the failure of male heirs, which made land available both to established families and to newcomers, links with the central government seem to have provided one of the most dynamic forces for change and development at the county level at this period. Without it most gentry families could look forward to at best stagnation and at worst decline.'[51] Whether public office-holding can quite carry the burden of ensuring knightly prosperity must be debatable. Only a relatively few local positions can in themselves have been particularly lucrative. It seems likely that the benefits of minor office holding were more often indirect, not least the fact that one became known at the centre. This opened up the possibility of patronage.

It can be shown then that the knightly landowners of the mid-thirteenth century enjoyed considerable advantages, albeit in varying degrees. This being so, there is more than a little irony in the fact that almost all commentators on the economy of the knightly class, including those who begin from the premise of a sound material base, have talked in terms of the difficulties they were able to overcome. Nicholas Vincent, for example, couches his study of the Whichfords in precisely these terms. This is a game in which the goal posts have been moved. For in place of Carpenter's materially secure landowners with a high standard of living we are in a world of 'resilience', 'careful management of resources' and surviving debtors. Vincent sees Robert de Whichford as a flourishing landowner. But how flourishing he actually was is unclear. The material position of the family which ultimately succeeded to his estates proves nothing. It is clear, as Vincent acknowledges, that he needed to pay careful attention to his estates.[52] Furthermore, like his father before him, he was accumulating debts. Robert, too, was cushioned – this time by the estates he had acquired through marriage.

It is, in fact, easy enough to list the factors that could propel a family into difficulty and, given an inadequate response, into debt. These include, in addition to problems of estate structure, personal inadequacy, the effects of

---

[50] Polden, 'A Crisis of the Knightly Class?', p. 49.   [51] *Ibid.*, p. 57.
[52] His negotiation of freedom from suit, which in one case since it involved view of frankpledge clearly extended to his tenants, has also to be seen in this light.

prolonged and costly litigation, an overlarge family to support including dowagers and younger sons, a heavy burden of knight service, the effects of overlavish monastic benefaction by previous generations, royal displeasure and political miscalculation.[53] Peter Michel, in his study of Sir Philip d'Arcy, has added what on the surface is a surprising ingredient. D'Arcy fulfilled the obligations of his military calling, fighting in the Gascon campaigns of 1242–3 and 1253–4. The effort of doing so cost him dear. Despite the king's support, manifested in a whole variety of ways, Philip's efforts propelled him into debt, on the second occasion quite seriously. He became involved with the Jews. Although the king's support blunted the impact of debt, at least in his own lifetime, his ardent royal service had been the root cause of it: 'The knight who plied his trade on horseback . . . was prone to fall off, financially speaking, although alternative sources of credit might defer the final day of reckoning.'[54]

It is abundantly clear that thirteenth-century landlords needed to pay careful attention to their estates. This was the age of treatises on estate management and accounting. Walter de Henley, writing *c.*1286, famously regarded those who did not pay such attention as feckless.[55] Nor were these needs new in the second half of the century. In the honour of Coventry, for example, landlords can be seen very clearly improving their estates from the 1230s onwards.[56] David Carpenter pointed to numerous Oxfordshire knights who did the same, including Sir Ralf Chenduit – the father of the impecunious Stephen Chenduit who later sold out to Walter de Merton – 'who reorganized the demesne of Cuxham into a contiguous area, and increased its extent by purchases from freeholders'.[57] We see smaller landlords, for example, extending their demesnes by assarting and buying out tenancies, we see them neutralising truculent free tenants, and we even see them updating their tenancies and increasing their rent rolls. As Kosminsky taught us, the knightly manors revealed by the 1279 Hundred Rolls tended on the whole to be small but demesne orientated.[58] What we cannot do, however, is to project the estates as constituted in 1279 too far into the past; '1279' is a snapshot, freezing the picture at one point in time, and many estates must have been subjected to either sudden shifts or steady improvements. On the other hand, Carpenter is surely correct to suggest that in most cases the changes were of degree rather than kind. Most of the knightly families of the 1220s whose

---

[53] The last is a subject which is worthy of more systematic treatment.

[54] 'Sir Philip d'Arcy and the Financial Plight of the Military Knight', p. 54.

[55] *Walter of Henley and other Treatises on Estate Management and Accounting*, ed. Dorothea Oschinsky (Oxford, 1971), pp. 308–11.

[56] Coss, *Lordship, Knighthood and Locality*, ch. 4: 'Seigneurial Economy and the Restructuring of Estates'.

[57] Carpenter, 'Was There a Crisis of the Knightly Class?', p. 743, drawing on P.D.A. Harvey, *Cuxham: A Medieval Oxfordshire Village* (Oxford, 1965), pp. 4–5, 21, 113–15.

[58] E.A. Kosminsky, *Studies in the Agrarian History of England in the Thirteenth Century*, ed. R.H. Hilton (Oxford, 1956), pp. 256–82.

estates can be studied thereafter seem to have drawn much of their resources traditionally from their home farms.[59] In some cases, these can be traced back to Domesday Book. Relatively few of them will have been wholly dependent upon fixed rents. At the same time, however, Peter Michel was right to warn against seeing what he calls 'the upper ranks of the English gentry as enjoying any kind of economic complacency'.[60]

How, then, should we interpret indebtedness among the landowning community? On the one hand it was a phenomenon which many landowners tended to live with. It was part, as it were, of the noble condition. One has only to think of the debts to the Jew Aaron of Lincoln, who died in 1186, some of whose debtors were among the noblest in the land.[61] One ingredient in such indebtedness was no doubt a socially governed tendency to conspicuous consumption. But there were other factors. The scale of indebtedness of tenants-in-chief to the crown soared during the reigns of Richard I and John, largely owing to the proffers they needed to make for marriages, wardships and reliefs.[62] Kathleen Biddick has argued that from the mid-twelfth century the increasing need for cash by the great landlords, largely to satisfy royal demands for war-orientated revenue, forced them into debt. Taking advance payments from merchants, they found themselves pushed more and more into increasing production for the market to meet their debts. Landlords were locked into a 'structural indebtedness' which was to characterise the period of English high farming.[63] As Carpenter and others have pointed out, debt could also be strategic. In 1198–9 Emma fitz Ellis borrowed money to finance litigation and gained the family three additional manors in consequence.[64] Others borrowed during times of difficulty and came away relatively unscathed. In the words of Anne Polden, 'what strikes one most forcefully about some of these histories is the variety of ways in which families could deal with financial pressures without seriously damaging their inheritance'.[65] Although indebtedness might in certain circumstances lead to disaster, it did not invariably do so. This is what one commentator, Peter Michel, has referred to as 'the ambiguity of debt'.[66] Moreover, as he says, much may have depended upon acquiring adequate and relatively unthreatening sources of credit. But it is equally the case that, for others, debt marched

---

[59] Carpenter, 'Was There a Crisis of the Knightly Class?', p. 745.

[60] Michel, 'Sir Philip d'Arcy', p. 50.

[61] See Holt, *The Northerners*, pp. 164–70; H.G. Richardson, *The English Jewry under the Angevin Kings* (London, 1960), pp. 89–91.

[62] See the recent review of this subject by T.K. Keefe, 'Proffers for Heirs and Heiresses in the Pipe Rolls: Some Observations on Indebtedness in the Years before Magna Carta (1180–1212)', *The Haskins Society Journal: Studies in Medieval History* 5 (1993), pp. 99–109.

[63] K. Biddick, *The Other Economy: Pastoral Husbandry on a Medieval Estate* (Berkeley, 1989), p. 51.

[64] Carpenter, 'Was There a Crisis of the Knightly Class?', p. 736.

[65] Polden, 'A Crisis of the Knightly Class?', p. 49.

[66] Michel, 'Sir Philip d'Arcy', p. 49. See also Polden, 'A Crisis of the Knightly Class?, p. 48.

relentlessly on. There are many examples of what has become recognised as a classic pattern: difficulties accumulating over more than one generation, minor and piecemeal alienations and then indebtedness to the Jews, until finally the families are forced to sell out. Of families who found themselves in this situation the better endowed naturally survived longer, not surprisingly, than did the materially weaker ones. Debt as a means of overcoming debt was always a dangerous procedure. Indebtedness, however, was not a feature only of the materially weak, but was found across the whole spectrum of knightly and once knightly families.

Young men may have been particularly inclined to borrow, especially before they came into their estates. This was not necessarily to cut a figure, although it may have been, but was often to further their own careers. Philip d'Arcy, it will be recalled, was an active Lincolnshire knight long before his father died in 1254. In 1247 he had purchased the wardship and marriage of the son and heir of the Yorkshire landowner Nicholas Quatremare, for the sum of £100. Unfortunately, Philip did not have the money and entered into a contract with the royal judge, Henry de Bath. The end result was protracted litigation between Philip and Henry in which the king finally intervened. According to the chronicler Matthew Paris, it was Philip d'Arcy who denounced the corruption of Henry de Bath before the king and queen in 1251, precipitating his fall.[67]

This is not to say that heirs to landed estates were necessarily without income and responsibilities of their own. William Durvassal, son and heir of Sir John Durvassal of Spernall in Warwickshire, had married Agnes, daughter of Geoffrey de Charlecote. With her came half of the manor of Whitley in Wootton Wawen. Between 1240 and 1252, however, the couple progressively alienated the property and by 1244–5 William had been in debt to the Jews. Whether this estate was already encumbered or whether William was himself responsible for the debts is unclear. What was extraordinary was the family's response. Unable, presumably, to find the cash to rectify the situation before it got wholly out of hand, Sir John found a solution which protected the future of his line. By a final concord concluded at Easter 1247 he conveyed the Spernall estate to his younger son, Roger, with the consent of William, his son and heir. When the small estate at Whitley finally passed into the hands of Peter de Montfort, in 1252, it was granted in return for the maintenance of William and Agnes in food for the rest of their lives.[68]

It seems very probable that many landowners suffered from a lack of liquidity. This was why extraordinary expenditure, such as the costs of litigation, was potentially hazardous. A good example of the run of the mill liquidity problems faced by landowners is provided by an incident in the life of Sir Ralf de Bracebridge, whose principal estate lay at Kingsbury in north Warwickshire. In

[67] Michel, 'Sir Philip d'Arcy', p. 51.   [68] Coss, *Lordship, Knighthood and Locality*, pp. 288–9.

1248 Ralf sought to buy out one of the freeholding families that so abounded in the area. They drew up an indenture whereby Ralf undertook to pay the sum of 19½ marks to Thomas de Cliff within the next twelve months. Thomas agreed to convey to Ralf his entire land and houses at Cliff at whatever point in the year he received the money. By a further agreement, in February 1249, Thomas formally demised the land for 20 marks to be paid by 1 August, of which 100s. was to be paid over at Easter. There were clauses relating to the exploitation of the land by both sides and the relevant charters were to remain in the custody of the Cistercian monks at Merevale until Ralf had actually paid. In brief, 'it was a strikingly elaborate arrangement to have undertaken in order to find a relatively modest sum of money for the purchase of what must have been an equally modest amount of land'.[69] Ralf, it seems, was too wily to borrow money for such an enterprise.

But it will not have been lost on men like Sir Ralf de Bracebridge that there was a strong contrast between their own situation and that of the *curiales*, with liquidity or at least ready access to liquidity, who were profiting so spectacularly on the land market, and often via the mechanism of the Jews: men like Geoffrey de Langley, Walter de Merton, Simon de Norwich, Paulinus Pever, John Mansel, Adam de Stratton and Lawrence de Broke. The role of ecclesiastical corporations was equally conspicuous.[70] The lay aristocracy, on the other hand, played a surprisingly small part in all of this, and that largely confined to keeping control within their own fees.[71] On the other hand, the two queens Eleanor of Provence and, more particularly, Eleanor of Castile were very much involved.[72] Monasteries and *curiales*, however, were merely the most conspicuous of those profiting on the land market. A marked, and accelerating, feature of the thirteenth century was the extent to which all manner of local as well as central administrators were investing in land – some of them knightly, many sub-knightly – often deploying money that was effectively recycled from rents and taxation.

That there were political repercussions is well known. In May 1258 the Petition of the Barons complained of the trafficking in Jewish debts by powerful

---

[69] For the incident and for a brief discussion of the Bracebridge estate see Coss, *Lordship, Knighthood and Locality*, pp. 180–7.

[70] For a recent review of ecclesiastical holdings in the Hundred Rolls of 1279 see Sandra Raban, 'The Church in the 1279 Hundred Rolls', in M.J. Franklin and C. Harper-Bill (eds), *Medieval Ecclesiastical Studies in Honour of Dorothy M. Owen* (Woodbridge, 1995), pp. 185–200.

[71] For a thorough review of the activities of the highest reaches of the aristocracy, in particular, see Sandra Raban, 'The Land Market and the Aristocracy in the Thirteenth Century', in D. Greenway, C. Holdsworth and J. Sayers (eds.), *Tradition and Change: Essays in Honour of Marjorie Chibnall* (Cambridge, 1985), pp. 239–61.

[72] See Margaret Howell, *Eleanor of Provence: Queenship in Thirteenth-Century England* (London, 1998), pp. 116, 263–4, 266, 277–8, and J. Carmi Parsons, *Eleanor of Castile: Queen and Society in Thirteenth-Century England* (New York, 1995), pp. 126–38 and Appendix 1. See also, Raban, 'The Land Market and the Aristocracy', p. 257.

men in the realm through which lesser men lost their land. From 1263 until the end of the civil war the Jews were under physical attack, while the Montfortian regime of 1264–5 came purposefully to the relief of the Jews' seigneurial debtors.[73] Nor did matters improve for the Jewish scapegoats after the war. Robert Stacey reports that from 1268 until their final expulsion in 1290 the Commons demanded legislation against the Jews as the price of taxation in almost every parliamentary session; the expulsion, moreover, came as just such a *quid pro quo*.[74] Entire or partial disinheritance made for desperate men. One such was Ralf Harengod. With a diminished inheritance, Ralf became indebted. After his failed attempt to reduce his tenantry to villeinage, he took to terrorising the free peasantry of east Sussex on behalf of himself and the prior of Hastings. He died fighting for Simon de Montfort at the battle of Lewes.[75]

However, as David Carpenter pointed out in 1980, only a minority of knights followed Simon de Montfort into rebellion.[76] Many, perhaps even the majority, remained as aloof as they could from this increasingly desperate conflict. Among those who stayed the whole course from reform in 1258 to civil war against the king in 1264–5 there was undoubtedly a disproportionate number of debtors, men with a particular stake in the continuance of the Montfortian regime. The spectre of debt was clearly a political issue, and the traffic in encumbered lands played a political role that was out of proportion to the incidence of serious debt. Moreover, from the very beginning of the 'revolution' in 1258 the baronial opponents of Henry III's regime had tapped into the manifold difficulties and discontents being experienced in the localities. What these tensions reflect is an acquisitive society and an atmosphere of competition for resources.

In short, recent research into the knightly class during the personal rule of Henry III has pointed to very mixed fortunes. There is no doubt that many families flourished, enjoying perhaps a higher standard of living than their forbears. A minority, on the other hand, suffered grave difficulties and succumbed to their debts. Others went through a process of adjustment to changing circumstances. Some of these experienced periods of major difficulty but nevertheless survived. Some suffered a reduction of their landed base, some a diminution in status. Nevertheless, the Postan thesis of a general economic decline of the knightly class is dead in the water. Indeed, it has been effectively dead ever since David Carpenter produced his study of Oxfordshire in 1980.

[73] Coss, 'The Crisis of the Knightly Class', pp. 31–4.
[74] Robert C. Stacey, 'Parliamentary Negotiation and the Expulsion of the Jews from England', in M. Prestwich *et al.* (eds.), *Thirteenth Century England VI* (Woodbridge, 1997), pp. 77–101. For a recent overview of Jewish activity in this period see the same author's 'Jewish Lending and the Medieval English Economy', in R.H. Britnell and B.M.S. Campbell (eds.), *A Commercialising Economy: England 1086 to c.1300* (Manchester, 1995), pp. 78–101.
[75] Searle, *Battle Abbey and its Banlieu*, pp. 163–5.
[76] Carpenter, 'Was There a Crisis of the Knightly Class?', pp. 751–2.

What then of the alternative thesis derived from Hilton? Was there a crisis in the knightly class in the way that he interpreted it? There is certainly a stronger *prima facie* case for this, not least because it can accommodate, and even explain, the variety of observable phenomena. In order to test the viability of this thesis, however, we must turn to the second strand of research undertaken since 1975, looking backwards from the list of knights ascertainable from the 1220s.

BACKWARD PROJECTION: THE HILTON THESIS

The debate on the fortunes of the knightly class led me to the realisation that the petty knight or *militulus* had been a widespread phenomenon in Angevin England. In 1980 David Carpenter traced the fortunes of fifty-three knights from a sample of seventy-one drawn from juries and panels of the 1220s. The remaining eighteen knights were, necessarily, set aside. Anne Polden was to follow the same procedure, omitting fourteen of her eighty-eight 'because no coherent picture of their lands or histories could be constructed from the evidence'.[77] Meanwhile, my own researches into Warwickshire had confirmed Carpenter's findings, forcing me to confront the problem of the missing knights. My analysis suggested that of the ninety-seven Warwickshire knights whose names were recovered from the eyre rolls and the *Curia Regis Rolls* between 1221 and 1232, no fewer than thirty-one, or almost a third of them, could be classified as men with only minor property interests in the county or whose property is no longer discernible. A second sample, drawn from the years 1200–14 – effectively as far back as one can go – has eighteen of forty-one knights in those categories; that is to say, not far short of a half were not the regular, well-established manorial lords that one expected to be studying.

Who were these knights? In general terms it would seem defensible to refer to them as *milituli*, knightlings or petty knights, echoing the famously snobbish retort from Henry II's justiciar, Richard de Lucy, that 'it was not formally the custom for every petty knight (*militulus*) to have a seal, which befits kings and great personages'.[78] In some cases, the interests of these knights proved to be wholly obscure. In many cases, however, their property can be discerned even if it cannot be measured.[79] Hugh de Essebroc, for example, had a homestead with meadow land and rents, in the parish of Kingsbury in north Warwickshire. He occurs in no extant lists of knights' fees. His interests – indeed, his very existence – are revealed only through local charters. Henry of Shuckburgh,

---

[77] Polden, 'A Crisis of the Knightly Class?', p. 30.

[78] Searle, *Battle Abbey and its Banlieu*, p. 42.

[79] For the full analysis see *Lordship, Knighthood and Locality*, ch. 7: 'Knighthood in Society'. Précis of my findings can be found in 'Knighthood and the Early Thirteenth-Century Court', pp. 53–4, and in *The Knight in Medieval England*, pp. 38–43.

a knight from the earlier sample, brought a case for four virgates of land at Shuckburgh before the Warwickshire eyre in 1221. The defendant was the grandson of Warin de Walcote, an itinerant knight who, back in Stephen's reign, had taken Henry's mother prior to wedlock and given her a son. The parties were brought into agreement by 'licence of the justices for God's sake, because they are poor'. That knights needed a property stake in the community in order to participate in these legal procedures is well known. It lay at the very heart of the grand assize, for example, where they were expected to hold some property within the neighbourhood in question. Jeremy Quick has pointed to a Hereford-shire case in 1220 where Sir Robert Vernay was disqualified from acting as one of the four knights sent to check that a litigant was suffering from bed-sickness because he was 'from a household and [did] not have any land'.[80]

However, this property stake need not have been extensive. In truth, these minor knights were being sustained by a variety of means. A very few were men with minor interests in the county, but stronger interests elsewhere. Prominent were younger sons and collateral members of knightly families. Prevalent, too, were interests acquired by marriage, to a dowager for example. A third signifi-cant factor was that of service. William de Flamville, for instance, was sometime steward to William de Hastings, William de Wilmcote a steward of the earl of Warwick. William Huse seems to have been in the service of Robert Marmion of Tamworth. One of the minor knights was a verderer of Feckenham Forest, while two others were royal falconers by profession. Of course, these factors were by no means mutually exclusive and two or even three of them might be combined in the same man. Their property then was of divers origins, from family, from marriage, and from the profits of service, either directly or through investment. Although the mere household knight was, properly speaking, excluded from juries and panels, in reality the distinction between property-holding knight and household knight may not have been so sharp. Relatively little is known about how household knights were sustained, except for the fact of their board and lodging. Grant G. Simpson's study of the *familia* of Roger de Quincy, earl of Winchester (1235–64), reveals at least one knight holding a *fief-rente* and another, tellingly, receiving rent from property under the lord's control.[81] The researches of Stephen Church into the household knights of King John, indi-cating that they were not as yet in receipt of regular wages, discourages us from going too far down this road.[82] On the other hand, it is surely probable that

---

[80] J. Quick, 'The Number and Distribution of Knights in Thirteenth-Century England: The Ev-idence of the Grand Assize Lists', in P.R. Coss and S.D. Lloyd (eds.), *Thirteenth Century England II* (Woodbridge, 1988), p. 116.

[81] Grant G. Simpson, 'The *Familia* of Roger de Quincy, Earl of Winchester and Constable of Scotland', in J.K. Stringer (ed.), *Essays on the Nobility of Scotland* (Glasgow, 1985), pp. 117–18.

[82] Church, *The Household Knights of King John*, ch. 4.

many received rewards other than direct enfeoffment, and there was nothing to stop them investing in rents and small parcels of land. Indeed, rent income was ideal in that it required little in the way of management to maintain, and could be treated as investment for the future. Those in ministerial positions and dealing with the lord's tenants were, of course, in a wholly different position and no doubt enjoyed many avenues of profit.

In short, the 'militulus was clearly alive and well in early thirteenth-century England'.[83] However, we do need to be cautious over the interpretation of such findings. We actually know nothing of the overall income of these knights and there may well have been considerable differences between them. Indeed, there may have been little difference in wealth between some of these milituli and some of the more established manorial lords. The reality was perhaps more of a continuum than is observable by us. Furthermore, we have little means of establishing relative status and influence in society, although one can be fairly sure that being the steward of a great lord, for example, carried some prestige. Angevin knighthood covered a wide spectrum: 'In truth, knighthood at this date was variously supported and had a variety of components, including a basis (whether exercised or not) in the profession of arms, an emphasis on service, and status conferred by wealth and/or relationship to the great.'[84]

How many knights were there then in early thirteenth-century England? And when and why did many of them jettison knighthood? As far as numbers are concerned, the first into the fray in recent times was Jeremy Quick. Working backwards from N. Denholm-Young's estimate of around 1,250 at any one time during the period 1266–1322, Quick looked specifically at the period from around 1200 to 1272. Examining twenty-seven counties and taking one eyre roll for each, he found a total of 1,539 knights involved in the grand assize. Allowing for the twelve additional counties, he came to the cautious conclusion that 'the number of knights who were involved in the administration of local government at any one time was probably somewhere around 1000–2000', adding that 'Although this number excludes barons, landless knights and those knights who successfully avoided grand assize service, it is difficult to believe that there could have been much more than 2000 knights in England at any one time.'[85] An important, if hardly surprising, finding was that the density of knights (per acre) tended to mirror the population and wealth of the counties, with ten counties heading the list: the midland counties of Bedfordshire, Buckinghamshire, Leicestershire, Northamptonshire, Oxfordshire and Warwickshire, together

---

[83] Coss, 'Knighthood and the Early Thirteenth-Century County Court', p. 54.   [84] Ibid., p. 48.
[85] Quick, 'The Number and Distribution of Knights', pp. 114–23. The quotation is from p. 119. For Denholm-Young's findings see his 'Feudal Society in the Thirteenth Century: The Knights', History 29 (1924), pp. 107–19; reprinted in his Collected Papers on Medieval Subjects (Cardiff, 1969), pp. 83–94.

with Norfolk and Suffolk, Surrey and Kent.[86] Quick saw his figures as broadly confirming Denholm-Young's findings, but by a different route. However, there is a major difficulty. The eyre rolls utilised by Quick range in date from 1202 to 1269, during which period the number of knights was in serious decline.[87] Aware of this and taking Quick's maximum of 2,000 as a starting point, I suggested in 1993 that the true figure at the beginning of the century was at least half as many again.[88]

It is now abundantly clear that a figure of 3,000 + knights in 1200 was itself an underestimate. The matter of numbers has now been put on a much firmer basis by Kathryn Faulkner in an important essay published in 1996.[89] Faulkner compiled a complete list of knights active in the various Angevin legal procedures between 1199 and 1216. The result was the 'remarkably high figure of 3,636'. Adjusting this figure to take account of the same name appearing in a contiguous county (but not further afield), she reduced this figure to 3,453, a figure at first sight very much in line with my guesstimate of 1993. In one sense this is a maximum figure, for it assumes that all of the men included were actual, not nominal, knights. As far as the majority of the knights and the majority of the procedures are concerned this seems to be a sound assumption. As Jeremy Quick noted, the electors of a grand assize jury in Dorset in 1207 were in mercy for choosing jurors who were not knights.[90] Moreover, it is quite clear that any lapse in correct procedure might be pounced on by either party to advantage in any case before the courts. This was shown, for example, in a Warwickshire case of 1225 when both parties objected in turn on the grounds that the four men viewing a defendant's bed-sickness should have been knights.[91] With such cases in mind, Jeremy Quick, Kathryn Faulkner and myself are agreed that the majority of electors and jurors of the grand assize and the viewers of bed-sickness must have been actual knights, although it is still highly likely that some non-knights none the less slipped through the net. In the case of two other procedures the matter is rather less clear cut: the appointment of men to hear the nomination of attorneys, and the twenty-four-man jury in a plea of attaint. Although the records often suggest that the men concerned were indeed knights, there is no guarantee that this was always so, most especially

---

86 Absolute numbers would, of course, produce a different list. K. Faulkner's list puts the following as highest yielding counties at the beginning of the century: Lincolnshire, Norfolk, Northamptonshire, Yorkshire, Suffolk and Essex, followed by Kent, Cambridgeshire and Buckinghamshire (see below, note 89).

87 Quick acknowledged, however, that his figures take no account of any decline in numbers during the century, but appears to have considered the rate of decline to have been of relatively little significance.

88 *The Knight in Medieval England*, p. 70.

89 Kathryn Faulkner, 'The Transformation of Knighthood in Early Thirteenth-Century England', *English Historical Review* 111 (1996), pp. 1–23.

90 Quick, 'The Number and Distribution of Knights', p. 14.

91 Coss, 'Knighthood and the Early Thirteenth-Century County Court', p. 47.

when the jury of attaint was to examine the verdict in one of the petty assizes where the original jury had not been knights. Faulkner, following C.T. Flower, argues that these men were generally knights and has included them in her calculations.[92] The most we can say, however, is that the majority were knights, at least at the beginning of the century.[93] It might also be objected that Faulkner makes no adjustment for the passage of generations, but this is of little importance given that, in practice, the great majority of the 3,453 knights come from the ten-year period 1199–1209.

In another, and more important, sense, however, this is very much a minimum figure. The important question is how does this figure drawn from the evidence of the Angevin legal procedures relate to the total number of knights in the country? Examining the Bedfordshire knights who were active in legal procedures between 1216 and 1230 and other prominent county knightly families, Faulkner argues that the number of knights recorded in 1199–1216 understates the number of knights available by 20 per cent. She suggests that the equivalent figure for Staffordshire is 25 per cent, but erring on the side of caution inflates her totals by only 20 per cent overall. More difficult are the distant counties where 'royal justice did not penetrate in the same way as in the heartland of the country', the counties for which there are no figures, and those counties where the numbers recorded appear to be artificially low. Her final figures, therefore, contain a fair degree of acknowledged guesswork: 'Doubling the figures for the peripheral counties of Cornwall, Lancashire and Northumberland, and trebling them for the more populous Devon, Worcestershire and Huntingdonshire would seem to be reasonable guesswork, as would figures of fifty apiece for Cheshire, Westmorland and Durham.'[94] Her revised total is 4,755 adjusted down to 4,515

---

[92] C.T. Flower, *Introduction to the Curia Regis Rolls*, Selden Society 62 (London, 1944), pp. 296, 398. Faulkner found twenty-four juries of attaint between 1200 and 1216. In twelve cases there is mention at some point that the jurors were knights, while in one case only (the second earliest) they are simply called men. In her view it was decided at some point shortly after this that attaint jurors should be knights. It may be, however, that they were simply expected to be knights wherever possible: 'The Transformation of Knighthood', p. 4.

[93] Examining the three attaint juries on the Gloucestershire eyre roll of 1248, John Mullan found that only eleven of the fifty-six jurors were knights. Most of the remaining jurors seem to have been relatively obscure individuals and their interests highly localised. He concludes, judiciously, that in contrast to the grand assize 'we must look at each attaint jury panel with an open mind and judge for ourselves what the sheriff was able to achieve and in the event, despite the tempting nature of attaint panels, it seems that we are unable to add to our pool of county knights by reference to this procedure'. John D. Mullan, 'Landed Society and Locality in Gloucestershire, *c.*1240–80' (Cardiff PhD thesis, 1999), pp. 41–4. A higher percentage of attaint jurors were probably knights earlier in the century, but this evidence suggests that it may never have been a rigid rule.

[94] Faulkner, 'The Transformation of Knighthood', p. 11. Her doubling of the thirty-nine recorded knights for Cornwall seems conservative. Mark Page finds seventy-two active knights from there (from sixty families) in the period 1250–75, and forty-two grand assize jurors in 1284: Mark Page, 'Cornwall, Earl Richard and the Barons' War', *English Historical Review* 115 (2000), p. 34.

to allow for duplication. As she points out, 'If knights who earned their living through the profession of arms, as household knights or mercenaries, were to be included as well as the knights available for administrative service, then the total number of knights in England must surely have been well in excess of 5,000.'[95]

Despite all the difficulties there is good reason for believing that it is of the right order of magnitude. Indeed, even this could conceivably be an underestimate. My own study of Warwickshire knights revealed a very low level of duplication between panels during the period 1200–14, strongly suggesting that the pool from which the knights were being drawn was larger.[96] Moreover, if we look closely at the honour of Coventry at the beginning of the thirteenth century, for example, we find that neither the earl of Chester's ministers who held property in the area nor the holders of the small manors around Coventry figure in Faulkner's lists, notwithstanding the fact that most of them were undoubtedly knights.[97] Particularly instructive are three knights – John Dive, John son of Benedict and Warin de Coundon – who witnessed a charter between two freeholders at Coundon at the very beginning of the century.[98] None of the three figures in Faulkner's lists and none of the three appears to have sired knights. Warin's son alienated his property during the early 1220s. The full extent and contours of his property are unknown. Although it was not extensive, it included both meadow and tenant land as well as urban interests. It constituted a tenth of a knight's fee. None the less, he may have lived in some style, possessing his own vivary. The Dive interest also disappeared subsequently. However, a descendant of the third knight, John son of Benedict, was still there in 1279 living as a free tenant on a tenth of a knight's fee. Judging by the extent of his holding it seems startling that his ancestor had supported knighthood. In all probability these three knights were associated with the Hastings lordship in the area. They were followed in the charter witness list by William the Huntsman, surely the ancestor of William le Venur who held a virgate on the Hastings manor of Allesley in 1279. They may all have belonged to the Hastings household, though of course they were not landless. Kathryn Faulkner is undoubtedly correct when she says that 'The existence of around 4,500 landed knights in England at the beginning of the thirteenth century means that knighthood changed less during the twelfth century, and more during the thirteenth, than has previously appeared to be the case.'[99] If we accept Denholm-Young's figure of 1,250 knights in England at the end of the thirteenth century as roughly correct, then, as she points out, numbers fell overall to a third or even a quarter of the total at its beginning.

---

[95] Faulkner, 'The Transformation of Knighthood', p. 12.

[96] For the details see *Lordship, Knighthood and Locality*, pp. 244–8.

[97] *Ibid.*, pp. 217–19. Walter of Coventry, one of the earl's stewards, was referred to as his bachelor, while his son and grandson were both knights.

[98] For what follows see Coss, *Lordship, Knighthood and Locality*, pp. 222–5.

[99] Faulkner, 'The Transformation of Knighthood', p. 23.

When did these numbers fall? Rather than a gradual decline, Faulkner argues for 'a fundamental change within a generation', that is between 1215 and 1230, with 'a widespread drop in numbers in the 1220s'.[100] On the face of it, there appears to be a case for this. After all, the first distraint to knighthood belongs to the year 1224. Taking samples of fifty knights for each of the counties of Bedfordshire and Staffordshire, drawn from her lists of 1199–1216, she suggests that nearly 50 per cent (twenty-four and twenty-one knights respectively) failed to produce knightly heirs. But is she in fact correct to posit such a short, sharp decline? There is a certain irony in the fact that Faulkner, an opponent of any crisis of the knightly class, envisages the number of knights literally plummeting over little more than a decade. A drop of such magnitude – and on her figures it should be well in excess of 50 per cent – is surely a phenomenon of crisis proportions. It is difficult to believe that this was possible, unless of course we really are dealing with notional knights, who could cease to regard themselves as knights, and cease to be regarded as knights, with comparative ease. As we have seen, an examination of the role of knights within the Angevin legal processes makes this conclusion extremely unlikely.[101] In fact, it is almost certain that the majority of these men were by this date dubbed as knights in a formal ceremony. The literary evidence strongly suggest that this was so across northern France from c.1180 and there is evidence that the knighting ceremony was well enough known in England.[102] Moreover, it was by no means confined to the highest levels of nobility. Indeed, the legal records themselves sometimes speak of belted knights, or knights 'girt with the sword', reflecting what was the essence of the knighting ceremony, at least in England.[103] In a famous lawsuit of the 1190s, for example, the abbot of Crowland complained of men being sent to view land who were neither of the military order, nor girt with the sword; nor, for that matter, could they speak French![104] Given that knighthood implied a ceremony and membership of a separate order, it seems rather odd to argue, as Faulkner does, that a sudden and wholesale abandonment of knighthood could have occurred without major disruption. For her, men simply abandoned knighthood – that is to say they failed to follow their fathers in taking it on – and they did so without regret. It was a matter not so much of opting out, she says, but of failure to opt in. To be sure, there is no direct

---

[100] *Ibid.*, pp. 15, 18.

[101] A case for this was in fact made by R.C. Palmer, *The County Courts of Medieval England, 1150–1350* (Princeton, 1982), p. 134. See, however, my comments in 'Knighthood and the Early Thirteenth-Century County Court', pp. 46–8.

[102] See, for example, J. Flori, 'Pour une histoire de la chevalerie: l'adoubement dans les romans de Chrétien de Troyes', *Romania* 100 (1979), pp. 21–53. For England see below, pp. 98–9, 137.

[103] See Robert Bartlett, *England under the Angevin and Norman Kings, 1075–1225* (Oxford, 2000), pp. 232–4.

[104] For a recent discussion of this case see *The Knight in Medieval England*, pp. 33–5.

echo of protest or of distress in the sources. But it is simply not true that knighthood lacked social status. Angevin knighthood was different, and more complex, than the full chivalric knighthood which superseded it, but there are many echoes of the knight's general status in the Angevin sources.[105] The idea of an order of knighthood was already strong, as indeed is implied throughout the Angevin legal procedures themselves. It was precisely the knight's social status that the procedures invoked. Even figures as relatively lowly as Warin de Coundon and his fellows clearly enjoyed some prestige within the community. As Hugh Thomas points out in his study of Angevin Yorkshire, 'few people relish downward mobility'. Moreover, the consequences of a decline in prestige could be severely practical, in reducing one's capacity to protect – let alone expand – one's interests.[106]

In fact, however, there is no need to posit a sudden dramatic fall in numbers during the 1220s. Faulkner's arguments are based on the knights recorded across the years 1199–1216. However, the bulk of them appear in the first decade of John's reign, 1199–1209. What she has, then, is essentially a ten-year base line, followed by a twenty-year period during which the next generation failed to take up knighthood. Moreover, a concentrated fall during the 1220s is not supported by other evidence. The Warwickshire eyres of 1221 and 1232, for instance, show a fall in the number of knights involved in the grand assize from sixty-five in the former year to forty-seven in the latter. Although this is an absolute fall it should also be borne in mind that there were only twelve cases in the latter year as against sixteen in the former, so that the ratio of knight to assizes was four:one in each case. That the number of knights was falling is clear enough, but it hardly suggests a catastrophic collapse during the 1220s. Moreover, numbers continued to fall during the 1230s and, indeed, beyond. As we have seen, detailed studies of three counties – Buckinghamshire, Oxfordshire and Warwickshire – have shown a high number of minor knights still flourishing through the 1220s, from families who subsequently jettisoned knighthood. In Warwickshire fourteen of the knights active in the 1232 eyre were still of the group whose property interests in the county have been designated as minor. In terms of distraint to knighthood, the crucial year was not 1224 but 1241, when the decision was made to extend it to all those with £20 land, whether held in military tenure or not, and irrespective of whom they held. By this date, the fall in the number of knights was being perceived clearly by the central government. Hitherto, distraint had applied only to those holding a full knight's fee and, with the probable exception of the first distraint in 1224, had applied only to tenants-in-chief. The timing of these early distraints make it clear that their primary

---

[105] For a discussion of the content of Angevin knighthood see Coss, *The Knight in Medieval England*, ch. 3.
[106] Thomas, *Vassals, Heiresses, Crusaders and Thugs*, p. 165.

purpose was military, and that they had much to do with the king's desire to recover his inheritance in France.[107] There are other indications, moreover, that the problem was first perceived as a serious one in the 1240s. It was in 1246 that distraint and avoidance of knighthood were introduced into the articles of the eyre as matters for judicial inquiry, and it was from the late 1240s that the king began to give more help to those intending knighthood.[108] Even these measures, however, failed to stem the flow. In Shropshire, whereas forty-one knights had participated in the grand assize at the eyre of 1221, only seventeen did so in 1256. In 1262 Warwickshire produced only twenty-nine knights for the grand assize, Bedfordshire only sixteen. However, caution is required here. The number of extant knights must always have been higher than the number functioning in the assize. Barons and *curiales* were among those who did not participate. During the 1250s the royal policy of selling respites and exemptions reached new heights. In addition to respite from knighthood itself, there were life-time exemptions from sitting on assizes, juries and recognitions and quittances of common summons to the general eyre.[109] In these circumstances it is not surprising that the numbers participating in the grand assize sometimes seem artificially low. On the other hand it is clear enough that in the 1250s sons of knights were still seeking to avoid knighthood, as the distraints of 1256, for example, show. In that year sixty men were found eligible in Shropshire and Staffordshire, sixty-two in Bedfordshire and Buckinghamshire, and thirty-three in Northamptonshire.[110] Seventeen Warwickshire knights fined for respite of knighthood in that year. Eleven of them were descendants of knights who had figured in the legal procedures between 1221 and 1232. All were from the better-endowed knights.[111] The knighthood of the *milituli* was irrecoverable by now. Everything suggests that the bulk of the retreat from knighthood had already occurred by the 1240s. Even so, numbers continued to fall. Numerically speaking, during the middle decades of the thirteenth century, knighthood in England had reached a low ebb.

---

[107] On this point see, especially, Michael Powicke, 'Distraint of Knighthood and Military Obligation under Henry III', *Speculum* 25 (1950), pp. 457–70, and the same author's *Military Obligation in Medieval England: A Study in Liberty and Duty* (Oxford, 1962), pp. 63–81. It was natural that the king should focus on the obligations of his tenants-in-chief.

[108] For details see *Lordship, Knighthood and Locality*, pp. 241–4, and *The Knight in Medieval England*, pp. 60–1, and references given there.

[109] See Waugh, 'Reluctant Knights and Jurors', pp. 937–86. Waugh calculates that Henry III issued nearly 1,200 charters to nearly 1,130 individuals granting them exemptions from jury service and office holding between 1233 and 1272 (*ibid.*, p. 966).

[110] Waugh, 'Reluctant Knights and Jurors', p. 52. The income level was set unusually at £15 rather than £20 in 1256, although it referred only to those holding by military tenure.

[111] Coss, *Lordship, Knighthood and Locality*, p. 256 and appendix 7.3. Sixteen men fined from Gloucestershire (Mullan, 'Landed Society and Locality', p. 63). Waugh calculates that in 1256 respite was granted to at least 370 men, and that during Henry II's reign 630 men bought respites.

Approaching from the opposite direction, however, one finds indications that the number of knights may already have been falling during the first decade of the century, if not indeed before. There was certainly an awareness of the indebted knight in the late twelfth century. The courtier Walter Map speaks of it, as do both the *Dialogue of the Exchequer* and the Assize of Arms.[112] Two chroniclers who wrote of the massacre of the Jews at York in 1190 spoke, no doubt with some exaggeration, of the widespread indebtedness and distress experienced by Yorkshire landowners.[113] Admittedly, this evidence is impressionistic. As we have seen, the pool of knights from whom the knightly jurors were drawn was larger the further we go back towards 1200. However, we have no means of detecting the extent to which numbers were already haemorrhaging by then. How many knights there had been in the mid to late twelfth century is, in fact, incalculable. T.K. Keefe noted 6,500 knights' fees assessed for scutage (i.e. payment in lieu of knight service) between 1190 and 1210.[114] But these are fees not knights. Knighthood at this time was often being sustained on fractional fees. It may well be that areas of economic growth and of strong freeholding communities, like the Forest of Arden, may have possessed correspondingly more *milituli* than older settled areas with tighter manorial structures. It is a subject that is worth further investigation. It is quite feasible that at its peak knighthood encompassed many more than 5,000 men.

In short, we do not know when the retreat from knighthood began, but the higher percentage of *milituli* in the earliest samples suggests that it began before the 1220s. It is observable in the 1220s and 1230s and it continued, undoubtedly at a slower pace, thereafter. By 1240 the retreat had made serious inroads into the number of knights in England. All the evidence suggests that the retreat from knighthood began, and was strongest, amongst the *milituli*, bringing an end to this phenomenon in England.[115] Judging from the witness lists to charters of the late 1230s and 1240s, chivalric knighthood had by now superseded the older Angevin amalgam.[116] It is likely, however, that this was achieved by a gradual but, no doubt, accelerating change, rather than by a sudden and very dramatic fall.

Why did it occur? In the past, three possible explanations have been offered for the retreat from knighthood: a decline in military service, the burden of

---

[112] Walter Map, *De Nugis Curialium*, trans. M.R. James (revised edn, Oxford, 1983), p. 8: 'knights . . . who either eat up their patrimony or who are shackled by debt'; quoted by Faulkner, 'The Transformation of Knighthood', p. 18. For the *Dialogue of the Exchequer* and the Assize of Arms see Coss, *Lordship, Knighthood and Locality*, pp. 212, 248.

[113] Thomas, *Vassals, Heiresses, Crusaders and Thugs*, p. 166.

[114] T.K. Keefe, *Feudal Assessments and the Political Community under Henry II and His Sons* (Berkeley, 1987), pp. 57–9.

[115] Faulkner herself agrees this point: 'The Transformation of Knighthood', p. 21.

[116] Coss, *Lordship, Knighthood and Locality*, pp. 214–17, 251. See also Fleming, 'Milites as Attestors to Charters in England', pp. 185–98.

administrative duties, and cost. The widely shared and complex nature of knightly status in Angevin England makes the first two unlikely, except perhaps as secondary factors, and there seems little doubt that the cost of knighthood holds the key.[117] More is known of the knighting of princes and magnates than of men from the shires. None the less, there are indications that by the beginning of the thirteenth century the knighting ceremony had become generally more elaborate. King John's own input into the knighting of a few of his household knights indicates this. In 1204 he spent £33 on 'three robes of scarlet, three of green cloth, two brocades, one mattress and other things necessary for making one knight'. In the same year, Thomas Sturmy of the royal household was given a robe of scarlet with a hood of doe skin, another of green or burnet, a saddle, bridle-reins, a cloak for wet weather, a mattress and a pair of linen sheets so that he might become a knight.[118] Of course, such evidence relates to the royal household and may not reflect the knighting ceremony in humbler circumstances. However, there are indications that it corresponds to the broader situation. Glanville tells us that an English lord was entitled to levy an aid from his tenants for the knighting of his eldest son, and this was acknowledged to be of general validity by Magna Carta. In reality, the king seems to have been responsible for knighting very few of his household knights. It was rare for them to serve an apprenticeship with him, and most entered the household as 'fully fledged knights'.[119] In other words they had received their training, and presumably their dubbing, elsewhere. Even in the case of Thomas Sturmy there is no direct evidence that the king was responsible for the knighting ceremony, as opposed to helping to defray the man's costs. The costs of the ceremony, moreover, constituted only part of the outlay. There was also the cost of armour and the cost of the warhorse, or destrier.[120] Furthermore, a man once knighted needed to maintain his dignity as a knight. He required not only destriers but also palfreys for himself and his squire. How far greater lords were taking responsibility for knighting and equipping their own knights is unknown, but it may well be that the costs involved in knighthood made many men, and especially the poorer ones, dependent upon them.

The cost of knighthood, however, is only one dimension. Clearly it is necessary to consider the question of income in relation to overall expenditure. How far were the retreat from knighthood and the financial difficulties

---

[117] For fuller statements see *Lordship, Knighthood and Locality*, pp. 252–5 and *The Knight in Medieval England*, pp. 62–9.

[118] *Pipe Roll 6 John*, pp. 213, 120; *Rot. Litt. Claus.*, vol. I, p. 3. See Bartlett, *England under the Norman and Angevin Kings*, p. 235, and Church, *The Household Knights*, p. 37. In 1209 the king spent over £21 on 'three silk robes and three robes of green cloth with deerskin and three coverlets and three mattresses and three saddles with reins and three pairs of linen sheets and three pairs of shirts and breeches and the other small trappings for making knights' (*Pipe Roll 11 John*, p. 10; cited by Bartlett, *England under the Norman and Angevin Kings*).

[119] For this point, and for what follows, see Church, *The Household Knights*, pp. 37–8.

[120] See R.H.C. Davis, *The Medieval Warhorse* (London, 1989), esp. pp. 67 and 82.

experienced by members of the knightly class interconnected phenomena? For Hilton, famously, they were indeed intimately connected: 'Those who disappeared were the ones whose incomes did not match their social pretensions.'[121] Although Kathryn Faulkner has recently argued that 'there was in reality very little correlation between financial strain and failure to take up knighthood', there remains a strong *prima facie* case for a connection between the *retention* of knighthood and a satisfactory level of income.[122] As far as the 1220s to 1240s are concerned, we have direct evidence not just of a connection between knighthood and financial embarrassment, but between knighthood and debt. In January 1227 Reginald de Mohun was granted a royal letter suggesting to his knights and free tenants that they contribute an aid towards his knighting. In 1233 Nicholas de Whichford was granted a similar letter to discharge the debts he had incurred through his knighting.[123] John de Carun, who was knighted in 1243, not only had borrowed money on the security of his land in order to finance it, but had found himself unable to repay the Jews as a consequence.[124] In view of this we need to look again at the question of knightly income and expenditure in the early thirteenth century.

In 1975 I linked the putative crisis of the knightly class with the great inflation of *c.*1180 to *c.*1220, arguing that lesser landowners who were living substantially off fixed rents and/or who lacked the wherewithal to shift to direct and market-orientated exploitation of their demesnes were in a potentially hazardous position given the prevailing economic climate. Recent work on the late twelfth- and early thirteenth-century economy has taken a revisionist turn, and it is necessary to ask how the new views affect the argument. Moreover, as Barbara Harvey has recently stressed, a new interpretation of economic change in this period is currently evolving, one which gives the dominant role to the market rather than population. In the commercialisation of English society, the century from around 1150 to around 1250 seems to have been of particular significance.[125] Historians are more inclined than they once were to see the twelfth century as a time of economic growth.[126] In consequence the years 1180 to 1220 have become more difficult to interpret. A review of the particularly

---

[121] Hilton, *A Medieval Society*, p. 51.
[122] Faulkner, 'The Transformation of Knighthood', p. 19. Her argument is based on some Bedfordshire families who continued to support knights into the next generation despite financial difficulties.
[123] *Lordship, Knighthood and Locality*, p. 249.
[124] A.C. Chibnall, *Sherington: Fiefs and Fields of a Buckinghamshire Village* (Cambridge, 1965), pp. 50–1.
[125] Barbara Harvey, 'The Aristocratic Consumer in England in the Long Thirteenth Century', in Prestwich *et al.* (eds.), *Thirteenth Century England VI*, pp. 17–18. For the commercialisation of society see, especially, R.H. Britnell, *The Commercialisation of English Society 1000–1500* (Cambridge, 1993), and Britnell and Campbell (eds.), *A Commercialising Economy*.
[126] See, for example, R. Faith, 'Demesne Resources and Labour Rent on the Manors of St Paul's Cathedral, 1066–1222', *Economic History Review*, 2nd ser., 47 (1994), pp. 657–78, and E. King, 'Economic Development in the Early Twelfth Century', in R. H. Britnell and J. Hatcher (eds.), *Progress and Problems in Medieval England* (Cambridge, 1996), pp. 1–22.

difficult price data for this period has been conducted by Paul Latimer.[127] After all the necessary caution has been expressed, and allowing for the fact that both the prices of individual commodities and the evidence through which we approach them tend to be governed by specific factors, his analysis reveals a broadly consistent pattern. Prices in general appear to move in broad accordance with those for grain and food-related livestock, that is to say, rather uncertainly during the last two decades of the twelfth century followed by a short, sharp price rise from c.1199 to c.1205. Thereafter, up to the mid-thirteenth century, prices remained relatively stable, but at a level generally higher than before the swift rise. However, the move to direct management of estates in this period now seems less universal than it used to, and some historians have doubted whether inflation really was the cause, or at least the sole cause of this shift.[128]

These findings, although they alter the perspective somewhat, do not, in fact, invalidate any argument based on structural difficulties for minor landowners. The argument around fixed rents and higher prices still remains, as indeed does the increasing market orientation of the economy. Moreover, the true scale of King John's taxation in its various forms is only now beginning to be truly appreciated.[129] As Nick Barratt has pointed out, John's attempts to maintain his position in the period 1210 to 1214 'represent the greatest level of exploitation in England since the Conquest'.[130] This tax burden hit the population at large. As is well known, the king bore down hard on his tenants-in-chief, particularly where the cost of reliefs, wardships and marriages was concerned.[131] But it should not be forgotten that this is likely to have had some knock-on effects for sub-tenants, as they in turn – as indeed Magna Carta suggests – may have been charged higher sums for relief. These and other factors, including the cost of litigation, made indebtedness to the Exchequer on the part of landowners endemic. All in all, there are very good reasons for thinking that some minor landowners, among others, may have found the first decade of the thirteenth century particularly difficult.

---

[127] Paul Latimer, 'Early Thirteenth-Century Prices', in S.D. Church (ed.), *King John: New Interpretations* (Woodbridge, 1999), pp. 41–73.

[128] See, especially, J.L. Bolton, 'The English Economy in the Early Thirteenth Century', in Church (ed.), *King John*, pp. 27–40. As we have noted, Kathleen Biddick has argued that from the mid-twelfth century the great landlords, in particular, were forced increasingly into structural indebtedness: 'Structural indebtedness locked the English agrarian sector into cash-cropping grain and wool for the expanding industrial sector of Flanders. As a response to this structural change, English agrarian lords moved abruptly toward direct management of their estates. The older arrangements of farming out estates and collecting food or its cash equivalent were unsuited to new forms of agrarian indebtedness and its demands for large-scale production' (Biddick, *The Other Economy*, p. 51).

[129] See Nick Barratt, 'The Revenues of John and Philip Augustus Revisited', in Church (ed.), *King John*, pp. 75–99.

[130] *Ibid.*, p. 87.

[131] See, most recently, Keefe, 'Proffers for Heirs and Heiresses', pp. 99–109.

Moreover, it may have been some time before conditions were measurably better. A new hypothesis by J.L. Bolton suggests reasons why this may have been so.[132] Bolton doubts the supposed size of the inflationary silver flow into England in the late twelfth and early thirteenth centuries. Not only does he suggest that the export of wool was less of a flood than a moderately flowing stream, but he argues that the value of these exports must have been partly counterbalanced by the level of imports. Although the underlying tendency was of an expanding, commercialising economy, the quantity of treasure being taken out to finance the royal wars – initially to pay for the cost of campaigning abroad and later, by King John, to stock-pile cash at his castle treasuries – must have had a depressing effect. This would explain, on the one hand, why the course of inflation was uncertain before 1199 and why, on the other, the inflation levelled off. That prices did not in fact fall back is explained by Bolton partly by population pressure and partly by an increased velocity of circulation of the coinage, as people made a scarce coinage work harder for them. In short, after the rise, prices were held at inflated but stable levels.[133] Indebtedness and a lack of liquidity may have been problems for some time. Although the economy was expanding again from the 1220s it may well have been the 1230s before it was really underway. The recoinage of 1247–51 was to put five times as much coinage in circulation. Like his father, Henry III inadvertently played a major economic role, though in the opposite direction: 'Henry III's ineptitude and resistance to royal exactions may have been just what an uncertainly expanding and commercialisng economy needed.'[134]

There is, in fact, evidence enough of knightly difficulties and indebtedness during the late twelfth and early thirteenth centuries. As we have seen, it is a feature in the honour of Huntingdon, where the Braybrookes were particularly active, and it is already present in the honour of Coventry, as witnessed by the dissolving interest of Warin de Coundon. As Edmund King has shown, Peterborough Abbey was particularly active in the land market created by declining knights in the generations before and after 1200.[135] It tended to be the less endowed families who were worst affected at this time. However, there are many cases where the fortunes of families who are later found chronically indebted

---

[132] For what follows see Bolton, 'The English Economy in the Early Thirteenth Century'.

[133] For Latimer the explanation of the price rise lies in a sudden dishoarding of what had become a suspect currency: Paul Latimer, 'The English Inflation of 1180–1220 Reconsidered', *Past and Present* 171 (2001), pp. 3–29. This leads him to explain the continuation of high prices rather differently from Bolton. For Latimer it was caused by the failure of the recoinage of 1205 to restore complete confidence together with taxation and of fear of taxation, all of which discouraged the holding of coin: 'The grim logic of the question, "Why collect coin so that the king can take it from you?" cannot have been entirely unappreciated' (*ibid.*, p. 26). He doubts the role of population pressure given that wages shared in the inflation.

[134] Bolton, 'The English Economy in the Early Thirteenth Century', p. 40.

[135] King, 'Large and Small Landowners'. See also the works cited in 'The Crisis of the Knightly Class'.

began to take a downturn during these years. Relatively safe alienation was often possible at this juncture because 'there was a good deal of play in the joints of the average fee'.[136]

Surveying the situation in Angevin Yorkshire, Hugh Thomas takes cognisance of improving landlords. He notes assarting, the expansion of demesne herds and the tapping of peasant surplus through the foundation of new mills. He notes, too, the opportunities offered by marriage and the advantages which accrued to honorial officials. In short, knightly incomes in Angevin England could be bolstered by exactly the same factors as we have seen at work in the England of Henry III. But Thomas also points to numerous examples of indebted knights.[137] As he says, a particularly evocative note is sounded by Roger Bret, who sold thirty-six acres of assarted land to Fountains Abbey for 20 marks, 20 shillings, one ox plough and one horse. He has done this, he says, in order to 'retain, for myself and my heirs, the remnant of our inheritance and not lose more or even all'.[138] Roger was one minor landowner who certainly knew the score.

Thomas, in fact, envisages a 'crisis of the gentry', as he puts it, beginning in the late twelfth century: a crisis, that is, in the sense of a period of difficulty and adjustment. For him, however, inflation is not the only, and perhaps not even the chief, cause. 'This was a time in which knights and other members of the gentry faced serious threats to their economic position and to traditional forms of behaviour, notably their generosity with grants of land.'[139] This generosity, to the church, to daughters and to younger sons, resulted in 'a tremendous transfer of resources away from gentry families and particularly from the main branches of these families'.[140] Traditional forms of behaviour may indeed have begun to catch up with knightly families. Nor should we forget Edmund King's observation from the Peterborough evidence that from c.1175 what we begin to see is the break-up in 'the integrity of the knight's fee'. One of the side effects of the assize of novel disseisin was to open what were once internal family arrangements to external validation. Families tended to lose control over what had traditionally been life-tenancies held by younger sons. In short, 'younger sons may have occupied in 1120 the same estates which were occupied by other younger sons in 1180. All that may have changed was that in this generation for the first time, such properties could no longer be recalled.'[141] This is an important observation, which has not been given the attention it deserves. The number of younger sons who figure among the knights of the grand assize in the early years of the thirteenth century, in particular, is very noticeable. Indeed it may have been the high-water mark for cadet knights in England.

---

[136] King, 'Large and Small Landowners', p. 37, quoting S.E. Thorne, 'English Feudalism and Estates in Land', *Cambridge Law Journal* 17 (1959), p. 205.
[137] Thomas, *Vassals, Heiresses, Crusaders and Thugs*, esp. ch. 6.   [138] *Ibid.*, p. 158.
[139] *Ibid.*, p. 166.   [140] *Ibid.*, p. 163.   [141] King, 'Large and Small Landowners', pp. 46–7.

But it was a potentially precarious position, both for cadet and for parent family. Some got themselves into difficulties. Others retrenched. By the second quarter of the thirteenth century knightly families were becoming noticeably less generous to the church. The transfer of advowsons to monastic houses, for example, seriously declined. Moreover, families began to regret earlier alienations and sought to retrieve them, most often unsuccessfully, through the courts.[142] Another casualty was knighthood. It is clear enough that in the process of retreat from knighthood, it was the minor knights – including many cadets – who tended to go first. As Hugh Thomas puts it, 'cost-cutting measures may have played a role in the rapid decline in the number of knights who as-sumed knighthood in the decades after the Angevin period', adding the highly pertinent observation that the 'avoidance of knighthood is likely to have been representative of wider sacrifices'.[143]

Knights, then, faced increased costs, but it is important not to see this solely in terms of externally generated economic factors impacting upon seigneurial families. It is hardly to be doubted that an important ingredient in the expand-ing, commercialising economy of the later twelfth and thirteenth centuries was aristocratic demand. This was reinforced by the stronger class consciousness that developed within aristocratic circles from the 1170s on. These changes are manifested in romance literature, for example, in the developing language of deference, in the crystallisation of heraldry and, of course, in the ceremo-nial aspects of knighthood.[144] It is not difficult to observe these expressions of social elitism and exclusion. It is more difficult to account for them. One can expect the English aristocracy to have been influenced by cultural trends in twelfth-century France, where Georges Duby famously saw a fusion between a higher and a lower 'aristocracy' in the face of perceived threats from above and below.[145] As far as England is concerned, it seems more likely that the magnates became increasingly assertive in the face of knightly aspiration from below, that is to say, from a lesser nobility that was fast consolidating its position.[146] David Crouch may well be right in suggesting that 'the use of prestigious, aristocratic trappings' was inspired precisely by the need to assert a social and cultural superiority and that in doing so the magnates created 'a superior knighthood for themselves'.[147]

Whether there was a deliberate intention to exclude the *milituli* from knight-hood is another matter. It is true that contempt for the rustic knight had been

---

[142] See J.E. Newman, 'Greater and Lesser Landowners and Parochial Patronage: Yorkshire in the Thirteenth Century', *English Historical Review* 92 (1977); Thomas, *Vassals, Heiresses, Crusaders and Thugs*, p. 164; Coss, *Lordship, Knighthood and Locality*, pp. 268–9.

[143] Thomas, *Vassals, Heiresses, Crusaders and Thugs*, p. 165.

[144] The fullest treatment of this subject is now Crouch, *Image of Aristocracy*.

[145] Duby, 'The Transformation of the Aristocracy', pp. 178–85.

[146] See above pp. 35–9.   [147] *Image of Aristocracy*, p. 153.

around for quite some time. It is possible that a factor in the decline of the *milituli* was the withdrawal of magnate support. Certainly by the middle of the thirteenth century aristocratic retinues had come to include more sub-knightly *valetti* and fewer knights. On the other hand, participation in tournaments and the crusades and the patterns of dissemination of heraldry all suggest that the retinue was the primary place where high-flown knightly values were forged.[148] The attitude of the magnates is likely to have been ambivalent. They may well have thought differently about their own followers from how they thought of the generality of lesser knights.

It is more probable that the thinning of knightly ranks was a consequence of noble behaviour rather than an intention, a by-product of cost and consumption patterns. It would be a mistake, though, to concentrate on specifically chivalric display to the neglect of all other aspects of aristocratic consumption. When we come to the thirteenth century we can see clearly that the real income of the higher nobility was increasing, even if the rise is less pronounced than if measured simply in cash. But their expenditure, reflecting an increasing standard of living, was steadily rising too.[149] They had their households and retinues to maintain and their passion for building to indulge. There was constant expenditure on diet, on stables, on textiles for clothing and furnishings, on armour, on furniture and plate. Their demand helped stimulate both imports and internal production.[150] It should not be forgotten that every aspect of aristocratic life involved display, honour and prestige. In the words of one commentator: 'Extravagant display, rich clothing, jewels, fine horses and dogs, and generous gifts were all essentials of day-to-day existence. And this only accounted for their relationship to the living. There were matching sets of obligations to the dead and the need to provide for their own souls.'[151] At the same time as the need to maintain standards – of generosity, hospitality and so on – there was also a need to keep control on expenditure. It is not surprising that the first household accounts date from *c.*1200, that is from the onset of inflation.[152] Nor is it surprising that Bishop Robert Grosseteste should have written his *Rules*, on how to guard and govern lands and household, for the benefit of the countess of Lincoln during the early 1240s.[153] Their level of routine expenditure has

[148] Coss, *The Knight in Medieval England*, pp. 51–60.
[149] See Christopher Dyer, *Standards of Living in the Later Middle Ages: Social Change in England c.1200–1520* (Cambridge, 1989), p. 37; see also Table 2, p. 36. Most of the extant figures, especially for the first half of the century, refer to ecclesiastical magnates, but they are no doubt indicative of a rising income among lay magnates too.
[150] On aristocratic consumption see, in particular, Dyer, *Standards of Living*, chs. 3–4. See also Harvey, 'The Aristocratic Consumer', pp. 17–37.
[151] Raban, 'The Land Market and the Aristocracy', p. 253.
[152] Dyer, *Standards of Living*, p. 92, quoting C.M. Woolgar, 'The Development of Accounts for Private Households in England to *c.*1500 AD' (University of Durham PhD thesis, 1986), pp. 32–55.
[153] *Walter of Henley*, ed. Oschinsky, pp. 388–407.

been suggested as part of the reason for the relatively low level of magnate involvement in the land market during the thirteenth century.[154]

It was in the nature of noble society that cultural patterns were disseminated downwards through a process of emulation, so that one can expect standards of consumption to have been rising below the level of the great lords. One thinks immediately of Chaucer's *Franklin*, in whose house it snowed with meat and drink, and whose literary forbears were the hospitable vavasours of twelfth- and thirteenth-century romance. Moreover, as we have noted, the higher nobility of the later twelfth century may already have been reacting against rising standards from below. Direct evidence of consumption patterns among lesser landowners, let alone the *milituli*, is difficult to find. The building and rebuilding of residences in the late twelfth and thirteenth centuries is one clue.[155] Particularly significant may be the widespread construction of moated sites, over 5,000 across the long thirteenth century, most of them constructed for minor landowners and the like. In some instances they suggest a relocating as minor lords distanced themselves socially from their free tenants. As Christopher Dyer tells us, moats 'represent a considerable outlay for a minor lord. Digging even a small moat would have involved moving 3,000 cubic yards of earth, and all of this work would have been carried out by wage labour, as few gentry would have commanded enough tenant labour services for such a task.' 'Perhaps', he adds, 'moat building as well as buying fine horses or other luxuries, tempted a minority of thirteenth-century gentry into debt.'[156] Horses were, in fact, a significant item of expenditure in their own right. The palfrey, in particular, was 'the staple riding-horse of lords, knights and officials', and 'constituted a normal and important expense for the upper ranks of society'. A sorry horse would have been immediately apparent. Because the palfrey was the most common horse found in the records, a reasonable price series can be constructed for it. Of course, examples are often few and the recorded prices were subject to fluctuations determined by quality, but the prices rose significantly between the 1180s and the 1240s.[157] The important point is that a knight had his own dignity to support and most knights will have had their own households to sustain.

When the first surviving household accounts from gentry families become available to us, from the 1340s, they show more or less what one would have expected.[158] Although much of their provisions were supplied from the resources of their home farms, they were none the less dependent upon the market

---

[154] Raban, 'The Land Market and the Aristocracy', p. 253.

[155] See Coss, *Lordship, Knighthood and Locality*, p. 307, and references given there.

[156] Dyer, *Standards of Living*, pp. 106–7.

[157] Latimer, 'Early Thirteenth-Century Prices', pp. 52–3.

[158] See, in particular, Christopher Woolgar, 'Diet and Consumption in Gentry and Noble Households: A Case Study from around the Wash', in Rowena E. Archer and Simon Walker (eds.), *Rulers and Ruled in Late Medieval England: Essays Presented to Gerald Harriss* (London, 1995), pp. 17–31.

for the more exotic items, including spices, wines, and certain varieties of meat and fish. It is clear enough that prestige attached to the consumption of certain foods and that there was an element of emulation involved: 'At Frampton, the young, knightly family of the Multons did its best to emulate the aristocratic lifestyle, concentrating most items from the elite range of foodstuffs, such as bitterns and a heron, for consumption around major feasts.'[159] That the table, its contents and, indeed, its service were matters of show at the knightly level is indicated pictorially by the Luttrell Psalter, which dates from the same period as the earliest gentry accounts. The Luttrells are shown dining *en famille* with their guests. Whereas the more mundane objects are viewed from the side, the more important items, 'representing the family plate', are shown from above. Particularly striking is the large, circular dish depicted in front of Sir Geoffrey Luttrell himself.[160] Members of the family are also shown dressed in the latest fashions. The steady stream of guests to a gentry household, witnesses to its standards of consumption, is shown clearly by the household books of Dame Alice de Bryene, dating from 1411–13.[161] Of course, this is a long way forward from the age of retreating knighthood but there is every reason to believe that the same social factors were in operation then.

Such was the social and economic climate within which both seigneurial failure and the retreat from knighthood occurred. It is difficult not to see them as connected phenomena. Knights with inadequate resources – such as the rent complexes observable around Coventry, or the small estates of east Sussex studied by Eleanor Searle – may have been among the first to suffer.[162] It is possible that there were more such failures in the early as opposed to the mid-thirteenth century, but they were a constant – always a minority feature – throughout the period. Beyond these, there were levels of difficulty and adjustment which are easy enough to observe but impossible to quantify. Looking from a broad chronological perspective, the new knighthood was both a cause and an effect of social change. The key factor was probably the need to preserve social distance in a time of increasing prosperity and expectations. Local seigneurs sought to increase the distance between themselves and the wealthier freeholders, just as the higher nobility sought to reinforce the gap between themselves and almost everyone else. But there were also other destabilising factors at work during the later twelfth and the early to mid-thirteenth centuries. For one thing, the retreat from the honour and the steadily increasing access to the central courts

---

[159] *Ibid.*, p. 31.

[160] See Michael Camille, *Mirror in Parchment: The Luttrell Psalter and the Making of Medieval England* (London, 1998), pp. 84–5.

[161] See, especially, ffiona Swabey, *Medieval Gentlewoman: Life in a Widow's Household in the Later Middle Ages* (Stroud, 1999), chs. 5 and 6.

[162] Coss, *Lordship, Knighthood and Locality*, pp. 222–4; Searle, *Lordship and Community*, pp. 154–66.

had taken some of the cohesion out of local society. Some of the problems came from the top down. Under the lax rule of Henry III, indulgent towards his relatives and other great lords, competition and resentment became political forces. The opportunities for increased wealth and standards of consumption that the thirteenth century provided did not ease matters so much as heighten tensions and disparities. There were difficulties at the level of the family, too. The common law, with its accent on protecting the tenant, made it difficult for families to behave in the old, informal ways, while legal strategies for protecting estates from biological extinction in the form of descent to heiresses had not yet been devised.[163] In short, although the rise and fall of landed families was a constant feature of medieval society, there are excellent reasons for believing that there were additional factors at work during the first half of the thirteenth century.

However, the retreat from knighthood showed that in the last analysis, whatever the advantages of knightly status may or may not have been, seigneurial survival counted for a great deal more. Once the trend away from knighthood had begun to accelerate, some of the sting may well have been taken out of the situation for the *milituli* and minor lords. For those who were more entrenched, however, the social consequences of losing knighthood became correspondingly greater. Some men whose membership was marginal strove hard to retain it. The retreat from knighthood continued, however, into the 1250s, with others weighing up its cost and pondering its advantages. Some of these were not so much abandoning membership as delaying their knighthood until a more appropriate or propitious time. Thus there was no natural water level, as it were, to which knighthood could flow down. The royal action of distraint to knighthood may have helped somewhat to stem the tide of retreat, but in the end society had to find its own equilibrium.

CONCLUSION: CRISIS OR TRANSFORMATION?

Where, then, does this leave 'the crisis of the knightly class'? To recap: in several key respects my 1975 essay was wrongly formulated. Principally, it failed to distinguish between the Postan and Hilton hypotheses. Although it was not my intention to champion any theory of decline, the rhetoric tended towards the Postan camp. This was compounded by a tendency to think solely in terms of external forces impacting upon the economy of the smaller landowner and by an over-concentration upon the period of Henry III's personal rule. A crisis theory which looks to a decline in the smaller landowners' share of England's land for its primary validation or which centres solely on the 1230s to 1260s alone has been shown to be untenable.

---

[163] For a recent discussion of these strategies see Eileen Spring, *Law, Land and Family: Aristocratic Inheritance in England, 1300 to 1800* (Chapel Hill, 1993), ch. 2: 'The Heiress-at-Law'.

But what of the Hilton hypothesis, that the achievement of full chivalric knighthood was accompanied by a social and economic crisis for the knightly class as a whole? There can be no doubt that this has several distinct advantages: it is able to accommodate the various social phenomena that have been observed, it envisages a medium- to long-term process at work, and it offers a central role for human agency. The problem lies with the terminology. However much one might regret it, the word crisis in this context carries Postan's indelible imprint, pushing one towards a concept of decline. Moreover, one normally thinks of a crisis as belonging to a specific moment in time rather than a prolonged process of change. Consequently, it is probably better to speak of a transformation rather than a crisis of the knightly class. Indeed, it is already present in the historiography. In 1993 I wrote of the transformation of Angevin knighthood, examining the changes that took place across the period from c.1150 to c.1250.[164] Kathryn Faulkner followed suit, in 1996, with 'The Transformation of Knighthood in Early Thirteenth-Century England'. There are echoes here, of course, of Georges Duby's salient essay on the transformation of the aristocracy in France.[165] It is important, however, that we, like Duby himself, use the concept not just as a description of what occurred but as an explanatory tool. As we have seen, it was not just knighthood that was transformed, but the knightly class itself. By the mid-thirteenth century it was no longer the same animal. Whether we choose to call the profound changes which occurred within the higher echelons of lay society in England between the late twelfth century and the mid-thirteenth the 'crisis' or the 'transformation' of the knightly class, the observable phenomena remain the same. The realisation of a more exclusive knightly class was an important stage in the development of the lesser nobility and a significant step towards the formation of the English gentry.

---

[164] Coss, 'Angevin Knighthood and its Transformation', this being chapter 4 of *The Knight in Medieval England*.
[165] 'The Transformation of the Aristocracy', pp. 178–85.

5. *Knights in politics: minor landowners and the state in the reign of Henry III*

The period from the Angevin legal reforms to the period of baronial reform and rebellion of 1258–67 has long been regarded as an important stage in the development both of the English state itself and of the relationship between the central government and local society. Whereas the Whig historians looked to Magna Carta as the foundation of English liberties, modern historians have looked to this period for the origins of the three-cornered parliamentary polity of the fourteenth century and beyond. From John Maddicott, in particular, we have learned to appreciate the contribution of the reign of Henry III to the developing interaction between the crown and provincial institutions.

It is not my intention to deny the significance of this interaction, nor indeed to deny the immense long-term consequences of the changes wrought in Angevin England. One has only to consider the rise of the common law and the concomitant steady growth of a direct relationship between the free man and the state. When it comes to the question of the gentry, however, a series of phenomena have tended to be taken out of context and combined in such a manner as to distort contemporary reality. The participation of county knights in the reform movement of 1258 has been seen as the outcome of cumulative office holding and judicial participation on the one hand and of a sort of collective responsibility on the other: the result of a heightened sense of public duty born of 'self-government at the king's command'. For R.F. Treharne, famously, the period of reform and rebellion marked a critical phase in the rise of a new class that 'had proved its worth, and had arrived, in national politics, at a position which gave it the opportunity of asserting itself in proportion to its economic and social standing, and to its experience in the practical work of daily government'.[1] This interpretation, I suggest, is not sustainable; or, at least, not without serious qualification. As we have seen, the Angevin legacy has been seriously misunderstood. The knightly class was by no means monolithic; and it was far from cohesive. On the contrary, everything suggests that

---

[1] Treharne, 'The Knights in the Period of Reform and Rebellion', pp. 1–12.

thirteenth-century society was characterised by insecurity and competition for power and resources. Increasingly high standards of consumption, a litigious mentality encouraged by the Angevin legal reforms and the effects of the decline of the honour as a social unit had all helped to create an atmosphere of tension and conflict.[2] The emergence of a new, more socially restrictive, knighthood may well have added to the tension. That there was a rising tide of discontent over the way the country was being run would be hard to deny. None the less, we should be extremely cautious in looking for any cohesive opposition to the crown at the knightly level. As far as the evolution of the gentry is concerned the significance of the period of reform lies more in what came out of it than in how it was generated.

I will argue in this chapter that the political relationship between the lesser landowners and the state has been seen through a distorted lens. I will begin with a close examination of that relationship during the turbulent years of 1225–7, and then move on to an examination of the contemporary meaning and significance of election and representation. The myth of the county court as a forum for the expression of specifically knightly or 'gentry' interests in this period will be exposed. Finally, I will turn to the significance of the period of reform and rebellion of 1258–67. Although my aim is revisionist, my purpose is far from being a negative one. A true appreciation of what *did* happen during these years is vital for a correct understanding of developments later in the century. First of all, then, the years 1225–7.

COLLECTIVE GRIEVANCES AGAINST THE STATE: THE YEARS 1225–7

Let us begin by establishing the context. In the summer of 1224 Louis VIII of France completed the conquest of Poitou. If Gascony were not to go the same way, the English had to put a major army in the field. There was no way this could be done without extraordinary taxation. However, Magna Carta had stipulated that in future extraordinary taxation could not be imposed without the consent of the realm. Hubert de Burgh, the justiciar, now proposed just such a tax. The magnates duly assembled in a great council at Westminster. As a result, a tax of one fifteenth of movable goods to be assessed on every person in the land was granted in return for the reissue of Magna Carta and the Charter of the Forests.[3] These were solemnly witnessed and sealed on 11 February 1225. A successful expedition was mounted, under the headship of the king's brother, Richard of Cornwall, which duly saved Gascony for the English crown. In order

---

[2] See Coss, *Lordship, Knighthood and Locality*, pp. 264–76 and John Hunt, 'Families at War: Royalists and Montfortians in the West Midlands', *Midland History* 12 (1977), pp. 22–5.

[3] See, in particular, F. Cazel, 'The Fifteenth of 1225', *Bulletin of the Institute of Historical Research* 34 (1961), pp. 67–81.

to ensure that the tax was used only for the specific purpose intended, the receipt and disbursement of the money was put in the hands of the bishops of Bath and Salisbury, presumably as a check on Hubert de Burgh. As we have seen in chapter 3, great care was taken with the process of assessment and collection on the ground.

Historians have been impressed with the efficiency and the yield of this tax, bringing in as it did a total of some £40,000.[4] David Carpenter has argued, justifiably, that the success of the tax was a tribute to the government of Henry III's minority, which had resurrected royal authority to a remarkable degree after the bleak years of the civil war and its immediate aftermath.[5] However, this is not how contemporaries are likely to have seen it. The reissue of the 1217 Charters in 1225 by the young king, of his own 'spontaneous and free will' and in return for his subjects' acceptance of extraordinary taxation, was a landmark in that it firmly established the charters within English political life. 'Thus the Charters of 1225 were always remembered as part of a mutual bargain between king and his subjects. This was why the king had a peculiar obligation to observe them.'[6] As Carpenter stresses, the Charters were purposefully and very effectively publicised. The sheriffs received their orders to proclaim and observe them and to organise the perambulation of the forests at exactly the same time (15 and 16 February) as the orders to set the assessment and collection of the tax in motion. Only a month or so later, on 29 March, the sheriffs were instructed to inform crusaders, who were normally exempt from taxation, that if they did not pay, they and their heirs would not be entitled to share in its provisions.[7]

But there is a danger, even today, of being rather starry eyed over this. Despite the impressive yield, there does appear to have been resistance in some quarters. London is conspicuously absent from the bishops' accounts, which may well explain its heavy tallage in the following year. There are no returns for the county of Chester, the county and bishopric of Durham, and the Marches outside of Herefordshire. A derisory sum came from Sussex, probably in consequence of the franchises enjoyed by the lords of its subdivisions, known as rapes. Given that the king threatened to exempt those who did not pay from the benefits of the Charters, it may well be, as Fred Cazel has suggested, that some of the great lords with major liberties felt that they had little to gain and were willing to take

---

[4] The bishops' accounts are published in *ibid.*, pp. 73–81. For the surviving, fragmentary returns from the counties see *Rolls of the Fifteenth . . . and Rolls of the Fortieth*, ed. F.A. Cazel and A.P. Cazel, Pipe Roll Society, new series, 45 (1976–7). Those for Lincolnshire appear to be some of the original returns vill by vill.

[5] Carpenter, *The Minority of Henry III*, ch. 10: 'Gascony, Taxation and Magna Carta'.

[6] *Ibid.*, pp. 382–4.

[7] *Pat. Rolls, 1216–25*, p. 572. The enrolled writ is directed to the 'justices' for Kent, though as usual no doubt it is intended to stand for all. The justices were ordered to restrain from allowing poor women to be harassed on the basis of their jewellery and such like. This suggests that the assessment was indeed being carried out 'diligently'.

that chance.[8] Even though it was assessed and collected diligently, one should not forget that this was a major imposition. The complexity of the process, most especially the two instalments, must have kept the tax in the forefront of people's minds over an extended period of time. Indeed, the yield itself may well have caused a stir. It is perhaps significant that the tax was one of the charges laid against Hubert de Burgh by the king in 1239.[9] There can be little doubt that men looked not for hot air but for some real and immediate benefits in return.

What did the men in the counties see as the principal benefits to them of the reissue of the Charters in 1225? What precisely did they expect to gain from it? Freedom from future extraordinary taxation, at least without consent, is implicit in the situation and perhaps goes without saying. But what else? It is clear from events during 1225 and 1226 that one of the principle benefits of the reissue was the opportunity it gave to put further limitations upon the 'depredations' of the sheriff and to keep him at bay. This comes across most clearly in the famous Lincolnshire case which surfaced in the central courts during 1226.[10] The particular dispute began when the sheriff, who had been unable to complete the cases before the county court in a single day, had ordered the court to reconvene on the following day. In the event the knights and stewards who turned up offered a direct challenge to the sheriff. They refused to enter the shire house, arguing that the county court was traditionally held for one day only. The sheriff promptly postponed the outstanding cases to the next wapentake court of Kesteven. This time, led by Theobald Hautein and Hugh de Humby, the knights and others responsible for making the judgements declined to do so outside of the county court. The sheriff, they maintained, was contravening Magna Carta.

At Westminster Hautein and Humby said that the Lincolnshire county court had traditionally met at forty-day intervals and that the sheriff was infringing custom by holding it more frequently and extending it beyond a single day. As they clearly knew, Magna Carta had protected the customary intervals. Similarly, they said, the sheriff had been holding wapentake courts only twice yearly,

---

[8] Cazel, 'The Fifteenth of 1225', p. 71. For examples of resistance to taxation across the period see Mitchell, *Taxation in Medieval England*, pp. 87–9.

[9] As reported by Matthew Paris in his *Liber Additamentorum* (*Chronica Majora*, ed. H.R. Luard, 7 vols., Rolls Series (London, 1872–3), vol. VI, p. 66). It may also be significant in this respect that both these charges and the near contemporary entry in *The Red Book of the Exchequer* considerably overestimate the yield from the tax. This may well reflect contemporary perceptions, recalled fourteen years later. The numerical error itself probably derives from a misreading by the clerks of marks for £.s.d. See Cazel, 'The Fifteenth of 1225', pp. 69–70.

[10] For this case see *Curia Regis Rolls*, vol. XII, nos. 2142, 2312, and *Bracton's Notebook*, ed. F.W. Maitland, 3 vols. (London, 1887), vol. III, no. 1730. It is discussed from various viewpoints in F. Pollock and F.W. Maitland, *The History of English Law before the Time of Edward I* (Cambridge, 1986), vol. I, pp. 549–50; Holt, *Magna Carta*, pp. 279–81; Maddicott, 'Magna Carta and the Local Community', pp. 33–4, 49; and Coss, 'Knighthood and the Early Thirteenth-Century County Court', pp. 48, 55.

in accordance with the Charter, but was now infringing this by taking county business to the Kesteven court. This, however, was a matter of interpretation. Magna Carta restricted not hundred and wapentake courts themselves to two per year, but only the great sessions known as the sheriff's tourn. But what if the quantity of ordinary business required more frequent meetings of the court? This particular matter was only finally settled in October 1234 when the king gave the sheriff of Lincolnshire a ruling. He had been told by his magnates that hundred, wapentake and magnates' courts had all met once a fortnight in Henry II's day. Given that the sheriff's twice-yearly tourn was inadequate for the quantity of business, the royal council had decided that all of these courts should meet every three weeks. However, only litigants and suitors would be required to attend. The general summons would be restricted to the sheriff's tourns.[11] Discussion of this episode has often focused on the wapentake court, but in fact the knights' treatment of the county court was very significant. Hautein and Humby were almost certainly very well aware that Magna Carta said nothing about the court being restricted to a single day. They were seeking to gloss the Charter in their own interests, and this tells us something important about what was going on in the wake of its reissue in 1225. Moreover, their interpretation suggests an attitude towards the county court which is at variance with a view which sees the county court as an institution valued by 'the gentry' as an organ for expressing their interests. They could hardly have valued it so greatly if they wished to restrict its incidence.

Lincolnshire was in some respects a special case, not least in the customary interval between its county courts. But the phenomenon which surfaced at Westminster was not restricted to this particular court, and the issues in contention went back to the previous year. Moreover, the sheriff of Lincolnshire was not the only one to experience such difficulties. In other counties, too, men were using Magna Carta to withdraw their suits from local courts. At the beginning of July 1225 the king wrote to the sheriff of Yorkshire to the effect that men were claiming additional liberties over and above those granted by the Charters. The sheriff was duly ordered to ensure that all royal liberties used in the time of King John and not included by specific mention in the Charters should be firmly observed and not assumed by anyone using the bad example of Lincolnshire. The volatility of the situation is indicated by a similar letter to the sheriff of Cumberland which contained one additional clause. This sheriff was to regulate the conduct of the county serjeants, so that they did nothing which could give offence to the good men of the county through immoderate behaviour or lack of prudence, or which could occasion even some greater malignity.[12]

---

[11] *Close Rolls, 1231–4*, pp. 588–9. For discussion of this see Maddicott, 'Magna Carta and the Local Community', pp. 34–5. This order replaced an earlier one, issued in August, giving the minimalist interpretation of twice only per year.

[12] *Rot. Litt. Claus.*, vol. II, pp. 48b–49.

What lay behind this is revealed by a subsequent letter from the king to the archbishop, bishops, abbots, priors, barons, knights, free tenants and all others of the county of Yorkshire. Issued on 7 July 1225, this firmly commanded them by virtue of the faith in which they were bound to their king to preserve all royal liberties that were not mentioned specifically in the Charters, including suits to the county court, to wapentakes and to ridings, admitting royal bailiffs and serjeants to the latter courts, and preserving royal rights as in the time of his ancestors. He reminded them that the liberties granted made no specific mention of these things by which royal rights and the royal dignity would be prejudiced. Once again, the same letter was issued to Cumberland.[13]

But the issue did not go away. Nor were problems confined to these three counties. The lawful remedy available to a sheriff faced with refusal to attend his courts was distraint, the detention of property to enforce compliance. That sheriffs were doing precisely this over the course of the next twelve months is indicated by a writ issued to six of their number on 22 June 1226. A meeting was fixed for 22 September at Lincoln to determine the contentions that had arisen between 'certain of the sheriffs' and the men of their counties over 'certain articles' contained in the charter of liberties that had been granted them. Each sheriff was ordered that if such contention had arisen between him and the men of his bailiwick and had involved the seizing of cattle, those cattle were to be returned (replevied), and that at the next county court he should say to the knights and good men of his bailiwick that they should choose four from among the more law-worthy and discreet knights among them to be at Lincoln on that day on behalf of the whole county to reveal the quarrel between him and them over the said articles. The sheriff was to be there himself to show why he had acted as he did. Eight counties were involved, including Lincolnshire and Northamptonshire, though not in fact Cumberland and Yorkshire.[14]

Although the meeting at Lincoln may not have actually taken place,[15] the instruction was repeated in very similar terms on 13 August 1227, and this time to twenty-nine sheriffs representing thirty-seven counties. Once again the knights were to be chosen in full county court, and although distraint was not specifically mentioned, it is very likely that the issue was the same. They were to come to Westminster three weeks from Michaelmas. However, seventeen of the sheriffs received an additional set of instructions. These concerned the forests. All foresters in fee were to be summoned to show from when, by whom and by what warrant they held. So, too, were all those who claimed hunting rights in the forest from before the granting of the Forest Charter. Furthermore, the sheriffs were to make diligent enquiry as to the names of those who had conducted the recent perambulation of the forest and had disafforested areas

---

[13] *Ibid.*, p. 79b.   [14] *Ibid.*, pp. 153–153b.
[15] Maddicott, 'Magna Carta and the Local Community', p. 34.

which had been forest before the coronation of Henry II. They were to make known to the king those woods and parts of the royal demesne which had been disafforested by these and without warrant.[16]

This last letter brings together, in fact, the two greatest issues of contention in the counties during the years 1225–6: the holding of the county courts and the question of disafforestation. On 16 February 1225, soon after the reissue of the Charters, the king ordered new perambulations of the forests throughout England. These perambulations were to be conducted by Hugh de Neville, chief justice of the forest, his deputy, Brian de Lisle, and Master Henry de Cerne, in association with two or more named men in each county.[17] As an afterthought, seemingly, the sheriffs and further 'justices' were associated with them. They were to meet with all of the knights in each county, taking them singly or together as they saw fit, and to begin immediately so that the whole thing could be expedited within a month from Easter. Metes and bounds were to be placed in the forests, indicating which areas were to be disafforested and which should remain, in accordance with the Forest Charter, and the results were to be enrolled. These results and the names of the knights who had conducted the perambulations were to be sent to the king under their seals of all commissioners, of the sheriffs and of the knights. No wood was to be felled or venison taken as a result of the perambulations until they had reached the king and the council had decided what was to be done. Within the counties twelve lawful knights who were well placed to know the truth were to be chosen and sworn; they would conduct the actual perambulations, in the presence of the foresters in fee and the verderers, and before the named justices.

Chroniclers record the enthusiasm with which the perambulations were greeted. 'All new forests throughout England were disafforested', exclaimed one monastic annalist.[18] According to the chronicler Roger of Wendover, after the confirmation of the Charters, 'all put their liberties into practice, making assarts, hunting game, ploughing the land which was formerly uncultivated, so that all did as they chose in the disafforested woods'.[19] The situation was reminiscent of that in 1218. The forest had been the greatest unresolved issue in 1215.[20] King John's failure to confront squarely the matter of the lands afforested by Henry II appears to have been a major reason for some of the northern barons continuing their rebellion after Runnymede. What Magna Carta *had* done was to provide for the election of twelve knights in each county whose task would

---

[16] *Rot. Litt. Claus.*, vol. II, pp. 212b–213a.   [17] *Pat. Rolls, 1216–25*, pp. 567–70.
[18] *Annales Monastici*, ed. H.R. Luard, Rolls Series (London, 1864–9), vol. I, p. 68 (Annals of Tewkesbury); C.R. Young, *The Royal Forests of Medieval England* (Leicester, 1979), p. 70.
[19] Matthew Paris, *Chronica Majora*, vol. III, pp. 94–5; Maddicott, 'Magna Carta and the Local Community', p. 39.
[20] For what follows see especially Young, *The Royal Forests*, ch. 4, and Carpenter, *The Minority of Henry III*, esp. pp. 80, 89–91, 168–9, 180–1, 385.

be to reform the evil customs of the forest and the malpractice of foresters. These commissions may well have functioned, as J.C. Holt suggests,[21] and their findings may well lie behind the Forest Charter issued in the name of the young king, on 6 February 1217, around the time that his government issued its modified version of Magna Carta. Like the baronial programme known as the Unknown Charter which antedated it, this involved the disafforestation of all new forests created by Henry II. On 22 February 1218 the sheriffs were sent copies of Magna Carta and the Forest Charter and told to have them read in the county courts, while on 2 April the chief justice of the forest and various sheriffs were ordered to have the Forest Charter sworn to and observed. There was a major difficulty, however, in that no procedures had been laid down for the implementation of the proposed disafforestation. In an extraordinary and fascinating example of self-help, two counties, Nottinghamshire and Huntingdonshire, proceeded to undertake their own, holding inquiries which effectively disafforestated the entire counties. At Leicester on 24 July 1218, in an effort to bring the situation under control, the regent ordered perambulations of the forest in each county by twelve law-worthy knights under the supervision of the chief justice of the forest. The results were to be forwarded to the king. Having found the results totally unacceptable – the men of Huntingdonshire, for example, having simply repeated their earlier and extreme findings – the government ordered a new perambulation in December 1219.[22] This time a group of important *curiales* was appointed to make inquiries through panels of twenty-four knights and free men in each county. The afforestations by Henry II were to be reported to the justiciar and council and they would take action as they deemed fit. If this was an attempt at producing a compromise it singularly failed. The juries of Oxfordshire and Buckinghamshire argued for disafforestation of their counties while that from Huntingdonshire stated baldly that Henry II had created the entire forest in their county. As David Carpenter has written, 'The Huntingdonshire remonstrance reveals, more forcefully than any other document of this period, the frustration felt in the counties at the failure to implement the Charter of the Forests or, as the government would have claimed, at the failure to pervert it. The perambulations equally reveal how strong feelings were over the issue amongst the knightly class.'[23] None the less, the perambulations were basically rejected by the government. In October 1224 the chief justice of the forest, Hugh de Neville, was ordered to have regards made within the forests

---

[21] Holt, *Magna Carta*, pp. 384–5. Letters patent had been issued on 19 June 1215 setting up the machinery for electing the knights (*Rotuli Litterarum Patentium*, p. 108b).

[22] To make matters worse, in July 1219 the government had appointed county commissioners to inquire into assarts made since the king's coronation. The assarters were asked to appear at Westminster in October. Not surprisingly, they came in hostile mood and proceeded to complain about the whole forest administration: Carpenter, *The Minority of Henry III*, pp. 150–1, 159, 163–4.

[23] *Ibid.*, p. 181.

observing the boundaries as in the time of King John, a direct contravention of the Forest Charter. This was just a few months before the great council at which the king was to seek his tax of a fifteenth on movables.

The king seems to have expected different results from the perambulations of 1225. On 12 March he wrote that the knights who made the earlier perambulations should not be proceeded against, whatever the findings of the most recent enquiries.[24] Once again the king was to receive the results of the perambulations and the royal council would decide what to do. And, once again, the perambulations were a serious disappointment to the crown. For a time the king gave in, and on 8 May 1225 the sheriffs were ordered to proclaim and observe the perambulations.[25] In February 1227, having declared himself of age and not bound by acts done in his name during his minority, Henry called the 1225 knights to Westminster to admit the errors they had made.[26] The chief of these had been the failure to recognise the difference between the forests which Henry II had newly created and those which had been lost during the reign of King Stephen and which Henry had revived, a contentious issue ever since 1217. In 1228 the sheriffs were ordered to proclaim that all forests were to remain as they had been under King John.[27] Counties were forced in practice to make their individual bargains with the king. Some, Northamptonshire among them, were gainers; others were back to square one. Not surprisingly, the issue of the forests was to surface again in 1237 when the king gained a tax of a thirtieth on movables, in return for confirmation of the Charters once more.[28]

After collection of the fifteenth and the confirmation of the Charters, the country was in a state of some excitement. One peculiar and rather extreme expression of this excited atmosphere was the attempt by an approver, Richard son of Nigel, to save his neck by bringing an appeal against three east midland landowners who had plotted, he said, to kill the king by having him poisoned.[29] The three were Ralf de Bray, William fitz Elias, and no less a knight than Vitalis Engayne, a prominent landowner with Northamptonshire lands at Blather-wycke, Rushton, Moulton and Bradden. The approver testified that he had first heard the three of them arranging this in Westminster Hall. He had heard Ralf and Vitalis speak of it again at the latter's house on his manor in St Neots.

---

[24] *Pat. Rolls, 1216–25*, p. 512.

[25] Carpenter, *The Minority of Henry III*, p. 385, notes the king's deliberate duplicity.

[26] The king magnanimously remitted their transgression in most cases, as having been made through ignorance. In a few cases he seems to have hounded them. On 15 January 1228 inquisitions in Warwickshire and Surrey were asked to name the perambulators who had disafforested areas that had been forest before the time of Henry II, while in March 1231 he was still seeking the men who had made the perambulation of Northamptonshire (*Close Rolls, 1227–31*, pp. 90, 579–80).

[27] *Close Rolls, 1227–31*, pp. 101–3.

[28] For the issues in 1237 see R. Stacey, *Politics, Policy and Finance under Henry III, 1216–1245* (Oxford, 1987), pp. 112–14.

[29] *Curia Regis Rolls*, vol. XII, pp. 215–16.

All of them had asked him to be an accomplice and had offered him a share of their lands if he would do so. Asked when this was, he said that it was at Easter a year ago (presumably 1224) when the king was at St Albans, lodging at the bishop's house on his way to London.

What is surprising, perhaps, is that the authorities took the case so seriously. At least two of the defendants, Vitalis Engayne and William fitz Elias, had been committed to the Tower during the proceedings. Vitalis, moreover, had offered to bring a Hundred knights to court in defence of his reputation. It is hard to believe that the approver had actually been party to such a plot. It is more likely that he was clutching at straws. Perhaps he felt that if you are going to tell a lie, tell a big one. On the other hand he may well have picked up a rumour which he proceeded to relay in a vain attempt to save his life. It may say something about the atmosphere of the time that this should have been remotely feasible. If the Ralf de Bray in question is the same Ralf who had been under-sheriff to the infamous Falkes de Bréauté who had been exiled from England only in 1224, the government's concern becomes a little more understandable, although even then one would have expected the intended victim to have been the justiciar, Hubert de Burgh, enemy of Falkes, rather than the young king himself.[30]

The events of 1225–6 have been related in some detail because they contain some important lessons for how we should envisage the relationship between the knights and the central government in this period. Two features are especially striking. The first is that the aspirations that surfaced in the counties were predominantly negative. The primary purpose was to keep the government at bay. This is seen in two principal directions. One is the attempt to limit the exactions of the sheriff, and the other is the demand for disafforestation. From early in John's reign through to the early 1230s the government was willing, in certain cases at least, to sell liberties. The counties of the south-west, in particular, purchased charters from King John that would give them the privilege of having a local man as sheriff, or even a particular nominee, rights that were reacquired during the 1220s. Occasionally, the same privilege was acquired elsewhere. In 1232, for example, the men of Nottinghamshire and Derbyshire secured Ralf fitz Nicholas as their sheriff for life.[31] As we have seen, disafforestation was also acquired on a county or regional basis. In both cases the purpose was essentially financial: the protection of resources against a rapacious crown.

---

[30]   For Ralf de Bray in this context see Carpenter, *The Minority of Henry III*, pp. 117, 393. Ralf was to enter the service of Ranulf III, earl of Chester. He was later restored to the king's service and was sent to Devizes to guard the now ex-justiciar, Hubert de Burgh: D.A. Carpenter, 'The Fall of Hubert de Burgh', *Journal of British Studies* 19 (1980); reprinted in Carpenter, *The Reign of Henry III*, pp. 47, 58.
[31]   Maddicott, 'Magna Carta and the Local Community', pp. 28–9.

The second feature of the relationship between government and locality in this era was its socially inclusive nature. As John Maddicott says, 'These grievances against the crown and its agents united local society in defence of local liberties. Issues such as the forest were not peculiar to any one class. They generated a widely shared sense of common interest and brought together barons, knights, freeholders and often churchmen in appeals to the Charters, and in fresh attempts to purchase privileges.' He gives the examples of Cornwall in 1225, when 'the bishop of Exeter, barons, knights and all the county' offered 800 marks for the disafforestation of the county, of which the bishop provided £140, the Cornish magnate Reginald de Vautort £133 and William Brewer, a west country baron, £25; and of the area between the Ouse and the Derwent, for the disafforestation of which 800 marks was given during the 1230s by the archbishop of York, the bishop of Durham, the abbot of St Mary's, York, and the earls, barons, knights and freeholders of the territory.[32] It is with justice that Maddicott sees echoes here of the type of county community which predated the Norman Conquest, when Anglo-Saxon magnates, ecclesiastics and thegns frequented the twice-yearly county courts.[33]

When knights were in conflict with the crown, moreover, magnates tended to be there in the background. In the famous débâcle in Lincolnshire, for example, Theobald Hautein announced that he had just returned from the royal court where he had spoken with the archbishop of Canterbury, the earl of Chester and other magnates. He and Hugh de Humby later told Thomas fitz Simon, a knight who had sided with the sheriff, that they would soon be seeing his lord and would tell him how his steward was conducting himself in the county court.[34] In the 1250s a later sheriff of Lincolnshire was prevented from holding wapentake and riding courts by no less a person than the bishop of Lincoln, the saintly Robert Grosseteste.[35] The interests of knights and barons were often at one. According to the chronicler Matthew Paris, the failure of the crown to honour the 1225 disafforestations was a major issue in the baronial rising against Henry III in 1227.[36] It may just be possible to contend, with Maddicott, that in these ancient county communities, 'the gentry found a voice'; but, if so, it was one voice among many. The evidence does not support the idea that the county was the political mouthpiece of the gentry.

This had certainly not been the case during the reign of King John. Even Hugh Thomas, the champion of an Angevin gentry, argues that the 'gentry had not yet achieved an independent voice through the county court or other means'.[37] He claims for them 'no independent voice or agenda' of the sort envisaged by John Maddicott during the later baronial revolt of the mid-thirteenth century.[38]

---

[32] *Ibid.*, pp. 48–9.   [33] *Ibid.*, p. 25.
[34] Coss, 'Knighthood and the Early Thirteenth-Century County Court', p. 48.
[35] Maddicott, 'Magna Carta and the Local Community', p. 35.   [36] *Ibid.*, p. 39.
[37] Thomas, *Vassals, Heiresses, Crusaders and Thugs*, p. 168.   [38] *Ibid.*, p. 190.

In fact, the views and interests of the lesser landowners would appear to have been channelled through the magnates. The contours of their participation in the Magna Carta rebellion is a matter of some debate. The *locus classicus* is Sir James Holt's incisive chapter in *The Northerners*.[39] Here he famously argues that 'the general impression created by the evidence is that the great rebel lords were followed by the men whom they might reasonably regard as their particular tenants almost to a man', from whom 'he probably expected, and certainly seems to have got, the succour and aid which a feudal lord would consider his due'. Nevertheless, within this broad context he allows for the 'complex influences' that were at work, including the bonds of neighbourhood and the role of major sub-tenants, proud and resourceful seigneurs in their own right. The point is that many lesser men had their own individual grievances against the crown, often similar to those of the barons. Neatly summarised by Hugh Thomas, these come down very largely to matters of resources, to the consequences, that is, of the fiscal policies of, and the burdens imposed by, the crown.[40] Although he questions the role of the honour in determining the actions of the feudal sub-tenants, Thomas argues that the barons rewarded their followers by gaining concessions for them in Magna Carta.[41] That the charter contained clauses of greater benefit to sectors other than the baronage is a truism of Magna Carta studies. Knights stood to gain, in particular, from the restrictions on the taking of aids (clause 15), the provisions over castleguard (clause 29), the protection offered tenants of escheated estates (clause 43), and the general extension of its provisions to sub-tenants (clause 60), together with the clauses bolstering the possessory assizes and the provisions over the forest which were of widespread concern. It seems undeniable that the barons, for reasons of practical politics if nothing else, sought advantages for their followers as well as for themselves. In other words they felt pressure from below.[42] It is worth reminding ourselves in this context that even in 1259, a chronicler tells us, it was 'the community of the bachelry of England', that is to say the magnate retinues, who forced the baronial reformers into publishing the more radical measures known as the Provisions of Westminster, measures which greatly benefited knights and free men. This was the primary means by which lesser men brought their influence to bear.

---

[39] Holt, *The Northerners*, ch. 4: 'The Northern Knights'.

[40] Thomas, *Vassals, Heiresses, Crusaders and Thugs*, pp. 180–8.

[41] *Ibid.*, pp. 44–7, 190–2. By contrast, K. Faulkner whilst arguing that 'the cocktail of ingredients was unique in each case', sees neighbourhood as generally more important than lordship in determining the decision to revolt: K. Faulkner, 'The Knights in the Magna Carta Civil War', in M. Prestwich *et al.* (eds.), *Thirteenth Century England VIII* (Woodbridge, 2001), pp. 1–12. The important question in the present context, however, is how the interests of the knights were factored in. It may well be justified to see opposition knights as 'politicised', but it is extremely difficult to see them as constituting a distinct 'party'.

[42] And see below, pp. 132–4.

How then should we see the county court in this period? All the indications suggest that, except when the royal justices were present for the general eyre, the county court was a lack-lustre affair, dominated by an increasing volume of routine administrative and judicial business.[43] The magnates themselves had ceased to attend, leaving their interests to be looked after by their stewards. Suit of court, that is to say obligatory attendance based on land tenure, was already declining in the early thirteenth century. Many of the tenurial obligations to attend would seem to have applied to the biannual great courts only, and with withdrawal of suit a constant factor there is every reason to believe that the number of suitors was declining throughout the thirteenth century. It is certainly not difficult to find evidence of low attendance by knights.[44] In 1211, for example, we hear of a judgement being put in respite in the Herefordshire county court because of the paucity of knights present and because of strife between those who were there: (*et quoniam pauci milites fuerunt ad comitatum tunc et contencio fuit inter illos qui interfuerunt, posuerunt judicium in respectum usque ad alium comitatum*). In Devon, in 1236, the defendants claimed that they had deferred judgement on certain matters in the county court because there were few knights there, and because the bishop and other barons and magnates were absent (*eo quod pauci milites tunc ibi fuerunt et episcopus loci et alii barones et magnates tunc absentes fuerunt*). During the famous Gloucestershire false judgement of 1212, it was twice stated that the case had been postponed in the county because of poor attendance at court. As John Maddicott has said, men found the meetings of local courts 'vexatious, expensive and open to exploitation', and this surely applied to county courts as much as any others.[45]

For the most part then, county courts were not large gatherings of knights and freeholders eager to take part in 'self-government at the king's command', and it would probably be truer to say that most knights avoided the detailed business of the court except where their interests, personal or shared, were concerned, and except when called upon to act when their status was specifically required – and not invariably even then. What we know supports Maitland's view that even the 'great counties' were not very large assemblies, let alone 'the thinly attended meetings that are holden month by month'.[46] As the events of 1225–7 make clear, sheriffs must have had increasing difficulty coping with the volume of business in the face of uncooperative suitors. In view of the stance taken by the likes of Theobald Hautein and Hugh de Humby in those years, it is very difficult indeed to envisage the county court as a significant forum of debate.

---

[43] For the routine nature of much of the judicial business see Palmer, *The County Courts of Medieval England*.

[44] What follows is taken from Coss, 'Knighthood and the Early Thirteenth-Century County Court', esp. pp. 45, 49, 54–5.

[45] Maddicott, 'Magna Carta and the Local Community', p. 36.

[46] Pollock and Maitland, *The History of English Law*, vol. I, pp. 542–3, 548.

ELECTION AND REPRESENTATION

What then of the question of election and representation? These are important issues because they can so easily carry anachronistic connotations. Indeed, as soon as we approach them we face an immediate problem. In our own minds it is difficult to disengage the concept of election from more modern ideas of suffrage, ballot, candidature, desire for office as a career move, and so on. And yet it is vitally important for us to try to rid our minds of these ideas if we are to enter into the spirit of thirteenth-century politics. What did election mean and what did it involve for contemporaries? It may be better, in fact, if we use the more neutral term 'chosen' in place of 'elected', although it is not always easy to do so. We need to see beyond the words used in the writs to the actual events, e.g. the sheriff should 'cause to be elected/chosen ... in full county court', but we have little evidence to enable us to do so.

The questions then are easier to ask than to answer. However, the case of the coroner is particularly instructive.[47] Although the writs appear to have been haphazardly enrolled, the Chancery's Close Rolls do give us letters to sheriffs requiring the election of new coroners from time to time and letters releasing individuals from office. It is clear that the coroners should be responsible knights (*de fidelioribus et discretioribus militibus eiusdem comitatus*) and that they should be elected to office in the county court (*in pleno comitatu*). The office does not seem to have been a particularly popular one. As one commentator has neatly put it:

> the office was demanding, financially unrewarding, and lacked opportunities for the exercise of power. It is hardly surprising that few men were willing to fill such a position ... Equally naturally, many of those men elected to the office immediately sought to evade it, using one of three excuses: old age and/or sickness, employment upon other business, and personal unfitness or insufficient qualification.[48]

Insufficient qualification meant, in effect, the lack of land from which to support themselves and on which they could be distrained. When first introduced in 1194, the coroners were to comprise three knights and one clerk in each county, although by as early as 1198 they appear to have been replaced by four knights. For much of the thirteenth century they do seem generally to have been knights. In 1275, however, the Statute of Westminster I sought to deal with the problem of 'mean persons' being elected to the office. The important point here is that, despite being chosen at the county court, men sought to evade the position. Now

---

[47] For the coroners see, generally, Hunnisett, *The Medieval Coroner*. See also the same author's 'Sussex Coroners in the Middle Ages', *Sussex Archaeological Collections*, vol. 95 (1957), 96 (1958), 98 (1960). For what follows see, in particular, *The Medieval Coroner*, ch. 9: 'Elections and Qualifications'.

[48] K.S. Naughton, *The Gentry of Bedfordshire in the Thirteenth and Fourteenth Centuries* (Leicester, 1976), p. 41.

it is true that one must be careful not to take the writs always at face value. There may have been a time lapse, even a considerable one, before a man objected to the office. Some probably enjoyed the work, at least for a time. Sometimes others sought to have a particular coroner removed. On the other hand, the fact that men so often sought release from it is of significance. Far from seeking office, many must have been unaware that they were being elected. They may not have been present in the county court, or have been consenting. It is to cover this that the writ to the sheriff ordering him to have a man elected specifies that he should know and should be willing (*qui ad hoc sciat et velit intendere*). They were expected to take an oath. None the less, men *were* elected against their will. Some were elected despite the fact that they held other offices or were absent on other business. In such cases it is clear that they could not have been present at their election. As early as 1202 there is an example of a man buying exemption, a process that reached its peak in the 1250s. There are also examples of coroners buying their removal from office and of men having to be distrained by the sheriff before they would take up their duties.[49] All of this has implications not only for the office of coroner but also for how we should see the process of election at the county court.

One wonders, in fact, how many so-called elections in the county court were actually nominations, either inside the court or without. Sometimes irregularities are reported on the central court rolls. In the Levelaunce case of 1225, for example, the sheriff of Warwickshire had managed to have only three knights elected for a view of bed-sickness and ordered a hundred serjeant to summon a fourth. As a result the whole procedure went awry.[50] More significant is the evidence recently discovered by John Maddicott of a few of the knights elected for the parliament of 1254.[51] It is most interesting to note that the Middlesex knights had not in fact been elected in the county court at all, as the writ to the sheriff had directed, but had been nominated by the sheriff as the only two he could find who were suitable. Moreover, the two knights he nominated – Sir Roger de la Dune and Sir Roger de Batchworth – were refusing to serve. The sheriff sought authority to distrain them. In the event, two knights of lesser significance – William fitz Reyner and John de Twyne – were ultimately returned. Now it is true, as Maddicott points out, that there were specific problems associated with Middlesex, where there were few resident knights and where the sheriff was a man of little stature who could not impose his will. It may also be the case, as he suggests, that the more significant men were making a political protest against financial pressures from the crown in refusing attendance, although it might seem a rather dangerous position to have taken up as they would

[49] Hunnisett, *The Medieval Coroner*, pp. 187–9.
[50] Coss, 'Knighthood and the Early Thirteenth-Century County Court', p. 47.
[51] J.R. Maddicott, 'The Earliest Known Knights of the Shire: New Light on the Parliament of April 1254', *Parliamentary History* 18, no. 2 (1999), pp. 109–30.

then have run a greater risk of another tax being imposed upon them. When all caveats have been made, however, the significant point is that two established county knights showed no willingness to participate in a national assembly. In the event two men of rather lesser social standing were returned, almost certainly nominated by the sheriff. Aside from Middlesex, we have only the names of the two knights who represented Northumberland and evidence that knights were chosen for one other county, Essex. Here, however, the sheriff received a writ telling him to substitute another knight for Walter de Bibbesworth, who was keeping the king's forest in the county. Even supposing that he had been elected in the county court, it is clear that he could not have been present to protest at his election and that his fellows elected an absent knight, unaware that his current duties would prevent his acceptance. Altogether it does raise doubts as to how seriously men took the idea of representation within the counties during these years.

What does seems clear is that election was essentially a device of the central government. It was employed, for example, in the possessory assizes and the grand assize, for forest perambulations, for the appointment of tax assessors at the local level, and for officials such as the coroners. It was also employed for meetings with the king. It can certainly be seen as an aspect of self-government at the king's command. It is worth re-emphasising, however, that this 'self-government' was only partial. As we have seen, there was an important distinction between the justices and the major financial agents of the crown, who were essentially interposed between the centre and the localities, and the generality of knights in the counties who were drawn on as jurors and such like. By and large the former were not elected but appointed direct. The plain fact is that election took place largely at the behest of the crown. Why was this so?

There were, I think, various reasons. One was efficiency, to ensure that people actually did undertake the necessary tasks. The county court was the obvious medium for this, especially as people needed to know who had been chosen. A second was to ensure that suitable men with the requisite knowledge were indeed chosen. A third reason was that in some circumstances men were required to speak on behalf of larger numbers of others and even to bind the larger body to any subsequent action. Hence the election of men to treat with the king and eventually to represent their fellows in parliament. The earliest summons to meetings at the centre were simply a device to give instruction. In August 1212 the king ordered the sheriffs to come with 'six law-worthy and discreet knights' from their counties 'to do what we tell them'.[52] Similarly, in May 1213 four knights from each county north of the Trent were to come before Brian de Lisle, the chief justice of the forest, to carry out what he should tell them.[53] In

---

[52] See Carpenter, 'The Beginning of Parliament' in *The Reign of Henry III*, pp. 390–2 for a recent discussion of these matters. See also, Holt, 'The Prehistory of Parliament', pp. 1–28.
[53] *Rot. Litt. Claus.*, vol. I, p. 219b.

November of the same year knights were again summoned to the king; as they were to come armed, the purpose was clearly connected with the general state of the realm. At the same time four knights from each county were to come 'to speak with us on the affairs of our kingdom'.[54] It seems very probable that this, too, was a euphemism for the receipt of instruction. Election and, in effect, representation (*pro toto comitatu*) do not figure explicitly until 1226 and 1227, when knights were summoned to discuss the case against sheriffs during the débâcle over the holding of courts and the interpretation of Magna Carta. And then, in February 1254, the sheriffs were instructed that two knights should be chosen in each county court to come 'in place of all and each of the county (*vice omnium et singulorum comitatuum*)' for the purpose of granting taxation, taxation that in the end was refused. The language of the writ was deliberately emphatic when it came to representation. Election then was a device used as circumstances warranted.

But what might election have meant to thirteenth-century knights themselves? Did they value it for their own reasons? The likelihood is that they, too, saw election as a useful device in appropriate circumstances. It appears in Magna Carta. As we have seen, in accordance with clause 48 twelve knights were to be elected in each county whose task was to reform the evil customs of the forest and to amend the malpractices of foresters. Clause 18 specified that the petty assizes were to be undertaken by the central court justices together with four knights chosen by the county. In practice this does not appear to have been carried out to the letter, and the government devised an alternative but less direct means of recruiting local men. Election *may* have been prized in its own right in the counties, but there is nothing to indicate it. It does not arise in the disagreements over the implementation of Magna Carta, and where alternatives were devised they seemed to work tolerably well. As far as one can see, it was more important in the counties that the sheriff should be a local man than that he should actually be elected.[55] In the end we have no means of knowing whether men actively sought to represent their fellows. However, the slight evidence from 1254 must at least give us pause.

Nevertheless, the fact of representation by knights in 1254 has been regarded by historians, justly, as significant in the evolution of parliament.[56] The circumstances are well known. Parliament met on 27 January 1254, with the king in Gascony and in urgent need of money. No agreement was reached, however, and a further meeting was called for 26 April. In the meantime the regents instructed the sheriffs to have two knights elected in each county to attend and

---

[54] *ad loquendum nobiscum de negotiis regni nostri* (*Select Charters*, ed. Stubbs, p. 282).

[55] Maddicott, 'Magna Carta and the Local Community', p. 29. But, see also p. 27.

[56] For what follows see J.R. Maddicott, ' "An Infinite Multitude of Nobles": Quality, Quantity and Politics in the Pre-Reform Parliaments of Henry III', in M. Prestwich *et al.*, *Thirteenth Century England VII* (Woodbridge, 1999), pp. 17–46.

to state what they were prepared to grant the king on behalf of their counties. Three days later, on 14 February, they wrote to the king saying that they thought it unlikely that 'the other laity' (that is to say the non-magnates) would grant an aid without a firm undertaking by the king to observe the Charters.[57] 'Many complain', they wrote, 'that the aforesaid Charters are not observed by your sheriffs and other bailiffs.' In many respects, this sequence of events seems to foreshadow later parliaments, where elected knights of the shire, in touch with opinion in the counties, were asked to grant taxation in return for the redress of grievances, even if – in this case – no taxation was actually granted.

However, the parliament of April 1254 may not have been the novelty it has been thought. Knights are reported to have been present at the parliament of May 1253 and, indeed, at several parliaments since 1237. How they came to be there is nowhere made clear. John Maddicott has argued that, in some or all of these instances, they may have been drawn directly from the shires. What had happened, he suggests, is that knights elected in the counties had replaced the lesser tenants-in-chief who had previously been summoned by the sheriffs. Clause 14 of Magna Carta had required the presence of the lesser tenants-in-chief as well as the greater men when the king sought extra taxation. The evidence suggests that the lesser tenants-in-chief were summoned by the sheriffs to what Maddicott calls 'taxation parliaments' in the reign of Henry III. From 1232 until 1257 there were at least fourteen assemblies where tax of the sort covered by clause 14 was considered, although the king was largely unsuccessful in acquiring it. Some of these lesser tenants-in-chief were on a par with other wealthy knights who did not hold directly of the crown, but very many of them were quite insignificant figures indeed. By means of election, more solid men would now replace some of the nonentities.[58] In other words election may well have been employed as a device to limit attendance and to produce a more sensible assembly, as well as producing one that would more effectively bind opinion in the counties.

If this interpretation is correct, the government's action directly reflected the social change that had been taking place in the counties. As Maddicott points out, this shift coincides with the change in distraint to knighthood away from tenure (knight's fee in 1224, tenants-in-chief in 1232 and 1234) to £20 landholders in 1241–2. It also coincides with the emergence of a more aristocratic knighthood. The knights of the 1240s and 1250s were in general more socially significant figures than their forebears, and their opinions mattered.

It may well be that the attendance of knights at the taxation parliaments – howsoever they came to be there – created one further channel through which

---

[57] *Close Rolls, 1253–4*, pp. 114–15; *Royal and Other Historical Letters Illustrative of the Reign of Henry III*, ed. W.W. Shirley, Rolls Series (London, 1866), vol. II, pp. 101–2.

[58] As he says, the resultant parliaments were in consequence not less but more aristocratic (Maddicott, ' "An Infinite Multitude of Nobles" ', p. 40).

Henry III's government became aware of discontent in the counties, although the general unwillingness to grant taxation may not have made it very receptive.[59] Once again, however, it is important to remain firmly within the contemporary context. There is nothing here which foreshadows the petitions which the later knights of the shire were to bring on behalf of their constituents, and nothing to suggest that the system was receptive to these.[60] When the baronial reformers opened up the floodgates of complaint in 1258, redress was to be achieved by traditional means, that is by the justiciar touring the country to 'do right to all persons'. Moreover, the role of knights, whether elected or not, should not be exaggerated. The 'long and acrimonious debates'[61] which took place in parliaments between 1237 and 1258 were essentially magnate affairs. And, when the reformers of 1258 established their new 'constitution', under the Provisions of Oxford, no mention was made of any elected representatives at the three annual parliaments.

With these several observations in mind let us examine the significance of the years 1258–67.

THE SIGNIFICANCE OF 1258–67

According to a long tradition in English historical scholarship the magnates who confronted the king in the parliament of April 1258 and imposed reforms upon him were acting, in a disinterested manner, to save the country from the consequences of his incapacity and to rule on behalf of the community of the realm. Recent work has overturned this rather naïve approach to the mid-thirteenth-century conflict and shown that the débâcle of 1258 was born of a more mundane struggle for influence over the king and for control of royal patronage.[62] It resulted from a split within the ruling caste, as one group of courtiers turned against another. The reforms enacted at the parliament held in Oxford in June 1258 gave them 'control over policy, appointments and patronage', as David Carpenter succinctly puts it.[63] In order to vindicate, and even in

---

[59] *Ibid.*, p. 42, brings together the inevitably exiguous evidence for the possible expression of grievances by representatives at these taxation parliaments.

[60] For what follows see Carpenter, 'The Beginning of Parliament', esp. pp. 384, 392, 405.

[61] The phrase is Carpenter's: *ibid.*, p. 387.

[62] The key works in this revision are: D.A. Carpenter, 'What Happened in 1258?', in J. Gillingham and J.C. Holt (eds.), *War and Government in the Middle Ages: Essays in Honour of J.O. Prestwich* (Woodbridge, 1984), pp. 106–19; D.A. Carpenter, 'King, Magnates and Society: The Personal Rule of King Henry III, 1234–1258', *Speculum* 60 (1985), pp. 39–70; H.W. Ridgeway, 'The Politics of the English Royal Court, 1247–65: With Special Reference to the Role of the Aliens' (Univ. of Oxford DPhil thesis, 1983); H.W. Ridgeway, 'The Lord Edward and the Provisions of Oxford (1258): A Study in Faction', in P.R. Coss and S.D. Lloyd (eds.), *Thirteenth Century England I* (Woodbridge, 1986), pp. 89–99.

[63] In D. Abulafia (ed.), *The New Cambridge Medieval History*, V: *c.1198–1300* (Cambridge, 1999), ch. 12: 'The Plantagenet Kings', p. 338.

a sense to validate, their stance they invoked the manifold grievances against the government and its agents which undoubtedly existed in the localities. As a result a wider movement of reform was brought into being. The collection of grievances known as the Petition of the Barons contained broader issues than those that directly concerned the great lords and seems to have been the product of wider consultation, while the Provisions of Oxford themselves reformed the shrievalty, a matter that was of wide concern in the counties.[64] Henceforth the sheriff was to be a vavasour, that is to say a substantial knight, of the county he administered, hold office for one year only at a time, and be supported in his office by the receipt of salary. Four knights were to be appointed in each county to collect complaints, largely against officials, and to present them to the justiciar who would hear them as he toured the country as part of the duties of this newly revived office. The predictable slowness of the justiciar's methodical eyre led to a slight change in procedure, so that when panels of knights were appointed in August they were instructed to bring the complaints to Westminster before the opening of the Michaelmas parliament. Here the Ordinance of the Sheriffs closely regulated that office. From the beginning, however, there had been a tendency to bring the magnates' own courts and agents under the same control as the king's, under what John Maddicott calls 'a principle of baronial self-denial'. 'It was a principle', he points out, which was 'partly rooted in the tactical need to win the support of local knights and freeholders: men whose backing was necessary to broaden the social basis of reform, confirm its permanence, and prevent any royalist recovery of power'.[65] It was, in any case, a hard principle for the reformers to resist, given that their initial action had been prompted by the notorious depredations of the king's Lusignan half-brothers and their agents, from whose behaviour they were seeking to dissociate themselves. Legislation was duly published in the spring of 1259, albeit at the cost of a split within magnate ranks, and in October 1259 the comprehensive Provisions of Westminster were enacted which both restricted the obligation to attend baronial courts and tackled the financial depredations of the justices in eyre. This, as Maddicott says, 'marked the zenith of the reforming movement'.[66]

It has generally been assumed that the instincts of the reformist barons were rewarded by a more or less spontaneous response from the counties and that an enthusiastic, if not zealous, movement for reform ensued. Indeed, traditional scholarship invested that response with an idealism which mirrored that detected in the actions of the barons themselves. In the words of R.F. Treharne,

---

[64] For a discussion of the legislation and its provenance, including the Petition of the Barons, see P.A. Brand, 'The Drafting of Legislation in Mid Thirteenth-Century England', *Parliamentary History* 9 (1990); reprinted in his *The Making of the Common Law*, pp. 325–67.

[65] J.R. Maddicott, *Simon de Montfort* (Cambridge, 1994), p. 167.   [66] *Ibid.*, p. 185.

In knowledge, competence and awareness of their responsibilities and powers, the knights of mid thirteenth-century England matched in the field of local government the public spirit and sense of responsibility shown by the magnates in the 'state of the realm' in 1258...The development of government in England between 1216 and 1258 provides several instances to show that a new principle was achieving recognition, by both the Crown and its officials on the one hand, and the knights on the other – the principle that government is for the sake of the governed, and not solely for the good of the rulers, with the corollary that good government must carry with it the goodwill of those who operate the system.[67]

Revisionist work is beginning to bring all of this into question too.

Dr Huw Ridgeway has recently attacked 'the analysis of Jacob and Treharne, that in 1258 the barons entered into an alliance on equal terms with the gentry of the localities, responding to pressure from below and permitting them to elect their own representatives and sheriffs'. This interpretation, he says, 'cannot be sustained'.[68] These earlier writers believed that the four knights empanelled in August 1258 subsequently chose their sheriff at the Exchequer, and that as these knights had themselves been chosen in the county courts this amounted to indirect election of the sheriffs. In fact, there is no contemporary evidence to suggest that the four knights appointed in each county to make inquiry into 'all excesses, trespasses, and acts of injustice committed in our realm' in August 1258 were actually elected in the county court. On the contrary, the instruction for the appointing of the knights suggests the opposite. It asks for their oaths to be taken either in the county court or before the sheriffs and coroners if the court was not to meet very shortly, suggesting that they were appointed in advance of any such court.[69] In some specific cases we know for certain that they were definitely not elected there. When the justiciar and chancellor were informed that two of the Devon knights were ill, the sheriff was told to find substitutes. In Shropshire the baronial reformer Peter de Montfort removed three of the knights 'because they are not fit' and himself substituted three others. Ridgeway is surely right to suggest that sheriffs 'with plenty of business to transact which required small juries of knights no doubt kept lists of potential appointees up their sleeves'.[70] They may well have drawn on these. There was the possibility – nay, probability – of baronial influence.

However the knights were chosen – and practice may have varied – it is very significant that the Provisions of Oxford, which called for these panels of knights

[67] Treharne, 'The Knights in the Period of Reform and Rebellion', pp. 9–10.
[68] H.W. Ridgeway, 'Mid Thirteenth-Century Reformers and the Localities: The Sheriffs of the Baronial Regime, 1258–1261', in Fleming *et al.* (eds.), *Regionalism and Revision*, pp. 59–86. The quotation is from p. 84.
[69] *Documents of the Baronial Movement of Reform and Rebellion 1258–67*, ed. R.F. Treharne and I.J. Sanders (Oxford, 1973), p. 115.
[70] Ridgeway, 'Sheriffs of the Baronial Regime', p. 68.

to be established in the first place, forbade any knight from excusing himself on the grounds of a royal charter saying that he is not to be placed on juries or assizes.[71] The government's sale of exemptions from county offices, including the shrievalty, on an 'unprecedented scale' during the 1250s now caused a major problem for the baronial government. This helps to explain why, *pace* Treharne, many of those who came forward as commissioners in 1258 could hardly be described as *buzones* of their shires, whatever that phrase may have meant. A recent study of four midland counties, for example, has shown that of the sixteen knights chosen to receive complaints in August 1258 only six had held office or received royal commissions prior to that year.[72] Moreover, only two of the others did so thereafter.[73] Indeed, when examined in the context of commissions and office holding some of them seem to have been remarkably obscure characters.[74] It is certainly hard to see them as the product of politically active county societies anxious to elect their most experienced men. It might be better to see their appointment as a reflection of the old Angevin legacy, previously described, which drew on the rank and file of knights when their status seemed appropriate.

Charters of exemption had sometimes to be overridden in order to find suitable sheriffs, as in the case of Robert de Meisy of Gloucestershire.[75] However, it is true that many of the 1258 sheriffs *were* genuine vavasours of their shires, and that some had solid administrative experience behind them. How were they chosen? Although there are two late examples, from February 1259, of sheriffs being nominated by the panels of knights, the likelihood is that in the majority of cases where the sheriff was replaced he was chosen by the baronial council, and generally from among those panels of knights. The fact that, in reality, a third of pre-existing sheriffs (nine out of twenty-six) were actually retained in office, for strategic and other reasons, suggests that there could have

---

[71] *Documents of the Baronial Movement of Reform and Rebellion*, ed. Treharne and Sanders, pp. 98–9; Ridgeway, 'Sheriffs of the Baronial Regime', p. 64.

[72] The six were: Eustace de Watford (Northamptonshire), Robert de Grendon, Nicholas fitz Ralf and Adam de Napton (Warwickshire), William de Boxworth (Cambridgeshire) and Robert de Haughton (Staffordshire). For profiles of the sixteen men see M.J. Fernandes, 'The Role of the Midland Knights in the Period of Reform and Rebellion 1258–67' (London PhD thesis, 2000), chs. 1.5, 2.5, 3.5 and 4.5.

[73] William de Waver (Warwickshire) and William Bagot (Warwickshire). I have discounted their appearance as jurors or litigants. Only eight of the sixteen appear to have been active during the Barons' Wars. Fernandes logs six as contrariants and two as royalists.

[74] Payne de Wasteneys of Staffordshire, Thomas de Lavenham and Philip de Insula of Cambridgeshire, for example, 'made virtually no impression on the sources whatsoever before or after 1258', while Thomas fitz Robert of Northamptonshire 'was struggling with debt by the 1260s, with limited demesne and no career to speak of' (*ibid.*, p. 320). C.H. Knowles, looking at the commissions in general, concluded that 'they were drawn overwhelmingly from fairly small knightly families holding lands in the counties where they were to collect evidence of abuses ('The Disinherited 1265–80', University of Wales PhD thesis, 1959, part II, p. 67).

[75] Ridgeway, 'Sheriffs of the Baronial Reform', p. 64.

been no widespread election, directly or indirectly, from within the counties. Furthermore, one would have expected the baronial regime to seek men who would be trusted by the magnates, and indeed many of the sheriffs can be shown to have had specific ties with them. In October 1259 the Provisions of Westminster provided for four knights in each county to review the wrongs committed by sheriffs, but nevertheless it was stipulated that the sheriffs for the ensuing year would be chosen by the barons of the Exchequer. Half of the men chosen were 'tried and trusted men', including some who had held office before 1258. The others were new men of the vavasour type, some of them once again with magnate connections. It *was* promised, however, that in the following year the sheriffs would be chosen at the Exchequer from the best of four men elected in each county court. In the event this did not happen, for the 1259 sheriffs remained in office. The barons claimed in their response to the king's charges of misconduct in April 1261 that the Exchequer officials were instructed to make shrieval appointments by means of election by the four knights, a claim that was repeated in their case to Louis IX at Amiens in 1264. It seems, therefore, that election of sheriffs was, indeed, an idea which had some contemporary currency, but it was one that was rarely put into practice. In 1259 the regime had reintroduced sheriffs' farms and increments, a policy that had caused so many problems pre-1258. It is difficult not to agree with Huw Ridgeway that: 'In the first flush of emergency, declarations of openness and reform may have been made, but a closer look at the baronial council shows it to have been as authoritarian in its dealings with the localities as any of its predecessors', and that it 'may be doubted whether they really consulted the political will of local society'.[76]

The involvement of county knights in the reforming activities of 1258–9 has many traditional elements, elements that are reminiscent of their activities during the troubled years of 1225–7 examined above. Once again their chief aspiration appears to have been a negative one, i.e. to keep a rapacious government and its agents at bay. There are other parallels too. When we see knights in political contention with the crown, magnates tended to be there in the background dictating direction. Since the chief target was the crown and its agents, it is less surprising than has sometimes been thought that the programme of action should have been a socially inclusive one, benefiting all the propertied from freeholders upwards. The accent on complaint and grievances, moreover, created something of a blame culture, aimed at the crown, courtiers and professional administrators. All problems tended to be seen in terms of defective lordship (either of the king or of others) and blameworthy and grasping agents. As a result, many of the difficulties and tensions experienced by lesser landowners occur only obliquely in the reform programme.[77] The fact that the

[76] *Ibid.*, pp. 84–5.   [77] Coss, *Lordship, Knighthood and Locality*, pp. 274–5.

reform programme placed a heavy emphasis on grievances against the crown is derived, in part at least, from the baronial genesis of the reform. This is not to deny, of course, that such grievances were very real and that men did not welcome the reforms. However, we should be very wary of seeing the legislation of 1258–9 as reflecting the political programme of an incipient gentry. That there was a broad community – using the term loosely – whose grievances could be tapped is clear enough. That there was anything like a monolithic knightly class which placed itself at the head of a spontaneous movement of reform and whose leadership was predicated upon several generations of selfless devotion to public service is not. Indeed, as we have seen, the history of the knightly class during the reign of Henry III strongly suggests otherwise.

What then should we make of the statement by the Burton chronicler that the Provisions of Westminster were finally promulgated in October 1259 because the 'community of the bachelry of England' had lobbied the Lord Edward, the earl of Gloucester and the other councillors appointed at Oxford? The barons had done nothing as yet, they said, 'for the utility of the republic', and unless they did so another way would be found.[78] The identity of these 'bachelors' remains uncertain, but the terminology used strongly suggests that they were members of the magnates' retinues, indicating once more that the retinue was the most important contemporary locus of knightly pressure, as opposed, that is, to the county.[79] Nevertheless, the clear implication is that the bachelors reflected what might be called knightly opinion, and suggests that some, at least, within knightly society had been politicised by the events of 1258–9. In other words, the 'palace revolution' of 1258 had raised a genuine expectation, in some quarters, of serious reform.

Arguably, what politicised opinion in the counties even more was the recovery of royal authority during the course of 1261 and its consequences. The king's new judicial eyre, of the old pre-reform type, was brought to a halt through local obstruction, and the large-scale replacement of the baronial sheriffs by *curiales* and household knights led to the appointment of rival 'keepers of the counties' subverting their authority. In other words, having tasted the fruits of the baronial-led reform some men reacted vigorously to preserve them. Once they had participated in the disruption of royal justice, moreover, they were politicised in a rather different sense, in that they now acquired a serious personal interest in the triumph of the baronial side. They may well have feared reprisals.

---

[78] *Annales Monastici*, ed. Luard, vol. I, p. 471.

[79] For a discussion of the various interpretations of the *communitas bacheleriae Angliae* see P.R. Coss, 'Literature and Social Terminology: The Vavasour in England', in T.H. Aston *et al.* (eds.), *Social Relations and Ideas: Essays in Honour of R.H. Hilton* (Cambridge, 1983), pp. 135–6. Most scholars have seen the bachelors as knights in the magnates' retinues. John Maddicott, however, believes that the bachelors comprised the knights who attended the Michaelmas parliament 'for whose attendance at this parliament this is the only evidence' (*Simon de Montfort*, pp. 184–5).

This was a time of considerable tension, as the two sides jockeyed for support. When, in September 1261, the magnate opposition summoned three knights from each county 'to treat with them about the common affairs of the realm' at St Albans, the king sought to divert them, under dire threat, to a meeting at Windsor.[80] For a time the king appeared to be winning an uneasy victory. However, the continuing discontent in the country coupled with a series of severe tactical errors on the part of the royal government, which offended some powerful vested interests, allowed Simon de Montfort to return to England in April 1263 as a 'popular' leader.[81] Violent attacks on the lands of royalists and others occurred across much of the country. Increasingly, the victory of one side or another was becoming a matter of keeping one's inheritance intact. The scene was set for the civil war of 1264–5 and for the disorder which persisted until 1267.

Nevertheless, the idea that there was considerable falling away of support for the reforming barons between 1258–9 on the one hand and 1263–4 on the other may be something of a myth.[82] It is predicated upon the assumption that enthusiasm for reform had been extraordinarily deep and widespread during those early years. The number of knights who were actively caught up in rebellion was in fact quite considerable, especially in the midlands and the eastern counties.[83] At the same time it is true that many others remained aloof from the Montfortian regime of 1263–5, or at least from armed conflict. It may well be arguable that Simon de Montfort died partly because insufficient numbers of knights supported him. However, this is not the same as saying that they had deserted his cause. In reality it is more likely that there were many who had not been especially fired with the desire for reform. If more knights had been attached to the reforming side in 1258 than later, it probably reflects the fact that more of the greater lords were.

The incidence of rebellion of mid-thirteenth-century knights can be subjected to the same sort of analysis as for the reign of King John. The key factors are lordship and neighbourhood. Opposition lords brought many of their followers into rebellion with them, and rebels are often found to have been numerically strong in areas of powerful opposition lordship. Minor barons – men like Peter de Montfort and Ralf Basset – played a key role in bringing knights into rebellion and sustaining support. Lordship, however, was not the sole factor. The power and example of a great lord did not necessarily suffice to sway opinion or

---

[80] *Close Rolls, 1261–4*, p. 490.

[81] For an excellent summary of these years see Maddicott, *Simon de Montfort*, ch. 6.

[82] For the putative slippage of support see Maddicott, *Simon de Montfort*, p. 237, quoting Knowles, 'The Disinherited', part II, pp. 80–3.

[83] Fernandes has shown that of the 123 grand assize knights of four midland counties that constituted his sample, no fewer than sixty-eight (or 55 per cent) were contrariants ('The Role of the Midland Knights', p. 322).

to determine action, especially in the case of royalist lords. Kinship and various forms of affinity were also factors. Lordship aside, however, the most powerful factor was undoubtedly locality. Intense pockets of rebellion are clearly identifiable.[84] The significance of these factors, however, rests on observation; it tells us little of motivation. This was a civil war and in such circumstances the mainsprings of action are multifarious. Some men must have had very specific reasons for rebellion – personal grievances against the crown, for example, or the hope of profit or relief from the Montfortian government. Some were certainly intimidated by their neighbours or by men more powerful than themselves. Some were driven by quarrels and rivalries which predated the era of reform but which helped to determine their alliances. Some, no doubt, sought local advantage. Just as magnates can be observed jockeying for personal advantage – and changing their loyalties to achieve it – and just as minor barons can be seen vying with others to extend or retain local power,[85] so the knights themselves must have been affected by purely local politics and configurations. Many men will have had to weigh a variety of local factors in the balance before jumping one way or another, changing sides or remaining resolute, even before staying aloof. For some – including men who had already committed themselves too far and men who had had their lands pillaged or seized by opponents – the struggle of these years must have seemed increasingly desperate. In short, as Mario Fernandes has aptly said, 'for all the influence the knightly class had in contributing to the Provisions of Oxford, few of the knights examined had the luxury of a free choice as to their role in the ensuing conflict'.[86]

Even so we should probably not dismiss the role of ideas entirely, and it has to be remembered that the counties were subject to a barrage of propaganda during these years. Ideals and personal profit are by no means mutually exclusive. After all, the career of Simon de Montfort himself has tended to be seen by historians in precisely this light. The important point is that when all allowances have been made for self-interest, for anachronism over elections and representation, and for the lingering effects of the Whig interpretation of history, county knights *had* participated in the implementation of a political programme of reform, a programme that centred on parliament. The events of 1258 have been referred to recently as 'the first parliamentary crisis in English history', and their importance in the development of parliament is indeed

---

[84] Fernandes, for example, identifies specific foci of rebellion in north and west Northamptonshire, in the south of Cambridgeshire around Bourn, in eastern Staffordshire on the border with Derbyshire, and in north and east Warwickshire (*ibid.*, p. 331). In Gloucestershire there was a particular concentration of rebels and rebel activity west of the River Severn. See Mullan, 'Landed Society and Locality', ch. 6: 'The Barons' War'.

[85] See, for example, the three-cornered contest for power between Ralf Basset of Drayton, Roger de Somery of Dudley and Philip Marmion of Tamworth in and around south Staffordshire: Hunt, 'Families at War', p. 27.

[86] *Ibid.*, p. 341.

considerable.[87] As we have seen, the involvement of knights is in many respects problematic. Their presence as representatives is clear only for the Montfortian parliaments of June 1264 and January 1265 and even then they could hardly have been the product of completely free elections. But the implications of the reform programme and its concept of a political community are inescapable. Things would never be quite the same again.

As significant as the role of county knights in the events of 1258–67, however, is the fact that the baronial programme of 1258–9 had linked reform at the centre with reform in the localities. This relationship was preserved in the legislation which followed the ending of hostilities, the Statute of Marlborough of 1267. Most importantly, the process of inquiry followed by legislation and law enforcement which had been adopted by the reformers was to become a cornerstone of the future Edwardian polity. This was, arguably, the most important bequest of the reform period. It was a process, moreover, which gave due recognition to the existence of a relatively wide political community. The fact that the 1258–9 programme had contained elements that were against the narrow sectional interests of the magnates and the split that occurred in baronial ranks during the process of implementation had shown that it was not so much the great lords but the knights and minor barons who tended to reflect the interests of that community.[88] All of this had major implications for the future.

Like the Angevin legal reforms of the later twelfth century, the real importance of the period of reform and rebellion in the evolution of the gentry is medium to long rather than short term. In one important respect, however, the effect of these years was not so much to enhance but rather to preserve the role of the county landowners within the system. The baronial regime and its Edwardian successor can be said to have revivified the crumbling edifice of Angevin government. Nothing could hold back the increasing army of professional administrators, but their wings were clipped a little and the influence of the commissioned county landowner was retained. Indeed, as we shall see, his role is readily observable within the Edwardian polity.

---

[87] By David Carpenter, in Abulafia (ed.) *New Cambridge Medieval History*, vol. V, p. 337.
[88] For this perspective see Maddicott, ' "An Infinite Multitude of Nobles" ', pp. 43–4.

6. *Knighthood, justice and the early Edwardian polity*

Let us take stock. In the preceding chapters I have explained in some detail why I think it is inappropriate to speak of a gentry in Angevin or in post-Angevin England. In particular, I have suggested that the relationship between minor landowners and both the judicial system and the state has been seriously misunderstood by historians and has been approached with a series of misconceptions. At the same time, however, I have argued that the changes which took place in and around the reign of Henry III were momentous. The development of a more exclusive knightly class marked an important stage in the evolution of the lesser nobility and provides an important foundation upon which the later gentry was based. The débâcle towards the end of the reign produced a heightened sense of political community and opened a new era in the relationship between the political centre and the localities.

It was during the decades that followed the period of 'reform and rebellion' that the stage was set for the transformation of the lesser nobility into the English gentry. These were the years when the full force of chivalric knighthood began to make itself felt, when knighthood became a more powerful vehicle than ever before for expressing the social and cultural hegemony of England's secular elite. They were also years when a more participatory governmental system – the Edwardian polity – was beginning to take shape. It was a polity within which a collectively wealthy and altogether more confident knightly stratum in the counties came to play a very significant part. If we are to understand the emergence of the gentry correctly we must pay close attention both to Edwardian knighthood and to the early Edwardian polity.

EDWARDIAN KNIGHTHOOD

In the competitive, divisive and rather unregulated society of the reign of Henry III even the new knighthood could hardly be expected to have created a more cohesive lesser nobility, at least not overnight. Given the climate that prevailed, its full effects were somewhat delayed. Nevertheless, an understanding of Edwardian knighthood takes us back of necessity to the middle decades of the century.

Much emphasis has been placed in recent years, and for very good reasons, upon the decline in the number of knights during the thirteenth century and upon the crown's policy of distraint to knighthood. But we should not neglect the other side of the coin. Some men were prepared to enter into debt in order to acquire knighthood.[1] More spectacularly, during the 1270s, Ingram de Oldcotes agreed to hand over his entire land to Roger d'Arcy in return for the latter agreeing to make him a knight and to maintain him in that estate with an esquire, two grooms and three horses for the remainder of his life.[2] Even if few men were prepared to go this far in order to secure knighthood, there is every reason to suppose that the majority of those landowners who did become knights did so willingly, even enthusiastically.

There can be no doubt that knighthood exercised a powerful ideological pull. The *Song of Lewes* shows that the panoply of ideas surrounding chivalric knighthood was thoroughly understood and appreciated in mid-thirteenth-century England.[3] A polished and utterly partisan poem on the side of the victorious Montfortian party of knights and barons who fought in the battle on 14 May 1264, it drew upon exalted notions of knighthood and its high moral purpose. 'Cleanness' will ensure that God is on your side:

> The earl's knights were for the most part striplings, novices in arms they knew too little of war. Now girt with his sword the tender youth stands at dawn in battle accustoming himself to arms ... Let the knight be girded with his sword upon his thigh, let there be no loosening, let there be no vile acts; the body of the new-made knight is wont to be bathed, so that he may learn to be cleansed from forbidden deeds.

Moreover, pictorial representations reveal an awareness of the concept of the knight of Christ, at least in some exalted circles. In MS Harley 3244, dating from *c.*1240–55, a treatise on the vices is preceded by a mounted knight with a diagram representing the Holy Trinity on his shield. His weapons and the horse trappings carry the names of the virtues. Just a little later the Lambeth Apocalypse depicts St Mercurius receiving his hauberk as he rises from the tomb. Angels present him with his sword, shield and pennon.[4] Most famously,

---

[1] See above p. 99.

[2] See P.A. Brand, 'Oldcotes v. d'Arcy', in R.F. Hunnisett and J.B. Post (eds.), *Medieval Legal Records Edited in Memory of C.A.F. Meekings* (London, 1978), pp. 64–113.

[3] For editions and commentary see *Thomas Wright's Political Songs of England*, ed. Peter Coss, Royal Historical Society (1996), pp. xxii–xxiii.

[4] See Richard Marks, 'Sir Geoffrey Luttrell and Some Companions: Images of Chivalry *c.*1320–50', *Wiener Jahrbuch für Kunstgeschichte*, Band 46–7 (1993–4), p. 353, and references given there.

a drawing added to the Westminster Psalter around 1250 shows a knight being armed before a king, probably Edward the Confessor. It may well commemorate the taking of the cross by King Henry III.[5]

On a less rarified, but none the less elitist, plane, one notes the emergence of rolls of arms at just this time, delineating membership of the new social elite. The earliest roll, in the true sense of the term, was Glover's Roll, dating from c.1253.[6] It contains 215 coats described in blazon, the technical language of heraldry which had already attained a level of sophistication.[7] After the king and his eldest son we find the arms of twenty earls, followed by 193 lords and knights. They include men from nearly all the counties. Belonging to the same period are the Matthew Paris shields. These, too, contain the arms not only of rulers, great magnates and courtiers, but of men of lesser importance, such as Gerard and William de Odingseles of Maxstoke, Warwickshire, and Robert Herring of Kent.[8]

Once we move into the 1270s and to the reign of Edward I, however, surviving rolls of arms begin to proliferate. On the latest reckoning no fewer than eighteen rolls, if we include the extraordinary heraldic poem, the *Song of Carlaverock*, belong to the reign of Edward I.[9] They continued to multiply thereafter.[10] Among the most interesting are the Occasional Rolls, which commemorate a specific event by listing in blazon the arms of those who participated in a battle, siege or tournament: the Falkirk Roll, for example, which celebrates the most prominent knights who fought there with Edward on 22 July 1298,[11] and the first Dunstable Roll which gives the names of the tourneyers of 1309.[12] The *Song of Carlaverock* gives 106 blazons of lords and knights who were at the siege there with the king in 1300. Perhaps most extraordinary of all is the Boroughbridge Roll, which commemorates the civil war battle of 1322 by blazoning the arms of those who were present on the royalist side.[13] Altogether 214 coats of arms are given. In addition the manuscript gives the names of 137 rebels, but

[5] Jonathan Alexander and Paul Binski (eds.), *Age of Chivalry: Art in Plantagenet England 1200–1400*, exhib. cat., Royal Academy of Arts (London, 1987), no. 26.

[6] It is based in part, however, upon some earlier material known as the 1240 Collection.

[7] For thirteenth-century blazon see Gerald J. Brault, *Early Blazon* (2nd edn, Woodbridge, 1997).

[8] For discussion see Coss, *The Knight in Medieval England*, pp. 73–6, and references given there.

[9] See *Aspilogia III: The Rolls of Arms of Edward I*, 2 vols., ed. Gerard J. Brault (Woodbridge, 1997), vol. I, pp. 39–40.

[10] For a list of the later rolls see *Aspilogia II: Rolls of Arms of Henry III*, ed. A.R. Wagner (London, 1967), pp. 260–2.

[11] Discussed in A.R. Wagner, *Aspilogia I: A Catalogue of English Medieval Rolls of Arms* (London, 1950), pp. 27–9. See also C.H. Hunter Blair, 'Northern Knights at Falkirk, 1298', *Archæologia Æliana*, 4th series, 25 (1947), pp. 68–114.

[12] See A. Tomkinson, 'Retinues at the Tournament of Dunstable, 1309', *English Historical Review* 84 (1959), pp. 70–89.

[13] Wagner, *Aspilogia I*, pp. 50–1.

without their arms. Perhaps the compiler thought that they had forfeited that honour.[14]

There were also Local Rolls, listing the knights of a specific region. The earliest of these is the Dering Roll of *c*. 1280, which consists mainly of knights from Sussex and Kent. Most informative of all, however, is the so-called Parliamentary Roll of Arms which belongs to the beginning of the reign of Edward II and which covers the whole of England county by county. Containing 1,100 names, it probably lists a very high proportion of the knights living and functioning at the time. After the king, thirteen earls and the bishop of Durham, it gives the bannerets, those senior knights who carried their own square banners into battle as opposed to the triangular pennons of the ordinary knights and who were often found commanding their own contingents in the field. Most of the remainder were ordinary or bachelor knights, listed according to the counties in which they resided.[15]

Knighthood is prominent wherever one looks in Edwardian England.[16] To the historian it presents itself patently on sepulchral monuments. The last quarter of the thirteenth century and the first half of the fourteenth witnessed the veritable colonisation of England's churches by the knightly effigy, both in wood and in stone.[17] From the beginning of the fourteenth century these were joined by full-figure brasses.[18] Despite their very considerable variety, what these representations have in common is a depiction of the military calling in combination with the celebration of social status. The relationship between the two is truly symbiotic. On the face of it, at least, there was no longer the same

[14] For a discussion of the historical accuracy of the roll see the study in *Complete Peerage of England, Scotland, Ireland, Great Britain and the United Kingdom*, 13 vols. in 14, ed. Vicary Gibbs *et al.* (London, 1910–59), vol. II, pp. 597–602.

[15] After no. 1034 there is a list of great men recently deceased, followed by various additions which seem to consist largely of men omitted from the county lists. For the manuscript (BL Cotton Caligula A.XVIII, fos. 3–21v) and for a list of editions see Wagner, *Aspilogia I*, pp. 42–50. Denholm-Young argued that the roll belonged to the time when Robert Clifford was acting marshal and assigned a date of *c*. 1308 ('The Song of Carlaverock, the Parliamentary Roll of Arms and the Galloway Roll', in *Collected Papers of N. Denholm-Young*, pp. 121–32). Wagner assigned a slightly later date (*c*. 1312) though on no very clear grounds. A new and thorough study is sorely needed.

[16] The following remarks are drawn from my essay 'Knighthood, Heraldry and Social Exclusion in Edwardian England', in Peter Coss and Maurice Keen (eds.), *Heraldry, Pageantry and Social Display in Medieval England* (Woodbridge, 2002), pp. 39–68, where a much fuller treatment may be found.

[17] As a rough guide, of the 143 knightly effigies assigned by Tummers to the thirteenth century more than half (seventy-seven) are said to belong to the very end of the century, with at least another nine assigned to the period 1270–90: Tummers, *Early Secular Effigies in England*, pp. 135–43.

[18] For the redating of the early figure brasses and the identification of styles see, especially, Paul Binski, 'The Stylistic Sequence of London Figure Brasses', in John Coales (ed.), *The Earliest English Brasses: Patronage, Style and Workshops 1270–1350* (London, 1987), pp. 69–132.

tension between the civilian and the military knight that one finds so often in the late twelfth and early thirteenth centuries.[19] True, moralists like the author of the *Simonie* or *Poem on the Evil Times of Edward II* might speak of the failings of contemporary knighthood – a penchant for fine clothing, for example, and cowardice in the field – but that is rather a different matter.[20]

It was through heraldry, though, that contemporaries most commonly experienced the ideological force of knighthood. It was literally everywhere, and by no means only in churches.[21] It was prominent on buildings, on seals and in manuscripts. It was to be found on dress, on domestic plate, on caskets and chests, on wall paintings and on tiled pavements. Within all of these media, antecedents of one sort or another are to be found during the mid-thirteenth century or, indeed, earlier.[22] It was in Edwardian England, however, that they coalesced to form a remarkably coherent and extraordinarily inventive display of heraldic art; one which encompassed an increasingly wide spectrum of the elite.

But heraldry was more than art. It was a living presence in Edwardian England. It was used to advertise the relationship between families, primarily through kinship and affinity. These associations were commonly shown by placing arms together in a series; on floor tiles for example, and on more private items, such as the famous Valence casket, which dates from the late thirteenth or early fourteenth century.[23] The historian of the county knights finds their associations depicted most often on tomb chests. An early example, from around the 1280s, is at Pitchford in Shropshire, where the wooden effigy of a sword-handling knight is accompanied by an integral tomb decorated with a series of seven shields (Fig. 1).[24] The knight is undoubtedly Sir John de Pitchford, who died in 1285.[25] The Pitchford arms were *sable, a cinquefoil or*. They are represented here twice, but in both cases differenced. They indicate John himself and his grandfather, Hugh, with the arms of their respective wives. John married

---

[19] For this tension see Coss, *The Knight in Medieval England*, ch. 3: 'Angevin Knighthood and Its Transformation'.

[20] *Thomas Wright's Political Songs*, ed. Coss, pp. xliii–v, 334–5 (lines 242–70): *And nu ben theih liouns in halle, and hares in the feld.*

[21] Indeed, on the basis of the evidence before the later fourteenth-century Court of Chivalry Andrew Ayton has pointed out that 'heraldic display was, if anything, an even more pervasive presence in aristocratic residences': Andrew Ayton, 'Knights, Esquires and Military Service: The Evidence of the Armorial Cases before the Court of Chivalry', in Andrew Ayton and J.L. Price (eds.), *The Medieval Military Revolution* (New York, 1995), p. 87.

[22] See J. Cherry, 'Heraldry as Decoration in the Thirteenth Century', in W.M. Ormrod (ed.), *England in the Thirteenth Century* (Stamford, 1991), pp. 123–34, and references given there. For effigies see Tummers, *Early Secular Effigies in England*.

[23] John Titterton, 'The Valence Casket and Its Original Owner', *Coat of Arms*, new series, 10 (1993), pp. 16–26.

[24] Shown in Tummers, *Early Secular Effigies in England*, plates 57–8.

[25] For what follows see, especially, W. Watkins, 'The Monuments in Pitchford Church', *Transactions of the Shropshire Archaeological Society* 53 (1949–50), pp. 186–97. See also R.W. Eyton, *The Antiquities of Shropshire*, 12 vols. (London, 1854–60), vol. VI (1858), pp. 267–84.

1. Oak effigy of Sir John de Pitchford, 1280–90, St Michael's church, Pitchford, Shropshire, with integral tomb decorated with seven shields. (Photography by David Turner, Turner Photography, Charlton near Telford)

Margaret Devereux, hence the shield bearing a fess and in chief three roundels. Hugh had married Burga de Baskerville, hence the shield bearing chevron between three roundels. The remaining three arms are undoubtedly those of Audley, Fitz Alan and Pembridge, families with whom the Pitchfords were in one way or another associated.[26] More unusually, at Cogenhoe in Northamptonshire, and from around the same date as the Pitchford effigy, one finds a series of arms sculptured discreetly in stone in the nave of the church. In the south aisle of the nave lies the effigy of a crossed-legged knight bearing the Cogenhoe arms, viz. *gules a fess between three mascles argent.*[27] He is in all probability Sir Nicholas de Cogenhoe, who is accredited with building the nave. Nicholas held one and a half knights' fees at Cogenhoe and Harrowden and was active in county affairs. He was dead by 10 June 1281.[28] On the capitals of his new nave pillars are displayed nine grotesque heads and ten small shields. Four

---

[26] The Audley arms are *gules fretty or*, while Pembridge are *barry or and azure*, and Fitz Alan *gules, a lion rampant or*. The relationship of these families to the Pitchfords is not entirely clear. John's son, Ralf, appears to have been married to an Audley, while John himself seems to have held the court at Oswestry and may perhaps have been a Fitz Alan steward. Two other monuments to the Pitchford family, at Albrighton, and of similar date, were made of stone and were even more lavishly heraldic. They are discussed in detail by Watkins (*ibid.*, pp. 164–85). One is lost, the other badly weathered. They appear to date from shortly after the wooden effigy.
[27] Tummers assigns a date of 1270–80 for this effigy: *Early Secular Effigies in England*, p. 137.
[28] *Book of Fees*, vol. II, pp. 931, 938; *Calendar of Inquisitions Post Mortem*, vol. II, no. 400.

of the shields display the Cogenhoe arms and one is blank. The other five are beyond doubt the arms of families associated with the Cogenhoes.[29] The scene is fascinating in terms of the way in which a not particularly wealthy or elevated Northamptonshire knightly family of the late thirteenth century projected itself.

However, it was not only on stone that relationships could be depicted. During the late thirteenth and early fourteenth centuries churches began to be glazed with a combination of grisaille and heraldic glass.[30] Discerning the precise association between families, or individuals, is often difficult. No doubt kinship was the most prominent factor, followed perhaps by lordship and service in one guise or another. But the sheer fact of neighbourhood led inevitably to various forms of association, some of them largely hidden from us. Perhaps, as Peter Newton suggested, a bond of friendship was sufficient.[31] There were, no doubt, very many heraldic manifestations of brotherhood-in-arms in medieval England.[32] The significant point is that interpersonal and interfamily relationships were displayed by means of heraldry; or, to put the matter another way, they were displayed through their joint celebration of knighthood.

The presentiality of heraldry in Edwardian England cannot be overstressed. Families would change their arms in the wake of an illustrious marriage. The famous Percy arms – *or, a lion rampant azure* – for example, are not the arms borne by the family in the thirteenth century. Henry de Percy, who bore the lion at Falkirk and Carlaverock, had adopted it following his marriage to Eleanor, daughter of Richard Fitz Alan, earl of Arundel, who bore *gules, a lion rampant or*. The traditional Percy arms had been *azure, a fess of five fusils or*.[33] The Lumleys of Chester-le-Street changed their arms twice in rapid succession following marriages, finally settling on *argent, a fess gules between three popinjays vert*, the arms of the Thwengs which they wore undifferenced as they came to replace this extinct family and to succeed to its lineage.[34] Examples

[29] For the details see Coss, 'Knighthood, Heraldry and Social Exclusion', drawing on Albert Hartshorne, 'The Cogenhoe Family and Cogenhoe Church, Northamptonshire', *Proceedings of the Society of Antiquaries*, 2nd series, 19 (London, for 1901–3), pp. 227–44.

[30] Extant examples include Selling in Kent and Norbury in Derbyshire. See Richard Marks, *Stained Glass in England during the Middle Ages* (London, 1993), figs. 119, 120 and 123.

[31] Peter A. Newton, *The County of Oxford: A Catalogue of Medieval Stained Glass* (London, 1979), p. 4.

[32] The classic treatment of this subject is Maurice Keen, 'Brotherhood-in-Arms', *History* 47 (1964), pp. 1–17; reprinted in Keen, *Nobles, Knights and Men-at-Arms in the Middle Ages* (London, 1996), pp. 43–62. For heraldic manifestations see S. Düll, A. Luttrell and M. Keen, 'Faithful unto Death: The Tomb Slab of Sir William Neville and Sir John Clanvowe', *Antiquaries Journal* 71 (1991), pp. 174–90, and Adrian Ailes, 'Heraldic Marshalling in Medieval England', in *Proceedings of VIII Colloquium at Canterbury, Académie Internationale d'Héraldique* (Canterbury, 1995), p. 18.

[33] Coss, *The Lady in Medieval England*, p. 40, and colour plate 13.

[34] *Ibid.*, pp. 40–1 (colour plate 13), and for a more detailed discussion of the Lumley case, P.R. Coss, 'Heraldry and Monumental Effigies in the North East', in T.E. Faulkner (ed.), *Northumbrian Panorama: Studies in the History and Culture of North East England* (London, 1996), pp. 7–17 and colour plate I.

could be multiplied. Changes in lordship could also result in new arms, as when both the Segraves and the Lacys changed their arms from the wheatsheafs of the defunct Norman lordship of Chester to the lion rampant, as a reflection no doubt of their new relationship with Edward I.[35] In the Segrave case this change was famous enough in aristocratic circles to be mentioned in the *Song of Carlaverock*.

New arms were brought into being to accommodate knightly younger sons. Some of these became established, signifying new lineages; others, however, were more transient. John de Grendon, a scion of the Warwickshire and Staffordshire family, seems to have changed his arms according to the retinue in which he served. He served, first, with Edmund de Stafford in Flanders in 1297–8, and bore the Stafford arms differenced with a martlet. He then served with Robert de la Ward and changed his arms to the Ward arms differenced with a bend.[36] In this age, military retinues could still provide the inspiration for new arms, just as they had done in the early days of heraldic dissemination. A revealing case is that of Eustace de Hatch who bore the arms *or, a cross indented gules*. Of unknown parentage, Eustace first appears as a trooper in Wales in 1276. He became a household knight and, eventually, a banneret. His lands, in Wiltshire and Dorset, were held in right of his wife. He was active in Edward I's Scottish wars and on two occasions the personnel of his retinue are known. Among his men-at-arms were three knights. All three seem to have borne his arms differenced. One of them, Nicholas Trimnol, was the son of his wife's first husband.[37] Another was his son-in-law, William de Hartshill, who abandoned his family arms in favour of the Hatch arms differenced with a *martlet vert* in the first quarter. William's son John, however, reverted to the family arms of *or, a chevron sable surmounted by an orle of martlets gules*. Both William's adopted arms and his family arms are found on his tomb at Saleby, Lincolnshire.[38]

The vibrancy of heraldic culture is best expressed, however, by reference to the famous Feast of the Swans, held at Whitsuntide (22 May) 1306. The context

---

[35] Coss, *The Knight in Medieval England*, pp. 80–1 (colour plate 10).

[36] *Or, a chevron gules, in dexter chief a martlet sable* followed by *vairy argent and sable, a bend or*. The Grendon arms were *argent, two chevrons gules*. For this and other examples see Robert Norton, 'The Arms of Robert fitz Roger and Others', *Coat of Arms*, new series 3, no. 110 (1979), pp. 161–3. See also *Aspilogia III*, ed. Brault, vol. II, p. 203.

[37] For the details see Robert Norton, 'The Arms of Eustace de Hatch and Others', *Coat of Arms*, new series 5, no. 121 (1982), pp. 18–19. Trimnol bore the Hatch arms differenced with a baston azure (or bend, according to the roll consulted).

[38] See H. Lawrance, *Heraldry from Military Monuments before 1350 in England and Wales*, Harleian Society 98 (1946), p. 21. The third knight, Robert Giffard, bore *or, a cross indented sable*. For further discussion of the knights concerned see also *Aspilogia III*, ed. Brault, vol. II, pp. 195, 218, 220–1, and 422. See also Andrew Ayton, 'Sir Thomas Ughtred and the Edwardian Military Revolution', in J.S. Boswell (ed.), *The Age of Edward III* (Woodbridge, 2001), pp. 115–18, for the dissemination of the Latimers' cross patonce among retinue members during the late thirteenth and early fourteenth centuries.

is well known.[39] At the banquet which followed the knighting of the king's son and heir, the future Edward II, the aged Edward I took an oath to avenge the murder of John Comyn and to wrest Scotland from the hands of the murderous Robert Bruce. Prince Edward vowed not to sleep in the same place for two consecutive nights before arriving in Scotland to help his father carry this out, and other knights took oaths the details of which are unrecorded. The Feast of the Swans was a superb piece of royal theatre. Historians are surely right to see it also in terms of the old king's military preparations for another campaign in Scotland, to boost knighthood and to increase noble participation. On 6 April he wrote to the sheriffs informing them of the impending knighting of Prince Edward, the heir to the throne, and ordering them to have it proclaimed that 'all those who are not knights and who would wish to be should come to London this side of Whitsunday next to receive the necessary equipment from the King's Wardrobe and at his gift, so that they might receive knighthood from him on the same day'.[40]

It was customary for princes and other young aristocrats to be knighted with other noble youths, kinsmen and friends. But this was to be something on an altogether different scale. The king was appealing, quite nakedly, to the snobbery that existed in English society. It was a startling success. The chroniclers note the knighting of 297–300 men, and the names of 282 of them have been recovered from the records.[41] They include many who were to play crucial parts in the reign of the future Edward II. However, most of the recipients of knighthood were county knights. In fact the Swan knights were a cross-section of England's nobility: earls, barons, bannerets and knights. For these last the appeal to their elitist instincts was twofold. They would be knighted not only with royalty but also with the leaders of aristocratic society. It was surely this as much as anything else which drew them to Westminster. Chivalric knighthood drew much of its mystique from the principle of association.

One of the young barons who was knighted was John de Somery, lord of Dudley in the west midlands. John was aged twenty-six or twenty-seven in 1306 and had just been summoned to Carlisle for military service against the Scots. He was summoned to parliament in 1308.[42] Particularly interesting is the number of other Swan knights who hail from the same part of the country.

[39] See especially Constance Bullock-Davies, *Menestrellorum Multitudo: Minstrels at a Royal Feast* (Cardiff, 1978).

[40] *Foedera*, vol. I, ii, p. 983.

[41] The list is given as an appendix by Bullock-Davies, *Minstrels at a Royal Feast*, pp. 185–7.

[42] *Complete Peerage*, vol. XII, part I, p. 114. For an outline of John's career see John Hunt, *Lordship and Landscape: A Documentary and Archaeological Study of the Honor of Dudley c.1066–1322*, BAR British Series 264 (Oxford, 1997), pp. 69–70. He died in 1322. Following the Hon. G. Wrottesley, I am assuming that he was the John de Somery who was a Swan knight. There is, however, a contemporary John de Somery, lord of Bygrave in Hertfordshire, who was pardoned in 1313 for his adherence to the party of Thomas of Lancaster and his consequent complicity in the murder of Piers Gaveston (*VCH Berkshire*, vol. III, pp. 212–15).

They include no less than three members of the Birmingham family – Henry, Richard and William – as well as Henry de Erdington, Richard de Edgbaston, Nicholas de Sheldon and George de Chastell. There were others with interests which were not too distant, including Giles de Astley of the Astleys of north Warwickshire and Leicestershire.[43] Surely we should see these young men as a contingent exercising a collective choice to attend the knighting at Westminster, and to attend, what is more, in the company of the illustrious young baron John de Somery.[44]

Noel Denholm-Young once wrote, famously, about the existence of 3,000 potential as opposed to 1,250 actual knights in the reign of Edward I.[45] By the end of the thirteenth century, however, knighthood was beginning to inhere within a comparatively restricted group of families. Moreover, it was by no means confined to heads of families as is sometimes supposed. One of the proudest features of wealthier knightly families was precisely their capacity to support several knights in each generation. The Parliamentary Roll of Arms, for example, shows us six la Zouches, two bannerets and four knights bachelor, listed under Leicestershire, all bearing variants of the family arms, viz. *gules, with bezants or.* The same county has four Segraves in addition to their two bannerets, while Staffordshire boasts five de Hastangs, bearing variants of *azure, a chief gules, overall a lion rampant or.*[46] Many families were represented by two knights. The Birminghams are one example with Sir William de Birmingham listed under the bannerets and Sir Thomas de Birmingham under Worcestershire.[47] There were also Henry and Richard de Birmingham who, together with William, were knighted with Prince Edward at the Feast of the Swans in 1306. It is difficult to doubt that their appearance at the feast advertised the family's capacity to support these young men in knighthood. Indeed, a score or so of families had two members knighted at this highly prestigious occasion. Four families had three. In addition to the Birminghams, they were the Lacys, the Corbets and the Bassingbournes.[48] In this last case all three knights do figure

---

[43] Among knights with Staffordshire interests, G. Wrottesley lists also: John de Weston, Ralf Bagot, Peter de Gresley, Roger de Somerville, John de Harcourt, Ralf Basset, William de Handsacre, William de Wrottesley and William Trussell. See 'An Account of the Military Service Performed by Staffordshire Tenants in the Thirteenth and Fourteenth Centuries', in *Collections for a History of Staffordshire*, William Salt Archaeological Society, vol. 8 part 1 (1887), p. 26.

[44] For a fuller treatment of these knights see Coss, 'Knighthood, Heraldry and Social Exclusion in Edwardian England', pp. 61–3.

[45] Denholm-Young, 'Feudal Society in the Thirteenth Century', reprinted in his *Collected Papers*, pp. 83–94. The validity of this suggestion depends upon what one means by 'potential'. Essentially, it is a backward-looking proposition. The age of a more inclusive knighthood had passed.

[46] See Coss, *The Knight in Medieval England*, plate opposite page 79.

[47] The latter's main interest seems to have been at Oldberrow, where he held in right of his wife: *VCH Worcestershire*, vol. II, pp. 424–5.

[48] See the list in Bullock-Davies, *Minstrels at a Royal Feast*, pp. 185–7.

in the Parliamentary Roll of Arms, where three versions of their spectacular gyronny are blazoned across three counties.[49]

In sum, there is abundant evidence to illustrate both the exclusivity and the binding force of knighthood in and around the time of Edward I. Having established this clearly, we can now turn to the early Edwardian polity and to the role of county knights within it.

THE EDWARDIAN POLITY

The foundations of the Edwardian polity during the 1270s and its debt to the baronial reform period have been brilliantly analysed by John Maddicott.[50] In many ways Edward I's government conducted a traditional reconstruction after a period of upheaval, restoring royal rights and rebuilding support. Inevitably much of the old system remained intact. 'Yet what happened in the 1270s was more than simply the expansion and culmination of ancient practice: it was closely grounded on the immediate past.'[51] The truth of this observation can be seen most clearly when it comes to the handling of local government, where Edward's reforms followed the same sequence as that adopted in 1258–60: enquiry, legislation and law enforcement. In 1274–5 royal commissioners were sent to the counties to investigate abuses. Their returns – preserved as the Hundred Rolls – were reflected in the Statute of Westminster of 1275. A general judicial eyre followed in 1278. In both the inquiries and the eyre the crown followed the earlier precedent in encouraging the *querela* or informal complaint. It also drew specifically upon knights. In some of the counties in 1274–5 knights were used to present evidence foreshadowing the knightly juries of presentment that were introduced into the eyres of the 1280s.[52] The idea was that it was easier for them to accuse high-ranking lords and their officials. The concept of the *querela* led directly to the petition to parliament. Petitioning probably began at the Easter parliament of 1275 and may well have been the result of a deliberate invitation to send *querelae*. The role of MPs as a channel by which the crown received petitions from their constituents was born around this time. It was in 1275,

---

[49] Sir John in Hertfordshire (*gyronny or and gules*), Sir Humphrey in Cambridgeshire (*gyronny argent and gules*), and Sir Warin de Bassingbourne in Lincolnshire (*gyronny or and azure*). Such knight-bearing lineages seem to echo romance. One thinks, for example, of Gawain and his three brothers, not to mention Lancelot, his brother Hector, his cousins Lionel and Bors and all the rest of his kin.

[50] Maddicott, 'Edward I and the Lessons of Baronial Reform', in Coss and Lloyd (eds.), *Thirteenth Century England I*, pp. 1–30. For a broad discussion of the first half of Edward's reign see also Michael Prestwich, *Edward I* (London, 1988), Part II.

[51] *Ibid.*, p. 28.

[52] *Ibid.*, p. 13. See also D. Crook, *Records of the General Eyre* (HMSO, 1982), p. 32 and *The Eyre of Northamptonshire, 1329–30, I*, ed. D.W. Sutherland, Selden Society 97 (s.l., 1983), n. 2. These juries became known as the 'triers'. In practice, however, they were not invariably made up of knights.

too, that the issuing of special commissions of oyer and terminer, to hear and determine specific complaints of wrongdoing, became prominent. As Maddicott has shown, there was a strong correlation between the holding of parliament and the issuing of such commissions. Much of what the king did was motivated by the need to police royal officials and to publicise his concern to promote best practice in the general interest. However, the use of the *querela*, the petition and the commission of oyer and terminer went well beyond the misconduct of officials, and the procedures fostered during the 1270s were there to stay.

The Michaelmas parliament of 1275 saw the first grant of taxation to this king and, significantly, it was accompanied by legislation, in this case the Statute of Jewry. It was an important precedent. Direct taxation on the laity had returned to England with the crusade tax of 1269,[53] but it was sought sparingly by Edward I during the first half of the reign. The fifteenth of 1275 was followed by the thirteenth of 1283 and the fifteenth of 1290. This helps to explain the absence of the county and borough representatives from many parliaments, although it seems that they were probably present more often than the records tell us. The king was an astute political manager, and the appearance of the representatives at Westminster played an important if intermittent part in his handling of his realm. The publicity value of the Commons was considerable. As Maddicott writes of the Easter parliament of 1275, 'The Statute of Westminster, promulgated in a crowded parliament, marked the growing importance of that assembly as a focal point for reform and for contact between king and subjects.'[54] The concept of the constituency was to grow gradually from this.

If the struggle against corrupt and overbearing officials was one major theme in thirteenth-century history, another was the steady expansion of the royal courts. People looked increasingly to the common law for redress. The work of Paul Brand shows that there was a doubling of the business dealt with by the Common Bench between 1200 and 1242–3, a second doubling between then and 1260, a further doubling between 1260 and 1280, a 78 per cent increase from 1280 to 1290, and another doubling between 1290 and 1306.[55] This increase partly reflects the development of new remedies and procedures – itself a consequence of increasing demand – and much of it was ultimately at the expense of other courts. Against this background it is hardly surprising that the operation of the common law was a matter of general concern. As is well known, the first half of Edward I's reign was an age of considerable legislative activity. A series of wide-ranging statutes made profound changes to the content and the operation of English law.[56] There seems no doubt that the central court

---

[53] See J.R. Maddicott, 'The Crusade Taxation of 1268–70 and the Development of Parliament', in Coss and Lloyd (eds.), *Thirteenth Century England II*, pp. 93–117.
[54] *Ibid.*, p. 16.   [55] Brand, *The Origins of the English Legal Profession*, p. 23.
[56] For a recent discussion of the statutes and the changes they wrought see Prestwich, *Edward I*, ch. 10.

judges made a major contribution to the drafting of this legislation. The judiciary became more secular and more professional during the course of the reign. It was symptomatic of broader changes, as lawyers in general became better educated. Indeed, a fully fledged legal profession may be said to have emerged at this time.[57]

In one area of life, however, the professionals were on the wane. From 1278 onwards county knights dominated the shrievalties. At last the demands of the Provisions of Oxford of 1258 had become a reality as henceforth the majority of the sheriffs would be 'loyal men and sound landholders', vavasours of their counties. The courtiers and the old professionals who moved from one county to another successively began finally to give way. Although men of this type continue to exist, and would be encountered for some decades to come, they were now a decided minority.[58]

In short, what we see in the Edwardian polity are the longer-term effects of the years of reform and rebellion. As Maddicott puts it,

> The reforms and disturbances of 1258–65 had given a new political prominence to the middling men of the localities whose exigent concern for good government and honest officials the king had now to recognise. Their emergence, as holders of local offices, petitioners for reform and representatives of their communities in parliament, was also the emergence of the late medieval English polity.[59]

However, we should be careful not to exaggerate either the degree or the speed of change. If the style of government was now a more inclusive one, the prolonged royalist reaction after the civil war and the underlying predisposition of the new king gave it a decidedly authoritarian slant. Edward I was concerned above all else with the maintenance of royal rights.

The early Edwardian polity was in many ways a conservative one. Social boundaries were barely affected by the reforms; indeed, during the decades following the civil war they may have continued to sharpen. Notwithstanding the king's concern at the usurpation of franchises, the magnates remained an extremely powerful and conservative force at the apex of society, while the indications are that the county knights had become an increasingly self-conscious elite, a process which had probably been strengthened more than anything else during the period of reform and civil war. Moreover, the process of redemption of forfeited estates after the war may well have produced, paradoxically, something of a closing of ranks, as landed society sought to preserve itself more or

---

[57] This subject is treated fully in Brand, *The Origins of the English Legal Profession*, which deals with the question up to 1307 and concentrates on the reign of Edward I. For some observations across a broader timespan see Anthony Musson, *Medieval Law in Context: The Growth of Legal Consciousness from Magna Carta to the Peasants' Revolt* (Manchester, 2001), ch. 2.

[58] For the series of steps which had made this change possible see Maddicott, 'Edward I and the Lessons of Baronial Reform', pp. 19–23, 27.

[59] *Ibid.*, p. 30.

less intact. For one thing, royalist landowners often had sisters and daughters who were married to Montfortians, not to mention wives who were themselves drawn from Montfortian families. In the end relatively few Montfortians lost their estates.[60]

What, then, was the role played by county knights within this political structure? Before examining this, it is necessary to reaffirm some important distinctions. As we have seen, the concept of 'self-government at the king's command' has tended to confuse the communal obligations placed upon members of the free laity on the one hand with the exercise of office and receipt of specific commissions on the other.[61] Communal obligations included suit of court to shire and hundred, presence at the general eyre when the king's justices toured the counties, and jury service. Although the responsibilities of knights and freeholders considerably overlapped, there were areas where the status of the knight had been specifically required, most notably the grand assize. However, many areas of communal responsibility were beginning to attenuate during the later thirteenth century. By the end of the century the grand assize, for example, was giving way to other legal procedures, while suit appears to have been of increasingly less consequence in the county courts as these became dominated by administrators and lawyers. The general eyre, into which the knightly, or supposedly knightly, 'trier' had been introduced in the 1280s, effectively came to an end in 1294. For knights, as for others, the exercise of communal responsibility was an occasional, intermittent and essentially declining one.

To a large extent the exercise of office and the receipt of specific commissions were also distinct. As is well known, local government – in the broadest sense of the term – became increasingly complex during the course of the thirteenth century. Both public and seigneurial administration employed increasing numbers of officials, many of them literate and well trained; so much so that it is possible to write of 'professional people' as a distinct sector of society.[62] Knights continued to play a part – as baronial stewards, for example – and in certain high-profile public offices, but the great majority of officials were lesser men seeking reward and advancement.[63] In terms of royal office, knights were especially in evidence exercising the still highly prestigious office of sheriff. No doubt it was still possible to see the office as a lucrative one, although many a county knight appears to have come unstuck in this respect. Other local offices, however, were much less attractive. Coroners, as we have seen, had tended to be

[60] See Clive Knowles, 'The Resettlement of England after the Barons' War, 1264–7', *Transactions of the Royal Historical Society*, 5th series, 32 (1982), pp. 25–41.

[61] See above pp. 44, 64.

[62] See Alan Harding, *England in the Thirteenth Century* (Cambridge, 1993), and the references given there.

[63] For the increasingly sophisticated arrangements between employer and employee see, for example, Scott L. Waugh, 'Tenure to Contract: Lordship and Clientage in Thirteenth-Century England', *English Historical Review* 401 (1986), pp. 813–39.

drawn from among the lesser knights during the first half of the century. What we find in Edwardian England is that the majority of coroners were no longer knights at all. It is difficult to gain a complete picture, as the chancery rolls record the names of coroners haphazardly and largely when a new election is ordered at the county court. This occurred officially because an existing coroner had become infirm or was deemed insufficiently qualified, but often, no doubt, it was because an existing coroner had had enough. In the eyre rolls, however, the names of all coroners functioning since the last eyre tend to be recorded, as their presence – always supposing they were still living – was required by the court. Of the eight Essex coroners listed in 1285, for example, only two appear to have been knights.[64] The Warwickshire eyre of the same year lists the coroners since 1272. The current coroners were William Herdwick, who had continued in office since the last eyre in 1272, Reginald de Atlebergh, Richard de Peydon and Robert Wandard. William Herdwick's original colleagues had been William de Upton, Thomas de Bler and Hugh de Agillun, all of whom were by now deceased. None of these men was a knight. Still living but no longer coroners were William Fundu, Henry de Edgbaston, Robert de Waver and Henry de Sheldon. Of these Henry de Sheldon certainly *was* a knight, while two of the others may have been.[65] When the Statute of Westminster of 1275 reaffirmed that coroners should be chosen from among 'the most wise and discreet knights' it was attempting to arrest a downward trend. Most coroners, by this date, were sub-knightly. An arduous office and one subject to election in the county court, it appears to have been increasingly avoided by the majority of knights. The same would appear to be the case with the forest officers, the verderers, in appropriate counties, and with the sub-escheators.[66]

But if few county knights in the time of Edward I exercised regular office, many others were in receipt of irregular commissions. In this respect they are reminiscent of the minority of especially trusted knights who had figured as justices, tax assessors and the like, particularly during the first half of the reign of Henry III. They continued to figure as justices of gaol delivery and in a variety of *ad hoc* commissions both judicial and administrative. For manpower

---

[64] J.S. Illsley, 'The Essex Gentry in the Reign of Edward I' (Cambridge MLitt thesis, 1971–2), ch. 4, p. 6. I have used the version which he generously put on the internet at http://www.history.bangor.ac.uk/esknights/gencon.htm.

[65] W. Dugdale, *The Antiquities of Warwickshire* (London, 1656), rev. W. Thomas (London, 1730), pp. 91, 894, 1003, gives Henry de Sheldon and Henry de Edgbaston as knights but not Robert de Waver, although he was the eldest son of a knight.

[66] For the status of early fourteenth-century sub-escheators see Nigel Saul, *Knights and Esquires: The Gloucestershire Gentry in the Fourteenth Century* (Oxford, 1981), pp. 140–1. They were appointed in any case neither by the government nor in the counties but by the two salaried escheators operating nationally, on either side of the Trent, and were probably paid by them. See Stevenson, 'The Escheator' in Willard, Morris *et al.* (eds.), *The English Government at Work*, vol. II part iii, p. 158. The office was suspended between 1275 and 1283, when the role was taken over by the sheriffs.

reasons the centre called upon them increasingly to supplement the work of the professional justices when it came to special commissions of oyer and terminer. Whereas the royal professionals had constituted 68 per cent of these justices in 1275 they were only 42 per cent in 1300.[67] Moreover, direct taxation had returned to provide another avenue through which county knights could function as agents of the state, although the incidence was not large before the 1290s. The office of sheriff aside, there can be no doubt that these commissions were the real tasks which many county knights coveted. They were the high-prestige roles that reflected their local status.

The county scene is best approached through the justices of gaol delivery. Although, as we have seen, the central court justices had gained a virtual monopoly over the assizes during the 1240s, local knights still found themselves sharing in the relief of gaols. After a hiatus in the records, the panels which were commissioned to deliver the gaols come to be recorded again more regularly on the Patent Rolls from 52 Henry III (1267–8) onwards. Serviceable lists of justices can be constituted for the twenty-year period from 1267–8 to 1287–8.[68] An increasing number of panels was probably commissioned, and certainly more are recorded, as these two decades progressed, and this may lead to some distortion in the analysis. None the less, sufficient evidence is available for us to be able to examine the composition of the panels.

The names of fifty-six justices of gaol delivery for Warwickshire have been drawn out of these sources.[69] Not surprisingly we find regular royal justices among them: Nicholas Grace (or le Gras), Walter de Hopton, Geoffrey de Lewknor, Roger Loveday, John des Vaux (*de Vallibus*). But the majority were not professional judges. Of the fifty-six justices for Warwickshire as many as thirty-one figured only once or in only one regnal year, while two others figured in consecutive years but only in the peculiar two-justice panels that were sometimes appointed instead of the normal four.[70] Some of these thirty-one appear to have had little direct stake in the county, although there were

---

[67] See Richard W. Kaeuper, 'Law and Order in Fourteenth-Century England: The Evidence of Special Commissions of Oyer and Terminer', *Speculum* 54 (1979), p. 753.

[68] Largely absent from the printed calendars, these panels can be resurrected by means of obsolete manuscript calendars and indexes still extant in the Public Record Office, and, for the first nine years of Edward I, from the appendices to the Reports of the Deputy Keeper of the Public Records for 1881–89. PRO OBS 1/465–7 are manuscript calendars from the Patent Rolls of 31–57 Henry III, while OBS 1/432–8 are manuscript indexes to the Patent Rolls of 10–16 Edward I. I am most grateful to Paul Brand for drawing these to my attention.

[69] For a complete list of the justices and their appearances see Appendix III, below.

[70] Sometimes they were commissioned to deliver a particular prisoner, for example Ralf de Arundel and Reginald Botereus who figure in 1269–70, Thomas de Foljambe who was commissioned to deliver a specific prisoner with John des Vaux in 1280–1, and Walter de Hopton who twice joined frequent Warwickshire deliverers for specific prisoners in 1284–5. On other occasions they sat on irregular two-man panels, e.g. Geoffrey Russell, sitting with the judge, Geoffrey de Lewknor, William de Careswell (on three occasions) and Odo de Hodinet (twice, on both occasions with William de Careswell).

others who were the heads of local landowning families, men like Ralf de Grendon, Hugh de Harborough, John de Ladbroke, John de Wilnecote and Peter de Wolverton.

By contrast, the twenty-three who appear in more than one regnal year and on one or more regular panels contain a higher proportion of local landowners. If we leave aside the judges, Lewknor and Vaux, and the Leicestershire knights, John de Folville and Anketin de Martival, we are left with a core of Warwickshire men. Among them are Walter de Bishopton, Robert de Hastang, Walter de Langley, Fulk de Lucy, Henry Murdak, Peter le Potter, William de Waver and Jordan de Whitacre. However, if we look more closely we find that a small core of eleven men constituted the mainstay of gaol delivery at Warwick in late Henrician and early Edwardian England. Eight of them were prominent county knights. They were Robert Burdet, Thomas de Charlecote *alias* Thomas de Haseley, Nicholas de Charnels, John de Clinton, Henry Huband, John Peche, Henry de Sheldon and Robert de Verdon. John de Digby and Henry de Nottingham, by contrast, were Leicestershire men.[71] However, this is not in itself very surprising given the close connections between these contiguous counties. Not only did the counties have great lords in common but they had long shared the same sheriff. The eleventh man, Robert le Waleys, was probably also more of a Leicestershire knight. He is presumably the Robert le Waleys, knight, who gave evidence at the proof of age of William Ferrers of Groby, Leicestershire, in March 1293, and whom Edmund earl of Lancaster had requested as one of the two justices to hear and determine trespasses in his forest and chases in 1280.[72] The appearance also of the knights Richard and William le Waleys on the commissions may suggest a family with a strong local presence.[73]

---

[71] John de Digby held the manor of Halstead in the parish of Tilton and a further estate at Billesden (*Cal. Close Rolls, 1279–88*, p. 182; *VCH Leicestershire*, vol. V, p. 9). John was an attorney for Nicholas de Segrave in 1271 and witnessed, as a knight, for Edmund, earl of Cornwall in 1288 (Charles Moor, *Knights of Edward I*, 5 vols., Publications of the Harleian Society 80–4 (London, 1929–32), vol. I, p. 285). Henry de Nottingham held a knight's fee of the Mowbrays at Thrussington and Ratcliff (*Cal. Inq. Post Mortem*, vol. III, no. 472). He also held commissions in Nottinghamshire (Moor, *Knights of Edward I*, vol. III, p. 270).

[72] *Cal. Inq. Post Mortem*, vol. III, no. 149; Kaeuper, 'Law and Order in Fourteenth-Century England', pp. 759–60, quoting PRO SC1/22/203. There seem, however, to have been several men of this name, and they are not easy to distinguish. A Robert le Waleys went to the Council of Lyons with the bishop of London in 1274 and another was king's parker at Odiham in 1275 (*Cal. Close Rolls, 1272–9*, pp. 120, 389). A Robert le Waleys was steward of Robert de Scales in Hertfordshire in 1293 (*Cal. Inq. Post Mortem*, vol. I, no. 1624). A Robert le Waleys held land at Wollaston, Northamptonshire, in 1247 and another in Essex in 1293 (*ibid.*, vol. I, nos. 49, 1616). Moor has the knight coming from Somerset and receiving commissions in Leicestershire, Derbyshire and Rutland (*Knights of Edward I*, vol. V, p. 143).

[73] A Waleys family held a manor at Shelfield in Aston Cantlow, Warwickshire, in the early fourteenth century when William le Waleys was its lord (*VCH Warwickshire*, vol. III, p. 38). Both William and Richard le Waleys appear in the rolls of arms for Edward I's reign. However, Richard seems to have been associated with Sussex. See *Aspilogia III*, ed. Brault, vol. II, p. 443. See also Moor, *Knights of Edward I*, vol. V, pp. 143–4.

Of these eleven men Charlecote, Peche, Verdon and Nottingham, in particular, figured throughout the entire period. If never quite forming standing panels, they nevertheless worked with one another over and over again. The most important point, however, is that the central government was still drawing upon a relatively small group of men from among the county's knights, men whom no doubt it thought it could trust, or ought to be able to trust, more than others. Sheldon, as we have seen, was a coroner, while Thomas de Charlecote and Robert de Verdon were sheriffs of the county. In fact if we look more broadly at the men who functioned as justices of gaol delivery in the county no less than ten of them – that is, a fifth of those who were not professional judges – figured as sheriffs at some point or another in their careers.[74] Some of them were certainly well known at the centre before they received their commissions. Five – William Bagot, Thomas de Bray, William de Careswell, Anketin de Martival and Henry Murdak – were pre-1278 sheriffs who received commissions of gaol delivery only after they had held office.[75] Another man, Walter de Langley, is a particularly interesting case. The eldest son of the infamous forest justice Geoffrey de Langley, he was employed only from 1274 when he succeeded his father as head of the Langley family. Although a landowner in his own right before this, he fails to figure until after his father's death. This suggests that the central government's old policy of drawing on men who were both locally powerful and known at the centre – either in some other capacity or through some affinity with a known personage – was still operative. There may, of course, have been some magnate recommendation. It is hard to doubt that the appointment of Richard de Amundeville in 1282 to help the sheriff preserve the peace had something to do with the earl of Warwick, given the close association between them.[76] Whatever had or had not changed in the meantime, however, something resembling the old post-Angevin system of control in the counties was still effectively in operation.

[74] William Bagot, Thomas de Charlecote, Thomas de Farndon, Fulk de Lucy, Anketin de Martivans, Henry Murdak and Robert de Verdon for Warwickshire and Leicestershire, Thomas de Bray for Buckingham and Bedfordshire, and William de Careswell and Roger Springhese who were both sheriffs of Shropshire and Staffordshire. For a study of the sheriffs of Warwickshire see Templeman, *The Sheriffs of Warwickshire.*

[75] Looking at the sheriffs of Hampshire between 1267 and 1278, T.E. MacIver found that they tended to have limited experience before becoming sheriff but that most of them subsequently received judicial commissions. The means by which the centre had prior knowledge of Hampshire sheriffs are generally clearer before 1278. It may well be, as MacIver suggests, that outgoing sheriffs made suggestions of likely successors, especially after 1278. Baronial influence may also have played a part. Richard de Aston, for example, who was sheriff in 1291, had been steward to Isabel de Fortibus. See T.E. MacIver, 'Aspects of the Gentry of 13th-Century Hampshire' (Oxford MLitt thesis, 1984), ch. 2, esp. pp. 155–93.

[76] *Cal. Pat. Rolls, 1281–92*, p. 30. In 1278 Richard had surrendered the manors of Berkswell and Lighthorne to the earl, his overlord, in return for these and the manor of Brailes for life. See, especially, Raban, 'The Land Market and the Aristocracy', in Greenway *et al.* (eds.), *Tradition and Change*, p. 249.

This impression is reinforced if we examine a second county. The same records reveal the names of forty-six men who were involved in delivering Northampton gaol across the same twenty-year period.[77] Many were involved on only one occasion. Sometimes this was to join a prominent royal justice in delivering a specific prisoner, as in the case of Walter de Grauntcourt, William de Colethorp and Thomas de Hewelton who functioned as a group with Hervey de Stanton in 1278–9. Others served on special two-man panels. Geoffrey Russell, for example, joined the justice Geoffrey de Lewknor, and is found acting regularly with him across several midland counties, delivering Northampton, Warwick, Bedford, Oakham, Oxford and Banbury.[78] Among royal judges, John des Vaux, Gilbert de Preston, Nicholas Grace and Roger Loveday also put in appearances.[79] The kings's serjeant, Robert de Colevill, occurs.[80] Robert le Baud and Eustace de Watford, who figure very prominently in the panels, were both sheriffs of the county, Robert in 1279 and Eustace back in 1258 and 1264. William de Turvill was later to be sheriff of Bedfordshire and Buckinghamshire. William Hay, who figures regularly across the early years, may have been the same William who was a verderer of Salcey Forest and who died in office in 1273.[81] Hugh de Goldingham, who makes two appearances, was sometime steward of Rockingham and Geddington Forests.[82] In the case of Northamptonshire, as many as four of the justices seem to have been coroners. William de Turvill and William de Colevill were functioning at the time of the 1285 eyre, while Guy de Morton and John de Lou were then said to have been in office at some point since the last eyre in 1272.[83]

Among those who make occasional appearances as justices of gaol delivery were some who were undoubtedly prominent county knights, men like John

---

[77] For the complete list of the justices and their appearances see Appendix IV, below.

[78] *Report of the Deputy Keeper of the Public Records*, vols. XLII–L (London, 1881–9).

[79] Assuming, as does the *Cal. Pat. Rolls*, that R. Loved (or Lovet) is Roger Loveday.

[80] For Robert de Colevill see Brand, *The Origins of the English Legal Profession*, pp. 58, 60–1, 189.

[81] In 1273 a verderer of Salcey was to be elected in place of William Hay of Quinton who had died (*Cal. Close Rolls, 1272–9*, p. 12). The last appearance of a William Hay as a justice of gaol delivery is of William Hay of Twywell. Clearly, there were two men of the same name. It is unclear, therefore, whether the justice who appears as William Hay without qualification was William Hay of Quinton or of Twywell.

[82] *Close Rolls, 1254–6*, pp. 85, 111, 289, 299, 340. In fact, he was steward of the royal forests between the bridges of Stamford and Oxford (*ibid.*, p. 50). Two other justices, Robert Mauncell and Ralf de Titchmarsh, or their namesakes, had been foresters or verderers in his time. See *Select Pleas of the Forest*, ed. G.J. Turner, Selden Society 13 (London, 1889), pp. 37, 100.

[83] There may also have been two John le Lous. On one occasion a justice of gaol delivery is called John le Lou of *Esse* (presumably for Easton). The 1285 eyre rolls give the following coroners since the last eyre: William de Morton, John Fauvel, Baldwin de Drayton and Simon Mallory who were deceased, Geoffrey de Trayly, Guy de Morton, Roger Beumeys and John le Lou who were alive but no longer functioning, and William de Colevill, William de Turvill, Ralf de Dyve and Robert de Hotot who were currently in office (PRO Just 1/620 m. 56). Anomalies in the election of coroners still occurred. In 1276 William de St Germain had been elected but could not function because bodily incapacitated (*Cal. Close Rolls, 1272–9*, p. 276).

de Beaufeu, Nicholas de Cogenhoe, Roger de Hackleton, William de Noers, William de Parles, Richard de Seyton and Ralf de Titchmarsh. Some of them figure in the same capacity elsewhere. Richard de Seyton was more prominent in the county of Rutland, but is also found delivering the gaol at Oxford. Nicholas de Cogenhoe appears with the central court justice Geoffrey de Lewknor delivering the gaol at Norwich.[84] We can assume that they were men generally known at the centre of government. The situation is best summed up by an instruction to the sheriff of Northamptonshire on 22 March 1276, to conduct an inquiry under oath over an assault on a royal bailiff. He was to take with him Nicholas de Cogenhoe, in effect a government nominee, 'and other knights whom he knows to be fit for the purpose'.[85] Nicholas had been one of the assessors and collectors of the fifteenth from Northamptonshire and Rutland in 1275.[86]

As with Warwickshire, however, a restricted group of men dominated the regular four-man panels over extensive periods. They were Robert le Baud, William de Colevill, John le Lou, Robert de Pavely, Philip fitz Robert, Robert fitz Walter, Eustace de Watford, and for shorter lengths of time William Hay and Geoffrey de St Mark. Once again we can see panels working together regularly, though never exclusively. For example, Robert fitz Walter, John le Lou, Robert le Baud and William de Colevill are found regularly together during the early to mid-1280s. Indeed, they can still be found as a group as late as December 1290.[87] They are also found delivering Peterborough gaol,[88] while three of them, together with Geoffrey de St Mark, provided the same service for Rutland's gaol at Oakham.[89]

Some of these men – Nicholas Cogenhoe, Robert de Pavely and Geoffrey de St Mark – had been royalists during the Barons' Wars.[90] However, the government was also employing ex-Montfortians; necessarily so, because Northamptonshire royalists had been thin on the ground.[91] At least nine men who had supported the baronial government figured among the justices of gaol delivery. They included

---

[84] *Cal. Pat. Rolls, 1272–81*, p. 341.   [85] *Cal. Close Rolls, 1272–9*, p. 276.
[86] *Parliamentary Writs*, vol. I, p. 4.   [87] *Cal. Pat. Rolls, 1281–92*, p. 395.
[88] On other occasions Peterborough gaol seems to have been delivered by men with a direct interest within Peterborough Soke. In 1270–1, for instance, it was delivered by Geoffrey de la Mare and John de Helpston together with Richard de Hemmington of Polebrook Hundred (which the abbot held) and Roger de la Hyde.
[89] On other occasions Oakham, too, was delivered by men with a local interest: Henry de Lynden, Simon de Lynden, Henry Murdak, William Murdak, John Sampson, Ralf Beaufeu, Richard de Seyton, Philip de Paunton, Robert de Sculthorpe, Peter de Wakerley, Richard de St Liz and Albricus de Whittlebury. Simon de Lynden had been sub-escheator for Northamptonshire and Rutland until October 1262, when the king accepted his resignation on the grounds of insufficient means (*Close Rolls, 1261–4*, p. 182).
[90] For what follows see Fernandes, 'The Role of the Midland Knights', ch. 1.6: 'The Northamptonshire Grand Assize Knights and the Barons' War'.
[91] Of the fifty-eight knights who functioned in the grand assize of 1261–2, Dr Fernandes identifies thirty-nine as contrariants and only eight as loyalists. He notes that the allegiance of the remaining sixteen is unrecorded.

three of the most prominent, namely Philip fitz Robert, Robert fitz Walter and no less a figure than Eustace de Watford, twice baronial sheriff, in 1258 and again in 1264.[92] His prominence as a gaol delivery justice may be symptomatic of the healing of divisions, but it is also indicative of the crown's need for experienced men on whom it could rely.

The situation in Warwickshire was similar. At least eight of the justices of gaol delivery had been supporters of the Montfortian regime, including the prominent justices Robert de Verdon and Henry Huband.[93] On the other side, Walter de Langley, the sheriffs Henry Murdak and William Bagot, and very probably Jordan de Whitacre, had been royalists. Bagot, who had been baronial sheriff in 1259, functioned for the crown in 1262 and again after Evesham. Another justice was Ralf de Grendon, son of the mercurial Robert de Grendon. A justice of gaol delivery in Warwickshire during the 1240s, Robert had been sheriff of Shropshire and Staffordshire from 1250 to 1255 and left office heavily in debt. The Shropshire eyre roll of 1256 contains a mass of complaints about his conduct. Ironically in 1258 he was one of the four commissioners for Warwickshire to hear and report complaints.[94] In February 1265 the Montfortian government made him sheriff of Staffordshire and Shropshire once again, and this was followed by the relief of the interest on his Jewish debts. However, he and William Bagot were the men responsible for taking the Warwickshire and Leicestershire lands of the rebels into royal hands after Evesham, and in 1266 he was given generous terms for the repayment of the debts to the crown.[95] Two qualities seem to have been at a premium when it came to membership of the gaol delivery commissions: experience and a solid presence within the local landholding community.

When we look at the relatively few judicial commissions of oyer and terminer and the like that are recorded for the first twenty years of Edward I's reign, we find a strong correlation with the commissions of gaol delivery. For Warwickshire we find William Bagot, Thomas de Bray, Thomas de Charlecote, Fulk de Lucy, Henry de Sheldon and Robert de Verdon,[96] while a few other gaol delivery justices figure in counties where they had stronger

---

[92] The others are: Roger de Hackleton, Richard de Hemmyngton, Roger de la Hyde, Geoffrey de la Mare, William de Parles and Ralf de Titchmarsh. For the career of Eustace de Watford see Fernandes, 'The Role of the Midland Knights', pp. 81–6.

[93] The others were Anketin de Martival, Robert de Hastang, William de Waver, and two men who managed to persuade the king of their innocence, Hugh de Harborough and William le Potere. For the details see Fernandes, 'The Role of the Midland Knights', ch. 2.6: 'The Warwickshire Grand Assize Knights and the Barons' War'. Of twenty-nine grand assize jurors in 1262, he identifies twelve as contrariants and five as royalists, with the remaining twelve classified under allegiance unrecorded (ibid., p. 145).

[94] The others being William de Waver, Nicholas fitz Ralf and Adam de Napton.

[95] For the career of Robert de Grendon see Fernandes, 'The Role of the Midland Knights', pp. 157–9, and Coss, Lordship, Knighthood and Locality, p. 289.

[96] Cal. Pat. Rolls, 1272–81, p. 341, and 1281–92, pp. 143, 308, 459.

interests.[97] Only three other non-professional justices are found for Warwick-shire, and they are relatively elevated figures.[98] There is a strong correlation with other commissions too. Henry de Nottingham and Henry de Sheldon, to-gether with the clerk John de Arundel, conducted the Hundred Roll survey in the counties of Warwickshire and Leicestershire in 1279–80,[99] while Henry de Nottingham was one of the two assessors for the same counties of the fifteenth of 1275.[100] Thomas de Charlecote was one of the assessors of the thirteenth of 1283, with John de Digby functioning for Leicestershire.[101] In 1287 Henry de Sheldon, Thomas de Charlecote and Fulk de Lucy were appointed with a fourth local knight, Thomas de Garshale, as keepers of the peace for Warwickshire.[102]

Once again the same characteristics are found in Northamptonshire. As far as other judicial commissions are concerned, the non-professionals comprise Robert le Baud, Nicholas de Cogenhoe, John le Lou, Robert fitz Walter – all gaol delivery justices – and very few others.[103] Nicholas de Cogenhoe, as we have seen, was one of the taxers in 1275.[104] In 1279 he was one of the three men appointed to inquire into the activities of Northamptonshire's sheriff with regard to distraint of knighthood.[105] John le Lou was among the keepers of the peace appointed for Northamptonshire in 1287.[106] If the situation was a little less incestuous here than in Warwickshire it may be because Northamptonshire

[97] Robert le Waleys in Leicestershire and Derbyshire, William de Careswell in Staffordshire and Roger Springhese in Staffordshire and Shropshire (*Cal. Pat. Rolls, 1272–81*, p. 407 and *1281–92*, pp. 100, 102, 103, 140, 205, 208, 212). William Bagot also figures in Staffordshire and Thomas de Bray in Leicestershire and Northamptonshire (*Cal. Pat. Rolls, 1272–81*, p. 465 and *1281–92*, pp. 100, 210).

[98] Andrew de Astley, Walter de Beauchamp and Nicholas de Segrave (*Cal. Pat. Rolls, 1272–81*, p. 409, and *1281–92*, pp. 406, 455, 459, 520).

[99] *The Warwickshire Hundred Rolls of 1279–80*, ed. Trevor John, British Academy Records of Social and Economic History, new series, 19 (Oxford, 1992), p. 25. The same men conducted the inquiry into the conduct of the sheriff over the matter of distraint to knighthood (*Cal. Pat. Rolls, 1272–81*, p. 342).

[100] The other was the sheriff, Osbert de Bereford, brother of the king's serjeant and later chief justice of the court of Common Pleas. Osbert was a cleric. See *The Earliest English Law Reports*, 2 vols., ed. P.A. Brand, Selden Society 112 (London, 1996), vol. II, pp. x–xii.

[101] Their associates, probably clerics, were Roger de Stoke and Peter de Leicester respectively (*Parliamentary Writs*, vol. I, pp. 12–13).

[102] *Cal. Pat. Rolls, 1281–92*, p. 265.

[103] *Cal. Pat. Rolls, 1272–81*, p. 341 and *1281–92*, pp. 46, 99, 140, 142, 203. Robert le Baud and John le Lou occur prominently. The others are John Fauvel, Master Henry de Bray, Thomas de Bray and Richard de Bray (*Cal. Pat. Rolls, 1281–92*, pp. 94, 210).

[104] The other was William de Perton, no doubt as clerk. The taxers in 1283 were Thomas de Farndon, justice of gaol delivery in Warwickshire and later sheriff of that county, and Richard de Bray (*Parliamentary Writs*, vol. I, pp. 12–13).

[105] The others were Ralf de Arden and William de Boyvill, sheriff of the county in 1270 (*Cal. Pat. Rolls, 1272–81*, p. 342). The latter was also one of the assessors of the thirteenth in Rutland in 1283. The fact that Henry de Nottingham, Henry de Sheldon and John de Arundel did this for Warwickshire and Leicestershire might suggest that Nicholas de Cogenhoe and his colleagues were also to conduct the Hundred Roll inquiry.

[106] The others were Ralf Peverel and John de Roseles (*Cal. Pat. Rolls, 1281–92*, p. 265).

boasted a higher number of knights at this time.[107] Nevertheless, the broad characteristics are the same, with a minority of knights predominating.

Studies of Northamptonshire and Warwickshire indicate that on the whole knights performed largely high-profile roles in early Edwardian England. Some of them also represented the counties in parliament, though sadly the names of MPs are almost entirely lacking at this date. Only a minority of knights, however, engaged in these public activities with any degree of frequency. The impression one has gained from a study centred on gaol delivery commissions meshes well with John Illsley's findings from Essex.[108] Looking across the reign of Edward I as a whole and at what he calls both 'executive and judicial administration', he identifies a central core of ten active knights who constitute the *buzones* of the county. This small group was less than 25 per cent of the sample of forty-two knights upon which his study was based, and certainly less than a quarter of the knights in the county.[109] Below these ten were a score of knights who played some part in the public life of the county, other than as jurors and private 'consumers' within the judicial system. Putting their public engagements in a broader perspective however, Illsley adds, judiciously, 'both the time spent performing these tasks and the number of tasks performed appear relatively modest by comparison with the time spent by the majority... in the pursuit or defence of their private interests'.[110]

He makes a second observation, that these *buzones* do not correspond automatically with a social elite. Alongside them in term of status and wealth he found an 'alternative elite' of knights whose interests were more military than anything else. In general they spent relatively little, if any, time on county-orientated activities. Some of them, indeed, were closer in lifestyle to the baronage: 'These men appear to have followed a more military style of life on the fringes of the baronial nobility and closer to the chivalric concept of knighthood.'[111] However, as he acknowledges, it is hazardous to identify hard and fast categories. Some of this 'alternative elite' are found attending parliament in the later part of Edward I's reign. In fact, as we shall see, such

---

[107] In response to the government's attempt to bring the broad swathe of landowners into its cavalry in 1297, the sheriff of Northamptonshire returned the names of ninety-seven earls and knights and forty-one *armigeri* who were sufficiently qualified, not counting the lands currently in the hands of widows (*Parliamentary Writs*, vol. I, pp. 288–9). Fifty-eight knights had figured in the grand assize at the 1262 eyre (PRO Just 1/616).

[108] For what follows see Illsley, 'The Gentry of Essex', esp. ch. 2, pp. 1–4, ch. 4, p. 15, ch. 5, pp. 7–8, 11–12, ch. 8, pp. 2–4.

[109] In 1295 a list was drawn up of all knights theoretically available for the defence of the coast of Essex. Of the 101 knights named, sixty-five held lands in the county but were not resident, twenty-five were resident, and eleven, though resident, were described as *impotens*. However, there are anomalies and some of those given as non-resident played some part in county affairs. Illsley's sample of forty-two is based, rather, on the fifty-seven knights listed under Essex in the *Parliamentary Roll of Arms*.

[110] Illsley, 'The Gentry of Essex', ch. 5, p. 12.   [111] *Ibid.*, ch. 8, p. 4.

distinctions were steadily eroded from the 1290s onwards as an increasing percentage of contemporary knights were drawn into service to the state.

But before we move on to consider the impact of the explosion in commissions which began in the 1290s, it is necessary to reflect on precisely why some knights should have been eager to involve themselves in the exercise of royal justice. Direct material rewards do not appear to have been great. They did not, of course, receive salaries. It is true that the chief taxers in the counties were allowed expenses by the Exchequer. However, even these were not very high and it may well be that they were expected to receive further remuneration in the counties.[112] There was the customary – and essentially legitimate – hospitality, which was widespread. Between this and corruption lay items which, as J.F. Willard put it, 'lay in a shadowy borderland'.[113] Much of this must also have applied to the justices of gaol delivery, although it can hardly have provided a major motive for participation on the part of later thirteenth-century knights.[114] There were also indirect rewards in the form of access to royal patronage, and the importance of this should not be underestimated. At its lowest levels it could help to achieve grants of free warren and the exercise of minor franchises.[115] It could also result in gifts such as timber and wine. The more fortunate or better placed might reap greater rewards, in the form of a wardship, for example, or the right to arrange the marriage of an heiress. Prestige within the lesser landowning ranks themselves may also have been a factor, not to mention advantages in terms of networks of power and vertical relationships with higher lords.

But there is a more basic reason why knights should have wanted to be involved in the exercise of royal justice. Courts, especially private courts, lay at the very heart of seigneurial life, for in the last analysis control over the tenantry was the real guarantor of seigneurial income. As is well known, the royal courts 'cast a longer and longer shadow over private and local jurisdictions'[116] as more and more business was drawn into them, by one means or another, during the course of the thirteenth century. Lords responded in a variety of ways. It has been suggested recently that the very appearance of manor court rolls during the middle decades of the thirteenth century is to be explained by the need on the part of English landlords to adopt the superior procedures of the royal courts, including the recording of proceedings, if they were to keep their free tenants coming to their courts, and that a variety of subsequent procedural

---

[112] See J.F. Willard, *Parliamentary Taxes on Personal Property 1290–1334: A Study in Mediaeval English Financial Administration* (Cambridge, MA, 1934), pp. 197–219.

[113] *Ibid.*, p. 205.

[114] Local offices like coroner were unpaid, which helps to explain why they seem to have been unpopular with most knights.

[115] For free warren see now David Crook, 'The "Petition of the Barons" and Charters of Free Warren, 1227–1258', in Prestwich *et al.* (eds.), *Thirteenth Century England VIII*, pp. 33–48.

[116] John S. Beckerman, 'Procedural Innovation and Institutional Change in Medieval English Manorial Courts', *Law and History Review* 10, no. 2 (1992), p. 197.

improvements are to be explained in this way.[117] A second response, affecting their broader tenantry, was to acquire view of frankpledge, the oversight of the mutual security system whereby groups of (usually) ten men, known as tithings, were responsible for producing any one of their number in court. Normatively this view was undertaken by the sheriff twice-yearly at the hundred courts. Private courts where view of frankpledge was exercised also received presentments of breaches of the peace and other offences. Moreover, there were additional minor franchises which had led directly to additional jurisdiction over the peasantry. There was the right to take the assizes of bread and ale for example, the right to a pillory and tumbril, and in some cases private gallows and the right to hang thieves. The right to have a weekly market and annual fair on one's land also involved the holding of a court to deal with trading matters.[118] These things could be quite lucrative and they naturally impacted upon the local perception of an individual's lordship, not least because a lord exercising such franchises was effectively the equivalent of a commissioned royal justice.[119] The inquiry that produced the Hundred Rolls of 1274–5 revealed the extent to which such franchises were being exercised and the degree to which manors were being withdrawn from suit to the hundred courts which, if unchecked, could presumably amount to much the same thing. In 1278 Edward I launched his famous *Quo Warranto* proceedings against the holders of franchises, proceedings which persisted until the suspension of the general eyre in 1294. As far as Warwickshire is concerned they reveal thirty-six lay lords claiming those franchises which directly impacted upon their tenants, while the Hundred Rolls of 1274–5 show fourteen claiming the franchises and another eighteen who were reported to have withdrawn the suit of communities under their jurisdiction.[120] Altogether some fifty families were involved. The list includes two earls and a good crop of minor barons and rich knights, but it also contains some relatively minor lords including a few who were sub-knightly.[121]

---

[117] Zvi Razi and Richard M. Smith, 'The Origins of the English Manorial Court Rolls as a Written Record: A Puzzle', in Razi and Smith (eds.), *Medieval Society and the Manor Court* (Oxford, 1996), pp. 36–68.

[118] One should also include free warren, for in granting minor hunting rights the crown effectively conveyed jurisdiction over poaching.

[119] See D.W. Sutherland, *Quo Warranto Proceedings in the Reign of Edward I, 1278–1294* (Oxford, 1963), p. 13.

[120] *Placita de Quo Warranto*, Record Commission (London, 1818), pp. 777–85; *Rotuli Hundredorum*, 2 vols., Record Commission (1812–18), vol. II, pp. 225–8.

[121] Of the gaol delivery justices there are proceedings against Richard de Amundevill, John de Clinton, Henry Huband, Fulk de Lucy and John Peche, as well as John son of Walter de Langley. Thomas de Charlecote was reported to have withdrawn suit from Haseley in 1274–5. Others failed to figure. However, one must be cautious. The sources do not necessarily reveal all the franchises that were being exercised. In Essex only fifteen of John Illsley's sample of forty-two knights are revealed as franchise holders, but he considers that others had managed to conceal them ('The Gentry of Essex', ch. 4, pp. 12–13). The 1274–5 Hundred Rolls show considerable numbers in Northamptonshire who were either claiming franchises or withholding suit. Again,

Minor franchises were exercised very unevenly, but what these records reveal is that a growing response to the exercise of royal justice was to harness it. It can hardly be doubted that it was precisely this response which determined the willingness of local knights to involve themselves in gaol delivery. There may also have been a growing realisation of the need for a broader plane of social control, given the increasing geographical mobility of the thirteenth century and a perception that royal and seigneurial justice were, in important respects, complementary. Whatever rights a lord succeeded in exercising in his own courts – and these varied considerably – there must have been considerable additional cachet in operating as a royal justice of gaol delivery.

A PROTO-GENTRY?

Should we then be speaking of a proto-gentry in early Edwardian England? Arguably there is a prima facie case for adopting this perspective. After all, the preconditions for the existence of a gentry seem to be largely in place at this time. Pre-eminently, the new knighthood had bequeathed an extremely powerful sense of elitism, strongly reinforcing the separatism of the nobility, both higher and lesser. As we have said, the gentry is predicated upon the existence of a lesser nobility. It also involves a strong sense of territoriality, a territoriality manifested by horizontal banding, partnership in government, collective control over the populace, collective identity and the articulation of a collective self-interest.[122] The roots of at least some of these phenomena are demonstrable in early Edwardian England. Out of the Edwardian polity there was to emerge, in due course, not only a forum for the articulation of collective interests, in the form of the House of Commons, but also a means of dialogue between the centre and the localities through its constituencies. The employment of knights on commissions was eventually to lead to a heavy reliance by the crown on lesser landowners as a whole and to a real partnership between local landowners and the state. A line of development can be traced from their delivery of the gaols to the existence of resident magistrates exercising public justice on behalf of their fellows. The acorns had been sown from which mighty oaks were to grow.

Other acorns can be identified too. In terms of the collective identity of the gentry, historians have traditionally put considerable emphasis upon the county. Notwithstanding the fact that the county court has been misunderstood, and used anachronistically by historians, it is still possible to argue that an attachment to

---

this includes some prominent gaol delivery justices while others fail to appear (*Rot. Hundred.*, vol. II, pp. 6–15). The *Quo Warranto* rolls for the 1285 Northamptonshire eyre have been lost, although the king's attorney seems to have had them in front of him when he challenged franchise holders at the eyre of 1329–30 (Sutherland, *Quo Warranto Proceedings*, p. 223). The records of this eyre show thirty-two lay lords claming such rights, including Robert fitz Walter and Thomas de Bray (*Placita de Quo Warranto*, pp. 499–521).

[122] See above, pp. 9–11.

the county could well have existed among resident knights and that it may well have grown during the course of the thirteenth century. The grand assize could conceivably have helped to produce this, especially as the number of knights declined and the notion of the locality as employed in the grand assize had of necessity to widen. The employment of a proportion of the knights on county-based commissions may also have had this effect, especially in the latter part of the century when the pool of knights from which the commissioners were drawn was much smaller than it had been in the immediate post-Angevin period. Such sentimental attachment can be supposed, even if it cannot be demonstrated.

It may also be possible to detect the first stirrings of territorial gradation in the thirteenth century. On several occasions we have referred, in passing, to clause 17 of the Provisions of Oxford of 1258 which determined that henceforth sheriffs should be vavasours of the counties they administered. Vavasour has been defined simply as 'substantial landowner'.[123] It is necessary, however, to expand upon this.[124] In origin the word vavasour seems to have meant a vassal of vassals (*vassus vassorum*) and it was commonly used in twelfth-century France to denote a sub-tenant (or *arrière-vassal*), separated by one or more rungs from the crown, or from a duke or count. In romance literature the vavasour is predominantly a mature knight, versed in the ways of chivalry but now living a sedentary life. He functions predominantly as a courteous and hospitable host to the knight-errant. As far as the twelfth century is concerned, the usage of the term in England mirrors, for the most part, that in France. It is found in charters, in legal sources and, indeed, in Anglo-Norman literature, though without the chivalric overtones. By the early thirteenth century, however, English usage had parted company with that of France. The treatise on the laws and customs of England, once attributed to Henry de Bracton, refers to 'vavasours' or 'magnates' as 'men of great dignity' (*viri magnae dignitatis*), and places them in the social hierarchy between barons and knights. This usage, moreover, is confirmed elsewhere. A royal writ of 1255, for example, ordered every sheriff in England that:

> with all haste they should cause to be proclaimed publicly throughout their bailliwick that all those who hold from the king in chief and owe him service should come to the king without delay with horses and arms and all their power to set out with him to Scotland, as they love the king and his honour, and indeed the lands and tenements that they hold from him; and the other vavasours and knights (*et alios vavassores et milites*) who do not hold in chief from the king should similarly come with horses and arms, as they love the king and his honour and wish to deserve his grace and favour for ever.[125]

---

[123] See above pp. 62, 128.

[124] For what follows see Coss, 'Literature and Social Terminology', in Aston *et al.* (eds), *Social Relations and Ideas*, pp. 109–50.

[125] *Cal. Close Rolls, 1254–6*, p. 218.

The vavasour, then, is more than a mere knight. Both are landowners and both may or may not hold directly of the crown. R.F. Treharne and Sir Maurice Powicke were wrong to interpret the word vavasour in the Provisions of Oxford as simply a synonym for county knight. Quite clearly it denotes the more substantial within their number. It was used to express a perceived difference among landowners below the highest rank, in terms of wealth and social standing. And, since the Provisions of Oxford refer to the vavasours of the counties, that perception was on a territorial basis.

Walter Map, writing at the court of Henry II, gives us a clue as to how this usage may have arisen when he pictures King Henry I in the company of his earls, his barons and his chief vavasours (*proceres vavassores*). In time the term may well have narrowed to denote only the most substantial among the erstwhile vavasours. Looked at from another angle, this shift in meaning may well have resulted from the very existence of the rather socially inclusive Angevin knighthood and the social tensions that ensued. In other words the origin of the peculiarly English usage of vavasour may well be yet another expression of that aristocratic drive for social exclusion which gave rise to the new knighthood of the thirteenth century. If so, it is an indication that the new knighthood itself did not immediately resolve the tensions within the landowning classes over the matter of social rank, nor did it create overnight a wholly cohesive knightly society.

The concept of the vavasour persisted in England through the thirteenth century. It was used, for example, by Pierre de Langtoft in his verse chronicle of Edward I's Scottish wars. Once again he used it in the Bractonian sense to denote men who occupied an intermediary position between baron and knight. But he also used it of individuals. Robert de Somerville, who died at the battle of Stirling in 1297, and Baldwin Wake, who was one of Simon de Montfort's lieutenants and a leader of the Disinherited after Simon's defeat and death at Evesham, are so described. Both of them, however, were really minor barons. Vavasour, though it does seem to reflect an embryonic sense of territorial gradation, was none the less a very imprecise term. By the end of the thirteenth century a much tighter knightly elite was in existence and in consequence the notion of the vavasour may well have become increasingly redundant. It did not long survive as a living term. It can hardly be a coincidence that it died out during the early to mid-fourteenth century, at the very time when a more precise system of social gradation was beginning to emerge.

In this, as in other key areas, there was still a long way to go by 1300. The difficulty with terms like proto-gentry is that they are teleological. Although we may legitimately identify tendencies and observe processes at work we must not at any point suppose that the emergence of the gentry was an historical inevitability. In order to avoid exaggerating the speed of change I would prefer to delay using the term proto-gentry until the fourteenth century. The reasons for this will become clearer during the course of the next three chapters, devoted respectively to the explosion of commissions which brought the great majority of knights on to the public scene, to the origins of true status gradation in the early to mid-fourteenth century, and to the maturation of a sense of identity amongst the emergent gentry.

7. The explosion of commissions and its consequences

It is time now to examine the explosion in commissions from the 1290s onwards, the development of a real partnership between the crown and county knights in terms of control of the populace, and the extension of that partnership to involve a broader local elite. We will then be in a position to understand the combination of factors which allowed the gentry to crystallise during the first half of the fourteenth century.

THE EXPLOSION OF COMMISSIONS

Although they continued to function as justices of gaol delivery, and very occasionally as tax collectors and the like, during the early years of the Edwardian polity there were not in reality very many high-level tasks for the county knights to perform. The full consequences of the rise of a more elite knighthood were masked as yet by the paucity of tasks which appealed to their elevated status.

This was to change with the explosion of commissions which began in the last two decades of the reign of Edward I. The major factor in this change was undoubtedly the impact of war. Taxation on personal property had returned with the twentieth of 1269, and Edward I levied further subsidies in 1275, 1283 and 1290. But, as Richard Kaeuper has remarked, 'once across the mid-1290s' dividing line, the change was marked'.[1] Six taxes were raised during the last fourteen years of his reign, and the pace continued through the reign of Edward II and into that of Edward III. More than a score of subsidies were raised between 1294 and 1340.[2] The taxes were collected by 'high men of local standing' appointed as commissioners by letters patent.[3] Very many of them were, of course, county knights.

---

[1] *War, Justice and Public Order: England and France in the Later Middle Ages* (Oxford, 1998), p. 35.

[2] For a recent, authoritative account, see M. Jurkowski, C.L. Smith and D. Crook, *Lay Taxes in England and Wales 1188–1688*, Public Record Office Handbook 31 (London, 1998), where details of the taxes and of earlier studies may be found.

[3] *Ibid.*, p. xxx.

The matter of subsidy necessitated the calling of the Commons to parliament. They had been present only spasmodically during the first half of the reign.[4] In a justly famous essay J.G. Edwards analysed thirty-four assemblies, 'variously styled parliaments or *colloquia*', to which the counties were ordered to send representatives between July 1290 and January 1327.[5] He successfully disposed of the idea that men were reluctant to attend and pointed to a relatively high incidence of re-election. In around a dozen parliaments the number of 'knights of the shire' who had been elected on previous occasions was exactly or approximately the same as those elected for the first time. In around ten cases, moreover, the number who had been returned before was actually higher than those elected for the first time. Of the 1,164 'knights of the shire' known to have been returned during these years, 507 were elected more than once. On the other hand, there were relatively few monopolists. Only seventy-nine men were elected five times or more. As a result 're-election to a series of immediately successive parliaments was unusual under Edward I and Edward II'.[6] In short, a considerable number of men had experience of representing the counties at Westminster.

War finance loomed large when the Commons were called to parliament and the costly nature of Edwardian warfare had an important impact on the deployment of the proto or incipient gentry. Nor was this impact confined to parliament and taxation. In addition to the cavalry which drew directly on the landed class itself, the king required considerable numbers of infantry. From the time of Edward I's 1282 campaign against the Welsh, the recruitment of foot soldiers was taken out of the hands of the sheriffs and given to specifically appointed commissioners of array.[7] The personnel involved changed during the course of the reign. Initially they were household knights, and these were followed by royal judges and councillors. It soon became clear, however, that men with direct knowledge of the particular counties were better placed to recruit than were royal officials. By the turn of the century knights were being employed alongside clerks, and by the end of the reign of Edward I the commissions of array were firmly in the hands of magnates and knights with military experience.

---

[4] For the early history of parliament, on which so much has been written, see especially, R.G. Davies and J.H. Denton (eds.), *The English Parliament in the Middle Ages* (Manchester, 1981). For a specific discussion of parliament in the reign of Edward I see Prestwich, *Edward I*, ch. 17.

[5] 'The Personnel of the Commons in Parliament under Edward I and Edward II', in *Essays in Medieval History Presented to Thomas Frederick Tout* (Manchester, 1925); reprinted in E.B. Fryde and Edward Miller (eds.), *Historical Studies of the English Parliament*, I: *Origins to 1399* (Cambridge, 1970), pp. 150–67.

[6] *Ibid.*, p. 159.

[7] For discussions of the development of commissions of array during the reign of Edward I see Michael Prestwich, *War, Politics and Finance under Edward I* (London, 1972), ch. 4, esp. pp. 99–101, and the same author's *Armies and Warfare in the Middle Ages: The English Experience* (London, 1996), pp. 123–5. For an older treatment see Powicke, *Military Obligation in Medieval England*, ch. 7. See also Kaeuper, *War, Justice and Public Order*, p. 25.

By this time, too, the commissions were generally based on single counties, and sometimes on even more restricted areas. In short, the task was increasingly entrusted to landowners with both local knowledge and military experience. As was the case with tax collection, however, much of the donkey work was done at local level under the general supervision of these socially elevated commissioners.

A fourth major role which came into the hands of county knights was that of keeper of the peace (*custos pacis*). Not a direct product of Edward I's wars – except in so far as war exacerbated crime and increased the public perception of spiralling disorder[8] – the keeper had complex roots. Although there were deeper antecedents, a major step in the evolution of this office had been the appointment of keepers of the peace in the counties by both sides, and largely for partisan reasons, during the Barons' Wars of 1263–5.[9] Their primary concern had been with security, including military matters. Keepers were again assigned to twenty-two counties, though on a piecemeal basis, during the restoration of order that dominated the country for two years following the battle of Evesham. In 1277 the king ordered the election of keepers in all counties from among the knights who were not accompanying him on his campaign in Wales. At this point, however, the emphasis began to shift away from military concerns to the arrest of malefactors.[10] A further development took place in 1287 when keepers were appointed to enforce the provisions of the Statute of Winchester of 1285 which was designed, as one historian has put it, to 'refurbish' the system of law enforcement in England.[11] The role of the keepers was essentially to supervise community policing, including the provision that every man should possess the arms appropriate to his wealth. The next general appointment of keepers, and the last of Edward I's reign, was born of political crisis. In 1300 the three

[8] One major problem was the pardoning of felonies in return for military service, which escalated from 1294. It has been calculated that in the last two decades of the reign over 2,000 felons were pardoned for war service. As Naomi Hurnard observed, 'Pardoning on this scale could not fail to have deplorable results' (*The King's Pardon for Homicide Before AD 1307* (Oxford, 1969), p. 317). See also Kaeuper, *War, Justice and Public Order*, esp. ch. 1 and pp. 126–7, who argues that Edward I moved England from a law state to a war state.

[9] A. Harding, 'The Origins and Early History of the Keeper of the Peace', *Transactions of the Royal Historical Society*, 5th series, 10 (1960) remains fundamental. See also the same author's *The Law Courts of Medieval England* (London, 1973) and his neat précis of thirteenth-century developments in *England in the Thirteenth Century*, pp. 211–14.

[10] That the keepers were already, at this date, taking inquests from local jurors is shown by a single survival. See Helen Cam, 'Some Early Inquests before "Custodes Pacis"', *English Historical Review* 40 (1925), pp. 411–19, and Harding, *England in the Thirteenth Century*, p. 212.

[11] Henry Summerson, 'The Enforcement of the Statute of Winchester, 1285–1327', *Journal of Legal History* 13, no. 3 (1992), pp. 232–50. Meanwhile, on 20 July 1282, there had been the isolated appointment of Richard de Amundevill 'to assist the sheriff of Warwickshire in the preservation of peace in these troubled times' and the appointment of Edmund of Cornwall as general keeper of the peace in the English counties with the power to appoint deputies (*Cal. Pat. Rolls, 1281–92*, p. 30; *Calendar of Chancery Rolls, Various, 1277–1326*, pp. 217–18; Harding, 'Origins and Early History of the Keeper of the Peace', p. 99).

knights chosen in each county to deal with infringements of the Charters were to double up as keepers upholding the Statute of Winchester. From the beginning and throughout the reign of Edward II keepers were appointed both to uphold the Statute and to pursue and arrest suspects. Sometimes they were given the additional power of gaol delivery, that is to say the right to try those indicted before them. More often such trial was reserved for the regular justices of gaol delivery and oyer and terminer. It was not until the next reign that the keepers were regularly afforded full judicial powers, turning them into justices of the peace. In many ways the keeper/justice of the peace was the most significant role that came into the hands of county knights at this time. As Alan Harding succinctly puts it, by the fourteenth century 'the shires were coming to be ruled by amateur landlord-magistrates'.[12]

It is apparent that by the beginning of the reign of Edward II the knightly participation rate in prestigious offices and commissions was already high.[13] The question is how high? This is a matter which must command our closest attention. Mere impressions are not enough. Our sources, however, are problematic and we must tread warily if we are to gain a full and accurate picture. One obvious approach is through the Parliamentary Roll of Arms, which gives lists of knights county by county. As Nigel Saul pointed out in his study of Gloucestershire, however, these lists are not entirely accurate. They include men who seem to have had no discernible connection with the county to which they were assigned, which strongly suggests that they were compiled by heralds, centrally, rather than through county returns.[14] Some knights appear to have been placed in a particular county through the coincidence of surnames, through similarity in arms or through forms of personal association. Nevertheless, the majority of the knights clearly do belong to the county in question, making the lists a useful starting point for the present purpose. For ease I will concentrate on one of the counties with which we are already acquainted. Under Warwickshire the roll lists thirty-one knights, with their arms blazoned. Of these, however, four are later additions.[15] Leaving these out of account, we have twenty-seven named knights. If we take the key roles of tax assessor and collector, commissioner of array and member of the peace commission as well as knights of the shire

---

[12] Harding, *England in the Thirteenth Century*, p. 219.

[13] In the study that follows I have made extensive use not only of Palgrave's *Parliamentary Writs* and other printed sources but also of the list holders of commissions and major offices for the counties of England compiled by Dr Richard Gorski. I am most grateful to Dr Gorski for giving me access to this material and for allowing the Warwickshire section to be reproduced as Appendix V to this study.

[14] Saul, *Knights and Esquires*, p. 30.

[15] The Warwickshire list is accessible in *Parliamentary Writs*, ed. Palgrave, vol. I, p. 418, drawn, accurately, from BL MS Cotton Caligula A.XVIII. The name of Richard de Limesy is interlined in the text in bolder ink, while three others – Thomas de Chiritone, Robert de Arden and Simon de Bereford – are added, again in a different ink, below the list.

elected to parliament, we find that seventeen out of the twenty-seven immediately figure: viz. John de Bishopton, William de Castello, George de Charnels, John de Clinton of Coleshill, John de Clinton of Maxstoke, Henry de Erdington, Thomas de Garshale, John de Ladbroke, Peter de Limesy, Simon de Mancetter, John Peche, John Percival de Somery, Ralf de Shirley, Richard de Turville, Robert de Verdon, Richard de Whitacre and Peter de Wolverton.[16]

This suggests a very high participation rate – 63 per cent in fact – among the county knights. Rather than accept this figure at face value, however, we should examine the remaining ten knights. The presence of some of them seems to be explained by anomalies in the roll. John de Charnels, for example, is placed next to George de Charnels. However, John's arms are wholly distinct from those of the Warwickshire family of that name who bore *azure, a cross engrailed or*. A John de Charnels was a tax assessor and MP for Nottinghamshire in 1313 and 1315 respectively.[17] His appearance at this point in the roll may be due to the association of the names by the compiler and hence a quirk of the roll. The roll gives a third John de Clinton in addition to the related Johns of Maxstoke and Coleshill. The sources appointing officials frequently, but not invariably, distinguish between the latter two. Where there is no indication, therefore, the man being commissioned could be either of these or, indeed, this third John. However, his Warwickshire interest is obscure. Once again, his arms bear no relation to the several branches of the great Clinton clan, suggesting that he was not related to them.[18] Roger Basset, on the other hand, is revealed by his arms – *or, three piles sable, with a quarter ermine* – as a member of the Bassets of Drayton Basset, whose head, Ralf, appears in the roll among the bannerets. The

[16] This is assuming that we are not crossing generations. In the case of John Peche, for example, it is not wholly clear whether the roll concerns John I or John II. A John figures prominently in commissions from 1317. In all probability he is John II and the John of the Parliamentary Roll. John I occurs as early as 1276 and appears to have been a knight (Moor, *Knights of Edward I*, vol. IV, pp. 25–6). Dugdale (*Antiquities of Warwickshire*, vol. II, pp. 954–5) conflates John I and John II but shows in fact that the former was a justice of gaol delivery 53 Henry III – 9 Edward I. The Boroughbridge Roll has two men of this name, father and son, the former being a banneret and almost certainly the John of the Parliamentary Roll. His son is shown bearing the same arms with a label. This John did not succeed to the family estates, however, John II being followed by his nephew, John III.

[17] He held £20 land in Derbyshire and Nottinghamshire in 1308 and had served in the Falkirk campaign of 1298 (Moor, *Knights of Edward I*, vol. I, p. 295, and *Aspilogia III*, ed. Brault, vol. II, p. 99).

[18] The Clintons of Maxstoke and Coleshill were descendants of Thomas de Clinton and bore variants of his arms, viz. *argent on a chief azure two mullets or* and *argent on a chief two fleurs de lis or* respectively. The third John bore *paly or and azure, a quarter ermine*. Moor suggests that he was John de Clinton of Baddesley Ensor, yet another branch of the family. The contemporary head of this family was James, who was succeeded by his son Thomas. A John de Clinton was shown as lord of Baddesley in 1316, but this is likely to have been John de Clinton of Coleshill (*VCH Warwickshire*, vol. IV, p. 16). James de Clinton sealed his documents with another variant of the family arms, showing on a chief two mullets pierced. (See below, ch. 9, p. 232.)

latter bore *or, three piles gules, with a quarter ermine.*[19] Roger is placed first in the Warwickshire section of the roll, immediately after the obscure John de Clinton. They bore closely related arms, John's being *or, three piles azure, with a quarter ermine.* Perhaps both men were closely associated with Ralf Basset, by retinue or affinity? What property, if any, Roger had in the county is unclear.

There are other cases, too, where a knight's stake in the county is tenuous. John de Grandone was probably related to the north Warwickshire family of that name, lords of Grendon. The head of the family was Ralf, who figures in the roll in the preliminary list of bannerets. Dugdale gives a pedigree showing a John de Grendon, an uncle of Ralf, who occurs in 55 Henry III.[20] However, the John of the roll bears entirely different arms (*vairy argent and sable, a baston or*) from those of the banneret (*argent, two chevrons gules*), while Robert de Grendon, Ralf's son, appears under Leicestershire bearing a label of vair. John was probably the man who held Grendon in Devon in 1288 and who had served with Edmund de Stafford in Flanders in 1297–8. He acquired a life grant of rent at Tysoe in Warwickskhire from the latter in 1307.[21] It seems that he bore the arms differenced of two successive lords with whom he campaigned, one being Stafford (as given in the Parliamentary Roll), and the other being Ward.[22] One might have wondered at the relationship between Nicholas de Turville and Richard de Turville, who follow each other in the roll, were it not for the fact that their arms are linked. Richard bore *gules, three chevrons vair*, Nicholas *gules, two chevrons vair.* Richard, who was lord of Wolston, was a Warwickshire coroner and MP. He was dead by 1316 when a Robert de Turville was the new lord of Wolston. A Nicholas de Turville had held at Burton Hastings in 1269 and the heir of Nicholas is mentioned there in 1348. Another Nicholas held at Pailton and Harborough in 1297 and may have been the man returned by the sheriff as a Warwickshire knight in 1324. He was undoubtedly the same Nicholas de Turville who was MP and tax assessor for Buckinghamshire and who had substantial properties both there and in Northamptonshire. His Warwickshire interests seem to have been comparatively minor and his activities in office reflect his greater interests elsewhere.[23] The appearance of William and Thomas le Blount under Warwickshire is more curious. Their arms do not suggest a relationship between them and they seem to have had little material interest in Warwickshire. In 1324 William was returned as a knight by the sheriffs of Worcestershire, Leicestershire and Rutland. He had strong property interests in

---

[19] Richard Basset of Weldon appears, as one would expect, under Northamptonshire and Rutland. He bore *palee de or and gules* [i.e. *or, 3 palets gules*], *a bordure azure with a bezant or.* The Bassets of Sapcote seem not to figure. There are also two Bassets given under Gloucestershire, with a William Basset figuring among the afterthoughts. *Parliamentary Writs*, ed. Palgrave, show a Roger Basset active in Somerset and Dorset during the reign of Edward I.

[20] Dugdale, *Antiquities of Warwickshire*, vol. II, p. 1101.

[21] See Moor, *Knights of Edward I*, vol. II, pp. 141–2.   [22] See above, p. 143.

[23] *Cal. Inq. Post Mortem*, vol. III, pp. 307, 309–10; Moor, *Knights of Edward I*, vol. V, p. 60.

the latter county for which he was MP, keeper of the peace and commissioner of array. In Warwickshire he held property amounting to a fifth of a knight's fee at Willoughby.[24] William le Blount and his brother Thomas had fought in the Falkirk campaign of 1298, though whether this was the Thomas of the Parliamentary Roll is far from clear.[25] A more prominent Thomas le Blount had Worcestershire and Gloucestershire interests. He was keeper of the peace for Worcestershire in 1322, and was probably the same Thomas le Blound who was steward of Edward II's household and who broke his staff in token of the king's abdication in 1327.[26]

A curious case is that of Richard de Amundeville. His arms fit those of the lord of Berkswell who in 1277 had sold out to the earl of Warwick in return for a life tenancy, both there and at Brailes. In a further agreement in 1297 he had given up the manor in return for £100 a year for life from properties in Worcestershire.[27] It seems unlikely that he was still alive at the time of the Parliamentary Roll of Arms. However, a father and son of that name seem to have been living in 1322 for a Richard de Mundeville is recorded on the Boroughbridge Roll bearing the arms of the Warwickshire family with a label gules. There was also a Richard who was MP for Suffolk in 1318 and 1319. All in all, however, it seems unlikely that the Richard de Amundeville of the Parliamentary Roll of Arms was holding any substantial Warwickshire interest. He would appear to have been assigned to the county either through family history or through an association with the earl of Warwick.

So far, then, our problem cases are either relatives of Warwickshire landholders, with little direct stake in Warwickshire themselves, or men with stronger connections elsewhere, a fact mirrored in their office holding activities. This leaves us with Nicholas de Eton and Edmund de Langley, both of whom may be instructive in other ways. Nicholas had purchased the manor of Ratley from the heavily indebted Thomas de Arden, head of the eldest line of one of the oldest landholding families in the county. His lack of involvement in local office may well reflect the way in which he was perceived as a newcomer, even as an interloper. He may be contrasted with his son, Nicholas de Eton the younger, who was to function as a commissioner of array in 1325. Edmund de Langley, lord of Shortley and Atherstone, was a grandson of the forest justice, Geoffrey de Langley. And yet he seems to have played no part in local office. In this respect he provides a strong contrast with his cousin, John de Langley, who was extremely active in both Warwickshire and Gloucestershire. The explanation is probably more to do with age than temperament. Not only was Edmund

---

[24] *VCH Warwickshire*, vol. VI, p. 263.   [25] *Aspilogia III*, ed. Brault, vol. II, p. 57.

[26] *VCH Warwickshire*, vol. II, p. 435. A Thomas le Blount held a half fee at Barcheston in right of his wife in 1325 (*ibid.*, vol. V, p. 5). The entry in Moor, *Knights of Edward I*, vol. I, p. 102, runs together several widely dispersed occurrences of the name.

[27] *VCH Warwickshire*, vol. IV, p. 29.

younger than his cousin, but he also predeceased him. In fact, he barely reached the age of forty, and was therefore hardly into the stage of life when men were expected to play a stronger role in the community.[28] It is also possible that he did not enjoy good health in his last years. In their various ways, then, these exceptions tend to prove the rule. The Parliamentary Roll of Arms, despite its obvious imperfections as a source, indicates that the participation rate in local office among knights was already very high at the beginning of the reign of Edward II. If we add to our seventeen the five knights who held office in other counties we reach a figure of 81 per cent. If we confine ourselves to the heads of Warwickshire families, the percentage is even higher.[29]

A clearer picture still can be gained from three sources spanning the period 1324–32. It is worth subjecting these, too, to detailed analysis. The first is the list of knights and men-at-arms in the county which the sheriff of Warwickshire, along with all the others, was asked to supply for the Great Council which was due to take place in May 1324. The central concern here was military, and the lists that survive are essentially as the sheriffs returned them. Thus there is no reorganisation or rationalisation such as the compiler of the Parliamentary Roll of Arms had attempted. The same men were returned from several counties. Identification, and in particular the separation of men of the same name, is sometimes difficult. Moreover, the sheriffs appear to have returned the names of minor barons as well as mere knights. Or, to put it in military terms, they included the names of bannerets as well as bachelors. The military purpose of the exercise also caused the names of non-knightly men-at-arms to be returned. Fortunately, the sheriffs kept the lists of knights and men-at-arms separate. The names of forty-two knights were returned for Warwickshire.

Despite the overarching military purpose of the exercise, it is striking how many of the men returned were also prominent as assessors of taxation, as members of the peace commission, as MPs, and indeed as sheriffs, as well as commissioners of array. In many cases they held multiple offices, although some (shown in brackets after their name) held only one. Those who performed these functions either for Warwickshire alone or for Warwickshire as well as one or more contiguous counties are as follows:

---

[28] See P.R. Coss, *The Langley Family and its Cartulary: A Study in Late Medieval Gentry*, Dugdale Society Occasional Paper 22 (Oxford, 1974), p. 5.

[29] The four additions to the roll do not greatly alter the picture. Richard de Limesy was related to Peter de Limesy. He bore the family arms of *gules, an eagle or*, but with *a baston of Montfort*.

Robert de Arden was the head of the branch of the Arden family whose main seat was at Hanwell in Oxfordshire. Although he had Warwickshire interests, Robert was more active in that county and in Northamptonshire. Simon de Bereford, to judge from his arms, belongs to the Warwickshire Berefords, the family of the chief justice of the court of common pleas, Sir William de Bereford. His own interests were centred on Lincolnshire, for which county he was MP in 1320 (Moor, *Knights of Edward I*, vol. I, pp. 11–12). For the judge and his family see *The Earliest English Law Reports*, ed. Brand, vol. II, pp. viii–xxi. Thomas de Chiritone is obscure. He may have come from Weston-by-Cherington where a Walter de Chiritone subsequently held a life interest from the Segraves (*VCH Warwickshire*, vol. V, p. 54).

Roger de Aylesbury
Ralf Basset of Drayton[30]
William de Birmingham
Ralf le Butler (peace commission – Staffordshire)[31]
John de Clinton of Maxstoke
Henry de Erdington
Nicholas de Eton (arrayer)[32]
Ralf de Grendon (arrayer)
John de Hastang
Richard de Hastang
Thomas de Hastang (arrayer)[33]
Richard de Herthill
John de Langley
William de Lucy
John Murdak
John Peche
John Percival de Somery (MP)
Thomas de Pipe
Ralf de Shirley
Robert de Verdon

Some twenty in all. In addition, however, perhaps as many as eleven others held office not in Warwickshire but in one or more counties where their interests were stronger, viz.:

William Botriaux (Cornwall)
Philip de Chetwind (arrayer – Staffordshire)
Alexander de Freville (Worcestershire)
John Gobaud (Lincolnshire)[34]
Philip de Hartshill (Buckinghamshire)
Hugh de Meynill (Derbyshire)
John de Mohun (Somerset)
John de Sudley (MP – Gloucestershire)

[30] Assuming that he is the Ralf Basset in question. He is designated 'of Drayton' in the peace commission for Warwickshire in 1328. A Ralf Basset figured in the peace commission for Staffordshire, and for Warwickshire and Worcestershire. He was an arrayer for Warwickshire, Staffordshire and Leicestershire. Ralf Basset of Weldon functioned in Northamptonshire and Rutland. Ralf Basset of Sapcote seems to have been dead by this date.
[31] This is probably Ralf le Butler of Wem. Ralf was MP for Warwickshire in 1309 and 1324, and on the peace commission for Staffordshire in 1320.
[32] Assuming that the 1324 knight is Nicholas de Eton junior, who was a commissioner of array in the following year, rather than his non-participating father.
[33] The forename is lost, but it seems almost certain that the third de Hastang is he.
[34] Assuming this is the John Gobaud who had functioned in Lincolnshire back in 1307 and 1309. On the other hand, the sheriff of Lincolnshire did not return him in 1324. He held an estate at Saltley, Warwickshire, in 1332.

Nicholas de Turville (Buckinghamshire)
John de Twyford (Derbyshire)
William la Zouche of Harringworth (Northamptonshire and Rutland)[35]

Thus, *in toto*, around thirty-one knights – that is, 74 per cent – can be shown to have been involved in major local office. A few – Ralf de Grendon, Thomas de Hastang, Philip de Chetwind, Nicholas de Eton – come across as essentially military figures, summoned for example to the Scottish wars, but they, too, were drawn in as commissioners of array.

Once again, there are names – in this case eleven – that are more problematic. Identification is difficult in the case of William le Butler. He could be William le Butler of Wem, who functioned in Shropshire and Staffordshire. More probably, he is William le Butler of Warrington whose family had long held an estate at Exhall, north of Coventry. He seems to have held no office in Warwickshire and his major interests were much further north. William de Grendon may be another member of the eponymous family of Grendon, but his independent interest is obscure.[36] Robert Marmion was probably the illegitimate son of Philip Marmion of Tamworth whose death in 1291 had brought his line to an end. By marriage Robert had gained two small manors, at Perry Croft and Glascote. It is possible that the role of these two men was military rather than anything else. This was certainly true of that great fourteenth-century success story William de Clinton. William, who later became earl of Huntingdon, was the younger brother of John de Clinton of Maxstoke. John de Napton appears to have been the younger brother of Robert de Napton, who had certainly held local office. John may have been a knight of the earl of Warwick. John de Somerville is presumably the man who held a half fee of the earl of Warwick at Birdingbury in 1316. He may well be the same man who had been MP as long ago as 1295 and tax assessor in 1295 and 1301. If so, he should be added to the twenty Warwickshire office-holders named above.[37] John de Oddingseles, lord of Long Itchington, on the other hand, seems to have been genuinely non-participatory in these major offices, and the same appears to have been true of Henry de Ladbroke, Guy de Mancetter[38] and Philip le Wolf. Most of these, however,

---

[35] Assuming that Zouche of Harringworth, with a Warwickshire estate at Weston in Arden (near Bulkington), is the man in question. There was at least one other William la Zouche, viz. William la Zouche of Ashby. He functioned in Rutland and Buckinghamshire.

[36] In 1306 Sir William de Grendon had been granted the marriage of Beatrice, widow of Roger de Clavering, should she be willing to marry him of her own free will and on condition that she stand trial for homicide should she be charged (Moor, *Knights of Edward I*, vol. II, p. 143). The Claverings held Aynho, Northamptonshire, as well as land in East Anglia.

[37] He may have been related to the Somervilles who held a manor at Stockton (*VCH Warwickshire*, vol. VI, p. 226), and to Philip de Somerville of Alrewas and Wichnir, Staffordshire, who was very active on Staffordshire commissions.

[38] Presuming we are dealing with him and not his father Simon. The forename is missing. Guy was definitely lord by 1327.

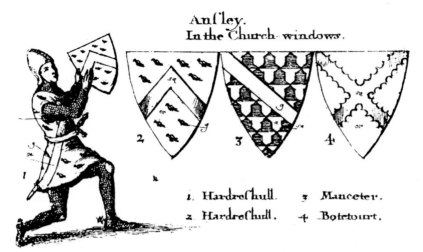

2. Ansley: lost early fourteenth-century glass showing the arms of Hartshill and Mancetter, from Dugdale's *Antiquities of Warwickshire*. (Photograph by John Morgan, Cardiff University)

were active in other spheres. John de Oddingseles and Philip le Wolf had both been summoned for service against the Scots, while Guy de Mancetter received protection going overseas in the retinue of John de Hastings in 1320 and 1324.[39] In 1324–5, moreover, Guy was in Aquitaine, serving in the retinue of Sir John de Hartshill (see Fig. 2). On 2 August 1324 he had his warhorse valued at £12, as did four of Hartshill's esquires. He was still in Aquitaine with two of those esquires on 9 November 1325.[40] It is the length of his absence from England which is striking. If this was mirrored at other times in his career it would totally explain his lack of commissions. It is possible to detect in the 1324 lists and in the Parliamentary Roll of Arms, then, the persistence of a militaristic and retinue-centred aristocratic culture which tended to eschew more mundane matters. It is undoubtedly true that retinues and military activities could enhance the social prospects and improve the lifestyle of less well-endowed younger sons and members of collateral branches of noble families, and indeed that some heads of landowning families were temperamentally unsuited to the role of tax collector. Men of this caste of mind no doubt preferred the keeping of castles to the delivering of gaols. None the less, many of them were drawn into the frame as commissioners of array. All in all it is remarkable that sources designed for heraldic or military purposes should show such a heavy involvement of early fourteenth-century knights in parliamentary representation and in royal commissions.

[39] Moor, *Knights of Edward I*, vol. III, pp. 60–1, 102, 280–1.
[40] PRO E101/16/38 m. 1d and BL Add MS 7967, fo. 33r. I am most grateful to Dr Andrew Ayton for these references and for drawing my attention to their significance.

And so we come to the Subsidy Rolls of 1327 and 1332, which will bring us even closer to the landholding and commission-holding gentry of Warwickshire.[41] Unfortunately, these sources have their problems too. For one thing they are not thorough in their use of designations. The same man appears as *dominus*, that is 'sir', under one entry and not under another. Clearly, knights may be present without the designation. Secondly, 'sir' may occasionally refer to a cleric. The subsidy roll of 1327 lists forty-two men designated 'dominus'. However, two of these are almost certainly clerics.[42] Clumsy expression renders the knighthood of one lay lord, William de Waver, uncertain and he has not been included in the analysis here.[43] We have, therefore, a total of thirty-nine named knights who contributed to the subsidy of 1327. However, this in itself produces a false picture. No less than nine of the knights who were returned by the sheriff in 1324 appear in the 1327 subsidy without designation.[44] Moreover, Sir John de Bishopton, as one of the assessors, did not appear in the body of the account.[45] Three others from the 1324 list (where they were designated knights) – Ralf Basset of Drayton, Henry de Erdington and William de Clinton – appear again, but undesignated, in the 1332 subsidy.[46] Coming from the other direction the only man designated a knight in 1332 who was present without

---

[41] The details that follow are taken from *The Lay Subsidy Roll for 1327*, Supplement to the Transactions of the Midland Record Society 6 (1902), and from *The Lay Subsidy Roll for Warwickshire of 6 Edward III (1332)*, ed. W.F. Carter, Dugdale Society Main Series 6 (London, 1926).

[42] These are John de Heth who pays as much as 6s. 8d. and follows the lord of the manor, Adam de Herthill at Baginton, and a Robert Gregory who pays 2s. at Hodnell where Richard Simound is given as lord. In the 1332 subsidy Sir Robert Gregory figures again at Hodnell, while there is now a Sir Richard the Chaplain at Baginton.

[43] The entry for each vill begins with its lord, designated *D'*, for *Domino*. Should he carry a title he is given *D' domino* [i.e. 'from Sir'] and his name, or *D' domina* in the case of the few ladies designated. At Cesters Over, William de Waver was given as *D' Willelmo domino Wave(re)*, i.e. *William lord of Waver*. He was probably not a knight. I have also ignored *D' domino de Haseleye*. Haseley was a manor of the earl of Warwick. On the other hand I have included Nicholas Peche who is rendered simply *Domino Nicholao Peche*. Although the first *D'* has been omitted, it seems that he is being called Sir Nicholas. It is, however, just possible that he was not yet knighted. But he was holding Honiley in his own right and had been since his father, who was still living in 1327, had granted it to him back in 1318–19.

[44] They are: William de Birmingham, Nicholas de Eton, Ralf de Shirley, John de Twyford, Philip le Wolf, John Percival, John de Hastang, John de Sudeley and John de Mohun.

[45] The other assessor was Robert du Val, who may also have been a knight. There is the additional problem of overlapping generations. Robert du Val was replaced as coroner in 1321, on the grounds that he was occupied in the service of various lords and, therefore, not continuously resident in the county (*Cal. Close Rolls, 1318–23*, p. 288). In 1322 Robert du Val, senior and junior, were in the service of Peter de Montfort. (See Moor, *Knights of Edward I*, vol. V, p. 86, and *VCH Warwickshire*, vol. IV, p. 250.) In 1325 one or other of these was a keeper of the peace. Although Robert du Val the taxer may well have been a knight, it seems safer to exclude him from the analysis.

[46] Ralf Basset of Draycote had life-tenure of the manor of Nether Whitacre. William de Clinton presumably already drew an income from the family estates before 1332. In that year he was holding the manors once of Thomas le Blount.

designation in 1327 was Henry Hillary. Given that he had already functioned as a commissioner of array, it seems fairly certain that he was already a knight in 1327. Adding these names to the thirty-nine and omitting the magnate Roger Mortimer, who was holding the estates of the young earl of Warwick, we have a total of fifty-two knights who are recorded as having a stake in Warwickshire in the year 1327. It is unlikely that many knights with an interest in the county have slipped through the net.

Of these fifty-two, twenty-nine knights, well over a half, held major office in Warwickshire alone or in Warwickshire and one or more contiguous counties:

Roger de Aylesbury
Thomas de Astley
Ralf Basset of Drayton
Edmund de Bereford[47]
William de Birmingham
John de Bishopton
Robert Burdet
John de Clinton (of Maxstoke)
Henry de Erdington
Nicholas de Eton
Ralf de Grendon (arrayer)
John de Hartshill (arrayer)
John de Hastang
Thomas de Hastang
Henry Hillary (arrayer)
William de Lucy
Peter de Montfort
John Murdak
Robert de Napton[48]
John Peche
Nicholas Peche[49]
John Percival
Thomas Pipe
John Ryvel

---

[47] Edmund was appointed to the peace commission and the commission of array for Warwickshire, Worcestershire and Oxfordshire in 1338 and on the commission of array for Oxfordshire alone in 1339.

[48] If this is the Robert de Napton who succeeded his father, Adam, at the age of twenty-two in 1292 he must have been sixty-two in 1332. He was said to have married Lucy, a daughter of Guy, earl of Warwick. He last figures in office, as a taxer, in 1319. Their son Adam and his wife made a settlement of the manor of Napton in 1348. Dugdale and the *VCH* give no other Robert, although it is possible that there is an intervening generation involved here.

[49] See above, note 43. Nicholas was arrayer in 1338 and taxer in 1348.

John de Segrave[50]
Ralf de Shirley
Robert de Verdon[51]
Thomas West (MP)
Richard de Whitacre

In addition, perhaps as many as fourteen functioned in other counties:

Thomas le Blount (Peace Commission – Worcestershire)[52]
John le Butler (MP – Gloucestershire)[53]
William le Butler of Warrington (Lancashire)
William le Butler of Wem (Shropshire and Staffordshire)
Roger Corbet (Shropshire and Staffordshire)[54]
John Gobaud (Lincolnshire)[55]
Hugh de Meynill (Derbyshire)
John de Mohun (Somerset)
John de Sudley (Gloucestershire)
Nicholas Trimenel (MP – Buckinghamshire)[56]
John Trussell (Peace Commission – Staffordshire)[57]
John de Twyford (Derbyshire)
William de Whittington (Gloucestershire)
William la Zouche of Harringworth (Northamptonshire and Rutland)

Thus far we have accounted for forty-three knights (twenty-nine plus fourteen), out of the fifty-two revealed as stakeholders in 1327, i.e. 83 per cent. This leaves us with just nine names. William de Clinton, soon to become earl

---

[50] This is probably John de Segrave of Caludon rather than his kinsman, John de Segrave of Folkestone, Kent, who held the manor of Weston by Cherington but whose interests remained in Kent.

[51] Robert was MP for the last time for Warwickshire in 1313 and last raised troops, in Buckinghamshire, in 1322. He was taxed at Bourton on Dunsmore in 1327 and was gone by 1332.

[52] Thomas le Blount functioned as a royal justice across several midland counties.

[53] John seems to have been a scion of the Butlers of Wem, since he appears at Middleton. He is probably identical with the John le Botiler of Lanulty, MP for Gloucestershire in 1323, 1332 and 1339.

[54] This is either Roger Corbet of Caus or Roger Corbet of Leigh.

[55] Sir John Gobaud had acquired the manor of Saltley with Anabel, daughter of Ranulf de Rokeby. He seems to have had little real interest in Warwickshire. In 1333 he and his wife leased their Warwickshire manor. The Gobauds were a Lincolnshire family and were active there. See *VCH Warwickshire*, vol. VII, p. 65; Moor, *Knights of Edward I*, vol. II, p. 122; *Aspilogia III*, ed. Brault, vol. II, p. 196.

[56] Nicholas Trimenel had been MP for Buckinghamshire in 1307 and had been summoned from there for military service in 1322. His main interests were in that county and in Oxfordshire. He held a manor at Moreton Morrell in Warwickshire, where he was succeeded by his son John. The latter was arrayer for Warwickshire in 1337 and 1338 (*VCH Warwickshire*, vol. V, p. 119).

[57] John was holding Billesley, the family's chief seat before they acquired the estates of the Pantulfs of Cublesdon in Staffordshire and elsewhere. He may be identical with the John Trussell of Thorpe Malsor who was very active in Northamptonshire.

of Huntingdon, was clearly a special case. William de Herle was a royal justice active in the midlands. He inherited Caldecote from his father but purchased a second Warwickshire manor, Burton Hastings, in 1316.[58] John Trillowe was another royal justice active in the midlands. In 1327 he was holding a manor at Haselor in right of his wife, Katherine Lyvet, a tenure that was short-lived in that she died without issue before 1332.[59] Sir William Vaugham is rather obscure. He seems to have had only a passing interest in the county. In 1327 he was holding the manor of Langley in Claverdon which had only recently left the hands of Henry de Ladbroke. By 1332 it belonged to Richard de Cloddeshale.[60] The remaining five knights appear to have been genuinely inactive members of Warwickshire's landowning class. Guy de Beauchamp belonged to the collateral branch of the Beauchamps which held a manor at Alcester. He was active as keeper of various castles during the years 1318–22 and was commissioner of array in north Wales.[61] He seems another of these essentially military figures whom we have encountered before. He was not, it seems, active in Warwickshire. The others we are already aquainted with. They are Henry de Ladbroke, Guy de Mancetter, John de Oddingseles and Philip le Wolf. In Henry's case the chief factor in his lack of involvement may once again have been age. He had succeeded his father by 1316 and was lord of Ladbroke in 1327. However, he appears to have been dead by 1332. The important point is that by this date we find ourselves seeking explanations not for *involvement* in local commissions but for *the lack of it.*

The developments which took place during the later years of Edward I, then, brought increasing numbers of county knights into major offices and commissions. If it can be argued that any monarch was 'the midwife' of the English gentry then surely it was not Henry II but Edward I? An argument along these lines, however, would be one dimensional, the product of a top-down approach to history. Status was not so much conferred by the receipt of royal commissions as confirmed; the prestige conveyed by office was incremental. To understand the emergence of the gentry correctly we must examine matters from the point of view of the landowners themselves. As we have seen, there are good reasons why local landowners should wish to participate in local office and, most particularly, in local justice. 'A knight, God protect me, will not rise to great heights if he enquires of the value of corn', said the author of a manual of chivalry in the early thirteenth century.[62] Such sentiments may have been fine on an ideological level, but it is unlikely in practice that many

---

[58] *VCH Warwickshire*, vol. IV, p. 40 and vol. VI, p. 57.   [59] *VCH Warwickshire*, vol. III, p. 111.
[60] *VCH Warwickshire*, vol. III, p. 72.   [61] Moor, *Knights of Edward I*, vol. I, p. 70.
[62] The Romance of the Wings (*Le Roman des Eles*), written by Raoul de Hodenc *c.*1210. The quotation is from Richard W. Kaeuper, *Violence and Chivalry in Medieval Europe* (Oxford, 1999), p. 274. For the text see *Raoul de Hodenc, Le Roman des Eles: The Anonymous 'Ordene de chevalrie'*, ed. K. Busby (Amsterdam, 1983).

knighted landowners of Edwardian England would have agreed. No landowner could afford to neglect his material base. Without his estates he and his family were nothing. The importance of estate management – and in some respects its precarious nature – are indicated, *inter alia*, by Walter of Henley's famous *Husbandry*, which we know circulated among landowners. Much could be left to subordinate officials, but those officials had always to be watched. Estates had also to be looked after in a legal sense. Over and above all of this, lords needed the co-operation of their tenants. A sensible lord neglected neither neighbourhood nor parish. He required both local prestige and a degree of social control of the populace. This is why the exercise of local office, especially judicial office, was so important.

The gentry undoubtedly came to see themselves not so much as officials of the crown – commissioned for this or that purpose – but as essential partners in government. This growing sense of partnership is most obvious when we look at the history of parliament. As is well known, a sea change occurred during the second half of Edward II's reign, when the Commons first became a serious force within English politics. Now, and for long after, it was the shire representatives who took the lead in opinion-formation. The immediate explanation for this change lies in the political circumstances of the reign, but there were other factors at work. One was the number of high-profile roles being undertaken by the knights. Another was the re-election of a heavy core of men to successive parliaments. This allowed for continuity in the opinions voiced, and encouraged the development of an *esprit de corps*.[63] During the 1320s and 1330s we begin to discern the formulation of Commons policy.[64] Their views may not have been wholly consistent – on questions of law and order for example – but they do appear to have been formed independently of both the crown and the magnates, the latter being the target of much of the Commons' criticism. From the middle years of Edward II's reign there was a considerable expansion in the number of petitions coming not from individuals but from the communities represented in the Commons. In 1327 the 'common petition' put forward in the name of the whole Commons became the basis of a general statute. This was also the year of the first known request from the Commons for the publication of the king's concessions in the provinces, and of the first instance of the circulation of an unofficial version of parliamentary proceedings.[65] As the Commons

---

[63] During the reigns of Edward I and Edward II a little over a third of parliaments had a majority of knights with previous parliamentary experience. Three fifths of Edward III's parliaments had such a majority. It was not a consistent trajectory however. Taking all three reigns, the largest number of returnees was in September 1313, when four out of five shire representatives had sat before. See K.L. Wood-Leigh, 'The Knights' Attendance in the Parliaments of Edward III', *English Historical Review* 47 (1932), pp. 406–7 and Maddicott, 'Parliament and the Constituencies', pp. 75–6.

[64] See, especially, Ormrod, 'Agenda for Legislation', pp. 1–33.

[65] Maddicott, 'Parliament and the Constituencies', pp. 79–87.

became a genuine forum for expressing opinion the two-way relationship between assembly and constituency came to have real meaning. Consequently, with the opening of the Hundred Years War and the return of heavy war finance, the county representatives were in a position to exert considerable pressure at the centre.[66]

When it came to partnership on the ground, though, the most significant role was that of keeper of the peace. Some seventy years ago Bertha Putnam subjected the transformation of the keeper into the justice of the peace to close scrutiny and her analysis quickly became an orthodoxy which has held sway almost to this day.[67] For Putnam and, so she believed, for contemporaries there was a stark choice to be made between centralised justice, staffed by the professional judges and serjeants of the central courts on the one hand, and devolved justice in the hands of local justices of the peace on the other. Concentrating on statutes and the forms of commissions rather than the personnel, she put great emphasis upon the acquisition (and intermittent loss) by the keepers of the peace of the power to determine indictments which effectively turned them into justices of the peace; all other judicial agencies she saw as competitors. Looked at from a purely legal angle, this was a struggle for jurisdiction over felony and trespass following the demise of the general eyre after 1294. But it was also a power struggle, with the gentry and the Commons on the one side and the crown, magnates and professional lawyers generally on the other. The end result was a victory for devolved justice and for the gentry.

It is a compelling picture. However, the reality was much more complex than Putnam had allowed for. In recent years her analysis has been subjected to considerable revision, primarily by Anthony Musson, and this revision must be taken on board.[68] For him the first half of the fourteenth century was

---

[66] The literature on parliament is of course considerable. For a broad survey of the relations between the crown and parliament see G.L. Harriss, *King, Parliament and Public Finance in Medieval England to 1369* (Oxford, 1975). See also the same author's 'The Formation of Parliament, 1272–1377', in Davies and Denton (eds.), *English Parliament*, pp. 29–60 and M. Prestwich, 'Parliament and the Community of the Realm in Fourteenth Century England', in A. Cosgrove and J.I. McGuire (eds.), *Parliament and Community* (Belfast, 1983), pp. 5–24. For recent discussions of the role of the representatives in the parliaments of Edward III see W.M. Ormrod, *The Reign of Edward III: Crown and Political Society in England 1327–1377* (New Haven and London, 1990), esp. pp. 163–9. Ormrod wisely warns against pushing the sense of partnership too far: 'The political negotiation of Edward's middle years may have been a bilateral affair, but it was not a dialogue between equals' (*ibid.*, pp. 201–2).

[67] B.H. Putnam, 'The Transformation of the Keepers of the Peace into the Justices of the Peace, 1327–80', *Transactions of the Royal Historical Society*, 4th series, 12 (1929), pp. 19–48; *Proceedings before the Justices of the Peace in the Fourteenth and Fifteenth Centuries: Edward III to Richard III*, ed. B.H. Putnam, Ames Foundation (London, 1938).

[68] Anthony Musson, *Public Order and Law Enforcement: The Local Administration of Criminal Justice, 1294–1350* (Woodbridge, 1996), esp. part I: 'The Evolution of the Justice of the Peace'. There is a useful précis of the revisionist position in Anthony Musson and W.M. Ormrod, *The Evolution of English Justice: Law, Politics and Society in the Fourteenth Century* (London, 1999), ch. 3: 'Royal Justice in the Provinces'.

characterised by experiment and improvisation as the central government sought to combat rising lawlessness, and the perception of lawlessness, and to devise an efficient system that would replace the once omnicompetent but unwieldy eyre. Treating the judicial system as a whole, he shows how the several agencies were complementary rather than competitive and that there was much more overlap between them in terms of personnel than Putnam had thought. Thus the acquisition of determining powers by the keepers had been taken out of context and given too much emphasis. Key episodes, moreover, were misunderstood. In 1314, for example, when separate commissioners were appointed to determine the indictments made before the keepers, half of these 'supervisors', as Putnam called them, were already keepers of the peace and hence were precisely determining their own indictments. Similarly in 1326, eighteen of the thirty-seven known 'supervisors' were already keepers.[69] In 1338, moreover, when genuine supervisors *were* appointed, there is little to suggest that they diminished the authority of the keepers, who did, in fact, have power to determine. Indeed, the magnates who were present among the supervisors seem to have been there largely for military reasons, while the overlap in personnel between the commissions was as high as a quarter.[70]

It is important, as Musson and Ormrod stress, not to make too much of a distinction between central and local personnel. The central court lawyers themselves enjoyed local interests and should be considered, in some senses, as belonging to local society. Indeed, the justices of assize were often appointed to circuits where their own property lay. Moreover, distinctions are blurred by the prominence of local men of law, defined (rather widely) by Musson and Ormrod as 'those whose profession was the law or whose involvement in judicial and administrative affairs enabled them to acquire some legal knowhow'.[71] Even when magnates were present on the peace commissions – as they were in the 1330s – they were there, it can be argued, not only as 'representatives of the great men of the realm or as close allies of the king' but as local men of influence in their own right.[72]

Moreover, the judicial role of the local landowners during the early decades of the fourteenth century was by no means confined to the peace commissions. For one thing, they were heavily involved in special commissions of oyer and terminer.[73] These originated, to all intents and purposes, in the years 1275–9 when they were used to relieve the pressure on the royal courts of litigation

---

[69] Musson, *Public Order and Law Enforcement*, pp. 34–9, 44–8. In 1332 when 'keepers of the county' were appointed they seem to have been hardly distinct from the keepers of the peace: 'Ninety-nine out of the 140 men commissioned as keepers of the peace in February 1332 were then assigned a month later as keepers of the county' (*ibid.*, p. 64).

[70] *Ibid.*, pp. 70–3.   [71] Musson and Ormrod, *The Evolution of English Law*, pp. 62–3.

[72] *Ibid.*, pp. 55–6.

[73] For what follows see the excellent study by Kaeuper, 'Law and Order in Fourteenth-Century England', pp. 734–84.

resulting from cases of trespass brought by *querela* (plaint or petition). Largely dealing with specific incidents or disputes, they became immensely popular from the later years of Edward I, reaching a peak in the middle years of Edward II and another at the beginning of the reign of Edward III, and tailing off thereafter. Especially popular among knights and other lesser landowners, the commissions were increasingly staffed by them. The proportion of cases tried by the central court professionals, by contrast, declined from 68 per cent in 1275 through 42 per cent in 1300 to 32 per cent in 1316–17.[74] Furthermore, the local men who occasionally exercised powers of determination as justices of the peace also exercised them through other judicial agencies. Despite the Statute of Fines of 1299, which gave the justices of assize the responsibility for delivering the gaols within their circuits, in practice local landowners continued to play a prominent part in gaol delivery and, during the reign of Edward II, local men also infiltrated the assizes.[75] As far as gaol delivery was concerned, a variety of commissions and agencies was in use. Most often they were delivered by justices appointed under special mandate. Sometimes, however, the power was given to the commissions of the peace. Other agencies were also involved. In the 1320s the justices of trailbaston, who were essentially commissioned to deal with violent crime and conspiracies, were given the task. Despite the statutes of 1328 and 1330, which tightened matters in favour of the professionals, local men were still figuring in commissions of gaol delivery during the 1330s. In that decade, however, the judicial role of the county landowners was being increasingly confined to the peace commissions. The power of determining was given to some of these and withheld from others. At this point some form of 'compromise' was required which would accommodate both county landowners and lawyers.

This 'compromise' was found in 1344 when the peace commissions were 'afforced' by the presence of men of law so that they could try the indictments, foreshadowing the *quorum* for felony. From 1351 the assize justices were formally appointed to all the panels within their circuits. Experimentation persisted in the years that followed. In 1362, for instance, the justices were required to sit four times a year, giving rise to the concept of the 'quarter sessions'. Sometimes additional authority was included, sometimes powers were taken away. But by now the fully fledged justices of the peace with power to hear and determine had become a mainstay of the judicial system. Thus: 'The essential change

[74] Kaeuper calculates that in 1275 nine justices were 'drawn from the ranks that provided knights of the shire, commissioners and later justices of the peace', twenty-nine in 1300 and seventy-five (covering 186 cases) in 1316–17 (*ibid.*, p. 753). Special commissions of oyer and terminer became, in fact, an instrument for the waging of gentry feuds.

[75] For a recent discussion of the justices of assize and gaol delivery in this period see Musson, *Public Order and Law Enforcement*, part II, pp. 85–122. The question is made more difficult for the historian in that the assize and gaol delivery commissions, given on the dorse of the Patent Rolls, have not been included in the published calendars for this period.

that occurred during the fourteenth century was the gradual replacement of... periodic provincial visitations with permanent judicial tribunals in the shires, and the resulting creation of a body of king's justices who lived and worked in the localities they served.'[76]

The revisionists have shown that the justice of the peace was the product of a complex evolution. We should be careful not to read England's judicial history backwards and place too much emphasis upon the peace commission in comparison with other agencies before the facts warrant it. But neither should we throw the baby out with the bath water. It is important to remember that experimentation and improvisation did not take place in a social and political vacuum. It may be valid to think in terms of a general response to a high incidence of crime, but people's responses are rarely socially neutral. The gentry had their own interests to pursue and Putnam's analysis was instinctively in tune with these. What they wanted, what they needed, was strong participation in the exercise of common law justice. Membership of the peace commission was not just a matter of ensuring that local society was properly represented in the measures taken by the crown nor of individual status within the broad peer group of the gentry, important though these things were.[77] As we have seen, the exercise of social control over the populace was a matter of vital concern to the gentry. This explains their eagerness to participate both in gaol delivery and in the keepership of the peace. The power to try indictments, through whatever agency it was exercised, was an important ingredient in how the populace perceived them, and indeed in how they perceived themselves. In a very important sense the members of the peace commissions embodied not only their own interests but also the collective interests of the gentry, and their responsibility was analogous to that of the knights of the shire who represented their communities in parliament. The representative role of the MPs grew famously from the middle years of Edward II's reign through to the early years of Edward III. It was reflected in the development of constituency feeling and collective petitions on the one hand and in the articulation of corporate interests and demands by the Commons on the other. At the same time we begin to discern the representative dimension to devolved justice. By the early 1330s a strong link had been forged between the sessions of parliament and the issuing of commissions of the peace, and there is an observable tendency for MPs themselves to serve among the keepers.[78] In 1338 the Commons demanded and formally achieved a say in their nomination. Ten years later they demanded that the members of the peace commission be chosen and sworn in parliament.[79] Even if no clear Commons agenda can be discerned in favour of justices of the peace in the relatively sparse records of the 1320s and 1330s, it was certainly there in the 1340s. Notwithstanding

---

[76] Musson and Ormrod, *The Evolution of English Law*, p. 42.   [77] *Ibid.*, p. 69.
[78] Musson, *Public Order and Law Enforcement*, pp. 60, 81.
[79] See the remarks in Saul, *Knights and Esquires*, pp. 128–35.

the mixed nature of the solution that was finally adopted, in which all interested parties – crown, gentry, magnates, professional lawyers and local men of law – had an input, a high measure of devolution had ultimately been achieved. Permanent judicial authority beyond the manor came to the gentry only with the triumph of the peace commission.[80]

That there was some opposition to the exercise of common law justice by local landowners is also certain, even if such opposition was intermittent. It would be surprising from what we know of the growth of professionalism among the justices and serjeants-at-law of the central courts from the time of Edward I if they had not wished to protect their role and expertise from the relative amateurism of some of their poorly trained counterparts.[81] It is difficult to comprehend the statutes which attempted intermittently to pull common law justice back into the hands of the professionals unless there was a lobby which advocated it. The Statute of Westminster of 1285, for example, officially confined special commissions of oyer and terminer to the central court justices.[82] Likewise the Statute of Fines of 1299 envisaged gaol delivery dominated by the professional justices of assize.[83] Both measures were defeated by manpower needs. The state was unable in practice to do without the services of the local landowners. It may well be the case, as Richard Kaeuper has suggested, that the gentry's constant feuding and the frequent use they made of special commissions of oyer and terminer in furtherance of this made the crown reluctant to entrust too much judicial authority to them.[84] On the other hand special commissions and the exercise of fundamental justice over the populace are very different matters, and it is uncertain that the crown and its advisers would have thought in that way. Perhaps one should think more in terms of a general reluctance to devolve too much power to men who – in comparison with salaried professionals – were more difficult to control. Whatever the case, a preference in favour of the professionals continued. The Statute of Northampton of 1328 confined the assize commissions to the lawyers and by the mid-1330s these were solely staffed by the royal justices and serjeants-at-law.[85] It may well have been the effective elimination of the gentry from the assize and gaol delivery commissions which caused the Commons of the 1340s to concentrate their demands and their rhetoric upon the justices of the peace.[86]

---

[80] Harding, 'Origins and Early History of the Keeper of the Peace', p. 103.
[81] See, principally, Brand, *Origins of the English Legal Profession*.
[82] Kaeuper, 'Special Commissions of Oyer and Terminer', pp. 744, 752.
[83] For the Statute of Fines and its effects see Musson, *Public Order and Law Enforcement*, pp. 96–8.
[84] See Kaeuper, 'Special Commissions of Oyer and Terminer', p. 784, and the same author's *War, Justice and Public Order*, pp. 178–9.
[85] See Musson and Ormrod, *The Evolution of English Law*, p. 58. A further statute of 1340 confined *nisi prius* to the same.
[86] As argued by Musson, *Public Order and Law Enforcement*, p. 82.

What all of this meant in practice, in terms of social power, can be seen in the class-based legislation of the years 1349–51, which was enforced by the justices of the peace.[87] Here we see the full realisation of the gentry's territoriality as it affected subordinate social groups and can take the true measure of what partnership in government might really mean. In the countryside prior to the Black Death, regulation of wages and enforcement of service was very largely a matter for manorial courts.[88] Tenants were by no means always quiescent, however, and landlords encountered resistance.[89] Hence the backing of the royal courts, especially in the matter of jurisdiction over unfree tenants, was a matter of some importance. Free tenants constituted a problem of a different order as this access could not be denied them, even though it could be tempered by the need to comply with village by-laws as well as by disparities in income. The general dislocation and, in particular, the dearth of labourers brought about by the plague tipped the balance – or at least threatened to tip the balance – of social power firmly against the landlord and caused the state to step in immediately to redress the balance. The Ordinance of Labourers of June 1349 forced all the able-bodied below the age of sixty to work and to work at customary wages. Mobility was restricted as lords were given priority over the services of their tenants, free as well as unfree. The Ordinance was reinforced and extended by parliamentary statute in 1351. Wage control became more specific and the provisions for enforcement were tightened. What is particularly significant is that the enforcement was undertaken by the gentry. As R.C. Palmer puts it, 'The enforcement of labor legislation was still primarily local, but local power was now more effectively exercised by lords representing central authority over all available workers instead of by lords exercising their own inherent authority over their unfree tenants.'[90] Nothing demonstrates more clearly than the

---

[87] Between 1352 and 1359 it was enforced under separate commissions by justices of labourers, but the personnel was essentially the same.

[88] See, especially, Elaine Clark, 'Medieval Labor Laws and the English Local Courts', *American Journal of Legal History* 27 (1983), pp. 330–9. See also W.O. Ault, 'Some Early Village By-laws', *English Historical Review* 45 (1930) and 'Open Field Husbandry', *Transactions of the American Philosophical Society*, new series, 55 (1965). These are quoted by Anthony Musson, 'New Labour Laws, New Remedies? Legal Reaction to the Black Death "Crisis"', in N. Saul (ed.), *Fourteenth Century Studies* (Woodbridge, 2000).

[89] See, most especially, R.H. Hilton, 'Peasant Movements in England before 1381', *Econ. Hist. Rev.*, 2nd series, 2 (1949), pp. 117–36.

[90] Palmer, *English Law in the Age of the Black Death*, p. 15. Palmer's thesis, however, is that the Black Death was responsible for a wholesale transformation of English law and of the means of governing the country, producing what he calls 'a government of inherent authority'. 'Governance after the Black Death was qualitatively different, exhibiting a government intent on using the law to control society, to preserve as far as possible the status quo' (*ibid.*, p. 5). In support of this thesis he offers another version of the gentry creation myth. In order to effect these changes the government quite deliberately and self-consciously called upon the local notables, empowering them, making them agents of the state in a way they had never been before, and transforming them into the gentry: 'The "gentry", substantial local people whose

Statute of Labourers and its implementation that the gentry and its partnership in government had come of age.[91]

THE CONTOURS OF A COMMISSION-HOLDING ELITE

The county knights were at the very apex of local society, and even the most casual glance shows that they dominated many local offices and commissions during the first half of the fourteenth century. But the same casual glance shows that they had no stranglehold over office. If we are to understand the emergence of the gentry correctly, and more particularly the role of office holding and justice within that process, then we must look more broadly at the contours of what we might call the commission-holding elite during the period.[92] We need to examine the part played by landowners who were sub-knightly, the sort of men who had for some time helped to keep the less prestigious offices of coroner, sub-escheator and the like afloat. We must also take account of the contributions made by administrators and men of law. Anthony Musson and Mark Ormrod have argued recently that we should see the personnel involved in the exercise of justice in fourteenth-century England less in terms of centre and locality or of amateur and professional and more in terms of the three categories of magnates, gentry and men of law. In doing so they resist what they call the 'conventional practice' of regarding local men of the law as part of the gentry, as this does 'less than credit' to their 'expertise and experience'. This is an interesting and important perspective in understanding 'the development of a county-based judiciary'. It is not, however, the most appropriate perspective when it comes to understanding the evolution of the gentry itself since, as Musson and Ormrod themselves acknowledge, for the most part 'such men came from the lesser aristocracy or (in the case of the practising lawyers) aspired to a place in the county elite'.[93] Nevertheless the role of established landowners, knightly and

position is strongly related to the exercise of state authority, replaces "the knightly classes" as the appropriate, if amorphous, designation of the lower ranks of the upper orders' (*ibid.*, p. 24). For a powerful critique of the Palmer thesis from the standpoint of legal history see Musson, 'New Labour Laws, New Remedies?', pp. 73–88.

[91] The crown supported landlords in other ways too. In 1348 the writ 'exception of villeinage' was reformed to make it easier for lords to combat men they considered their serfs challenging them in court. In 1352 the Commons secured a restriction in the use of the writ 'proof of liberty' by which former villeins could avoid being repossessed. See Ormrod, *The Reign of Edward III*, p. 147. There can be no doubt that the 'upper classes coalesced after the Black Death to preserve as well as they were able their position in traditional society' (Palmer, *English Law in the Age of the Black Death*, p. 13). As he points out, it is surely no accident that in 1350 the crown not only gave the keepers of the peace the power to deal with offences under the Ordinance of Labourers, but at the same time surrendered the power to hear and determine felonies and trespasses, thereby reversing the government's opposition to parliamentary demands for fully fledged justices of the peace (*ibid.*, p. 23).

[92] In what follows I have drawn very extensively on Dr Gorski's list of the holders of commissions and major offices in Warwickshire, 1290–1348 (Appendix V).

[93] *The Evolution of English Law*, pp. 62–3.

sub-knightly, was supplemented by administrators and lawyers, and due weight must be given to these. Just what were the contours of this office-holding elite during these most formative decades of the early fourteenth century?

When we examine the members of the peace commission during the first half of the fourteenth century we see immediately just how far the county knights dominated. The calendared Patent Rolls reveal the names of forty men who were involved in the peace commissions for Warwickshire between 1300 and 1345.[94] They include Thomas de Beauchamp, earl of Warwick, Hugh le Despenser and Chief Justice William de Shareshill who were there as magnates. Of the remaining thirty-seven, no fewer than eighteen have already been revealed by our sources as Warwickshire knights:

Thomas de Astley
Roger de Aylesbury
Ralf Basset of Drayton
Edmund de Bereford
William de Birmingham
John de Bishopton
John de Clinton of Coleshill
John de Clinton of Maxstoke
Henry de Erdington
Thomas de Hastang
John de Ladbroke
William de Lucy
Peter de Montfort
John Peche
John Ryvel
John de Segrave
Robert de Verdon
Richard de Whitacre

To these, however, we can add eleven more knights whom our earlier sources failed to reveal. Nicholas de Astley and John de Cantelupe fell between our 1308 and 1324 sources.[95] William de Careswell, by contrast, who held the Langley

---

[94] Ralf Basset and Ralf Basset of Drayton have been regarded as the same man, as have William de Birmingham and William de Birmingham the elder, John de Clinton and John de Clinton of Coleshill, John Ryvel (*alias* Revel) and John Ryvel of Newbold, William Trussell and William Trussell the elder, Richard de Whitacre and Richard de Whitacre the younger. John de Peyton has been taken as an alternative form of John de Peyto and Robert de Wardon as an alternative form of Robert de Verdon. Less obviously, Robert de Perham and Robert de Knoll have been regarded as the same man.

[95] Nicholas was the uncle and immediate predecessor of Thomas de Astley. He was taken prisoner at Bannockburn (*VCH Warwickshire*, vol. IV, pp. 77, 211; vol. VI, pp. 17, 165). Sir John de Cantelupe was lord of Snitterfield and Wolverton (*VCH Warwickshire*, vol. III, pp. 168, 194).

inheritance in right of his wife, was not a knight until the 1330s.[96] Robert de Herle, similarly, was a knight during the 1330s.[97] He joined the peace commission in 1345.[98] Despite his Warwickshire and family origins, Richard de Edgbaston had been returned by the sheriff as a Leicestershire knight in 1324. William Trussell, a member of a clan with property stretching across several counties including Warwickshire, was returned in 1324 under both Leicestershire and Northamptonshire. Philip de Gayton was primarily a Northamptonshire knight. He was sheriff of Warwickshire and Leicestershire in 1300.[99] Thomas de Chaworth was a knight of Leicestershire and John de Harrington of Leicestershire and Rutland. Their peace commissions covered Leicestershire as well as Warwickshire. John de la Lee was a Shropshire knight.[100] On balance Robert du Val seems to have been a knight at the time of his involvement in the peace commission in 1325, although the evidence is not quite secure. The family were lords of Luddington and of great antiquity. There is a problem here in distinguishing between generations. He was John de Bishopton's co-assessor of the subsidy of 1327 and may well have been the same Robert who had ceased to be coroner on account of other business in 1320. He was not credited with knighthood in the 1332 subsidy, but none the less occurs as knight in a charter of the same year.[101]

This takes us to a total of twenty-nine knights and leaves us with only eight members of the peace commission who were probably not knights. Two of

Dugdale says he was a knight in 9 Edward II and gives his arms as *three leopards heads jessant flower de Lis, or* (*Antiquities of Warwickshire*, pp. 661–2). He was on the peace commission in 1308, 1314 and 1316.

[96] He was holding the manors of Pinley and Milcote in the 1332 subsidy but was not designated knight. The Langley Cartulary suggests that he was not a knight at this point but shows that he was in 1339 (*The Langley Cartulary*, ed. P.R. Coss, Dugdale Society Main Series 32 (Oxford, 1980), no. 515.) He had in fact been knighted by 1338 when he appears as a knight on a horse inventory. He was serving with Hugh le Despenser (PRO E101/35/3 m. 1). I am most grateful to Dr Andrew Ayton for bringing this to my attention. And 1338 was the very year in which he served on a peace commission.

[97] A horse inventory shows that he was a knight by May 1337. He was in Scotland with the earl of Warwick (PRO E101/20/17 m. 7d). Once again I owe this reference to the kindness of Dr Ayton.

[98] Grandson of Robert de Herle who held a manor at Caldecote, Robert was a knight in 1349. He had succeeded his father, William de Herle, in 1347. The latter may have been the justice of that name (*VCH Warwickshire*, vol. IV, pp. 40, 107; vol. VI, pp. 57–8).

[99] Lord of Gayton, he was returned by the sheriff of Northamptonshire as a knight in 1297. He was on the peace commissions of 1300 and 1307. For his Warwickshire interests see *VCH Warwickshire*, vol. III, pp. 66, 118.

[100] He may be identical with the John de Leigh who held a manor at Kingston (*VCH Warwickshire*, vol. V, p. 42), although he was not credited with knighthood in the lay subsidies.

[101] *Langley Cartulary*, ed. Coss, no. 323. Dugdale says he was a knight in 1334 and gives his arms: *a Fesse chequy betwixt 3 Lions rampant* (*Antiquities of Warwickshire*, pp. 703–4). Dugdale considered the Robert du Val who was assessor of the subsidy of 1309 as an earlier man but identical with the coroner. He logs this man also as a knight. Curiously no Robert du Val figures in either the Parliamentary Rolls of Arms or the 1324 lists.

these, John de Peyto the elder and John de Peyto the younger, were father and son. They were drawn from what we might call sub-gentry stock. Successive members of the family had built up a considerable estate at Drayton near Stratford-upon-Avon during the second half of the thirteenth century. They were aided by advantageous marriages. John de Peyto the elder married one of the heiresses of Hugh de Harborough, acquiring estates at Harborough, Pailton and elsewhere.[102] John de Peyto the younger was one of the assessors of the 1332 subsidy and seems to have disposed of even greater resources. He was in receipt of a £30 a year pension from Wolstan de Braunsford, bishop of Worcester, before 1339, in which year he took on a life-long lease of the manor of Stratford-upon-Avon from the bishop at a rent of £60 per annum. In 1349–50 he built a chapel at Sheldon where a priest was to pray for his soul, and for those of his wife Beatrice and his father, John de Peyto the elder.[103] There is no indication that either man was knighted, and although John de Peyto the younger was identified as eligible by the distraint of knighthood in 1334 he still did not become a knight.[104]

John de Merington, who was appointed to the peace commission in 1345, was of merchant stock; or rather, he was a member of one of the greatest mercantile/financier families of fourteenth-century Coventry who had made their fortunes primarily through the export market in wool.[105] The family, including John's father Hugh, had arrived in Coventry during the 1290s and had made the city the centre of their operations for several generations.[106] Meanwhile, in 1321 John de Merington, with his brother Henry and their parents, had taken the lease of Newbold Grange from the monks of Pipewell Abbey. John was the largest taxpayer at Newbold in 1332. In 1360 he had licence for an oratory at his manor of Little Lawford. In short, though the Merington operation remained in Coventry, John had joined the ranks of the county gentry. His son, Thomas, who succeeded him at Little Lawford, was classed as an esquire in the Poll Tax returns of 1379.

---

[102] *VCH Warwickshire*, vol. III, p. 266, and vol. VI, pp. 100, 259, 168, 176.

[103] *VCH Warwickshire*, vol. III, pp. 258–9, and vol. IV, p. 205. John de Peyto took on other leases and received a £40 pension in Haselor (*VCH Warwickshire*, vol. III, p. 111, and vol. IV, pp. 202, 223.). On his death in 1373 he held a manor at Luddington in right of his wife, Beatrice (*VCH Warwickshire*, vol. III, pp. 258–9).

[104] PRO C47/1/13 (Chancery Miscellanea). In the witness list to a charter of 20 April 1340 John de Peyto the elder and John de Peyto the younger appear immediately after four named knights (*Calendar of Ancient Deeds*, vol. V, no. 10711). By contrast, their successor, yet another John, was indeed a knight. He was the nephew of John de Peyto the younger. His father William had married the Langley heiress to Wolfhamcote. John, by marriage to yet another heiress, acquired the manor of Chesterton which was to be the long-term family seat (*VCH Warwickshire*, vol. V, p. 42 and vol. VI, p. 269).

[105] See R.A. Pelham, 'The Early Wool Trade in Warwickshire and the Rise of the Merchant Middle Class', *Transactions of the Birmingham Archaeological Society* 63 (1944).

[106] *The Early Records of Medieval Coventry*, ed. P.R. Coss, British Academy Records of Social and Economic History, new series, 11 (Oxford, 1986), pp. xl, xlii.

Robert de Saddington was a professional lawyer. An attorney as early as 1317, he was a serjeant in the Northamptonshire eyre of 1329–30. He seems to have originated in Saddington in Leicestershire and this dimension explains his membership of the peace commission for Warwickshire and Leicestershire in 1336. Robert went on to greater things. He was later to become chief baron of the Exchequer and ultimately chancellor.[107] He was one of only two or three members of the peace commission who might seriously be considered as local men of law.

John de Heyford and Robert de Stoke are among the professionals whom Robert Palmer identified operating in the Warwickshire county court at the beginning of the fourteenth century.[108] John de Heyford was undoubtedly a pleader, or serjeant, active in the county court. But he was also active in the central courts, acting as attorney in the court of common pleas 165 times between 1288 and 1306 and on ten occasions in the Exchequer of Pleas. He had regular clients in the county, both lay and ecclesiastical.[109] He featured as a justice of gaol delivery for the county between 1312 and 1315.[110] His keepership, in 1332, belongs to a later stage in his life, by which time he was a moderately wealthy man in the county.[111]

Robert de Stoke, on the other hand, does not appear to have been a pleader in the county court.[112] Essentially a professional administrator, he was in the service of the prior of Coventry for an extensive period from the 1280s onwards and was named as his steward in 1293 and 1300. He seems to have remained in this position until about 1310. He came from Stoke near Coventry and by then he had greatly extended his property in the area.[113] Whether he should also be considered a professional lawyer is a matter of some debate. Though he appeared on six occasions as an attorney in the court of common pleas between 1302 and 1305 and was appointed general attorney for two abbots, his work in this respect was not as extensive as that of John de Heyford.[114] He was to feature regularly as a justice of gaol delivery in Edward II's reign, and was

---

[107] For Robert's career see *The Eyre of Northamptonshire 3–4 Edward III*, ed. Sutherland, vol. I, p. lxvii.

[108] R.C. Palmer, 'County Year Book Reports: The Professional Lawyer in the Medieval County Court', *English Historical Review* 91 (1971), pp. 776–801, and Palmer, *County Courts of Medieval England*, ch. 4. All citations here are to the latter.

[109] Palmer, *County Courts of Medieval England*, pp. 102–3.

[110] Musson, *Public Order and Law Enforcement*, p. 161.

[111] He contributed handsomely to the 1327 and 1332 subsidies at Ratley,

[112] Reviewing the evidence Paul Brand finds that of the thirteen or fourteen 'pleaders' identified by Palmer only six can be safely regarded as practising in the court (*Origins of the English Legal Profession*, p. 194).

[113] For Robert's local position and property see Coss, *Lordship, Knighthood and Locality*, pp. 312–14.

[114] Palmer revised his original opinion (of 1971) on Robert of Stoke and in 1982, with more details on his career, classified him as a professional lawyer: 'County Year Book Reports', pp. 793–4; *County Courts of Medieval England*, pp. 109–10.

a justice of assize at Coventry in 1316.[115] By this time, too, he had become involved in peace commissions, and he seems to have been much trusted by the central government.[116] Perhaps we should consider him to have moved on from an administrative to a legal career. At the same time it should be recognised that by the time he was appointed to commissions he was a fairly wealthy and much respected figure in the county.

The qualifications for office, as it were, of the last two members of the peace commission are more difficult to discern. Richard de Stoneleigh was a contributor to the 1332 subsidy at Wormleighton. He acquired further property at Chadsunt, Kineton and Stoneleigh where his purchases caused the abbot of Stoneleigh to take a case against him to Westminster.[117] Ralf de Perham was a member of the peace commission in 1314 and 1329. In 1314 he is found leasing a major part of the manor of Solihull from one of its heiresses for £20 a year, and presented to the living at Sheldon in 1318.[118] At the very end of Edward I's reign he had leased the manor of Knowle from the monks of Westminster, which strongly suggests that he and the equally obscure commissioner in 1331, Ralf de Knoll (i.e. Knowle), were one and the same. It is possible that these two men, Richard de Stoneleigh and Ralf de Perham, also possessed some legal expertise.[119] None the less, the evidence presented indicates that before the 'compromise' of 1344 the peace commission was very heavily the preserve of the county knights and of a few men who could approach them in terms of local prestige.

That the knights played a major part in the special commissions of oyer and terminer is also clear, although here their role was matched by that of the professional lawyers. If we look at the Warwickshire cases between the years 1300 and 1340 we find a heavy preponderance of professional lawyers – central court justices, serjeants-at-law and regular assize justices – on the one hand and established knights on the other. Among the latter are thirty-three knights whom we have already met, together with the two John de Peytos. There are additional knights from other counties, some of whom, like Robert de Arden of Northamptonshire, do have clear Warwickshire interests. We find, for example, Richard de Baskerville (Herefordshire), William de Harcourt, William Motoun, Ralf

[115] Musson, *Public Order and Law Enforcement*, p. 156.
[116] He was included in the 'special' commission of 1314 to determine the indictments of the keepers in Warwickshire and Leicestershire and in the trailbaston commission later in the year. He was appointed keeper in 1318 and 1320. In 1322 he was keeper of the lands and castles of rebels in Warwickshire, Oxfordshire, Bedfordshire and Northamptonshire.
[117] *Warwickshire Feet of Fines*, ed. Stokes and Drucker, vol. II, nos. 1881, 1869, 1901; *The Stoneleigh Leger Book*, ed. R.H. Hilton, Dugdale Society Main Series 25 (Oxford, 1960), pp. 19, 122–3, 152.
[118] *VCH Warwickshire*, vol. IV, pp. 204n, 218.
[119] Richard is found acting as an attorney. See *Feet of Fines Warwickshire*, no. 1700.

de Stanlowe, Hugh de Prestwold (Leicestershire), James de Audley (Staffordshire), John de la Lee (Shropshire) and Miles de Rodborough (Gloucestershire). Perhaps 50 per cent of the hundred or so commissioners were county knights. From the central court judges we find Robert de Ashill, Roger Belers, Henry de Hambury, Ralf de Hengham, Roger Hillary, Thomas de Radcliffe, John de Stonor and Richard de Willoughby. Other central court lawyers include: Roger de Bankwell, John de Foxley, Thomas de Hampton, Robert de Mablethorpe, Robert de Saddington, Robert de Scarborough, Roger de Scotter, Henry Spigurnel and Nicholas de Warwick. From 1290 until 1307 Nicholas was the king's serjeant-at-law.[120] In a very specific sense the two groups were not exclusive, in that judges and other successful lawyers often became knights. Nicholas de Warwick, moreover, had strong interests in Warwickshire, his county of origin. As far as commissions of oyer and terminer were concerned, however, the professional lawyers do not seem to have been operating on a single county basis. In fact, very few of the justices could be said to be local men of law operating in Warwickshire. Among those who might lay claim to such status are, once again, John de Heyford and Robert de Stoke, together with Thomas Boydin, Robert de Warwick and perhaps William de Catesby.

Thomas Boydin of Stretton on Dunsmore was a pleader in the Warwickshire county court at the beginning of the fourteenth century and seems also to have been a professional attorney in the court of common pleas, being appointed 144 times between 1299 and 1308.[121] He was general attorney for two successive heads of the Hastings family. Robert de Warwick is perhaps best described as a lawyer/administrator.[122] He first appears on the scene as an attorney in the court of common pleas in 1294, although he is found there infrequently until 1300. From then until 1304 he was appointed attorney in that court no less than 168 times, so that his professional capacity can hardly be in doubt. During 1302–4, however, he was under-sheriff of Warwickshire and Leicestershire. In 1310 he became under-sheriff of Worcestershire for its hereditary sheriff, Guy de Beauchamp, earl of Warwick, making him the effective sheriff of the county. His association with the earl probably put him on the wrong side of the dominant regime and he received several pardons in the years that followed. After the earl's death, in 1315, he is found as a Warwickshire coroner[123] and as a justice of gaol delivery at Warwick, often in association with Robert de Stoke.[124] He had been MP for both the county and the borough of Warwick

---

[120] Brand, *Origins of the Legal Profession*, p. 104. See also *Select Cases in the Court of King's Bench V*, ed. Sayles, pp. xliii–xliv, cix–cxi.
[121] For Boydin see Palmer, *County Courts of Medieval England*, pp. 103–5.
[122] For what follows see Palmer, *County Courts of Medieval England*, pp. 97–101.
[123] *Cal. Close Rolls, 1318–23*, p. 264.
[124] Musson, *Public Order and Law Enforcement*, p. 161.

before his death in 1332. He was hanged for felony. His main estate was at Claverdon, but he also enjoyed property in Kenilworth and Warwick.[125]

William de Catesby was of prosperous peasant stock. His father, John de Hull of Flecknoe, made numerous acquisitions of land at Ladbroke in south-east Warwickshire. It was William, however, who seems to have assumed the name Catesby, a village two miles to the south of Flecknoe but across the border in Northamptonshire. William was the real founder of the family's fortunes. However, his early career is unclear and it is not known whether he had any formal legal training; his son John, by contrast, certainly did have. William de Catesby became an increasingly prominent figure following his election to parliament for Warwickshire in 1339 and again in 1340. In the latter year he became escheator for the five counties of Warwickshire, Leicestershire, Nottinghamshire, Derbyshire and Lancashire and was commissioned to arrest a malefactor, one Umfray of Church Lawford.[126] In the decades that followed William was extremely active in public life, being *inter alia* justice of labourers, sheriff, escheator again for Warwickshire and Leicestershire and MP for Warwickshire on four further occasions. William and his son John acquired a string of manors, principally in south-east Warwickshire, as well as a major interest in the town of Coventry. Their spirited and skilful defence of the manor of Ladbroke has been the subject of a major study.[127]

The life of William de Catesby shows that election as MP could itself be a major factor in upward mobility. However, before we turn to the members of the Commons we need to look briefly at the other offices. As has been noted already the knights continued to play a prominent role in gaol delivery.[128] The commissions of array, for very obvious professional reasons, were wholly dominated by them. Indeed the list of commissioners of array between 1297 and 1345 reads like a roll call of local knights.[129]

[125] He also had property in Worcestershire (*Cal. Close Rolls, 1313–18*, pp. 76, 471; Palmer, *County Courts of Medieval England*, p. 99).

[126] *Cal. Pat. Rolls, 1340–3*, p. 88.

[127] J.B. Post, 'Courts, Councils and Arbitrators in the Ladbroke Manor Dispute, 1382–1400', in R.F. Hunnisett and J.B. Post (eds.), *Medieval Legal Records* (London, 1978), pp. 290–339. For a wider appreciation of their property interests see N.W. Alcock, 'The Catesbys in Coventry: A Medieval Estate and Its Archives', *Midland History* 15 (1990), pp. 1–36, and Jean Birrell, 'The Status Maneriorum of John Catesby, 1385 and 1386', in *Miscellany I*, Dugdale Society Publications (Oxford, 1977), pp. 15–28.

[128] We find, for example, John de Clinton, Henry de Erdington, Philip de Gayton, John de Harrington, William de Lucy, John Peche, Thomas le Rous and William Trussell as well as John de Peyto the elder operating alongside the lawyers (*Cal. Pat. Rolls, 1301–7*, p. 478, *Cal. Pat. Rolls, 1313–17*, pp. 226, 493–4, and *Cal. Pat. Rolls, 1321–4*, pp. 59, 370). Dugdale adds further names from the dorse of the rolls, among them Robert Burdet, John de Cantelupe, Richard de Edgbaston, Richard de Herthill, John de Ladbroke, John de Langley, Ralf de Shirley, Robert du Val and Richard de Whitacre (as assize justice): Dugdale, *Antiquities of Warwickshire*, pp. 210, 230, 503, 662, 704, 833, 846, 891, 899, 954.

[129] Altogether forty-seven arrayers have been logged. Definite knights are: Andrew de Astley, Thomas de Astley, Roger de Aylesbury, Ralf Basset of Drayton, Edmund de Bereford (when

As far as MPs are concerned, however, knightly domination was a noticeable feature from 1290 to *c*.1320 but was not sustained thereafter. Up to 1322 almost all of the members representing Warwickshire were drawn from the county knights we have already met. Twenty men fall into this category.[130] Another eight were largely drawn from the same social bracket, and most if not all of them were probably knights. John and Robert Fitz Wyth, father and son, were lords of Shotteswell and Bubbenhall. John, who had been a justice of gaol delivery early in the reign of Edward I, had fought in both Wales and Scotland. Dugdale believed Robert to have been a knight. The family's arms were *gules, two bends or*.[131] John de Somerville, of Stockton and Birdingbury, was essentially a Staffordshire knight.[132] Hugh de Culy seems to have been a Leicestershire knight whose family had Warwickshire interests.[133] Thomas de Clinton was presumably a relatively obscure member of the great Warwickshire clan. He flourished briefly in 1315–17 when he was twice MP, taxer and arrayer, the latter in itself suggesting that he was a knight. John de Dene was returned as a Northamptonshire knight in 1297 and figures on the Parliamentary Roll of Arms under Leicestershire. Seven times MP for Warwickshire between 1309 and 1321 he was also sheriff on five occasions. He was also sheriff and MP

sheriff in 1341), William de Birmingham, William de Careswell, George de Castello, Nicholas de Charnels, John de Clinton, Thomas de Clinton, Richard de Edgbaston, Henry de Erdington, Nicholas de Eton the younger, Ralf de Grendon, John de Hartshill, John de Hastang, Thomas de Hastang, Robert de Herthill, John Huband, John de Langley, John de la Lee, William de Lucy, Peter de Limesy, Peter de Montfort, John Murdak, Robert de Napton, John Peche, Nicholas Peche, Thomas de Pipe, Hugh de Prestwold (of Staffordshire), Thomas le Rous (of Staffordshire), John de Segrave, John de Somery, William Trussell, John Triminel, Richard de Whitacre and Roger la Zouche. Array was included in some of the peace commissions during the 1330s and 1340s. This brought in the earl of Warwick and the justice William de Shareshill, for example, in 1332 and 1338. William de Ferrers was an arrayer across several counties in 1322 while the earl of Lancaster functioned in Leicestershire and Warwickshire in 1339. A few men were included who have not been noticed as knights and seem to be just below the knightly level: John de Peyto the elder, William de Peyto, Guy le Breton and John Comyn. John de Peyto was there as of the peace commission. Guy le Breton was distrained for knighthood in 8 Edward III and may have succumbed to it. He was an arrayer in 1336.

130 We find: John de Bishopton, Ralf le Botiler, Robert Burdet, George de Castello, George de Charnels, John de Clinton of Maxstoke, Philip de Gayton, Richard de Hastang, Richard de Herthill, William de Lucy, Peter de Limesy, Simon de Mancetter, John Murdak, John Perceval de Somery, Ralf de Shirley, John de Somery, Richard de Turville, Robert de Verdon, Richard de Whitacre and Peter de Wolverton.

131 *VCH Warwickshire*, vol. V, p. 148 and vol. VI, p. 46; Dugdale, *Antiquities of Warwickshire*, p. 48.

132 John comes between Robert de Somerville who had a grant of free warren at Stockton in 1290 and his son Roger who died in 1338. Robert had at least five sons of whom John was one; he was probably older than his brother Roger who seems to have succeeded him. Another brother was Adam, MP for Warwickshire in 1327 (*VCH Warwickshire*, vol. VI, pp. 38, 226; Dugdale, *Antiquities of Warwickshire*, pp. 341–2).

133 The family, though not it seems Hugh, held at Marston Culy, and he acquired a manor at Dunton near Curdworth (*VCH Warwickshire*, vol. IV, pp. 36, 64). His Leicestershire manors were at Gilmorton and Radcliffe on Soar (*Feudal Aids*, vol. III, pp. 99, 126; *Cal. Inq. Post Mortem*, vol. III, no. 116; *Cal. Inq. Misc.*, vol. II, no. 540).

for Staffordshire, twice MP for Huntingdonshire where he was also a taxer and a member of the peace commission. He later figured as a commissioner of array for Huntingdonshire, Cambridgeshire and Northamptonshire. He acquired the Warwickshire manor of Monkspath in 1304.[134] Hugh de Croft had been sheriff of Shropshire and Staffordshire in 1309 and commissioner of array in the latter county in 1314 before becoming MP for Warwickshire in the following year. Geoffrey le Irreys, MP in 1302, was very probably lord of Ansty, north of Coventry. His predecessor there, Thomas le Irreys, had certainly been a knight.[135]

The first member who was clearly of sub-knightly stock was Richard de Barcheston, who was Sir John Murdak's fellow MP in 1322. Richard was lord of Barcheston and although he was of an ancient family it had borne no knight since Simon de Barcheston back in the early thirteenth century. Richard was returned as an *armiger*, or man-at-arms, by the sheriff in 1324, an indication of the social bracket from which he came. A man of similar stock was John Comyn, four times MP between 1327 and 1332. His family had long been lords of Newbold Comyn but without knightly pretensions. He, too, was returned as a man-at-arms in 1324.[136] Guy le Breton was the head of a family who had held the manor of Bascote in Long Itchington since the twelfth century. Henry de Lyle had inherited the manor of Moxhill, where his family had held since the early thirteenth century. He was given a boost by his marriage to Joan, daughter of John de Wilmcote, with whom came manors at Wilmcote and Bentley.[137] William de Sutton, MP three times during the 1320s and again in 1338, seems to have owed his position largely to his marriage. His wife was Margery, widow of William de Spineto of Coughton who died in 1316. By means of a jointure William de Sutton held the manor until his death in 1338, when he was succeeded by his wife's son, another William de Spineto.[138] A commissioner of oyer and terminer in 1323, William de Sutton was also among those who were commissioned to survey the state of Warwick castle in 1327.

The presence of such men in parliament should not surprise us. As early as 1322 some counties had expressly elected *valetti* as members, and it seems that a man of this status was entitled to only 2s. per day expenses as opposed to the 4s. per day which the knight could command.[139] *Valettus* was a term that had

---

[134] *VCH Warwickshire*, vol. V, p. 168.
[135] *VCH Warwickshire*, vol. VIII, p. 43. However, Henry le Irreys, who was lord of Ansty in 1316, was not. He was listed as an *armiger* in 1324.
[136] *VCH Warwickshire*, vol. VI, p. 158.
[137] *VCH Warwickshire*, vol. III, p. 38, and vol. IV, pp. 211, 260.
[138] *VCH Warwickshire*, vol. III, p. 80.
[139] See Helen Cam, 'The Community of the Shire and the Payment of Its Representatives in Parliament', in her *Liberties and Communities in Medieval England* (Cambridge, 1944; reprinted London, 1963), p. 239; Saul, *Knights and Esquires*, p. 15 and more generally pp. 6–29.

long been in use to describe a man of gentle stock who was either permanently or temporarily sub-knightly. It was the term used for would-be, or rather should-be, knights when it came to distraint to knighthood, for example. But it is also found more widely in both civilian and military contexts.[140] With the use of *valettus* the concept of 'knight of the shire' as a technical term was born. Henceforth, a knight of the shire was not necessarily expected to be a knight.

Needless to say, however, these men did not replace the traditional representatives of the shires. The Commons of the 1320s still found room for knights like Roger de Aylesbury, John de Bishopton, Robert Burdet, Richard de Hastang, William de Lucy, John Murdak and Thomas West.[141] But the social spectrum from which MPs were drawn was now rather wider. It was wider, moreover, than the traditional *valetti*. Robert de Warwick, who seems to have been a genuine 'local man of law', was elected in 1330. Of higher stock, perhaps, was Thomas Blancfront, who seems to have been a younger son made good. He was most probably a scion of the Bedfordshire Blancfronts, who also held a manor at Offord in Wooton Wawen.[142] Thomas was royal farmer of Kineton Hundred in 1317. He purchased an estate at Alvechurch, Worcestershire, from the lawyer Nicholas de Warwick. He was a knight of Roger Mortimer and was captured at the battle of Boroughbridge in 1322.[143] Sheriff in 1328, under the Mortimer regime, Thomas seems to have had himself elected to parliament in the same year, a not uncommon phenomenon.[144] John Croupes who was elected in 1328 may be the man of that name who contributed to the 1332 subsidy at Warwick and, less substantially, at Pinley. He may therefore have had urban, or urban/ministerial, origins.[145] John Sotemay, on the other hand, who was elected in 1330, was certainly from Warwick where he contributed to the 1332 subsidy from both within and without the walls.[146] A tendency for the election to parliament of some relatively humble men has been noticed elsewhere.[147] Beginning

---

[140] For a fuller discussion of the meanings attached to *valettus* see below, pp. 225–8.

[141] It is not clear whether Adam de Somerville, brother of the late John de Somerville, should be added to the knights.

[142] *VCH Bedfordshire*, vol. III, p. 422; *VCH Warwickshire*, vol. III, p. 200. William Blancfront was a Warwickshire coroner in 1322 (*Cal. Close Rolls 1318–23*, p. 387).

[143] *VCH Warwickshire*, vol. V, p. 1; *VCH Warwickshire*, vol. III, p. 255; *Parliamentary Writs*, ed. Palgrave, vol. II, pt 2, p. 196.

[144] John de Dene had done the same back in 1311, although his status in the community may have been higher. For a classic discussion of this phenomenon see K.L. Wood-Leigh, 'Sheriffs, Lawyers and Belted Knights in the Parliaments of Edward III', *English Historical Review* 46 (1931), pp. 372–88.

[145] A Richard de Croupes had contributed to subsidies at Stratford- upon-Avon in 1309 and 1313. Curiously there is no Croupes recorded in Warwick, nor indeed Stratford, in 1327. However, the surname is found at Edstone and Tiddington. Equally, John (de) Croupes may be related to the family of Whittington, Gloucestershire. See Saul, *Knights and Esquires*, p. 33.

[146] But solely from without in 1327.

[147] Saul, *Knights and Esquires*, pp. 120–2. Saul points to the same phenomenon not only in Gloucestershire but also in Somerset and Bedfordshire. See the works cited there.

in the 1320s, it becomes a more noticeable phenomenon during the following decade.

Of the twenty-eight or twenty-nine[148] men known to have been elected to the Commons from Warwickshire between 1332 and 1348, only seven or roughly 25 per cent were knights.[149] Nicholas de Charnels now joins the select company of Roger de Aylesbury, John de Bishopton, John de la Lee, William de Lucy, John Ryvel and Ralf de Shirley. Others were traditional manorial lords who are perhaps classifiable as *valetti*. To Henry de Lisle, William de Sutton and the two John de Peytos (who are in any event rather difficult to classify) we might add Gerard de Seckington who held a small manor at Seckington which seems to have been of some antiquity,[150] John de Coningsby who inherited a manor at Morton Bagot from his father and was returned as a man-at-arms in 1324,[151] and Robert de Lalleforde who was holding the erstwhile Heyrun manor at Church Lawford.[152]

Two men held their estates by marriage to widows in the manner of William de Sutton: John de Compton at Bearley and John de Saunderstede at both Chesterton and Moreton Daubeny. The legal devices of jointure and entail could now be used to create a life tenure for the husbands of widows even when they had no issue by them. In the case of a younger man marrying a middle-aged widow, this would keep her heir from his inheritance for some considerable time. John de Saunderstede seems to have turned this into an art. A settlement of Chesterton in 1334 gave him and Elizabeth de Loges, widowed way back in 1300, life tenure there with reversion to her grandson Nicholas de Warwick. In 1349 a settlement along the same lines confirmed John's tenure of Moreton Daubeny with reversion to Henry de Pipe.[153]

Four others might be thought to belong to this same broad stratum. William de Sheldon was presumably of the eponymous knight-bearing family which had long held Sheldon, although his own tenurial position is unclear.[154] Roger de la Launde was presumably a scion of the sub-knightly de la Laundes of Lea Marston and Dosthill, although his own property was at Clifton on Dunsmore

---

[148] There are thirty names recorded. However, John de Newbold appears to be a synonym for John Ryvel (of Newbold). If Henry de Idle is an error for Henry de Lisle (Isle) then the number is reduced to twenty-eight.

[149] Assuming that John de la Lee of Kingston is the same John de la Lee who was a knight in 1324.

[150] *VCH Warwickshire*, vol. IV, p. 199.   [151] *VCH Warwickshire*, vol. III, pp. 135–7.

[152] *VCH Warwickshire*, vol. VI, p. 147; Dugdale, *Antiquities of Warwickshire*, p. 30. Whether this was by purchase or inheritance is not wholly clear. He may well have held by reversion as Dugdale believed. The chronicle of Pipewell abbey makes a point of saying that he held by purchase and not by inheritance, which suggests, in fact, that it was matter of dispute.

[153] *VCH Warwickshire*, vol. V, pp. 42, 119.

[154] In 1327 Henry de Sheldon and his wife granted a ten-year lease of the manor to the bishop of Ely, and ten years later it was leased to John de Peyto junior and his wife for life. In each case the lessee paid £10 per year. However, William de Sheldon paid substantially to the lay subsidy there in 1332.

where he paid substantially to the lay subsidies of 1327 and 1332. Henry Miles and Henry de Hockley were similar contributors at Brookhampton and Stretton on Dunsmore respectively.

Of the remaining MPs, Adam de Stivington was a Stratford burgess,[155] while William de Catesby and William Erneys were lawyers.[156] So, too, were Robert de Warwick and, possibly, Richard de Stoneleigh whom we have met before. This leaves only Nicholas de Stratford, whose name suggests his ultimate origins but whose interests are unknown, and the wholly obscure John Worthin and Henry de Idle, unless, as seems likely, the latter is simply an error for Henry de Isle, or de Lisle.

The history of royal taxers in Warwickshire follows a similar trajectory to that of its MPs. A total of fifty men have been logged as royal taxers for Warwickshire between 1295 and 1348.[157] Sixteen of them figured in or before 1332, when the lay subsidies were assessed on individuals for the last time. They were overwhelmingly knights.[158] In fact, the local administrator/man of law Robert de Stoke, taxer in 1308, 1309, 1316 and 1319, was very much an exception during these years. From 1334 onwards the personnel is more mixed. Of the thirty-four men who figure as taxers between then and 1348, only ten were knights or at least of knightly stock.[159] Fifteen of the others were of the type we have described as *valetti*. Nine, including the two Peytos, we have already met.[160] To these we must add William de Peyto, brother of John de Peyto the younger and the successor to the Langleys at Wolfhamcote, John Durvassal, head of the once knightly family who were lords of Spernall,[161] William de Spineto, lord of Coughton,[162] John of Upton near Ratley,[163] Roger de Culy, son of Hugh, and Richard de Clodeshale. The latter inherited estates acquired by his father and grandfather in Warwickshire and Worcestershire and continued to

---

[155] Where he contributed to subsidies in 1313, 1327 and 1332.

[156] For William Erneys see below pp. 246–7.

[157] I have left out of account occasions when the same taxers were appointed for several counties, as in 1304 and 1312.

[158] We find: John de Bishopton, Thomas de Clinton, Richard de Edgbaston, Henry de Erdington, Thomas de Garshale, Richard de Herthill, John de Langley, Robert de Napton, Ralf de Shirley, John de Somervill and Robert du Val, as well as the Northamptonshire knight Lawrence de Pavely. The others were a clerk, Ralf de Bolemere, Stephen de Rabaz of Northamptonshire, taxer in 1297 and sheriff in 1300, Ralf de Perton who, as we have said, is probably identical with Ralf de Perham (*alias* Ralf de Knowle) the keeper of the peace, and Robert de Stoke.

[159] Roger de Aylesbury, Richard de Hastang, Richard de Herthill, grandson of the taxer of 1301 and 1302, John Huband, lord of Ipsley, John de la Lee, Nicholas Peche, John Ryvel, Ralf de Shirley, John Torville and Richard de Trussell.

[160] The others were: Guy le Breton, John Comyn, Henry de Hockley, Robert de Lalleforde, Henry Miles, John de Saunderstede and William de Sutton.

[161] *VCH Warwickshire*, vol. III, pp. 172–3. See also Coss, *Lordship, Knighthood and Locality*, pp. 237, 259, 288–9.

[162] *VCH Warwickshire*, vol. III, p. 80.

[163] See Coss, *Lordship, Knighthood and Locality*, pp. 188, 199–200, and *VCH Warwickshire*, vol. V, p. 145.

make acquisitions himself.[164] He was later caught by the distraint to knighthood of 1356–7.

So far, by knights and *valetti*, we have accounted for twenty-five of the thirty-four taxers. The others included two ecclesiastics – the abbot of Stoneleigh and the prior of Kenilworth – and one serving sheriff, Robert de Bereford. Three were of merchant stock. In addition to John de Merington, we find Roger de Bray of Coventry, another wool merchant, and Richard de Shirington of Birmingham.[165] This leaves only one Adam de Holeway, whose interests are unclear,[166] Roger de Guilsborough, who was probably from Northamptonshire, and the seemingly obscure John Worthin. In short the taxers were appointed almost exclusively from men who had status in the county, most of them of traditional landed stock.

In sum, an analysis of the members of parliament and commission-holders for Warwickshire during the first half of the fourteenth century confirms the heavy involvement of county knights and, indeed, the involvement of the majority of resident knights. As one would expect, they had a near monopoly of commissions of array but were joined by men of law when it came to commissions of a judicial nature. During the early decades their domination as county MPs and taxers was near total. From the 1320s, however, this elite began to broaden. We see it first of all with the return of *valetti* as 'knights of the shire'. Most of these were drawn from traditional sub-knightly landed stock. Increasingly, however, we find knights and traditional *valetti* being complemented by lawyers and lawyer/administrators and by men of urban, even mercantile, origins. What is true of the MPs becomes true of the taxers, too, after 1332. Meanwhile, the commissions of the peace and of oyer and terminer had also broadened. What is especially noticeable, however, is that men of a professional background are found in increasingly prominent positions once their stake in the land has been enhanced, betokening their absorption within the social elite.

Some sense of the dimensions to this elite can be gained from the men who in 1323 functioned as mainpernors or guarantors for the fines totalling 800 marks which were owed to the crown by the chief taxers, their clerks and the sub-assessors in respect of misdemeanours during the collection of the last four subsidies. These included the surviving taxers themselves (Henry de Erdington, John de Langley, Ralf de Perham, Ralf de Shirley, Robert de Stoke and William

---

[164] *VCH Warwickshire*, vol. IV, p. 262, and *VCH Worcestershire*, vol. III, pp. 25, 201 and vol. IV, p. 346.

[165] I assume he was of merchant stock. He was a contributor to the 1332 subsidy in Birmingham in 1332.

[166] He may well have been descended from John de Holeweye who was returned as lord of Newbold Pacey in the subsidy of 1327. However, he paid only 9d to the tax, and an eponymous family of Pacey is otherwise recorded here (*VCH Warwickshire*, vol. V, p. 122). The return for Newbold Pacey is defective in the 1332 subsidy roll. The surname also occurs among substantial tenants in the 1332 subsidy at Princethorpe, Wolfhamcote and Kineton.

de Sutton), other county knights and men of knightly stock (such as Roger de Aylesbury, Robert Burdet, Ralf de Grendon, Richard de Herthill, Henry de Ladbroke, William de Lucy, John Ryvel, Robert du Val and William de Waver), the non-knightly MPs (Richard de Barcheston, Guy le Breton, John Comyn, Henry de Hockley, Henry de Lisle, John de Peyto, Gerard de Seckington and Adam de Stivington), and the 'men of law' (John de Heyford and Robert de Warwick). Although one would hesitate to translate such a list directly into a functioning social elite, given its judicial provenance, at the very least it illustrates the several backgrounds from which the members of the resident elite, or elites, within the county will have been drawn.[167]

Two further dimensions need to be explored before we turn, finally, to the crystallisation of the gentry. One is the development of a strong sense of identity centring on the county. The other is the origin of the social gradations that were such an important characteristic of the gentry. First, the question of identity.

---

[167] The case against the Warwickshire men is in PRO Just 1/1389. It is translated in *Lay Subsidy Roll for Warwickshire of 6 Edward III*, ed. Carter, as appendix D (pp. 96–9). For the national dimension see Willard, *Parliamentary Taxes on Personal Property 1290–1334*, pp. 219–29. Altogether 108 men were named as mainpernors; most of them are readily identifiable, from the lay subsidies of 1327 and 1332, as landowners or major freeholders in the county. It seems probable that the list bears some relationship to the contemporary county court.

8. *Identity and the gentry*

Central to the formation of the gentry, I have argued, is a developed sense of territorial identity: a collective identity which both involved the expression of shared interests and led to the development of status gradations. The county was crucial to the process, and its role was considerably enhanced when it came to interact with the Commons in parliament. As the Commons emerged as a real political force during the 1320s and 1330s, so the county's capacity to articulate local interests was correspondingly strengthened.

This argument may be thought, at least at first sight, to be moving against the grain of recent studies. The notion of the shire as the embodiment of social cohesion in the localities has taken something of a hammering of late. Robert Palmer's powerful and influential study of the county court has shown how it was dominated, most notably by the reign of Edward I, by lawyers who were often also the stewards and bailiffs of lords.[1] These were the men who were largely responsible for the judgements of the courts, and who 'made the county court a professional and legally respectable institution, rather than the amateur court presented by historians'.[2] Looking at the early thirteenth century I have suggested that local society operated at some remove from the county court, and that most knights avoided its detailed business except when specifically called upon.[3] Arguably, historians in the past have overstressed the county as a factor of social cohesion during the first hundred years of the Angevin reforms, and 'in consequence have seriously underestimated alternative loci of social power'.[4] Michael Prestwich, surveying the thirteenth century as a whole, finds that despite the reform movement of 1258–65 and its aftermath, the reign of Edward I shows few signs of independent action by county communities. Rather, he argues that the county was immensely useful administratively to

[1] Palmer, *The County Courts of Medieval England*, chs. 3–5. [2] *Ibid.*, p. 112.
[3] Coss, 'Knighthood and the Early Thirteenth-Century County Court', p. 55, and see above p. 122.
[4] Coss, *Lordship, Knighthood and Locality*, pp. 3–5.

the crown, militarily for example, and in the collection of taxation.[5] Most recently, Christine Carpenter has launched a scathing attack on the usefulness of the county community as an analytical tool, arguing that it should be removed from the historian's vocabulary.[6] She warns against taking the petitions and protestations of the Commons at face value, suggesting that the existence of this institution and its relationship to the crown has tended to distort our vision. She argues further that the existence of a county community implies the identification of a county elite; and this, she claims, it is hard to find. What I want to do in this chapter, therefore, is to look more closely at the role of the county in the formation of the gentry. I wish to address three questions specifically. First, what other forms of territorial identity existed in our period and how did these relate to the county? Second, can we discern a growing identification with the county, especially post-1258? And, finally, if so, does this identification with the county become sharper during the 1320s and 1330s?

It is arguable that we come closest to the mentality of the lesser landowners in the cartularies and estate books which they left behind. Severely practical in purpose and in content, for the most part, they reveal the intense localism of much gentry life. As Philip Morgan has pointed out, although their attitude to lineage is heavily patrilineal in form, in practice 'it is the ownership of place that is more important than the true descent of the lineage', necessarily so given the importance of marriage in the transmission of estates.[7] Thus, family histories as revealed in these sources are often the conflation of more than one family. The Hotots of Clapton, Northamptonshire, are a case in point. The first of the two Hotot estate books begins with the basic history of the Clapton family's estate and then moves to Sir Richard de Hotot's consolidation of his holding there.[8] His son, Sir Thomas de Hotot, lord from 1250 to 1280, wrote a substantial part of this in his own hand, and was responsible for a second estate book. This contains some snippets of sensational family history. They are, however, intensely local in tone. We hear, for instance, how William de Clapton returned home with his bride from near Newark to find his hall and chambers and all that he had prepared for the wedding celebrations in flames. This was said to be a punishment from God for cutting down a grove from the churchyard to build his manor house.[9] The Hotots spent much time building up a second estate at Turvey, Bedfordshire, and their time was not spent in one locality only; but the

[5] M.C. Prestwich, *English Politics in the Thirteenth Century* (London, 1990), ch. 3.

[6] C. Carpenter, 'Gentry and Community in Medieval England', *Journal of British Studies* 33 (1994), pp. 340–80.

[7] P. Morgan, 'Making the English Gentry', in P.R. Coss and S.D. Lloyd (eds.), *Thirteenth Century England V* (Woodbridge, 1995), p. 25.

[8] *Estate Records of the Hotot Family*, ed. E. King, in *A Northamptonshire Miscellany*, Northamptonshire Record Society 32 (1983), pp. 3–58.

[9] *Ibid.*, pp. 5, 46–7.

overall impression the estate books give, not surprisingly, is of lives revolving around manor and parish.

The same features come across even more clearly in the estate books left by Henry de Bray of Harlestone, also in Northamptonshire. Henry tells us that he wrote the second of his two books in his own hand and finished it in 1322.[10] He arranged his little work (*opusculum*), he says, for the benefit of his heirs, and the concerns that feature most prominently in the two manuscripts are material ones. Henry is revealed as a figure of some substance, holding a sub-manor at Harlestone:[11] the sort of man who would later come to be called 'esquire'. Henry was active in every way in preserving and extending his interests. None the less, the greater part of Henry's property was inherited. In addition to the history of properties, and quarrels over property, there is much family history here. Henry's daughter and heiress, Alice, was married to John Dyve of Little Brampton in 1308 and consequently he has a good deal to say about the history of the Dyve family too. In 1325, Henry de Bray tells us, Harlestone parish church was rebuilt, and the cost of this was born by Henry himself and two other local figures: his son-in-law John Dyve and Roger de Lumley. As Henry de Bray supplied the stone and timber for this work, his editor suggests that the sculptured heads at the base of the arch on the inner side of the porch may represent Henry and his wife Mabel.[12] This may be fanciful, but it is entirely consistent with his strong parochial interests, indicating one level of perception of self.

But it is, of course, only one level of perception. Henry was at some point in his life steward to the prior of St Andrew, Northampton, and an escheator. He must also have had wider horizons. Have we any access to these? At the end of Henry's second book there is a list entitled *De obitis vicinorum*.[13] Many of the deaths recorded are those of relatives (both Brays and Dyves), of tenants at Harlestone and of neighbouring lords like the Boketons of Boughton and Pitsford, John de Holdenby and Hamo de Vieleston and his wife Isabel. Some deaths of national significance are also noted.[14] The list of deaths was not compiled as they happened, however, but added later. Not surprisingly perhaps, given his age, Henry was interested in longevity. He tells us that Peter de

---

[10] *The Estate Book of Henry de Bray*, ed. D. Willis, Camden Society, 3rd ser., 27 (1916). The editor has collapsed Henry's two books into one, rearranging the material under broad headings.

[11] Henry's rent-roll of 1329 records £11 16s. 10½d. from his tenants, besides boon services. The list of his expenses for 1289–1309 shows that he built himself a substantial manor house, including a hall, north and south chambers and a courtyard with outbuildings.

[12] *Estate Book of Henry de Bray*, ed. Willis, p. xxi.   [13] *Ibid.*, pp. 60–2.

[14] He noted the death of Edmund, earl of Cornwall, at Ashridge in May 1300. Part of Harlestone was, in fact, held of his honour of Berkhampstead. He also noted the beheading of Piers Gaveston at Blacklow on 19 June 1312, the killing of Sir Roger Bel(l)ers at Leicester on 19 January 1325 (*recte* 1326), the murder of the bishop of Exeter and the grisly executions of the two Despensers in 1326. Henry de Bray may well have begun his calendar year at Lady Day.

Welles and William Breton of Teeton were both octogenarians, and that Hamo de Vieleston was a septuagenarian. Some of the information is also found elsewhere in the two manuscripts, as in his list of expenses where we find, for example, that John de Holdenby died on 10 September 1306 at the time that Leycroft was planted with acorns. The expenses list notes a number of marriages and deaths (some of which are not included in the list of obits) and the coming of the justices of trailbaston in 1305.[15] Altogether these details suggest overwhelmingly parochial concerns, with an occasional glance at what is happening nationally.

However, this is not the whole of the story. In the midst of the obits are two lists of deaths which are of wider interest. There is a list of thirteen men who died in 1314 or 1315, and this is followed by four further deaths noted together under 1318. These deaths do not figure elsewhere in the texts, and their source is therefore unknown. The names are largely those of lords of the broader locality, and might, perhaps, derive from prayers for the dead at the abbey of St James, Northampton. They seem to reveal an entirely different dimension to Henry's knowledge and interest. In addition to Sir Richard Basset, who held the barony of Weldon in Corby Hundred, we have the names of landowners, mostly knights, of central to south Northamptonshire, reminiscent of a grand assize jury in their geographical spread, with Harlestone itself more or less central. There are six landowners to the north,[16] three to the south-east[17] and four others south of Watling Street, including, right on the Warwickshire border, the unfortunate Sir Thomas Murdak of Edgecote and of Compton in Warwickshire who was murdered by his wife and his own servants.[18] Towards the Leicestershire border, centred on Crick, lay the interest of Sir Nicholas de Astley. The head of an important knightly family with manors at Astley and elsewhere in Warwickshire, and in Leicestershire and Northamptonshire, Nicholas had been captured at Bannockburn and was to die a prisoner.[19]

To be sure, Henry de Bray records nothing of these details, and his lists cannot be said to reveal a range of contacts; none the less they illustrate his wider awareness of society. This awareness operates, in fact, on two territorial levels beyond that of the manor and parish. For want of a better terminology, they might be distinguished as the 'immediate neighbourhood' and the 'broader

---

[15] *Estate Book of Henry de Bray*, ed. Willis, pp. 48–51.

[16] Sir Thomas de Verdun of Brixworth, Hugh lord of Cransley, Sir Nicholas de Seyton with interests at Draughton and Maidwell, Thomas de Arden, lord of Spratton, Sir Nicholas de Wymall, lord of Wymall, and Sir Robert Boutvilein of Cottesbrooke.

[17] Theobald, lord of Gayton, Sir Hugh Wake, the justice of the peace, lord of Blisworth, and William de Combe Martin of Alderton and elsewhere in Cleyley Hundred.

[18] The others were Lady Elena de Lucy of Bradden and Slapton, Sir Thomas Lovel of Snorscombe, and Sir Thomas Wale, lord of Eydon. For the murder of Sir Thomas Murdak see Coss, *The Lady in Medieval England*, pp. 131–7.

[19] For the Astleys, see *VCH Warwickshire*, vol. VI (1965), p. 17, and Dugdale, *Antiquities of Warwickshire*, vol. I, pp. 106–9.

locality'. It is easy to believe that the former had a greater impact upon the lives of the likes of Henry de Bray than it did for more elevated men. But we should also reflect on men like Nigel Saul's Sir William de Etchington IV, and how he chose to spend his time. William was a

rich, well connected knight, a man in his later years summoned to parliament as a lord. He knew the earl of Surrey; and he had attended the funeral of Lady Tregoz. There is no denying his standing in society. Yet the men with whom he went hunting in 1308/9 were not these grander sort but his tenants and immediate neighbours Alan and Thomas Buxhill.[20]

When we turn to the broader locality, what is strikingly apparent is that its range is much narrower than the county, even though it takes account of some figures with cross-county interests.

These, and indeed other forms of association, and therefore of identity, can be seen to co-exist. Among the most elusive, however, is that broad local-ity to which Henry de Bray's obits can be seen to allude. Thirteenth-century sources tend to reflect this in the terminology they use: *patria*, for example, and *visnetum*.[21] The notion of *visnetum* is used, of course, in the assizes. The pro-cedure of the grand assize, whereby knights formed the jury in cases before the royal court over the right to disputed land, emphasised that the jurors should be from the locality in question.[22] Studies of grand assize juries from the early thirteenth century show that, in the early days of the assize at least, this stip-ulation was carried out to the letter. A case I have drawn attention to from the Worcestershire eyre of 1221, for example, shows the great majority of the jurors holding property within an 8 mile radius of the disputed land at Little Wolverton.[23] Kathryn Faulkner has demonstrated the point very clearly from Bedfordshire, where all sixteen jurors (as well as three of the four electors) in a case concerning Meppershall held land within a 10 mile radius, as did thirteen out of the sixteen (and all four electors) in a case concerning Sharnbrook. These places are located in the north-west and east of the county respectively and, most interestingly, only one man served on both juries.[24] The relatively numerous cases from Northamptonshire during the first two decades of the century reveal the same characteristics.[25] A local jury with some knowledge of the disputed property and its history was, of course, highly desirable. It was also likely to reflect the views, the prejudices even, of the locality. One should bear in mind

---

[20] Nigel Saul, *Scenes from Provincial Life: Knightly Families in Sussex, 1280–1400* (Oxford, 1986), p. 64.

[21] For a discussion of these terms see Coss, *Lordship, Knighthood and Locality*, pp. 8–10.

[22] For the operation of the grand assize see above, pp. 45–51.

[23] Coss, *The Knight in Medieval England*, pp. 36–8. 'Jurors' in this context means, to be precise, 'potential jurors', for the electors generally chose a larger number (usually around sixteen) from which the final jury of twelve was later drawn in court. See also the case over land at Maidwell, Northamptonshire, in 1201 (above, pp. 48–9).

[24] Faulkner, 'The Transformation of Knighthood', pp. 1–23.   [25] See above, pp. 48–50.

that these jurors had themselves local interests, so that an outsider might find it difficult to get justice. Where the disputed property lay near the border between two counties, the defendant could seek to have a jury composed of knights from the two counties. What this meant in practice was knights from two localities. It is not, of course, evidence for a strong county identity.[26]

In this context, it is worth examining the progress of the grand assize jury. One would expect the serious decline in the number of knights that occurred during the middle decades of the thirteenth century to have radically altered the situation. If it became more difficult to put together knights from a locality in any real sense, notwithstanding the elastic nature of the term, one would expect the jurors increasingly to be knights of the county rather than of any specific neighbourhood; but this does not appear to have happened, at least in Northamptonshire. A case from 1231 over land and meadow at Norton, in Fawsley Hundred, close to Watling Street, shows a very heavy concentration of knights from south and south-central Northamptonshire.[27] Moving forward to the 1247 eyre, a dispute over land at Houghton, in Wymersley Hundred, a little to the east of Northampton, involved six jurors with land in the same hundred, while almost all of the remaining jurors came from within a 15 mile radius.[28] Similarly, a case over land at Paston, in the extreme north of the county, brings a very heavy concentration of knights from the northern hundreds of Corby, Willybrook and Huxloe.[29] Even as late as 1262 a case over land at Duston, west of Northampton, produced at least thirteen jurors with property relatively

---

[26] For an example, see Coss, 'Knighthood and the Early Thirteenth-Century County Court', pp. 56–7.

[27] *Curia Regis Rolls, 1230–2*, no. 1769. The jury included: Henry de Dyve of Brampton, [Henry] de Alneto of Maidford and Adstone, Reginald de Lyons (*Leonibus*) of Warkworth, Simon de Turville of Croughton, Simon de Pinkeny of Moreton Pinkney and Weedon Lois, John Fauvel of Weston Favell, John Malesovers of Collingtree, Henry Gubiun of Yardley Gobion, William de Hocton of Houghton, Ralf Barre of Billing and Richard de Besevill of Hardingstone. The main estate of Aimery de Noers, on the other hand, was at Lowick, away to the north. However, Robert de Noers was later said to have land at Norton in Fawsley (see note 30 below) and it may be that Aimery had enjoyed property there too. One can rarely be sure that knights whose main property was at a distance did not have additional interests nearer to hand.

[28] PRO, Just 1/614B m. 27d. Those with land in the hundred were: William de Wichenton of Whiston, Nicholas de Cogenhoe of Cogenhoe, John Malesovers of Collingtree, Robert de Pavely of Easton Neston (in neighbouring Cleyley Hundred) who had land in Houghton, Luke de Colum of Wootton and Roger de Hackleton of Hackleton. The others included Eustace de Watford of Watford, Richard de Irchester of Irchester, Geoffrey de Waudevill of Everdon and Bradden, Richard de Newton of Newton and Coton and William Cardun of Winwick, together with Robert Basset and Hugh de Goldingham, who both had property at Rushton, and Henry de Drayton with land at Addington, Drayton and Islip.

[29] PRO, Just 1/614B m. 5. The jurors included Robert de Colevill of Brampton, Robert de Lindon of Easton, Thomas fitz Robert of Brampton and Dingley, William de Dyve with property at Cranford, Maurice de Andevill of Addington, William de la Musche of Aldwinkle, Henry de Drayton of Addington, Drayton and Islip, John Malesovers with property at Middleton and Walter de Denford of Denford, together with Hugh Fauvel of Weston Favell, somewhat further south.

close to the disputed land, that is to say within a 10 mile radius, although four of the others held their main estates in the northern hundreds of the county.[30] In short, electors endeavoured to find knights from the part of their county where the disputed property lay, whether south, centre, north or whatever, and to include knights with property in the immediate vicinity. And if they latterly had to include men from further afield, they nevertheless continued to achieve a measure of success.[31] One is reminded of the perception of local society suggested by Henry de Bray's obits. Of course, the view presented by the grand assize is a false one, in that it is restricted to knights. It also tells us nothing directly about social cohesion and it fails to reveal any precise geographical bounds to these loose territorial 'groupings'. But in this respect the picture is not entirely inaccurate; for the most part there are unlikely to have been any such bounds.

It is true that a focus may sometimes have been provided by a lordship, or component of a lordship, especially in the early thirteenth century, when the honour could still retain some vestiges of its former vitality. And, of course, local society, notably in its higher reaches, might gravitate around a magnate, a centripetal attraction which often went beyond tenurial or formal retainer links: the Montfortian heartland is a classic case in point.[32] But aristocratic society was dynamic, not static, and its affinities formed and dissolved,[33] making any capacity to inculcate a true territoriality within the broader landowning classes very limited. An ecclesiastical lordship might also provide a focus. An entry in the first Hotot estate book tells us that the thirty-third year of Henry III was 5,448 years from the beginning of the world, 1,249 years from the birth of Christ, 1,216 from the death of Christ and 644 years from the building of Peterborough [Abbey],[34] which seems to locate the author not only in time but also in space.

---

[30] PRO, Just 1/616 m. 21. The long list of potential jurors here (twenty-one in all) includes William de Welton, with property at Norton in the hundred of Nobottle Grove, Philip de Daventry of Daventry, Robert Mauntell of Hartwell, Roger de Lyons of Warkworth, Robert de Pavely of Houghton and Potterspury, Hugh Fauvel of Weston Favell, Robert de Noers with land at Norton in Fawsley Hundred, Philip de Couele of Holdenby and Ravensthorp, Nicholas de Cogenhoe of Cogenhoe, Roger de Hackleton of Hackleton, Ralf Throp with property at Staverton and Welton, John Sampson of Litchborough and Robert Mallore of Welton in Fawsley Hundred. By contrast, the main interests of Robert de Hotot and Simon de Watervill were in Corby Hundred, at Carlton and Ashley respectively, Ralf de Titchmarsh came from Titchmarsh in Navisford Hundred, and Hugh de Goldingham had property at Rushton in Rothwell Hundred.

[31] Northamptonshire, it has to be admitted, was reasonably well endowed with knights. There were at least fifty-four functioning in the 1247 eyre, fifty-two in 1253 and fifty-eight in 1262 (PRO, Just 1/614B mm. 2, 5–6, 14, 2d–3d, 11d, 27d; Just 1/615 mm. 20, 22d, 25d, 28d; Just 1/616 mm. 4–6, 8, 10, 21, 2d–3d, 6d, 10d–11d, 13d, 16d). The pool of knights naturally varied from county to county and even within counties. It is possible, therefore, that this exercise might produce differing results elsewhere.

[32] For Simon de Montfort's affinity see, most recently, Maddicott, *Simon de Montfort*, pp. 59–76, and works cited there.

[33] Saul, *Scenes from Provincial Life*, p. 60.

[34] *Estate Records of the Hotot Family*, ed. King, pp. 22–3.

Perhaps, too, localities may be partly determined by geographical features. They could also be underpinned by units of administration, as Nigel Saul suggests may have been the case with the rapes of Sussex and the lathes of Kent.

What Saul shows is that the sort of sub-county connections which we have glimpsed through various means in the thirteenth century persisted into the fourteenth. The knights and esquires of east Sussex, for example, 'had few ties with their peers from the western half of the county'.[35] It is these local forms of association, among others, which are likely to be revealed by network analysis, although this is methodologically much more complex than is sometimes supposed.[36] Saul may well be justified in opening up the possibility of a 'county of communities'.[37]

And so, at last, we come to the county. I wish to begin my discussion of it with a paradox. It is always easy, at first sight, to overestimate the role of the county, precisely because it tends to be the prism through which we see. At the same time, however, as Saul has pointed out, the 'sentiments and reactions aroused by the county' are hard to identify.[38] As far as the first half of the thirteenth century is concerned, despite all the correctives we have made, the county must have contained some resonance, not least among the knights who were called upon for the grand assize and similar purposes. Notwithstanding the importance of the locality and, indeed, a certain reluctance to serve, it must at least have begun to influence men to regard themselves as a knight of this or that county. It is a curious feature of the grand assize that relatively few knights are to be found functioning in more than one county.

Nevertheless, it was the period of reform which opened in 1258 which, arguably, was crucial. County knights were called upon to channel complaints and criticism to the government in parliament. In the time of Edward I petitions came regularly and increasingly to parliament. A series of seminal works by John Maddicott has shown how this strengthened the concept of representation and how it provided a regular channel of communication between government and localities.[39] From 1275 onwards we can see a clear coincidence between sessions of parliament, the receipt of petitions and the setting up of commissions of oyer and terminer, often to investigate the very complaints named in the petitions.[40] As Maddicott writes, this petitioning began 'to create a wider public awareness of national politics and of the political remedies for complaint'.[41] As yet, however, the role of the county can still be exaggerated. As Prestwich

---

[35] Saul, *Scenes from Provincial Life*, p. 61.

[36] For an enthusiastic espousal of network analysis see Carpenter, 'Gentry and Community in Medieval England', pp. 365–74.

[37] Saul, *Scenes from Provincial Life*, p. 60.   [38] *Ibid.*, p. 57.

[39] Maddicott, 'The County Community and the Making of Public Opinion', pp. 27–43; 'Parliament and the Constituencies', pp. 67–87; 'Edward I and the Lessons of Baronial Reform', pp. 1–30.

[40] See above, pp. 146–7.   [41] Maddicott, 'Parliament and the Constituencies', p. 62.

has recently stressed, the number of petitions coming from the counties as such during the reign of Edward I was actually quite small, an average between 1290 and 1307 of one per parliament. Little concerted political action can be seen coming through from the shires, and in parliament it was the baronage who continued to act on behalf of the community of the realm.[42]

What then was the role of the county at this time? Christine Carpenter suggests that the significance of the county was dependent upon its role as a court:

As long as the county court remained an important local judicial tribunal it is quite possible that a significant body of local landowners would habitually have attended, and that would explain why it was used as a forum to publicize instruments like the Confirmation of the Charters in 1297 and Articles on the Charters in 1300. But after the legislation of 1278, landowners of any substance were unlikely to have business with the court, unless it concerned their tenants. We should therefore not see the courts as a focus of shire unity in the later Middle Ages but rather as a remnant of a time when they had perhaps rather more significance.[43]

This seems to be, in fact, an inversion of the truth. The shire's judicial competence had been reduced, right enough,[44] but on her own admission the value of the county in terms of the transmission of information easily survived the decline in the range of its ordinary judicial business. The part which the county played in the political life of the fourteenth century was manifestly not derived from its judicial role.

It would be a mistake, I think, to underestimate the impact of the county's administrative functions. The duties imposed on the shire were considerable. To take just one example, it was here that the government launched its periodic attempts to force all those with land valued over a certain figure to pay a fine or to take on knighthood.[45] The administrative importance of the county not only impacted upon people's consciousness, but also spawned records. The thirteenth-century canon of Barnwell Priory who was able to visit Cambridge castle to make a copy of the sheriff's list of local landowners and their obligations which was kept there, is well known.[46] In fact, considerable detail on county landowners must have been known locally as a result of government demands. In 1278, for example, sheriffs were ordered to distrain to knighthood all those

---

[42] Prestwich, *English Politics in the Thirteenth Century*, pp. 57–8 and ch. 8.

[43] Carpenter, 'Gentry and Community in Medieval England', pp. 347–8.

[44] Writs of false judgement, trespass against the king's peace and cases involving more than 40s. had all been reserved for the royal courts (Maddicott, 'County Community and the Making of Public Opinion', p. 29). For a detailed discussion of the jurisdiction of the county court focusing on the reign of Edward I see Palmer, *County Courts of Medieval England*, chs. 8–9.

[45] The inquiry into persons failing to take up knighthood in Bedfordshire and Buckinghamshire in 1344–5, for example, was taken in full county court: Ormrod, *The Reign of Edward III*, pp. 161, 245.

[46] Maddicott, 'The County Community and the Making of Public Opinion', p. 36.

with £20 land. The writ to the sheriff of Northamptonshire is endorsed with the names of the two men who were elected by the county (that is, in the county court) to undertake an inquiry. The return lists thirty-eight men with their mainpernors or guarantors, together with a further fifteen who had taken knighthood since the receipt of the writ, and ten men with £20 land within the liberty of Peterborough. To these lists the sheriff added, gratuitously and somewhat officiously one would have thought, a further list of twenty-two names of men who had (or who were claiming to have) less than £20 of land, giving the actual value and indicating, in many instances, that he suspected they had more elsewhere.[47] The gathering and maintaining of information of this kind on local landowners must surely have strengthened their own perception of the significance of the county. Nor does there seem any reason to make the existence of a sense of county society dependent upon regular attendance at the ordinary business of the county court. Men were surely quite capable of keeping tabs on what was going on without constant encroachment on their time. And, if many meetings of the county court were thinly attended and dominated by lawyers, others were quite large gatherings. For example, when the sheriff of Northumberland drew up his list of all those distrained to knighthood in the county court, with their mainpernors, in 1278, the total came to 171 names.[48] Had the county court really been outside most men's normal orbit most of the time, then it hardly seems plausible that the crown would have used it so much for the transmission of information and general instructions. Whether we are dealing with the early thirteenth century or the early fourteenth, sheriffs must often have found themselves in difficulties through non-participation and, perhaps, we should sympathise with them. Frequently, no doubt, they preferred to act on their own initiative, but perhaps they had to do so. But the action of the court, or more correctly action at the court, could bring them up sharp.[49] County society may not have been strongly cohesive, but it could act when it wanted to. The very importance of the county administratively, and the persistent interaction with parliament, can hardly have failed to have an effect. At this point we might recall Henry de Bray and his registers. The first of these, written after 1309, begins with a *Descriptio Mundi*, and then goes on to list the thirty-nine shires of England (which include London), before giving the bishoprics and archbishoprics and then the kings of England.[50] This does seem to suggest that the idea of the county lay at the forefront of his mind.

[47] PRO C47/1/2 no. 4. The sheriff also lists five clerics who have £20 land.

[48] *Hec conscripcio facta fuit in pleno Comitatu Northumbr'*: *Parliamentary Writs*, ed. Palgrave, vol. I, pp. 214–15, quoted by Maddicott, 'County Community and the Making of Public Opinion', pp. 29–30. Compare Ormrod, *The Reign of Edward III*, p. 161: 'In practice, the attendance figures probably fluctuated widely depending upon the size and social structure of the shire and the nature of the business being transacted.'

[49] As happened, for example, in Lincolnshire in 1226. See above, pp. 112–13.

[50] *Estate Book of Henry de Bray*, ed. Willis, pp. 3–4.

Whatever else the county was or was not in this period, it was certainly a 'community of the mind'.[51] That the community of the shire existed in the minds of contemporaries must be beyond dispute. How else could it figure in that 'multitude of fourteenth-century petitions' which 'begin with some variation on the words "the community of the county of Bedford complains to the king and his council" or "the men of the community of the county of Lincolnshire show" '?[52] Which brings us to what Christine Carpenter calls the 'parliamentary context'. This she plays down, on the grounds that little is known about attendance at elections. However, cumulatively we do, in fact, know quite a lot about the parliamentary context. We know that by ancient custom the representatives to parliament should be chosen by the worthier men of the county in full county court (*per probiores homines comitatus in pleno comitatu*).[53] We know a good deal about the transmission and receipt of petitions.[54] We also know that the county was reactive and could become the focus of resistance to the government. In January 1327 the Commons requested the right to publish an account of their petitions and the answers they had received in their counties.[55] At the parliament of October 1339 the Commons requested consultations with 'the commons in their counties' before they would submit to an aid.[56] In short, as Maddicott says, 'No longer is the county predominantly the passive recipient of instructions and information; it also reacts, electing, representing, petitioning, and expressing its views in parliament, where the conversation of the marketplace and the manor house finds a more influential audience.'[57]

[51]   Christine Carpenter seems to deny this in explicitly seeking 'communities of the mind' elsewhere ('Gentry and Community in Medieval England', pp. 366–7).

[52]   Maddicott, 'The County Community and the Making of Public Opinion', p. 40.

[53]   As was stated in king's bench in 1338 when irregular returns by successive sheriffs of Cambridgeshire were reported. (See M.M. Taylor, 'Parliamentary Elections in Cambridgeshire, 1332–8', *Bulletin of the Institute of Historical Research* 18 (1940–1), pp. 21–6.) As J.S. Illsley has pointed out, we learn about electoral procedures when such irregularities had occurred. Rather than accepting these as reflecting the norm, should we not see them as exceptions which prove the rule? (J.S. Illsley, 'Parliamentary Elections in the Reign of Edward I', *Bulletin of the Institute of Historical Research* 49 (1976), pp. 24–40.) Similarly, the evidence for magnate control at this point can be stood on its head. The most quoted instance is 1297 when the sheriff of Sussex reported that the knights and freeholders who had been summoned to make an election refused to proceed because the archbishop of Canterbury and others, including bishops, earls, barons and knights, were absent on the king's business abroad (*Parliamentary Writs*, vol. I, p. 60). But this was an abnormal year, when there was passive resistance to the king's demands. Moreover, while it is true that the magnates are invoked, the sheriff also makes it quite clear that knights and freeholders were involved in the elections. For the contrary view see Simon Payling, 'The Widening Franchise – Parliamentary Elections in Lancastrian Nottinghamshire', in D. Williams (ed.), *England in the Fifteenth Century: Proceedings of the 1986 Harlaxton Symposium* (Woodbridge, 1987), pp. 167–85.

[54]   Maddicott, 'Parliament and the Constituencies', pp. 66–72.

[55]   *Ibid.*, p. 81. After 1340, copies of the statutes and taxation schedules were regularly given to the knights of the shire to take back to their constituents for discussion. On this point see Harriss, *King, Parliament and Public Finance*, p. 365, and Ormrod, *The Reign of Edward III*, p. 162.

[56]   Maddicott, 'Parliament and the Constituencies', p. 81.

[57]   Maddicott, 'The County Community and Public Opinion', p. 43.

There is good reason to suppose then that by the 1320s a sense of identity with the county is likely to have grown stronger. This may be discernible in the way sheriffs responded to government writs seeking information about landowners within their jurisdiction or bailiwick. They had long been asked to supply the names of men with sufficient land who were avoiding taking on knighthood. Edward I had asked them for lists of landowners, in 1297 and 1300 for example, from which he could issue a military summons. Rarely, if ever, did the sheriffs distinguish between those men who merely held the appropriate amount of land in their county and those who actually lived there; indeed, there was no reason why they should do so. By the 1320s, however, we can see this distinction coming through. In 1322, when they were asked to send knights and others who were active militarily but who were not currently serving in retinues to the muster at Newcastle and to return the names, the sheriff of Rutland supplied not a straightforward list but details against the name of each man, sometimes indicating that he was old or ill, or that he was not presently in the county or that he did not in fact live there.[58] One can understand why a sheriff might respond in this way. He was explaining why it was that some of these men had not been personally summoned. The sheriff was presumably placing bounds upon his own responsibility in order to avoid criticism from the government. More instructive are the sheriffs' returns when asked to summon knights and men-at-arms in their counties to a Great Council in 1324. Proclamation was to be made in the county court and elsewhere as the sheriffs saw fit. They were then to bring lists of the knights and men-at-arms in their bailiwicks. Most of the sheriffs did precisely as requested. The sheriff of Lincolnshire responded as the sheriff of Rutland had done two years before, with details against the name of each man not expected to attend. A number of the sheriffs, however, produced separate lists distinguishing between men who actually dwelt in the county and men who did not. The sheriffs of Worcestershire, Surrey and Sussex, Bedfordshire and Buckinghamshire and Middlesex all separated out those knights who were *commorantes* (co-dwellers) within their counties. The sheriff of Wiltshire differentiated the resident knights (*milites residentes*) from the rest.[59] What is striking about these returns is that the sheriffs were supplying information that the government had not requested. One might argue that they were attempting to cover themselves against all eventualities; indeed, some of the other sheriffs indicated in their lists where men were old or ill. Nevertheless, it is probably significant that sheriffs were able to say so easily and confidently who was resident and who not. Significantly also, there was no differentiation among the men-at-arms; it was assumed that all would be resident. They sent, however, more exclusive lists of men-at-arms for

---

[58] *Parliamentary Writs*, vol. II.2, pp. 594–5. For a broader discussion of these returns see below, pp. 220–5.
[59] *Parliamentary Writs*, vol. II.2, pp. 647–8, 652–4, 657.

the Great Council in 1324 than they had for the general muster in 1322. It seems likely that the sheriffs were reflecting wider perceptions of identity within the counties themselves, especially if these lists emanated from the county court. In other words, in a very real sense, the resident knights together with the restricted men-at-arms constituted county society.

This evidence is very fragile, and clearly it cannot be pushed too far. If residence was increasingly a factor, there were also factors working against the county. As is often pointed out, landowning cuts across counties and it may well be that those major knights and minor barons with strong interests in several counties belonged rather to extra-county or even regional elites.[60] Actual political solidarity may have been achieved only sporadically at county level. One way of approaching this issue, in fact, is to ask why genuine political solidarity should in practice have been difficult to achieve. Much of the responsibility lies with the gentry themselves, of course, and with the higher nobility, but part of the explanation lies also with the crown. As is well known, despite the fact that the crown had to work through local agents, it was unwilling to concede full judicial power to the gentry. Naturally enough, the government would wish to employ principally those it felt it could trust; and this might or might not coincide with local sensibilities. Something of the complexity of the situation is revealed by the evidence surrounding the appointment of justices of the peace in 1338, recently offered by Anthony Verduyn in support of his view that the Commons played little part in their appointment up to and including this time.[61] His evidence can also be employed in a different direction however. In February of that year, after a meeting of parliament but not necessarily connected with it, individual men (for the most part knights) were called upon from the counties to attend meetings in April. These meetings concerned peace-keeping and 'other weighty business', probably the array of men for war and coastal defence. One of the interesting features of this is that these men were not elected, as were the members of parliament, but were selected by the king and council. The number varied from two to five per county. The government seems to have been calling upon the men it wanted. As a result of the meetings, these men sent in their nominations for keepers of the peace for their respective counties. The Chancery records preserve the returns for nineteen counties. Some of these show that in practice the knights indulged in consultation, with those described as the leading men of the county, the leading residents (*sic*) or the *plus suffisauns*. For five other counties there are actually original returns, which survive among the classification of petitions. Two of these suggest that the knights made the

---

[60] As pointed out, for example, by Carpenter, 'Gentry and Community in Medieval England', p. 362.

[61] A. Verduyn, 'The Selection and Appointment of Justices of the Peace in 1338', *Historical Research* 68 (1995), pp. 1–25.

selection themselves, but the other three are returns in the name of the county community.[62]

The government clearly wished to avoid, as far as possible, election and representation. In reality most of the knights preferred consultation of some sort, even if this was not with a formal county community. Moreover, the wording implies the existence of an elite within the county landowners whose voice counted more than that of others. A few members of the higher nobility were nominated, but the great majority were men we would regard as gentry. In some cases the knights nominated themselves, but most did not. Most interestingly of all, perhaps, is that only 40 per cent of the men nominated were actually appointed, and 40 per cent of those finally appointed were neither the knights themselves nor their nominees. The king and council seemed determined to have the major say, even to the extent of overriding the views of those they had themselves called upon to make the choice. What this underlines is that by this time notions of community and representation did indeed exist in the counties, whether exercised at the county court or not, and that the government wished to keep them, as far as possible, at bay.

Undoubtedly, the real focus for the political aspirations of the gentry at this time was not the county court but parliament. A full-blown political forum was vital to the realisation of the gentry, but that realisation was predicated upon the county. To put it another way, the collective identity of the emergent gentry found its ultimate expression in parliament, but its penultimate expression in the county. The evidence suggests that the territoriality of the gentry and perceptions centred upon the county marched hand in hand.

[62] *Ibid.*, pp. 6, 24: *la comune del counte de Salop; la commune de mesme le counte* [Dorset]; *gentz de countee de Hereford.*

9. *Knights, esquires and the origins of social gradation in England*

One of the abiding characteristics of the English gentry has been its system of social gradation. And yet the origins of this system have received relatively little attention from historians.[1] Of course, we are well used to describing a local society of knights and esquires in the fourteenth century and of accommodating the addition of gentlemen, albeit with some hesitancy, in the fifteenth. Historians have highlighted the sumptuary legislation of 1363, which points to the gentility of the esquire, and the Statute of Additions of 1413 which gives legal recognition to the mere gentleman. We may understand that neither piece of legislation is to be taken entirely at face value. Nevertheless they are recognised to be significant markers in the evolution of a graded gentry.

As to the highest gradation – that of the knight – we are now on relatively firm ground. We know that knighthood changed significantly in character during the early to mid-thirteenth century and that the rise of chivalric knighthood had a profound effect upon the elite mentality of the emergent gentry. Precise numbers continue to elude us, but even here we have a clear trajectory. Numbers were much higher at the beginning of the thirteenth century than was once thought and, indeed, a recent study by Kathryn Faulkner points to the existence of at least 4,500 to 5,000 knights in the counties during the reign of King John.[2] Numbers were probably already falling by then, and they reached their nadir in the middle decades of the century. They would seem to have risen somewhat in the time of, and as a result of the activities of, Edward I. None the less, both the so-called Parliamentary Roll of Arms and the summonses to the Great Council of 1324 suggest that Denholm-Young's estimate of 1,250 actual knights within the counties at this time was of the right order of magnitude. Knights had become a small elite.

The significance of chivalric knighthood would be difficult to overestimate. Not only did it provide an element of cohesion between higher nobility and

---

[1] See, however, the important study by Saul, *Knights and Esquires*, ch. 1.
[2] See above, pp. 91–3.

local society, but it also inculcated ways of thinking and behaving which penetrated steadily downwards as the English gentry took shape. What is much less understood, however, is the rise of the esquire as a gradation and it is this that I wish to explore in this chapter. Our understanding of this important phenomenon tends to rest on one major assumption, viz. that esquire takes shape as a residual category to occupy the space left by the retreating knights – to satisfy, that is, the aspirations of those heads of families and collaterals whose forebears had abandoned knighthood. *A priori* this assumption has a lot going for it: it appears to be what happened in much of France; the English government under Edward I and Edward II recruited sub-knightly cavalry from landowners under terms such as *armiger*, often translated as esquire; the sheriffs' returns of men-at arms summoned to the Great Council of 1324 contain many heads of once-knightly families. In Warwickshire, for example, of the nineteen non-knights returned, four were subsequently knighted, six were men whose ancestors had been knights and another five shared the surnames of contemporary knights.[3]

On closer examination, however, the matter is by no means so clear cut. We do not find in England men described in charters as N of X *armiger* (or variants), as we do in France, comparable to *dominus* N of X *miles*.[4] Does this simply reflect an insularity in diplomatic fashion, or was the esquire as a social grade late in developing in England? Let us begin by looking at the evidence arising out of Edward I's military concerns. The government of Edward I continued the policy of distraining to knighthood adopted by his predecessor and there are some surviving returns. Over and above this, however, the government repeatedly sought military service from those with £20 or more in income from land and rent and required sheriffs to provide lists of landowners at and above specific income levels.[5] In May 1297 sheriffs were ordered to return the names of all those holding £20 land and rent. In his return the sheriff of Northamptonshire differentiated between categories of landowner. He gave a list of ninety-seven knights (two of whom were in fact earls) and another of forty-one *armigeri*, as well as ladies, clerics holding lay fees, and a list of abbots and priors.[6] The list of forty-one *armigeri* comprises a broad range of men. In some ways it is reminiscent of the lists of knights we can put together from legal sources earlier in the century. Moreover, it produces similar problems. In some cases the men are obscure, that is to say they are not revealed by the manorial descents given in county histories nor by the national records revolving around

---

[3] For the details see Coss, *The Knight in Medieval England*, p. 129.
[4] For a recent summary of the French evidence see Crouch, *Image of Aristocracy*, pp. 169–70. As he points out, English society ceased to be international, except at its highest levels, and this may help to explain the differences.
[5] On this subject see, especially, *War, Politics and Finance under Edward I*, ch. 3.
[6] The sheriffs' returns are published in *Parliamentary Writs*, ed. Palgrave, vol. II.2, pp. 288–90, drawing on BL MSS Harley 1192 fo. 8b and Cotton Claudius C.II fo. 56.

the knight's fee. Nevertheless, the majority are readily identifiable. They include heads of families who have not, or who have not as yet, taken up knighthood. They include collaterals of families whose main line had traditionally furnished knights and who would themselves have provided additional knights in the past. They include heads of some families which had not been knightly, they include men holding by marriage or by succession and they include men who had risen through service. There is, however, one fundamental difference between the 1297 list of *armigeri* and the lists of knights of the grand assize. Inclusion here is founded upon income rather than status. There are likely to have been many men whose actual status in society was similar but who did not reach £20 per annum, or at least not according to the sheriff's returns.

Lists such as these provide a convenient entrée into county society, as Nigel Saul has shown particularly eloquently for contemporary Gloucestershire. But are we entitled to conclude that *armiger* or esquire was in actual use as a status term, as a courtesy title for a non-knight? In a similar writ of 14 January 1300 the government used different terminology, when it instructed sheriffs to summon knights, *scutiferi* and others holding land and rents amounting to £40 per annum to come with horses and arms to Carlisle, and to supply the names to the Wardrobe. This, of course, is not an insuperable problem. If we look for terminological exactitude in medieval sources we are likely, as often as not, to be disappointed. A word can be used in more than one sense, while different words can be used in the same sense.[7] Edward I recruited large numbers of non-knightly cavalry for his wars. One of the several words used to describe such a man was indeed *armiger*, which in origin meant armour-bearer; another was *scutifer* or shield-bearer. To be sure, *armiger* was the Latin word most often used to translate the French *écuyer* or *escuier*. In the present context, however, *armiger* and *scutifer* may mean nothing more than mounted man-at-arms. As the government endeavoured to draw upon a wider spectrum of landowners for its wars, it naturally called upon the sons of knights who were not themselves knighted, upon members of cadet lines of established families and upon members of families which had shed knighthood during the thirteenth century. *Armiger*, with its military connotations, was perhaps a useful term to use for those laymen who came within the royal purview and were not knights. In all probability the king was not employing a social category as such but rather indicating that these men had exercised or could exercise arms as cavalrymen. When addressing people for other purposes in its writs to the localities, the government seems not to have used such terms, suggesting that their usage was as yet restricted. Below knights we hear rather of *probi homines, bones gentz*, even of free tenants.[8] When military service is required, however, it is sought

---

[7] Government departments, for example, differed from one another in their employment of terminology to describe men-at-arms (Saul, *Knights and Esquires*, p. 15).

[8] See, for example, *Parliamentary Writs*, vol. I, pp. 53–4; vol. II.2, pp. 408, 501, 738.

from earls, barons, knights and other men-at-arms, and it is in this context that we find terms like *armigeri* and *scutiferi*.

Esquire, moreover, has other and humbler connotations. As is well known, esquire in origin denoted a knight's servant with particular responsibility for his horses and arms.[9] As the romances show, it was an ideal situation for a trainee or apprentice knight, but many esquires were never in this category; less so, it seems, the farther we go back in time. No doubt there was prestige in having an esquire of high social rank and of obvious breeding. Not all esquires, however, were of gentle stock, even in the thirteenth century. Nevertheless, the personal service involved in such a position could be prestigious and could bring material rewards. In the late twelfth century, for example, Gilbert Picot gave land in Coventry to Robert Calvin, his esquire (*armiger*). Robert was later to convey this property, amounting to three messuages, to Combe Abbey for the good of his soul.[10] One can imagine, moreover, that many men may have been more than content to have themselves described as the esquire of some important personage.

But, however prestigious it might be, esquire was none the less a service role. We see this clearly enough in the Statute of Arms of 1292, which attempted to regulate the role of esquires and other servants at tournaments.[11] They were allowed to play only a limited role in the fighting. Significantly, only those esquires who were accustomed to carve their lord's meat were to attend the festivities afterwards, and this reminds us, too, that esquire had household connotations.[12]

A neglected source for the study of aristocratic society which reveals the position of the esquire is the forest eyre; in particular the evidence for lordly poaching or, to be technically precise, offences against the king's venison.[13] For example, Gerard de Furnivall was found guilty of poaching in Northamptonshire in August 1283 with William de la Hurst his *armiger*, Robert de Bradefeld and many others of his household (*familia*), while Robert de Beaumond and John de

---

[9]   See, in particular, Matthew Bennett, 'The Status of the Squire: The Northern Evidence', in C. Harper-Bill and R. Harvey (eds.), *The Ideals and Practice of Medieval Knighthood I* (Woodbridge, 1986), pp. 1–11.

[10] *Early Records of Medieval Coventry*, ed. Coss, p. 355.

[11] See Juliet R. V. Barker, *The Tournament in England, 1100–1400* (Woodbridge, 1986), pp. 57–60.

[12] For *armigeri* and *esquiers* in households see Kate Mertes, *The English Noble Household* (Oxford, 1988), p. 26 and *Household Accounts from Medieval England*, ed. C.M. Woolgar, British Academy Records of Social and Economic History, new series, 17–18 (Oxford, 1992–3), part 2, no. 25. See also Denholm-Young, *Seignorial Administration*, p. 25 and G.A. Holmes, *The Estates of the Higher Nobility in Fourteenth-Century England* (Cambridge, 1957), pp. 58–9. According to Mertes, however, the word most often employed for honourable service in the household from around 1300 was *generosus*, meaning noble or gentle man.

[13] See Jean Birrell 'Who Poached the King's Deer?', *Midland History* 7 (1982), pp. 9–25 and 'A Great Thirteenth-Century Hunter: John Giffard of Brimpsfield', *Medieval Prosopography* 3 (1994), pp. 37–66.

Cawynton, knights, had committed a similar offence with two of their *armigeri* in Sherwood Forest in 1329.[14] Equally significant is an offence committed in the Forest of Dean in 1275 and reported in 1282. Walter de Beauchamp, knight, was convicted of poaching with John de Sapy and others of his household. John, it is said, was at that time Walter's esquire, but is now a knight (*qui tunc fuit armiger eius et modo est miles*).[15] The idea of esquire as trainee knight was clearly very much alive at this date.

But this *cursus* was presumably not open to all esquires, many of whom were on a more menial plane. The role of the esquire as an attendant is revealed in some of the early indentures of retainer. The 1297 indenture between Aymer de Valence and Sir Thomas lord Berkeley stipulates that Thomas will remain in his household (*mennage*) with his banner and five knights (i.e. himself plus four), receiving £50 yearly, in both peace and war, and robes for his knights. In addition to the fee and the robes, however, there will be food at Aymer's table for himself and the knights, for two esquires (*esquiers*) to serve him and for an esquire for each of the knights.[16] Similarly, in an indenture of the same date between the Earl Marshal and Sir John de Segrave, the latter agreed to serve with fifteen knights throughout the earl's life. When they were summoned to be with him, there would be *bouche à court* for Segrave and his knights, and for the esquires, and wages for the grooms.[17] The position of esquires is once again indicated in the indenture between Aymer de Valence and Robert fitz Pain in 1303. Robert promised to serve at tournaments with two knights from Christmas 1303 to Easter 1305 for £100. He was to have *bouche* for himself and the knights, for his three valets and for two esquires for each of his knights.[18]

The relative position of valets and esquires is something to which we will need to return. Meanwhile, however, let us move forward to the more concentrated evidence from the 1320s. In October and December 1321, writs were sent to the sheriffs summoning knights and *armigeri*. On 7 February 1322 writs were issued enforcing the Statute of Winchester. These referred to knights, *armigeri* and other *homines equites* as well as *homines pedites*. On 20 June 1322 sheriffs were instructed to send all bannerets, knights, *armigeri* and other *homines ad arma equites*, who are not in retinues, to the muster at Newcastle.[19] Does

---

[14] PRO E32/76 m.13 and E32/132 m.16. Many such examples could be cited.

[15] PRO E32/30 m.14.

[16] *Private Indentures for Life Service in Peace and War 1278–1476*, ed. Michael Jones and Simon Walker, in *Camden Society Miscellany XXXII*, Camden Fifth Series 3, Royal Historical Society (London, 1994), no. 4. The timely appearance of this volume has allowed me to be sparing in my citations. Unless otherwise indicated, the full text and references are to be found there.

[17] *Indentures for Life*, no. 5. The text is in Denholm-Young, *Seignorial Administration*, pp. 167–8.

[18] *Indentures for Life*, no. 11. For a recent discussion of the early indentures of retainer see also J.M.W. Bean, *From Lord to Patron: Lordship in Late Medieval England* (Manchester, 1989), ch. 2.

[19] *Parliamentary Writs*, vol. II.2, pp. 540, 542, 545, 586.

this mean that by this date there was a clear distinction between *armigeri* and men-at-arms, that is to say that the esquire as a social category has actually arrived?

In this respect, the sheriffs' returns are in fact rather disappointing. They responded variously. Some gave a single list, others did not include all categories.[20] Some ran categories together. The three sheriffs of Bedfordshire and Buckinghamshire, Hertfordshire and Essex included all categories but returned the names of *armigeri* and men-at-arms in an undifferentiated list.[21] Of the surviving returns, only those from the sheriff of Oxfordshire and Berkshire listed *armigeri* and *homines ad arma* separately. It is worthwhile examining these closely.

In 1322 the sheriff of Oxfordshire and Berkshire returned the names of eighteen *armigeri* and nine men-at-arms in the former county, and of four *armigeri* and ten men-at-arms in the latter who were not already attached to retinues; that is to say, men who constituted an additional pool of potential cavalrymen which had not been tapped.[22] What was it that distinguished the *armigeri* from their fellows? Were they the sons of knights? Had they perhaps recently succeeded to their estates and would in the course of time become knights, or were expected to become knights? Or were they the heads of more established families, of more illustrious ancestry, or more entrenched in the county? A host of detailed family histories would be out of place here, but the plain fact is that on all counts these men fail our test. As far as the *armigeri* are concerned, their knightly credentials are variable and not all were of ancient stock, and if some of the men-at-arms are newcomers on the county scene, there were others who were of distinguished ancestry and the sons of knights. If the *armigeri* tend on the whole to come from more established families than the men-at-arms, there is none the less considerable overlap. In Oxfordshire, for example, the men-at-arms include Richard de Abberbury, who belonged to a rising administrative family and ultimately of peasant stock; but they also included Ralf des Préaux whose family had held at Great Tew since it was bestowed upon them by Earl Ranulf III of Chester in 1206 and which had been settled upon him by his father Sir John des Préaux in 1304.[23] On almost any reckoning he should have been placed on the upper side of a dividing line. As far as Berkshire is concerned, in each case against some of the criteria, the men-at-arms Andrew de Hautot,

---

[20] *Ibid.*, pp. 586–95. Original returns survive as PRO C47/1/9.

[21] This is readily understandable, for in a sense all these were men-at-arms. On 24 June 1322 the sheriff of Northamptonshire received a writ ordering him to send the names of the men-at-arms in his county via William la Zouche of Harringworth. He duly returned an undifferentiated list (*Parliamentary Writs*, vol. II.2, p. 596).

[22] *Ibid.*, p. 593.

[23] For the Abberburys see Simon Walker, 'Sir Richard Abberbury (*c.*1330–99) and His Kinsmen: the Rise and Fall of a Gentry Family', *Nottingham Medieval Studies* 34 (1990), pp. 113–40. For Ralf des Préaux and his ancestors see *VCH Oxfordshire*, vol. XI, p. 229.

Peter le Botiler, Aimery Fettiplace and Richard de Coleshill[24] have a claim to be considered socially as in as high a bracket as the *armigeri* Philip de Englefield and Robert Punchardon,[25] let alone the less elevated William Pluckenet and Peter de la Huse.[26] Perhaps there were factors inhibiting full acceptance, the ultimate bourgeois origins of the Fettiplace family for example – Aimery was the grandson of the rich burgess Adam Fettiplace, mayor of Oxford. If the divide between *armigeri* and men-at-arms in these counties is a genuine social divide, which of course it may yet prove to be, then all one can say is that the basis of that divide is by no means clear to us.

However, we must countenance the possibility that separate categories of *armiger* and man-at-arms did not actually exist in the counties, i.e. that the sheriff of Oxfordshire and Berkshire responded in the way he did simply because this is what the writ asked him to do. In this respect, it may be indicative that most of the other sheriffs fudged the distinction. When in 1324 the same sheriff was asked, with the others, to send the names of knights and men-at-arms (*homines ad arma*) in his counties to meet with the prelates, earls, barons and *proceres* at the Great Council to be held at Westminster on 30 May, he responded, once again, precisely under the required headings. In fact, he submitted two lists, one of knights for the two counties and one of men-at-arms, again running the

---

[24] Andrew de Hautot seems to have been the son of a knight. He was lord of West or Great Shenford which had been acquired by Sir Richard de Hautot in 1274. Richard de Coleshill, lord of Coleshill, was probably the grandson of a knight. The family had held Coleshill at fee farm of the abbess of Winchester since the late twelfth century. They were, in fact, something of a professional family, having produced sheriffs of several counties over generations. Almaric Feteplace, of North Denchworth and Padworth, was the son of a knight. Philip Feteplace had been MP in 1302. Peter le Botiler, of Basildon and elsewhere, was the younger son of a knight who had succeeded his brother in 1318. His brother, Thomas, had been MP for Gloucestershire in 1305. Peter le Botiler himself was returned as MP for Berkshire in 1325 but *in loco militis*. Richard de Coleshill and Peter le Botiler had recently succeeded to their estates and could have been considered as candidates for knighthood as much as the *armigeri*, if this had been the criterion for the higher status. For the family histories see *VCH Berkshire*, vol. III, pp. 415, 459; vol. IV, pp. 239, 290, 519–20. See also the relevant entries in Moor, *Knights of Edward I*.

[25] Philip's family had held at Englefield since the twelfth century. He had recently succeeded Roger de Englefield, MP in 1307 and 1312, who had been living in 1316 (*VCH Berkshire*, vol. III, pp. 405–6). Robert was the grandson of Sir Oliver Punchardon who had married one of the two heiresses to Stanford Bingley and had died in 1282. Robert had succeeded his father, another Oliver, only recently (*VCH Berkshire*, vol. IV, pp. 111–12). Oliver Punchardon junior and Roger de Englefield had been summoned to military service by Edward I on a property qualification, but then so had Richard de Coleshill senior and Thomas le Botiler. See *Parliamentary Writs*, vol. I, pp. 485, 544, 583, 795.

[26] The Pluckenets had held at Chipping Lambourn since the twelfth century. William had succeeded his father in 1311 and had proved his age in 1319 (*VCH Berkshire*, vol. IV, p. 253). They may have been related to the illustrious knight Sir Alan Pluckenet, whose landholding stretched across seven counties. Peter de la Huse certainly had a wealthier relative, in Sir John de la Huse. He had land in Hampshire as well as at Finchampstead in Berkshire where Peter's father and John had married two heiresses, daughters of William Banister, by 1299. Peter had succeeded his father back in 1306 (*VCH Berkshire*, vol. III, pp. 243–4). See also the relevant entries in Moor, *Knights of Edward I*.

two counties together.[27] Three of the 1322 Berkshire *armigeri* figure among the men-at-arms in 1324, Peter de la Huse alone being missing. Interestingly enough, only two of the 1322 men-at-arms – Richard de Coleshill and Aimery Fettiplace – are now included. Were the others now considered too insignificant, given that these returns were associated with the Great Council? These two men were certainly among the wealthiest of the 1322 men-at-arms. Significantly, the sheriff's returns for Oxfordshire conform to the same pattern. In 1322 he sent the names of eighteen *armigeri* and nine men-at-arms. In 1324, thirteen of the eighteen *armigeri* figure among the men-at-arms, while only one of the nine erstwhile men-at-arms does so.

Does the distinction, then, mean anything? After all, as we have seen, in 1322 most of the sheriffs ran the categories together. Sheriffs often tended to obey writs as literally as possible. When in 1324, by contrast, they were asked for lists of men-at-arms they sent lists of men-at-arms, but these included a majority of men listed in 1322 as *armigeri*.[28] The sheriff of Warwickshire and Leicestershire, however, sent a list not of men-at-arms as in the writ but of *armigeri*. Did he consider that for all intents and purposes the terms were identical? The sheriff of Sussex, having listed the knights in his county, gives the names of other men-at-arms or *armigeri* (*nomina aliorum hominum ad arma vel armigerorum*). Was he aware of any distinction?[29]

Two more sheriffs acted distinctively. The sheriff of Lincolnshire returned a list of *armigeri* who exercise arms (*qui exercent arma*) while the sheriff of Worcestershire returned, in addition to those who are knights, the names of those in his county who *had* exercised arms (*qui exercuerunt arma*). If we can extrapolate from this, it would seem that the sheriffs were returning not men who arguably ought to go to war, by reason of their social position, but in fact those among the most substantial landowners, below the level of knights, who were or who had been militarily active; in 1322 they had returned a somewhat broader group. But the designations were not significant. They seem not to have corresponded with any precise status divisions within the counties.

But, notwithstanding the way the sheriffs reacted, the government itself must have meant *something* by these categories. Moreover, a writ in French sent out in December 1324 ordered the selection of *chivalers, esquiers & autres gentz darmes* for service overseas in the spring of 1325.[30] At this time we hear a lot about hobelars, lightly armed horseman, e.g. *hobelours mountez a*

---

[27] *Parliamentary Writs*, vol. II.2, pp. 656–7, where they are given solely, but incorrectly under Berkshire.

[28] The writs and the sheriffs' returns are printed in *Parliamentary Writs*, vol. II.2, pp. 636–57. The originals survive as PRO C47/1/10.

[29] The sheriff of Norfolk and Suffolk, however, returned for both of his counties lists of *armigeri ad arma* and lists of other men-at-arms.

[30] *Parliamentary Writs*, vol. II.2, p. 687.

chivalx.[31] These, however, were recruited on a different basis and it seems most unlikely that they are the men-at-arms referred to in the sources under discussion. Moreover, non-knightly cavalrymen drawn from county landowners can hardly have varied much in terms of the military equipment they brought or in terms of their military training. Perhaps the clue to what lay in the government's mind is contained within the 1322 writ itself. The sheriffs were asked to send the names of those who were not already serving in retinues.

Not all of the sheriffs, however, did as they were asked. The sheriff of Rutland gave information on twenty-eight individual men, explaining their circumstances as he knew them and what action he had been able to take in pursuit of the writ.[32] He included men who were actually serving in retinues as well as those who were not. Of the twenty-eight, ten are given as knights, one is given as a cleric and six are given as *armigeri*. Against the other eleven there is no designation.

As we have come to expect by now, the *armigeri* are of varying backgrounds, and there is no need to rehearse this. In the course of his comments, however, the sheriff of Rutland conveys some important facts. Two of the six *armigeri* were actually currently serving in retinues. John de Wittlebury was in the retinue of Ralf Basset of Drayton, while Robert de Helewell was in the retinue of William la Zouche of Harringworth.[33] Moreover, a third *armiger*, Robert de Sheldon, elderly now and ill, is said to hold his land of the gift of Ralf Basset, one of the lords of retinues already mentioned. Everything suggests that he was a life retainer. His 100s. land at Exton is precisely of the right order in this context.[34] These six, however, are probably not the only *armigeri* in the sheriff's return. The return was presumably made on the basis of hundreds and all six are from Alstoe Hundred.

The returns from the other hundreds are less punctilious over designations. In all, eleven men are without designation. They fall, however, into two categories. The first includes Ralf Basset and William la Zouche themselves, together with three other comparatively elevated figures.[35] Of the remaining six men, all but

---

[31] *Ibid.*, p. 689. For the hobelars see Philip Morgan, *War and Society in Medieval Cheshire 1277–1403* (Manchester, 1987), pp. 38–48.

[32] *Parliamentary Writs*, vol. II.2, pp. 594–5.

[33] John was lord of Wittlebury while Robert held a manor at Whissendine (*VCH Rutland*, vol. II, pp. 158, 160).

[34] This, for example, was the sum Aymer de Valence contracted to provide for life for John Darcy from his manor of Gainsborough, Lincs., in their indenture of 1309. See below p. 226. The other three named *armigeri* were: Richard de Harington of Whissendine, who was said to be infirm and unable to work, John de Bussy, lord of Thistleton, and Bernard son of John de Brus of Exton. Richard de Harington was the son of Sir John de Harrington, lord of Glaston (*VCH Rutland*, vol. II, p. 183). Also included in the sheriff's return, he was said to be over eighty.

[35] They are Edmund de Passelewe, the royal justice who was lord of Empingham, and two barons of parliament, John la Ware, lord of Woodhead and Great Chasterton, and John de Crombwell, lord of Essendine. The latter, the sheriff tells us, was serving in the royal retinue. Ralf Basset,

one are said to be currently in retinues. We are not told anything of their status. However, there are indications that some of them at least were not casually recruited men-at-arms. Brice le Daneys is said to be over seventy years old. It seems hardly likely that he would have been with John de Segrave on a casual basis.[36] He sounds like a long-standing retainer. Thomas de Greenham had latterly been in the wardship of Roger de Northburgh, bishop of Coventry and Lichfield, who had recently arranged his marriage.[37] His choice of retinue is thus readily explained. It would seem that Thomas was in fact a member of the bishop's household. The young Richard Seintliz, who had just succeeded to his inheritance, may similarly have been in the Segrave household.[38]

A case can be made, then, for suggesting that the distinction in the 1322 writ (and in some of the sheriffs' returns) between *armiger* and man-at-arms took its meaning from the retinues. That is to say, *armigeri* were distinguished from other men-at-arms precisely because either they were regular members of households or they had been formally and individually retained. Could it be that the *armigeri* the government hoped to recruit via the sheriffs were men who had formerly participated in retinues or whose fathers had done so and who were therefore expected to follow suit? Did it mean by men-at-arms, in contrast, those who participated on a more ad hoc basis – for example, they were among those whom retainers brought with them to war?

The early indentures of retainer can be used to give support to this idea. There is, however, an immediate problem over terminology. The indentures are, for the most part, in French, and the word most commonly used for a sub-knightly retainer is not esquire, the expected vernacular equivalent of *armiger*, but valet (*vadlet, vallet*).[39] In 1297, for example, Sir John Bluet retained William Martel, *seon vallet*, for life.[40] In addition to his fee, William was to receive two robes annually and to be provided with food and drink as a *gentil homme*, with two grooms. William undertook to serve John loyally as a valet in the current war

---

Edmund de Passelewe and John la Ware were all summoned to the Great Council from Rutland as knights in 1324 (*Parliamentary Writs*, vol. II.2, p. 649).

[36] Brice held the manor of Tickencote (*VCH Rutland*, vol. II, p. 276).

[37] Thomas is said to hold around £10 land in Ketton. His father had died in 1316 and his wardship was eventually sold to Bishop Roger de Northburgh who married him to Alice, daughter of Roger de Sulgrave of Helpston, Northants. Thomas obtained seisin, in fact, in 1322 (*VCH Rutland*, vol. II, p. 256).

[38] Richard is said to have around £15 land in Seaton and to be in the retinue of Sir John de Segrave. He had succeeded his father William by the summer of 1321 (*VCH Rutland*, vol. II, p. 215). The others without designation were: Walter de Yarmouth, said to hold £10 land in Cottesmore and to be in the retinue of Bernard de Brus (lord of Exton); John Hacluyt, said to be in the royal retinue, who held the manors of Braunston and Leighfield in Oakham and was keeper of the forest of Rutland (*VCH Rutland*, vol. I, p. 254; vol. II, pp. 16, 33); and John de Boyvill who held the manor of Ayston (*VCH Rutland*, vol. II, p. 59).

[39] The problem is compounded by the translation of valet as yeoman in calendars and the tendency for historians to follow suit.

[40] *Indentures for Life*, no. 7.

between the kings of England and France and in any future war. Similarly in 1309 Aymer de Valence, earl of Pembroke, retained John Darcy for life in peace and in war.[41] He was to receive his sustenance and suitable robes as did the earl's other *valletz*, together with his horse and armour in time of war. John was to receive 100s. rent, but on taking up knighthood Aymer was to enfeoff him of thirteen and a half marks in land and rent when he would serve as one of the earl's bachelors.[42] In these examples then, valet has both household and military connotations, and a natural progression is indicated from valet to knight.

Valet was undoubtedly a term regularly employed by the magnates to denote retinue membership. Among the muniments of Earl Thomas of Lancaster noted after the battle of Boroughbridge was a list of the names of the *Contes*, *Barons*, *Chevalers* and *Valletz* of his retinue.[43] Indentures, moreover, sometimes specifically mention valets in the provision of service. In 1311, for example, Sir Nicholas Hastings contracted to stay in the service of Ralf, lord FitzWilliam 'for the term of their two lives'. He was to come with two valets and ten grooms when summoned in time of war, with the two valets and only four grooms in time of peace.[44] In 1318 Hugh le Despenser the younger retained Hugh de Neville of Essex with two additional knights and seven *vadletz*.[45]

When we move back from the vernacular into Latin, even in documents which refer to the same milieu as the indentures, for example household accounts, we find ourselves back with *armiger*. The surviving household account of Thomas of Lancaster, for 1313–14, speaks of livery given to seventy knights and twenty-eight *armigeri* as well as clerks, officials, grooms, archers, minstrels and carpenters.[46] Administrative officers often seem to have been called valets. Thomas of Lancaster gave a life-grant to William Galon, valet, in 1319. William was no less a person than the earl's receiver at Embleton who had custody of Dunstanburgh Castle.[47] Thus a valet can be called an *armiger* and it certainly looks as though this was the case in the sheriffs' returns of 1322.

What, then, was the relationship between the terms valet and esquire? The latter was occasionally used in place of valet in indentures of retainer. When Henry, earl of Lancaster, retained Philip of Castle Martin for life in 1333, he

[41] *Ibid.*, no. 15. See also no. 17.

[42] The Darcy situation does not appear to have been in any way unusual. Sir Bartholomew de Enfield, who contracted with the earl of Hereford in 1307, had made a previous agreement with him before he became a knight and by which he received a life-interest in an estate. See Bean, *From Lord to Patron*, p. 67, n. 14, citing *Cal. Pat. Rolls, 1292–1301*, p. 84.

[43] Printed in Holmes, *Estates of the Higher Nobility*, pp. 140–1.

[44] *Indentures for Life*, no. 19.   [45] *Ibid.*, no. 29.

[46] J.F. Baldwin, 'The Household Administration of Henry Lacy and Thomas of Lancaster', *English Historical Review* 42 (1927), pp. 198–9.

[47] Holmes, *Estates of the Higher Nobility*, p. 71; J.R. Maddicott, *Thomas of Lancaster 1307–22: A Study in the Reign of Edward II* (Oxford, 1970), pp. 14, 21.

undertook to treat him *aussicom un autre des esquiers le dit counte*.[48] Similarly, when Ralf Basset of Drayton retained Philip de Chetwind for a year's service in 1319, he undertook to treat him as he did his other *esquiers*. However, should Philip take the order of chivalry within the year, i.e. become a knight, he would take service with Ralf before any other, but on renegotiated terms.[49] The words appear to be used synonymously when Hugh le Despenser the younger retained Hugh de Neville in 1318. The two knights bachelor and seven *vadletz* with whom Neville undertook to serve are referred to as his *bachilliers et esquiers avantditz* in the subsequent clause giving *bouche à court*.[50]

Like esquire, valet had strong service connotations. It, too, could be employed on a relatively low level. The 1297 indenture between Aymer de Valence and Thomas of Berkeley refers, in addition to the latter's knights and their esquires, to three *vallez de meyster* who carry the packs (*males*) of Thomas and his knights.[51] And this example does not stand alone. In 1328 Henry lord Percy retained Ralf lord Neville with twenty men-at-arms, of whom five were to be knights.[52] He was to receive robes and saddles for himself and his knights. In time of war, he and his *gentiz gentz* would eat in hall with six *vallez de mester*. What is interesting here is that these *valets de mestier* seem to be below the level of gentility. We cannot expect uniformity in terminology and usage. Perhaps they would be called grooms (*garcons*) elsewhere. In preference, however, and especially where it was used without qualification, the word valet was employed to denote a man of some significance.

That significance was most often derived from a vertical association with a higher lord.[53] Its origin was the Latin *valletus*, meaning 'little vassal'.[54] This word is found in the mid-thirteenth century to denote non-knightly household retainers.[55] True enough, it was also used regularly by the crown in the thirteenth century for those who ought to be knights or who were avoiding knightly status, and it was later used to describe members of parliament for the counties who were not knights and should, therefore, receive expenses at a lower rate.[56]

---

[48] *Indentures for Life*, no. 35.

[49] *Ibid.*, no. 30. See also M.C. Prestwich, 'An Indenture between Ralph, lord Basset of Drayton, and Philip de Chetwynd, 4 March 1319', *Stafford Historical and Civic Society, Transactions* (1971–3), pp. 18–21. I am most grateful to Professor Prestwich for supplying me with a copy of this publication.

[50] *Indentures for Life*, no. 29.   [51] *Ibid.*, no. 4.   [52] *Ibid.*, no. 33.

[53] For a letter of receipt by Roger de Merdesfen, *valletus* of Aymer de Valence, dated 7 June 1303, see PRO E213/13. I owe this reference to the kindness of Mr Adrian Ailes.

[54] Crouch, *Image of Aristocracy in Britain*, pp. 164–6.

[55] See, for example, Jacob, *Studies in the Period of Baronial Reform and Rebellion*, pp. 127–8, citing *Cal. Pat. Rolls, 1266–72*, pp. 146–7.

[56] *Crown Pleas of the Wiltshire Eyre*, ed. Meekings, pp. 31, 38–9; Helen Cam, 'The Community of the Shire and the Payment of Its Representatives in Parliament', in her *Liberties and Communities in Medieval England* (Cambridge, 1944; reprinted London, 1963), p. 239. And see above, pp. 196–7.

Although the terms were sometimes treated as synonymous, valet was often employed in preference to esquire to denote a man who enjoyed some social status, perhaps because the latter had more obvious, or more exclusive, service connotations. But equally, valet was employed as a term of convenience; it was not a title or a social rank.

By contrast, the term man-at-arms was employed more generally. In 1319, for example, William lord Latimer agreed to serve Earl Thomas of Lancaster for life with forty men-at-arms (*hommes darmes*).[57] Clearly the status of the men-at-arms would vary, and ten of those who were knights (the number is not stipulated) were to receive robes and saddles from the earl. In 1317 the same earl contracted with Sir Adam Swillington and Sir John Eure. In each case they were to come with ten men-at-arms in time of war. The ten had to include three knights, and these were to receive robes and saddles. All were entitled to *bouche à court*.[58] In 1327 Henry, earl of Lancaster made a similar agreement with Sir Philip Darcy who was to bring seven men-at-arms.[59] The indentures between magnates and the king for specific campaigns were also generally for service with a specified number of men-at-arms.[60] The term men-at-arms then, in such documents, encompasses men who were knights, those who were otherwise known as or retained under the name of valet or occasionally esquire, and presumably men who were neither.

In short, the word *armiger*, traditionally translated as esquire, could equally be synonymous with valet. It certainly seems to be the case that the Latin term had a wide and by no means consistent usage; it was used as an approximation, one might say, or as a catch-all. We cannot assume that when we meet *armiger* in our documents we are meeting the esquire as a social rank. Indeed, all the indications are that we are not. I am not suggesting by this that no social distinctions existed below the level of knight, but only that there is as yet no general rank of esquire.

Thus far, I have spent a good deal of time attempting to prove a negative. So when did the esquire emerge as a social gradation? The inevitable benchmark is the sumptuary legislation passed by parliament in 1363, which attempted to regulate the apparel which the different social strata should be allowed to wear. We find two levels of esquire. There were those who were on the same level economically as knights and their immediate families, who were to be treated in broadly the same way, and there were other esquires and all manner of gentle men below the estate of knight (*esquiers & toutes maneres de gentils*

---

[57] *Indentures for Life*, no. 31. The text is in Holmes, *Estates of the Higher Nobility*, pp. 122–3.
[58] *Indentures for Life*, nos. 24, 27.   [59] *Ibid.*, no. 32.
[60] See, for example, M.C. Prestwich, 'Cavalry Service in Early Fourteenth-Century England', in J. Gillingham and J.C. Holt (eds.), *War and Government in the Middle Ages: Essays in Honour of J.O. Prestwich* (Woodbridge, 1984), pp. 156–7.

gentz desouth lestat de chivaler). In other words the legislation was based upon status groupings but was forced to recognise that these cut across actual income levels. Esquire is now a social position.

There is other evidence about this time confirming the emergence of the esquires. The Scrope–Grosvenor case in the Court of Chivalry *c*.1385 makes reference to Sir Robert Laton's lost roll of arms dating from *c*.1370 which included esquires as well as knights. This was taken by Denholm-Young to signal the heraldic arrival of the esquires.[61] The evidence is fragile and the reality a good deal more complicated than this.[62] Some sub-knightly landowners were certainly employing heraldic devices on their seals well before this date. But clearly 1370 is another convenient *terminus ad quem* for the social emergence of the esquire.

The evidence of sepulchral monuments also points in this direction. At Lambourn in Berkshire, for example, there is a brass of two figures with an inscription indentifying them as John de Estbury, *armiger*, founder of St Mary's chantry, who died 25 October 1372 and Thomas his son. The date of the latter's death is not filled in except that it is post 1400.[63] Once again, this evidence is from later than the date concerned; nevertheless, it was understood that John de Estbury had enjoyed the status of esquire and that this was something to be celebrated.

Moving forward a few years, the poll tax of 1379, being a graded tax, naturally gives designations. The preamble distinguishes between three types of esquire, each to be taxed at different rates. The esquire who by estate ought to be a knight pays 20s., the esquire of lesser degree 6s. 8d. and, finally, the esquire not in possession of lands, rents or castles who is in service or has been armed 3s. 4d. We are reminded that esquire still retains some of its service connotations even though it has also gone, so to speak, 'out of court'. To take one county as an example, the fragmentary returns for Warwickshire yield the names of nineteen esquires or *armigeri*.[64] One of them, Thomas de Bishopton, pays 20s.[65]

---

[61] N. Denholm-Young, *Country Gentry in the Fourteenth Century* (reprinted Oxford, 1969), p. 5.

[62] See Saul, *Knights and Esquires*, pp. 20–3.

[63] Thomas was living in 1408 and the date of the brass is thought to be *c*.1410. See W. Lack, M. Stuchfield and Philip Whittemore, *The Monumental Brasses of Berkshire*, Monumental Brass Society (London, 1993), p. 86. See also *VCH Berkshire*, vol. IV, p. 235.

[64] PRO E179/192/23 7 24. At the time of writing Professor R.H. Hilton kindly loaned me his transcript of these returns. They are now published in *The Poll Taxes of 1377, 1379 and 1381, Part 2*, ed. Carolyn C. Fenwick, British Academy Records of Social and Economic History, new series, 29 (Oxford, 2001), pp. 641–89.

[65] For the Bishoptons see *VCH Warwickshire*, vol. III, p. 261; vol. IV, p. 223; vol. V, p. 80. Heads of this family had enjoyed knighthood from the early thirteenth century through to the time of Sir John, who was living in 1337. Whether Thomas himself became a knight is unclear. The line ended with Sir William, who died in 1447.

Seven pay 3s. 4d.[66] The majority, however, pay at the rate of 6s. 8d.[67] These are the standard esquires as it were. A few of them are heads of families which were once knight-bearing: John de Langley of Ettington,[68] George de Castello of Withybrook,[69] John de Clopton[70] and Robert Turvill of Wolston.[71] Most of them, however, are not. Annabel Comyn was the widow of an esquire, John Comyn, the last of a sub-knightly family which had long held a small manor at Newbold Comyn.[72] Thomas de Merington of Little Lawford belonged to a family of mercantile origins,[73] while William de Catesby of Shuckburgh was of peasant stock.[74] Roger Harewell of Wootton Wawen was described as keeper of the estates of the Wootton Wawen Priory in 1373.[75] The others were Henry

---

[66] They are: Edmund Compton of Stratford, Philip de Aylesbury [D(a)lusb(ur)y] of Lapworth, John Fulwode of Tanworth, Richard Kynton of Compton Wynyates, Richard Gay of Halford, John Bretford of Rugby and Thomas de Clifton of Stretton under Fosse.

  The preamble's statement that the esquires at this level were without land or rents should not be taken literally. Men who were presumably the forebears of Richard Gay and John Bretford contributed to the 1332 subsidy at Halford and Rugby respectively. The Fulwodes held a manor in Tanworth (see below), while Philip of Aylesbury was a member of the family who held a manor at Lapworth and may have been its head who bore that name (*VCH Warwickshire*, vol. V, pl. 10). The status of these men can hardly have been very different from that of the men who follow.

[67] The sum paid by Robert de Turvill is lost, but it was most probably 6s. 8d.

[68] This is almost certainly the man later known as John de Langley of Atherstone-upon-Stour. He was the grandson of Sir Edmund de Langley, and the head of a family no longer knight-producing and now in straitened circumstances. See Coss, *The Langley Family and Its Cartulary*, pp. 19–20.

[69] His ancestor, William de Castello, had succeeded the knight Nicholas fitz Nicholas at Withybrook but had respite of knighthood himself in 1256 (Coss, *Lordship, Knighthood and Locality*, p. 263; *VCH Warwickshire*, vol. VI, pp. 265–6). A later Sir William de Chastel appears on the Parliamentary Roll of Arms bearing *goules a ii barres e un quarter en lun quarter un chastel de sable*.

[70] John de Clopton of Clopton in Stratford-upon-Avon was the son of Walter de Clopton, himself the son of Walter de Cockfield who had acquired the manor from the eponymous Cloptons. He may have been related to them, although the families bore different arms. Robert de Clopton had been a knight in the early thirteenth century, but the family (with a small manor) had ceased to be knight-bearing (*VCH Warwickshire*, vol. III, p. 262; Coss, *Lordship, Knighthood and Locality*, pp. 236, 258).

[71] This branch of the Turvill family, which had held at Wolston since 1240, was about to become extinct. Sir Richard de Turvill, who was described as of Wolston in 1309, may have been its only knight. In 1314 he was discharged of the office of coroner as infirm (*VCH Warwickshire*, vol. VI, p. 275). According to the Parliamentary Roll of Arms he bore *goules a iii cheverons de veer*; while Sir Nicholas de Turvill of Pailton bore *goules a ii cheverons de veer*.

[72] *VCH Warwickshire*, vol. VI, p. 158.

[73] For the origins and early history of the Meringtons see above, p. 190. For the Merington estate at Little Lawford see *VCH Warwickshire*, vol. VI, pp. 188–9.

[74] His father was John de Hull of Flecknoe, 2 miles north of Catesby, which name he seems to have assumed. The family's rise was through the usual means of good marriage, legal training and administration. See above, p. 194. William acquired his manor at Shuckburgh in 1353 (*VCH Warwickshire*, vol. VI, p. 217).

[75] He acquired property at Wootton Wawen through marriage, and was succeeded by his son whose effigy is in the church there. According to Dugdale, Roger was the brother of John Harewell, bishop of Bath and Wells (*Antiquities of Warwickshire*, vol. III, p. 198; *ibid.*, vol. II, p. 809).

Standyche of Clifford[76] and Thomas Rich[77] and Henry de Sidenhale, both of Tanworth in Arden. In short, the esquires of 1379 were of very mixed ancestry. However, some (probably rather loose) differences in degree and service connotations notwithstanding, their existence as a social rung is now open to view.

Once again, we can set this evidence against that from indentures of retainer. During the 1330s to 1350s esquire and valet continue to co-exist. In 1337 William son of John de Roddam of Northumberland agreed to serve Henry lord Percy with 'a sufficient companion' when summoned in peace or in war. During the latter he and his companion were to receive robes like other valets.[78] Valet continued to be used of administrative officers in particular. The roll of the liveries of cloth and fur made in the household of lady Elizabeth de Burgh in 1343 includes ninety-three esquires. One of these is John de Hertford, called elsewhere *notre cher vallet Johan de Hertford notre seneshal de Clare*.[79] As late as 1356 the Black Prince ordered £10 to be given yearly for life to his valet, William Greenway, his chamberlain of Chester, whom he had retained in peace and war.[80]

On the other hand, the word esquire was coming increasingly to the fore. In 1353 Sir John de Sully was retained by the Black Prince for life, to serve with an esquire, both of them enjoying *bouche à court*.[81] In 1365 the prince retained Sir Geoffrey de Warburton with two esquires for peace and war. Two years later, he retained Sir Baldwin de Bereford, who was to find two sufficient esquires in time of war.[82] In other words we are finding the word esquire where valet would once have been preferred. Esquire could now be used as a title, as when Humphrey de Bohun, earl of Hereford, retained William de Stapelton, *nostre bien ame esquier*, in 1370, or Thomas de Beauchamp, earl of Warwick, retained John Russell, esquire, in 1372.[83] From their beginning John of Gaunt's indentures were with esquires as well as knights.[84] The first of his esquires for whom an indenture survives is Nicholas Atherton. This dates from March 1370. There are three more from 1371 and no less than twenty-three for 1372. Clearly,

---

[76] Clifford is Ruin Clifford near Stratford, but Henry's ancestry is obscure. He sealed heraldically in 1383 (Gregory Hood Deeds, Shakespeare Birthplace Trust, no. 479). His seal carried a saltire with a border engrailed.

[77] Occasionally, the tax returns lapse into the vernacular, so that Thomas Rich is described not as *armiger* but as *squier*. Similarly we find Thomas *of* Bishopton and John *of* Clopton.

[78] *Indentures for Life*, no. 36.

[79] Holmes, *Estates of the Higher Nobility*, p. 58. See also *ibid.*, pp. 68–70 for other examples from the Bohun estates.

[80] *Register of Edward the Black Prince*, ed. M.C.B. Davies, 4 vols. (London, 1930–33), vol. III, pp. 475–6. See also Bean, *From Lord to Patron*, p. 60.

[81] *Indentures for Life*, no. 41. See also *Register of the Black Prince*, vol. IV, p. 91, for Sir Edmund de Manchester who was similarly retained with an esquire two years before.

[82] *Indentures for Life*, nos. 49, 51.   [83] *Ibid.*, nos. 53, 62.

[84] See the list in Bean, *From Lord to Patron*, appendix III.

however, the status of men like Atherton extended beyond the household. They formed the nucleus of the army of knights and esquires which Gaunt contracted to provide for the king's wars.[85] Gaunt's Register also shows letters of protection being granted to men styled esquire as well as to knights who were going off to war overseas in the summer of 1372.[86] The word valet, found in an equivalent sense in the early indentures, seems to have gone out of fashion.[87] Perhaps this shift is coterminous with the emergence of the esquire as a social grade.

Everything seems to point then to the decades *immediately before* the sumptuary legislation of 1363 as the crucial stage. There is one further line of approach to the question, and that is through the use of heraldic seals. The social history of the seal is still in its infancy in England, but the work of Paul Harvey and Andrew McGuinness has already indicated the dividends it is going to pay in the study of this particular period, notwithstanding its methodological complexity.[88] The increasingly common borrowing of seals, for example, means that we can accept a seal as a grantor's only when it explicity says so or where we can deduce this with certainty from additional documents. None the less, some important general points can be made. It is not surprising that amongst the earliest examples of non-knightly heraldic sealing should be some from collaterals of knightly families. One example that has been noticed is Robert de Langley, lord of Wolfhamcote in Warwickshire and younger brother of Sir John de Langley. He was not himself a knight but he sealed with the Langley arms in 1317.[89] Another example is that of James de Clinton of Baddesley Clinton. Around 1300 James sealed two documents with what the legend to one of them says was his own seal. It was a shield bearing *upon a chief two mullets pierced*.[90] He was, in fact, the fourth son of Sir Thomas de Clinton of Coleshill (d. 1277). The Parliamentary Roll of Arms of *c*.1308 reveals clearly that James was sealing with one of several variants of the Clinton arms, or differenced to use the correct terminology. Sir John de Clinton of Maxstoke, that is the head of the eldest line, bore *argent od le chef de azure a ii molets de or*, while another Sir John, undoubtedly the second of Thomas's four sons, bore *argent od le chef de azure a ii flures de or*. A second type of individual

---

[85] *John of Gaunt's Register, 1372–6*, 2 vols., ed. S. Armitage-Smith, Camden Society, 3rd series, 20–1 (1911), vol. I, p. 35.

[86] *Ibid.*, vol. I, pp. 31–5.

[87] It was already travelling downwards, socially. See, for example, Saul, *Knights and Esquires*, pp. 16–20.

[88] P.D.A. Harvey, 'Personal Seals in Thirteenth-Century England', in Ian Wood and G.A. Loud (eds.), *Church and Chronicle in the Middle Ages: Essays Presented to John Taylor* (London, 1991), pp. 117–27; P.D.A. Harvey and A.F. McGuinness, *A Guide to British Medieval Seals* (London, 1995).

[89] See Saul, *Knights and Esquires*, pp. 20–2.

[90] Calendar of Baddesley Clinton MSS, Shakespeare Birthplace Trust, nos. 11, 17. Two slightly later deeds, of 1318 and 1322, show him to have been lord of Baddesley Clinton. He died in 1323.

who began to seal heraldically was the head of a knightly family who was not himself, or at least not yet, a knight. Before 1300, certainly, such men had sealed with what were in effect signets. However, this was to change. In 1342 John de Langley son of Sir Edmund used the family arms on his own seal although he was not, and did not become, a knight.[91] The chronology, however, remains unclear, and a great deal of work remains to be done on this particular issue. It is not an easy matter, for so many seals have been lost or defaced.

The most intriguing and potentially rewarding category of all, however, is the family which has not been knightly but whose head will come to be called esquire in the fourteenth century. In order to be able to interpret seals in this context we need collections of original charters of sufficient size from sub-knightly families. One such collection is that of the Archers of Tanworth in Arden, Warwickshire. Tanworth is a large parish with a number of small manors held since the twelfth century by just such non-knightly tenants. In the king's hands in 1086, it came to Henry de Newburgh when he was made earl of Warwick. The Archers themselves originate with Robert the archer (*sagittarius*) who, according to Dugdale, received Umberslade in Tanworth from Henry de Vilers and Roger de Hulehale as a gift to himself and his wife during the reign of Henry II. Robert's son, William, received additional land from Earl Waleran (1184–1204). He was allowed a chapel here in 1234–5. His son, John, acted as a champion for Earl Thomas (1229–42) from whom he received extensive rights of hunting and hawking in the territories of Tanworth, except in the earl's park, in return for twelve broad arrowheads and two capons yearly.[92] It seems almost certain, therefore, that the Archers were in the earl's service.

With the aid of the Archer pedigree we can examine the changes in their seal usage. The earliest example of heraldic sealing by a member of the family is in 1321 when John le Archer of Tanworth gave the manor, no doubt as the first step in creating a settlement, to Brother Thomas le Archer, prior of the hospital of St John of Jerusalem, who seems in fact to have been John's brother, and to Nicholas le Archer, another kinsman. The document carries two seals, undoubtedly those of John and Thomas. They used similar seals, viz. three arrows and three arrow heads respectively on a shield. The latter has the legend L'ARCHER.[93] That it belonged to Thomas is clear from the identical device with which he sealed a quitclaim to his nephew John le Archer a few years later.[94]

---

[91] Gregory Hood Deeds, Shakespeare Birthplace Trust, no. 342.

[92] For the Archers and for the history of the various manors in Tanworth see *VCH Warwickshire*, vol. V, pp. 168–71 and Dugdale, *Antiquities of Warwickshire*, pp. 780–4.

[93] Archer Deeds, Shakespeare Birthplace Trust, no. 416.

[94] Archer Deeds, no. 455. It carries the legend: FRATER THOM-E —CHER. The seal was Thomas's personal seal and not the seal of the order. On this point see E.J. King, *The Seals of the Knights of St. John of Jerusalem* (London, 1932), pp. 63, 99, 106–8 and plates xvii and xviii. For the confused state of the order during his time as prior see *The Knights Hospitallers in England; Being the Report of Prior Philip de Thame to the Grand Master Elyan de Villanova*

It corresponds with the family's later known arms: *azure three arrows or*.[95]

Extant thirteenth-century seals, by contrast, show no sign of heraldry. William Archer sealed with an eagle, John Archer with a device which appears to be an insect on his own seal *c*.1225. Two late thirteenth-century deeds of John le Archer and John le Archer son of John le Archer are sealed with the owners' seals, respectively a stag passant and a bow and arrow being drawn.[96] Unfortunately, there are no deeds from the first two decades of the fourteenth century to pinpoint the change more precisely. It may be added that Robert de Hulehale of the same parish, who was of similar station to the Archers, sealed with his own seal bearing a sheaf of corn in 1282.[97] The Hulehales sold their manor of Monkspath (with property at Bedsworth) in Tanworth to John le Archer before the end of the thirteenth century. Clearly the Archers were growing in prosperity, and this may have influenced their early adoption of arms.

The deed collection, moreover, contains seals from the other sub-knightly families with manors in the parish. The family of Crewenhale, for example, of the manor of that name, also sealed heraldically. Their seal is in evidence in 1349 when Robert de Crewenhale seals with his own seal, viz. a shield *vairy upon a fess, three arrows pointing downwards* (see Fig. 3).[98] Robert, moreover, lent his seal to his neighbours. It was used in 1340, for example, when William de Sidenhale granted land in Tanworth to Henry de Sidenhale and his wife.[99] The Sidenhales held the manor of that name in the parish. By 1365 Henry de Sidenhale had his own heraldic seal: on a shield *a fess between two crescents*.[100] Henry de Sidenhale paid 6s. 8d. as an *armiger* in the 1379 poll tax.

---

for A.D. 1338, ed. L.B. Larking wth an historical introduction by J.M. Kemble, Camden Society, old series, 65 (1857), pp. lvii, 215. By 1328 he had ceased to be prior. He died 28 Aug. 1329. Two other Archers, John le Archer senior and John le Archer junior, were preceptors of the order in 1338 (*ibid.*, pp. 11, 65, 208). I am most grateful to Dr Anthony Luttrell for his help on these points.

[95] These arms reappear in 1392 when Thomas le Archer granted his manors to four feoffees. The seal carries three arrows pointing downwards on a shield and bears the legend SIGILLUM TOME DE . . . CHER (Archer Deeds, no. 800). Meanwhile he, or an earlier Thomas, had sealed heraldically on four occasions between 1366 and 1385 but with borrowed arms (Archer Deeds, nos. 709, 734, 751, 772). However, another member of the family, Simon le Archer, who belonged to a collateral line, had sealed with a complex heraldic (or quasi-heraldic) device in 1328 and 1340: a lion rampant debruised by a shield with a martlet in chief, three scallops in fess and three arrowheads pointing down in base (Archer Deeds, nos. 462, 452). The seal was his own. John le Archer's widow, Margery le Tracy, had sealed in 1325 with three crosses on a fess between a bird and three arrowheads, the latter presumably reflecting her husband's arms (Archer Deeds, no. 452).

[96] Archer Deeds, nos. 42, 47, 251, 283.   [97] *Ibid.*, no. 268.   [98] *Ibid.*, no. 659.

[99] *Ibid.*, no. 557. The Crewenhale seal was also used by Robert de Bentforde of Tanworth in 1365 (*ibid.*, no. 703).

[100] *Ibid.*, no. 704. We find him using the device again in 1383 and 1395; in the former case the legend once again says the seal is his. In these last cases, however, there are three crescents not two (*ibid.*, nos. 765, 811). Thomas le Archer had on one occasion used the Sidenhale seal.

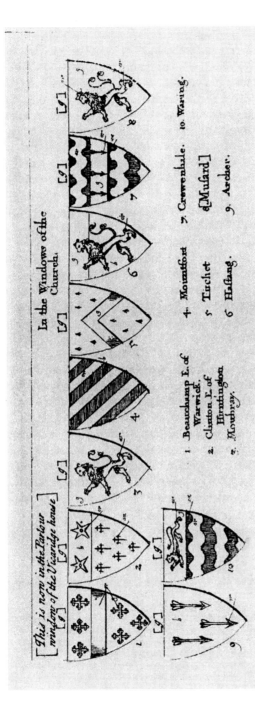

3. Tanworth-in-Arden: lost heraldic glass including the arms of Archer and Crewenhale, from Dugdale's *Antiquities of Warwickshire*. (Photograph by John de Morgan, Cardiff University)

The Fulwodes, again residents of the same parish, are also instructive, for John de Fulwode was also given as an *armiger* in the same poll tax. The Fulwodes held the manor of Fulwood or Clay Hall.[101] John de Fulwode sealed non-heraldically in the 1360s, but heraldically in 1383 and 1399. We find a paschal lamb in 1366, a bird and a stag's head in 1368; there is nothing to indicate that these are personal seals, and the paschal lamb for example is commonly found in the collection.[102] By contrast the seal of 1399 is said on the legend to be his. It is a shield *crusily, three buckles on a bend*. The 1383 seal is also crusily with a bend.[103] Two other members of the Fulwode family appear to have sealed heraldically, however, as early as 1349, viz. *within a bordure a bend between six mullets*.[104]

The limitations of the evidence from a single, though quite extensive, deed collection are obvious. The lack of earlier deeds for some of these families makes proof difficult, but the evidence points clearly to the increasing adoption of heraldic seals by them during the middle decades of the fourteenth century. The Archers appear to lead the way, as early as 1321, and it may be significant that they had become more prosperous in recent times. However, the status of Brother Thomas, as prior of the Hospital of St John, must also have been a factor. The Archers were followed by Robert de Crewenhale who had an heraldic seal by 1340, and by Henry de Sidenhale and the Fulwodes thereafter. John de Fulwode, Henry Sidenhale and Thomas le Archer all figure as esquires in the 1370s.[105] In the preceding decades they had become heraldic. None of the families was ex-knightly. It would seem then that by the 1320s heraldic seals were already being used sporadically by men of such station, and that this became commoner from the 1340s.

Despite its limitations, the evidence appears, cumulatively, to be reasonably clear. The appearance of esquire as a social rung can be dated to the middle third of the fourteenth century. Esquire as we perceive it more clearly in the 1360s and 1370s is a fairly inclusive category. This may help to explain the delay in its development. There is evidence from the early fourteenth century, if not before,

---

[101] According to Dugdale the Sidenhale manor passed to them by marriage in 1330, but this is clearly in error. John de Fulwode had licence for a private oratory in 1395 and the family did well in the fifteenth and sixteenth centuries.

[102] Archer Deeds, nos. 706, 718, 720.

[103] *Ibid.*, nos. 764, 823. A crusily is a variety of field semé, that is powdered with charges; in this case with crosslets.

[104] One is an agreement between Robert de Fulwode, perpetual vicar of Tanworth and Simon son of Robert de Fulwode and his wife, while the other involves Ranulf son of Robert de Fulwode (Archer Deeds, nos. 635, 662). John's father, however, appears to have been William de Fulwode who had used a variety of non-heraldic devices during the 1340s, and possibly earlier (*ibid.*, nos. 475, 516, 602, 603). The pedigree is unclear.

[105] According to Dugdale, Thomas was an esquire of the earl of Warwick at this time (*Antiquities of Warwickshire*, p. 780). He may well be the man who is called Thomas Rich in the 1379 poll tax returns.

of status consciousness below the level of the knight. We can discern it in the growing fashion for heraldic sealing and we seem to perceive it in the relatively restricted groups who were summoned to the Great Council in 1324. It would be very surprising had this not been the case within the localities. But, of course, there were no rites below knighthood to generalise any differentiation and there was a lack of clear social terminology. The emergence of a broad category of esquire may well represent something of a retreat from narrower and more exclusive feelings of social superiority.

What it represents, arguably, is the triumph of a territorial conception of status. It can hardly be coincidental that this development followed hard upon the emergence of the Commons as a significant political force and that it was concurrent with the maturation of the justice of the peace. In short, the development of the esquire is symptomatic of the formation of the English gentry.

The rise of the esquire as a social category did not, of course, fix matters for all time. Although the category was a wide one, it did not include all those with a claim to gentility, as the sumptuary legislation of 1363 makes clear. Tension around this issue may well have increased towards the end of the century. One has only to think of Chaucer's Franklin.[106] By the first decade of the fifteenth century, moreover, the status of esquire was being explicitly celebrated in funeral monuments. In addition to the Lambourn brass already mentioned, there is the brass to John Mulsho, esquire, and his wife at Geddington, Northamptonshire, dated 1400, for example, and the brass to Thomas Seintleger, esquire, at Otterden, Kent, of 1408.[107] Among early stone effigies which make reference to the status is that to John Wyard at Meriden, Warwickshire, of around 1405.[108] Despite the Statute of Additions of 1413, the social acceptance of the mere gentleman took some time to achieve.[109] A spirit of social exclusion may help to explain the appearance of esquire as a designation in witness lists during the 1420s and 1430s.[110] One must be wary, though, of taking diplomatic fashion too much at face value. The status of esquire had been well recognised for some considerable time. When Thomas le Archer of Tanworth in Arden conveyed his manors to feoffees in 1392, the transaction was witnessed by Thomas Maureward, knight, and by Henry de Sidenhale and John de Fulwode. Although we know

---

[106] See Coss, *The Knight in Medieval England*, pp. 153–8 and the essays cited there.

[107] See M. Norris, *Monumental Brasses: The Memorials*, 2 vols. (London, 1977), vol. I, pp. 55, 58; vol. II, fig. 67, and the same author's *Monumental Brasses: The Craft* (London, 1978), fig. 60.

[108] See Brian Kemp, 'English Church Monuments during the Period of the Hundred Years War', in Anne Curry and Michael Hughes (eds.), *Arms, Armies and Fortifications in the Hundred Years War* (Woodbridge, 1994), p. 200 and plate xxxi. For the inscription see Dugdale, *Antiquities of Warwickshire*, p. 987. I am extremely grateful to Professor Kemp for his advice and for saving me from error in these matters.

[109] For recent confirmations of this, see Acheson, *Leicestershire in the Fifteenth Century*, p. 34, and Carpenter, *Lordship and Polity*, p. 44.

[110] *Ibid.*, p. 48.

Henry and John to have been esquires from the 1379 poll tax returns they are lacking here in any designation. By contrast, however, two of the feoffees are named, in the body of the text, as William Bracy of Warmington, esquire, and John Charnels, esquire.[111] Although the fifteenth century was to see much readjustment before social gradation reached full maturity, by the middle of the fourteenth century the process was well underway.

[111] Archer Deeds, no. 802.

10. *Crystallisation: the emergence of the gentry*

The gentry finally crystallised during the first half of the fourteenth century. How should we account for this? Clearly, a full explanation has to encompass both social and institutional factors. I intend to approach the subject first by examining the structure of the gentry, and secondly by looking again at the characteristics of the gentry as outlined at the beginning of this study.[1]

THE STRUCTURE OF THE GENTRY

When the gentry finally took shape towards the middle of the fourteenth century the county knights became its highest gradation. Their history has sometimes been written, however, as though they had occupied this position long before: as the highest grade in advance of gradation. On this reading the corpus of thirteenth-century knights was simply subdivided to form the fourteenth-century ranks. But this is to read history backwards. Moreover, it simplifies a complex evolution and it assumes a predetermined outcome. Among other things, it fails to account for the delay in the emergence of a second rank, the esquires. In fact, a sociologist observing the English nobility around the year 1300, and without the value of hindsight, could be forgiven for thinking that it was evolving along the same lines as the French noblesse, so intense was the sense of difference expressed by and around knighthood.

Nevertheless there were factors pulling this exclusive knighthood asunder. Most obviously, there was the existence of a higher nobility. The line of demarcation between higher and lower nobility had never been particularly clear. It has been calculated recently that there was something in the region of eighty to ninety men who could be truly described as magnates at any one point during the thirteenth century.[2] They were distinguished by their wealth and the

---

[1] See above, pp. 9–11.
[2] By Barbara Harvey in 'The Aristocratic Consumer', p. 19, refining David Crouch's estimate of around 100 which was based on Glover's Roll of Arms of *c*.1250. In 1200 there were about 160 baronies but they were subject to fragmentation. See Crouch, *Image of Aristocracy*, pp. 22–3.

widespread nature of their estates, as well as by their tendency to receive a personal summons to military campaigns and to parliaments. There were others who held their lands by barony, but this alone did not convey an automatic right to parliamentary summons. On the contrary, the summonses in the time of Edward I have been justly described as haphazard.[3] Of the fifty-three summoned in 1295, for example, twenty-two did not hold by baronial tenure and six were not even tenants-in-chief of the crown.[4] The most important criterion appears to have been a magnate's standing with, and value to, his monarch. K.B. McFarlane calculated that in 1300 there were at least 136 families whose heads had been summoned on one or more occasions.[5] There can be no doubt, however, as McFarlane stressed, that the higher nobility became less fluid and more exclusive during the course of the fourteenth century and that a personal summons to parliament became the hallmark of membership.[6] The notion of precedent produced in effect a parliamentary baronage, the 'peers of the realm'. From the middle of the century it was becoming clear that a personal summons to parliament for someone outside the traditional ranks was an act of social and political promotion. A long-standing demarcation within English society had been strongly reinforced, and the net result was a neater, smaller and even more exclusive elite. As McFarlane put it, 'a nobility of a type peculiar to England, having little in common with the French noblesse and the German Adel, first came into existence and established itself in that position of dominance in English society which it was to retain and exploit for several centuries'.[7] In the end only the parliamentary peers were to be considered truly noble. The rest of the nobility – the English gentry – enjoyed mere gentility, in effect a watered-down version of nobility.

However, the beginnings of this exclusive parliamentary peerage are detectable quite early in the fourteenth century. The term 'peers' was used in a parliamentary context as early as 1312.[8] As the study by J.E. Powell and K. Wallis showed, the list of those receiving a personal summons was already showing a strong tendency towards standardisation by the time of the battle of Bannockburn in 1314, even though it was periodically revised during the course of the century.[9] Although the actions of kings played a large part in these developments, there are major factors emanating from the baronage itself. These families had long practised endogamous marriage, for example,

---

[3] J.E. Powell and K. Wallis, *The House of Lords in the Middle Ages* (London, 1968), p. 309.

[4] Michael Prestwich, *The Three Edwards: War and State in England 1272–1377* (London, 1980), p. 140.

[5] K.B. McFarlane, *The Nobility of Later Medieval England* (Oxford, 1973), p. 144.

[6] For what follows I am much indebted to the judicious discussion by Given-Wilson, *The English Nobility*, ch. 2.

[7] McFarlane, *Nobility*, pp. 268–9, quoted by Given-Wilson, *The English Nobility*, p. 55.

[8] Prestwich, *The Three Edwards*, p. 140.

[9] Powell and Wallis, *The House of Lords*, pp. 312–15.

and most specifically of their heirs, reinforcing their sense of social exclusion. The development of new legal procedures in the fourteenth century, especially the form of entail known as tail male, allowed them to manipulate and restrict the descent of their estates in ways that had not been possible before. Most importantly, the lords claimed the right to be tried and judged by their own peers in parliament, a right which was validated by statute in 1341.[10]

But the distinction between earl and baron on the one hand and knight on the other was not the only distinction. There was also the distinction between the knights bachelor and the bannerets, those 'senior' knights who led their own contingents in the field.[11] Bannerets were of considerable importance within the king's military household. They were significant, too, within magnate retinues, as illustrated by indentures of retainer. In 1317, for example, when as we have seen Sir John de Eure contracted to serve for life with the earl of Lancaster, it was specified that he would receive exactly the same liveries as the earl's other bannerets. Sir Nicholas Cryel undertook that if he became a banneret after inheriting his estates he would continue to serve Sir Stephen Segrave as he had done before while a bachelor.[12] To be sure this evidence suggests that the difference was 'one of degree rather than kind'.[13] Nevertheless, it was of considerable social significance. We see it in the Parliamentary Roll of Arms, where the bannerets are listed separately. We see it also in those rolls of arms known as Occasional Rolls. And we see it again in their memorials where some men explicitly celebrated the rank of banneret.

It is hardly surprising, then, that banneret came to be considered a social as well as a military distinction. Although some bannerets earned their position on the battlefield, the rank had always had a tendency to reflect prior wealth. A knight like Nicholas Cryel was much more likely to become a banneret than one of more modest endowment. The king, however, could promote a man to the rank of banneret socially as well as militarily. In 1335, for example, Edward III granted Reginald Cobham of Sterborough 400 marks a year 'for his better maintenance in the estate of banneret... until the king provide for him four hundred marks yearly in land and rent for life'.[14] Men were summoned from among the bannerets to join the barons in parliament, although a distinction remained between them.[15] This distinction was to fade away with the word itself during the early fifteenth century to leave merely 'peers'. In the meantime, however, banneret had been recognised in the sumptuary legislation of 1363

---

[10] Given-Wilson, *The English Nobility*, p. 57.

[11] The argument which follows has been rehearsed in outline in Coss, 'Knighthood, Heraldry and Social Exclusion', pp. 66–8.

[12] *Indentures for Life*, nos. 13, 27.   [13] *Ibid.*, p. 20.

[14] *Cal. Pat. Rolls, 1334–8*, p. 346; Given-Wilson, *The English Nobility*, p. 62.

[15] A good example was the highly successful soldier, Thomas Ughtred, who was granted an annuity of £220 per year for life in 1347 and was summoned regularly to parliament and councils thereafter. See Ayton, 'Sir Thomas Ughtred', pp. 107–32.

and the poll tax preamble of 1379, and for a time it looked set to become a permanent social rank.[16]

The development of a rather precarious social rank of banneret and the hiving off of some of its more favoured members into the lords had the effect not of binding the lesser and the higher knighthood together but of reinforcing their separation. This separation continued to be reinforced, moreover, by the lingering service connotations of knighthood. To be a knight bachelor, in particular, was to be someone else's man. To be a knight bachelor was to be a member, actually or potentially, of another man's retinue, while the knighthood celebrated by the *Song of Carlaverock* and the Falkirk Roll was very largely the knighthood of those who brought their own retinues, that is to say of bannerets and above. Noble society was cohesive on one level – in that it was cemented by deeply shared values and ideals – but it was also deeply imbued with the notion of rank.

Of at least equal significance for the emergence of the gentry was the relationship between knights and those directly below them socially. Just as knights fought with bannerets, so they fought alongside other mounted men-at-arms including those normally referred to in indentures of retainer as *valetti*.[17] As the indentures make clear, such men were generally considered to be *gentils hommes*, and they tended to be recruited from the landowning families who had ceased to be knightly but whose military potential Edward I and Edward II tried hard to tap. Despairing perhaps of substantially increasing the number of knights, the crown sought to recruit the missing landowners, by compulsion if possible, under other names. These were the *scutifers*, *armigers* and the like, the sub-knightly cavalry who figure in the accounts of government departments. Many of them were of gentle rank, or at the very least on the margins of gentility. The Edwardian period as a whole saw what Andrew Ayton has aptly described as 'the "re-militarisation" of the gentle-born',[18] a re-militarisation which culminated in the high participation of the English gentry in the armies of Edward III.[19] The sheer numbers involved during the 1340s and 1350s underlines the significance of the sub-knightly soldier. According to the most recent calculations there may have been as many as 4,000 English men-at-arms at the siege of Calais in 1346–7, and well over 3,000 in the army that Edward III took

---

[16] For some recent observations on the rise and subsequent decline of the bannerets see Nigel Saul, *Death, Art, and Memory in Medieval England: The Cobham Family and Their Monuments 1300–1500* (Oxford, 2001), pp. 136–42.

[17] See, especially, Michael Prestwich, 'Cavalry Service in Early Fourteenth-Century England', pp. 147–58.

[18] Andrew Ayton, 'English Armies in the Fourteenth Century', in Curry and Hughes (eds.), *Arms, Armies and Fortifications*, p. 29.

[19] For a recent review of the evidence for this see Andrew Ayton, 'Edward III and the English Aristocracy at the Beginning of the Hundred Years War', in Matthew Strickland (ed.), *Armies, Chivalry and Warfare in Medieval Britain and France* (Stamford, 1998), pp. 173–206.

to France in 1359.[20] Well might Ayton say that 'the active warrior aristocracy extended well down the social hierarchy, beyond the knightly community, to rest squarely in the ranks of the lesser gentry'.[21] As Maurice Keen has recently pointed out, this increasing military experience has a direct bearing not only on the choice of the term esquire – with its strong military connotations – to designate the second rung of the gentry, but also on the squirearchy's adoption of 'heraldic' culture as the primary expression of its rise to social acceptability.[22] Warfare, he has no doubt, was the major stimulus to their adoption of arms: 'War . . . was where the esquire first and foremost needed a coat, and the close association between arms, gentility, and military service was integral to the mental world of the fourteenth century aristocracy, greater and lesser.' Arms will have been further diffused, he aptly suggests, by a process of 'acculturation', as those who had not been to war followed their neighbours who had in adopting coats.[23]

It was not only in war, moreover, that knights rubbed shoulders with other *gentils*. The indentures themselves remind us that lords required service in time of peace. Within aristocratic social life knights mixed with other men who were considered to be of gentle stock. Moreover, the term *valettus*, in common use since the middle of the thirteenth century to describe non-knightly household retainers, was also used to denote those landowners who were wealthy enough to be knights or who were avoiding knighthood.[24] By 1320, as we have seen, it came to be used of those members of parliament for the counties who were not knights and whose expenses were paid, therefore, at a lower rate. All of this reflects the existence of the 3,000 landowners whom Denholm-Young thought of, rather anachronistically perhaps, as potential knights. He deduced this principally from the thinning of knightly ranks in the thirteenth century, from the fact that at any one time a percentage of knightly families would have their male heirs under age, and from the continued existence of distraint to knighthood. In fact, although there was continual adjustment to cater for shifts in wealth and for the unusually ambitious, by 1300 knighthood was fast becoming the preserve of a restricted range of families. None the less, Denholm-Young's analysis highlights an important social reality. Non-knightly lords were often the seigneurial neighbours of knights. They lived cheek by jowl. And they shared many of the same concerns: with estates, with tenants and with a system of social control.

---

[20] See Ayton, 'Knights, Esquires and Military Service: The Evidence of the Armorial Cases before the Court of Chivalry', p. 83.

[21] *Ibid.*, p. 96. See also Morgan, *War and Society in Medieval Cheshire*.

[22] Maurice Keen, 'Heraldry and Hierarchy: Esquires and Gentlemen', in Jeffrey Denton (ed.), *Orders and Hierarchies in Late Medieval Europe* (Manchester, 1999), pp. 98–100.

[23] See Dr Keen's important new book, *The Origins of the English Gentleman* (Stroud, 2002), most especially ch. 5: 'The Rise of the Esquires'. I am most grateful to Dr Keen for allowing me to read this book in advance of publication.

[24] For the *valetti* see above, pp. 225–8.

On the ground the new knighthood of the mid to late thirteenth century had created something of an artificial divide.

That divide was bridged to some extent by the development of social gradation. As we have seen, the appearance of the esquire as a social rung belongs to the middle third of the fourteenth century. Heraldry, once again, provides the key to observing important social changes. The heraldic accommodation with the new squirearchy does not appear to have been achieved easily, or indeed overnight. It is not until the late fourteenth century that rolls of arms came to include substantial numbers of men who were not knights. The lost roll of Sir Robert Laton (c.1370) may well have been the first.[25] The first steps towards the acceptance of the esquire were taken with the wider use of heraldic seals. By the beginning of the fourteenth century the rule that only knights could seal their documents heraldically was already beginning to break down. In the first instance, however, the dam was breached by the male relatives of knights, cousins and younger brothers of knighted heads of families, a development which perhaps tended to reinforce traditional distinctions.[26] But it was also being breached sporadically by others, including household *valetti* of the great lords who were using seals that reflected the arms of their masters.[27] By the time we come to the 1330s and 1340s, however, we find heraldic sealing spreading rapidly downwards to encompass not only ex-knightly families of ancient stock but also those, old and new, who had never been knightly. That the dam remained intact for so long is a tribute to pride in lineage and to the exclusive nature of chivalric knighthood.

There was more happening here, however, than the belated rehabilitation of excluded landowners. As we have seen, the emerging squirearchy contained men of diverse origins, including the ex-knightly, the sub-knightly and administrators/men of law. As I have argued above, it is not helpful in this context to distinguish 'men of law' from the gentry. 'Man of law' is a slippery concept, and 'local man of the law' is more slippery still. Musson and Ormrod, as we have seen, define such men as 'those whose profession was the law or whose involvement in judicial and administrative affairs enabled them to acquire some legal knowhow'.[28] It is the generous second half of this definition which is contentious. Arguably, more than legal 'knowhow' is required before we classify someone as a 'man of law'. Stricter definitions are available. Robert Palmer, for instance, writes as follows:

> I consider a person involved in legal activities a professional lawyer when, for a period of years, that person appears to be spending the major part of his time in legal functions and deriving the greater part of his income from

---

[25] Keen, 'Heraldry and Hierarchy', p. 99.   [26] See above, pp. 232–6.

[27] See Adrian Ailes, 'Up in Arms: The Rise of the Armigerous *Valettus*', in A. Curry (ed.), *Thirty Years of Medieval Studies at the University of Reading: A Celebration* (Reading, 1996), pp. 9–15.

[28] Musson and Ormrod, *The Evolution of English Law*, pp. 62–3. And see above, p. 182.

those activities or, at least, from the investments made from that income, and when that person possesses a specialised knowledge differentiating him from laymen.[29]

If we follow this definition we should confine local man of law, *stricto sensu*, to those professional serjeants and, less certainly, professional attorneys operating in county and other local courts from late in the reign of Edward I.[30] Perhaps we might include as 'local men of the law' those professional attorneys operating in the central courts who drew the majority of their business from a single county.[31] We might also conceivably refer to the central court professionals as local to the counties where they originated and/or maintained or developed a strong material base. But to regard all those administrators who deployed some knowledge of the law in the service of their lords or who ever acted as attorneys as 'men of law' is surely to stretch an elastic term too far. Most county knights must have possessed some legal knowledge; they could hardly have protected their own property without it. And those knights who delivered the gaols must have possessed the necessary 'knowhow' to have been able to do so. But one would hardly wish to call them 'men of law'. Pushed to the limits 'man of law' becomes redundant as a distinctive social category. Nevertheless, lawyers and administrators *did* play a significant role in the emergence of the gentry.

If we are to understand that role correctly we need to view them from a longer perspective. Bailiffs, stewards and other administrators had been around for centuries. However, the demand for service greatly increased during the course of the thirteenth century. As Scott Waugh has stressed, 'local offices multiplied as kings asserted their legal, feudal and fiscal powers' whilst landowners required an 'army' of professionals as they responded to the changes set in train by the late twelfth-century shift towards the direct exploitation of estates.[32] Service became more sophisticated. In this increasingly literate society, treatises proliferated to instruct on best practice when it came to stewardship, management of husbandry, accountancy and so on.[33] There was even a school of business-training

---

[29] Palmer, *County Courts of Medieval England*, p. 89 n. 1. Paul Brand's definition is similar: 'For me a "professional lawyer" is someone recognised by others as having a special expertise in legal matters and who is willing to put that expertise at the disposal of others, who is paid for doing this and who spends a major part of his time in this professional activity' (*Origins of the English Legal Profession*, p. vii).

[30] For a review of the evidence see *ibid.*, pp. 83–5. For a different, and rather maximalist, view of the role of professionals in local courts see R.C. Palmer, 'The Origins of the Legal Profession in England', *The Irish Jurist*, new series, 11 (1976), pp. 126–46. See also the same author's 'County Year Book Reports', pp. 776–801.

[31] Brand, *Origins of the English Legal Profession*, p. 75. By 1300 almost two-thirds of professional attorneys operating in the Common Bench fall into this category.

[32] Waugh, 'Tenure to Contract', p. 815.

[33] On literacy see especially M.T. Clanchy, *From Memory to Written Record: England 1066–1307* (2nd edn, Oxford, 1993), ch. 7: 'Literate and Illiterate'. For the treatises see *Walter of Henley*, ed. Oschinsky.

operating on the margins of the university at Oxford.[34] The most profession-alised area of all, however, came to be the law. The increasing complexity of the common law and an appetite for litigation among the propertied classes gave rise to the professional lawyer. Paul Brand puts the matter succinctly: 'once we reach the reign of Edward I, it begins to make sense to talk about the existence of a legal profession in England'.[35] By 1300 professional pleaders and attorneys had long been operating at Westminster. By the early fourteenth century the former can be seen practising in the county courts, and professional attorneys may well have been there too. They are certainly in evidence a generation later, in the early 1330s. Lawyers were trained in the courtroom. But they were also being instructed in the classroom and through private reading, as the surviving treatises indicate. In fact, 'it seems clear that there was a market in the second half of the thirteenth century for elementary legal instruction and probable that among the persons comprising this market a considerable number were intend-ing to practise as professional attorneys'.[36] But, by implication, not all of them. Indeed, it had become important for any successful administrator, as indeed for any landowner, to possess some legal 'knowhow'. It is hardly surprising that people of property increasingly employed and contracted with lawyers and men who were versed in the law. Service was almost invariably profitable and not sur-prisingly there have been many studies of the upward mobility it engendered.[37] Famously, a man could move from seigneurial to royal service in search of in-creased advancement. Nevertheless, the horizons of many a thirteenth-century administrator must have remained very local. Formal education and the magnet of Westminster was to broaden those horizons. As the fourteenth century pro-gressed, moreover, some local administrators and lawyers began to play a wider role, as commissioned justices for example and as MPs, where they operated alongside entrenched, and largely knightly, landowners.

Two Warwickshire men make the point eloquently. One is William Erneys, the descendant of Richard son of Ernis who was a tenant of the prior of Coventry in the late twelfth and early thirteenth century.[38] During the 1240s Richard son

---

[34] H.G. Richardson, 'Business Training in Medieval Oxford', *American History Review* 46 (1941), pp. 259–80.

[35] Brand, 'Origins of the English Legal Profession'; reprinted in his *The Making of the Common Law*, p. 11.

[36] Brand, *Origins of the English Legal Profession*, p. 117. For the early history of legal education in England see the same author's 'Courtroom and Schoolroom: The Education of Lawyers in England prior to 1400', *Historical Research* 60 (1987); reprinted in his *The Making of the Common Law*, pp. 57–76.

[37] Two good examples are G.G. Astill, 'Social Advancement through Seignorial Service? The Case of Simon Pakeman', *Transactions of the Leicestershire Archaeological and Historical Society* 54 (1978–9), pp. 14–25, and Walker, 'Sir Richard Abberbury', pp. 113–40.

[38] For what follows see Coss, *Lordship, Knighthood and Locality*, pp. 149–54 and Coventry Priory Register (PRO E164/21, fos. 45b, 58b, 59, 195). I have used the forthcoming edition by Joan Lancaster Lewis for the Dugdale Society.

of Richard Ernis exchanged his property in the town for land at nearby Sowe (now Walsgrave on Sowe), which he was to hold of the prior on favourable terms. Richard became a member of the prior's ministerial team, and he seems to have possessed some legal expertise which was placed at his lord's disposal. He was particularly associated with the prior's premature attempt to unite fully his two jurisdictions in Coventry during the 1260s. Needless to say, Richard prospered and, through a series of purchases, added to the nucleus of his estate at Sowe. The centre of his operations was Attoxhall on the edge of the wastes. It was here that the family possessed the moated dwelling with its orchard and grove, known in the fifteenth century as *Erneysplace* and in later times as Moat House Farm. Erneys Green was nearby. No doubt it was a sumptuous dwelling which functioned as a status symbol differentiating Richard Ernis and his de-scendants from their newly acquired tenants. Richard was a thirteenth-century success story of a familiar kind. His interests, however, were intensely local.

The family continued to prosper and, for a time, they continued to serve the prior. William Erneys, whom we have encountered already in our survey of Warwickshire commissions, was in the same mould as Richard Ernis, who was probably his grandfather. He, too, was an effective administrator as well as a farmer of some substance. During the years 1332–5 he was royal escheator across five counties,[39] moving on to become a steward of Queen Isabella. Ironi-cally, given his family background, he played a major part in – and very probably masterminded – the campaign of harassment which wrested the prior's lord-ship over Coventry from him.[40] Between 1334 and 1340 William was four times MP for Warwickshire. We might well classify him as a local administrator/man of law, and equate him with his ancestor, Richard Ernis. But, unlike this Richard, he was able to represent his county at Westminster and to play a role on the national scene.

Robert de Stoke – steward, attorney, royal taxer, gaol deliverer and justice of the peace – was of a similar background to William Erneys and from the same area.[41] As he demonstrated at the 1285 eyre, Robert could trace his ancestors back, in direct line, to the limits of legal memory, that is to say to one Ivo living in the time of Richard I. The family had held directly of the earls of Chester, with whom they would seem to have had a service association.[42] Although their association with a major lordship may have involved some local prestige,

[39] Warwickshire, Leicestershire, Nottinghamshire, Derbyshire and Lancashire. See *Lists and Indexes PRO*, no. 72, p. 168, and *Cal. Close Rolls, 1330–3* and *1333–7*.

[40] For his local activities see, especially, Arthur and Eileen Gooder, 'Coventry before 1355: Unity or Division?', *Midland History* 6 (1981), pp. 16–19 and note 108. His interests were at Attoxhall, Sowe, Foleshill and Wyken.

[41] For what follows see Coss, *Lordship, Knighthood and Locality*, pp. 52, 312–14, and above pp. 191–2.

[42] Their remote ancestor was very probably the Robert de Stoke who had witnessed a charter for Earl Hugh II back in the 1150s.

in terms of income from land at least, the thirteenth-century Stokes were hardly more than wealthy freeholders, living, one might say, on the margins of gentility. Robert de Stoke, through his commissions and his increased wealth, brought them in from those margins. A series of purchases between c.1290 and 1309 made him a major figure in the area as well as the undoubted lord of Stoke. By the time he became a justice of the peace in 1314 he was a landowner of some significance as well as a successful professional. Robert and his successors lived very comfortably at Stoke. In the mid-fourteenth century their stylish manor house comes into view, with its garden, 'knight's chamber', and elaborate gatehouse with a chamber over. The absorption of 'new' families must often have been uneasy. Perhaps the erstwhile service connotations of knighthood itself, whose echoes are found even in the fourteenth century, helped to make it easier. It was certainly facilitated by the increased territoriality of the lesser nobility and by the associated phenomenon of horizontal banding. The inclusion of lawyers and administrators certainly gave the gentry one of its enduring characteristics. The capacity to absorb the upwardly mobile contributed greatly to its strength as a ruling class.

THE CHARACTERISTICS OF THE GENTRY

This study began by defining the characteristics of the gentry as a social formation. In the first place, the gentry was a type of lesser nobility. It enjoyed a powerful elite culture. Built initially around an exclusive knighthood, this was transmitted downwards but without losing its essence. Secondly, although based on land, that is to say upon ancient forms of property, it was nevertheless able to accommodate the influx of professionals. The remaining four characteristics are the components of territoriality: collective identity, status gradation, local public office and authority over the populace. They are significant not only in themselves but also in their interrelationship, in their interdependence, and in their interaction with the social factors discussed above. Let us examine these interconnections whilst reviewing our major findings, beginning with the growth of collective identity.

The identity of the gentry begins essentially with the county. The county, of course, had deep roots in English society, but it was during the second half of the thirteenth century that it began to play a crucial role in the emergence of the gentry. The experience of the grand assize seems likely to have caused knights to think of themselves as knights of specific counties, and the thinning of knightly ranks can only have enhanced this. The demand in the Provisions of Oxford that sheriffs be vavasours of the counties they administered points to the existence of a purely territorial elite. The territorial elite was enhanced during the second half of the century as judicial and other commissions fell to a more restricted sector of the community. Other factors came into play.

The development of the county as a parliamentary constituency was of vital importance. The reformers of 1258–9 and the Montfortian rebels politicised the counties to an extent that had hardly happened before, but it was the longer-term consequences of the period of reform and rebellion which were of most significance, principally the interlocking of parliament with the localities. The explosion in commissions during the second half of the reign of Edward I brought an increasing proportion of the knights into service, including men of the more militaristic type who hitherto had tended to remain aloof. Judicial commissions, in particular, enhanced the territoriality of their social power with its implication of collective control over the populace. There can be little doubt that the concept of county elites was growing during this period. Of course there were knights, as there long had been, whose wider interests transcended county boundaries. Even among these, however, there was a tendency to identify principally with one county or another. That this sense of identity had become much stronger by the 1320s is suggested by sheriffs' returns to royal writs in which they specified which knights were resident in their county.[43]

There were other significant developments in these years. The troubles of Edward II's reign considerably enhanced the role of the Commons in parliament. It can hardly be coincident that the broadening of the social base from which MPs were drawn followed swiftly on from this. Until the 1320s knights dominated the parliamentary representation of Warwickshire, as we have seen. What was true of Warwickshire, moreover, was true elsewhere. Margery Basset noted that thirteen out of the fifteen known representatives for Bedfordshire during the reign of Edward I were certainly knights at the time of their election and that the other two are observable as knights sometime thereafter. Of the nineteen new members during the following reign, fifteen were knights on election and one other was knighted thereafter. By contrast, only two thirds of the thirty-seven new members during the reign of Edward III were knights.[44] In Northamptonshire thirteen of the fifteen men elected between 1290 and 1306 were returned by the sheriff as knights in 1297.[45] Moreover, it is not only in the midlands that this phenomenon is found. It is observable in counties as far apart as Kent and Northumberland.[46] By 1320, in contrast, the parliamentary *valettus* had appeared on the scene. What is especially interesting is that, the occasional man of law aside, the sub-knightly landowner figures in the Commons *before*

---

[43] See above, pp. 213–14.

[44] Margery Basset, *Knights of the Shire for Bedfordshire during the Middle Ages*, Bedfordshire Record Society 29 (Bedford, 1929).

[45] The other two were John de Lyons, returned by the sheriff as a man-at-arms (*armiger*) in 1297, and Stephen Rabaz who was sheriff of Warwickshire and Leicestershire from 1290 to 1293.

[46] See Rev. J. Cave-Brown, 'Knights of the Shire of Kent from A.D. 1275 to A.D. 1831' in *Archæologia Cantiana* 21 (1985), pp. 198–210 and C.H. Hunter Blair, 'Members of Parliament for Northumberland (October 1258–January 1327)' in *Archæologia Æliana*, 4th series, 10 (1933), pp. 140–211.

he figures on royal commissions. That is to say, by and large the county knight was prepared to elect him before the crown was prepared to appoint him taxer or keeper of the peace. In one way this should not surprise us. For some time the counties had been electing non-knights as coroners. But member of parliament was a trust of a different order. Their election here suggests that, for all the differences of status, county society was coalescing.

It is important to stress that the crown did not create the graded gentry. Indeed, when it came to appointments to offices and commissions its attitude tended to be a conservative one. But it did have to take account of social changes. A recent study of the fourteenth-century sheriff by Richard Gorski has shown that the 'premeditated transfer of sheriffs from one county to another, still a feature in the opening decades [of the fourteenth century], has all but ceased by the accession of Edward III'.[47] So, too, it seems, had the employment of relatively obscure men, that is to say men whose material interests in the county are difficult to reconstruct.[48] It is probable that the strength of contemporary opinion had some part to play in this. Moreover, opinion in the counties was beginning to regard certain types of interest as inadequate for major office. In a famous case in 1318, for example, the crown was petitioned by the men of Leicestershire that their sheriff, William de Neville, should be removed, as the only land he held in the county was his wife's dower.[49]

The consequences can be seen in subsequent decades as the crown responded to manpower needs and to changing attitudes. We have seen the effects in the membership of the various commissions. Looking not only at the shrievalty but also at MPs and the other major offices, Gorski detected a major shift away from heavily knight-dominated administration towards the employment of both knights and esquires: 'Thus, if lists of the busiest local officials in the 1330s can at times resemble a roll call of English knights, by 1360 the situation in most counties was very different.'[50] The speed of change was variable. Southern and south midland counties were very much in the van, with northern counties, Norfolk/Suffolk and Somerset/Dorset lagging behind. But the direction of change was unmistakable. The reign of Edward III saw 'the emergence of esquire officials scattered throughout the kingdom'.[51]

[47] Gorski, 'The Fourteenth-Century Sheriff', pp. 39–40.

[48] 'They are "obscure" in the sense that little or nothing survives about their estates, and they appear in almost every county, particularly in the opening decades of the century' (*ibid.*, p. 55). However, Gorski also makes the point that their obscurity may be due to the inadequacies of our evidence (*ibid.*, pp. 55–6).

[49] Saul, *Knights and Esquires*, p. 114. The same attitude may have lain behind opposition to the sheriff of Nottingham, John de Oxenford, in 1334. See J.R. Maddicott, 'The Birth and Setting of the Ballads of Robin Hood', *English Historical Review* 93 (1978), pp. 276–99. For the Devon examples of Hildebrand of London and Hervey Tyrel in 1335 and 1341 respectively, see Gorski, 'The Fourteenth-Century Sheriff', p. 66.

[50] *Ibid.*, p. 79.

[51] *Ibid.*, p. 80. Overwhelmingly, the public careers of members of the gentry, their 'political activities' as Gorski calls them, were closely tied to their property. This can be seen not only in

In its attempts to regulate the clothing that the various 'estates' should wear, the sumptuary legislation of 1363 illustrated the fact that, socially speaking, the esquire had come of age. But, in doing so, it reflected far more than this. In reality, it was not just the esquire but the gentry that had come of age. What it reflected were the profound changes that had occurred during the first half of the fourteenth century. This is not to say, of course, that the gentry was fixed for all time. On the contrary, as is well known, it continued to evolve. The fact that the sumptuary legislation spoke of other gentle men below the esquires reminds us that there was a third, as yet inchoate, grade of gentry in the making, whose precise contours were to be determined, in part at least, by the complex social changes which followed in the wake of the plague. The status of gentleman was to be recognised by act of parliament in 1413.[52] There were other changes too. During the later fourteenth century, for example, the emergence of smaller 'administrative communities' in the counties, with a balance of esquires and knights, has been discerned.[53] The justice of the peace continued to evolve, and quarter sessions seem to have become a rival focus to the county court. Some historians of the fifteenth century speak of the social gulf that existed between greater and lesser gentry.[54] And so on. Nevertheless, by the middle of the fourteenth century all of the major ingredients which constituted the English gentry were in place. There was a central forum for the articulation of its interests, allowing opinion to take shape in the localities and to be effectively communicated. There was a powerful elite culture. There was a strong measure of control over local justice which would ensure the gentry's social pre-eminence. And, finally, there was a system of social gradation which allowed for significant differences while at the same time expressing a collective identity.

THE GENTRY AS AN IDEAL TYPE

The English gentry emerged as a part society.[55] It is necessary to ask how it related to the other parts. One of the current trends within later medieval English history stresses the community of interests which existed between crown, higher

the careers of men of ancient lineage but also in cases where public responsibilities followed in the wake of estate building. It also worked in the opposite direction, as men faded from public view: 'if the administrative responsibilities of the gentry mirrored the acquisition of their lands, then the same applied when their estates were fragmented or lost' (*ibid.*, p. 43). Thus, if men held office in more than one county this was because they had strong interests in both.

[52] On the subject see now Keen, *Origins of the English Gentleman*, esp. chs. 6–8.

[53] *Ibid.*, p. 80.

[54] See the works cited in 'The Formation of the English Gentry' above. However, see also C. Moreton, 'A Social Gulf? The Upper and Lesser Gentry of Later Medieval England', *Journal of Medieval History* 17, no. 3 (1991), pp. 255–62.

[55] The analogy is with peasant society as seen by Kroeber and Redfield. For a summary of this position see T. Shanin (ed.), *Peasants and Peasant Societies* (Harmondsworth and New York, 1971), p. 14.

nobility and gentry, and which extended, even, to lesser freeholders.[56] As a corrective to more conflictual models, the consensual approach has much to recommend it. This was, to be sure, a sophisticated society in which there was much to be consensual about. All property owners had a stake in preserving good order and ensuring that serious conflicts should be contained. There were also class interests to be considered. It is surely significant that the keepers of the peace finally secured their powers to determine at the very time that the need to assert control over the rural tenantry and workforce was particularly acute, that is to say in the aftermath of the Black Death.

Nevertheless, the interests of crown, higher nobility and gentry, however much they interlocked, by no means always coincided. The very fact that historians analyse the later medieval polity in these terms implies this. Christine Carpenter, for example, despite seeing an essentially symbiotic relationship between (higher) nobility and gentry, none the less shows their vantage points to have been different. The former, she writes, in order 'to offer the right sort of protection to their clients, needed to control the whole county'.[57] Magnate rule was a particular type of rule with an accent upon vertical ties and personal subordination to a great lord. Members of the gentry co-operated with great lords for a variety of reasons, including self-interest, and often, no doubt, because they had little choice in the matter. The fact that magnate rule, when it was effective, needed to accommodate the gentry's own network of associations and alliances indicates that it was not the only way to order the localities. Running counter to the higher nobility's traditional practice of vertical territorial control based on personal dependence was the principle of local office dominated by local men looking to the crown. The triumph of this principle, it has been argued, was potentially injurious to the higher nobility unless they could effectively control it.[58]

But, in fact, it is also the case that the position adopted by the crown and the position occupied by the gentry on this issue were by no means always the same. The crown's version of self-government at the king's command contained the capacity to call upon whomsoever it wished (and wished to favour) *as individuals* and for them to answer the call. As Richard fitz Nigel wrote in the *Dialogue of the Exchequer* (completed 1179): 'It is the king's prerogative as chief of the executive that any man in the kingdom, if the king need him, may be freely taken and assigned to the king's service, whose man soever he be, and whomsoever he serves in war or in peace.'[59] Despite concessions where necessary to the principle of representation – when knights were asked

---

[56] See, pre-eminently, Gerald Harriss: 'Political Society and the Growth of Government in Late Medieval England', *Past and Present* 138 (1993), pp. 28–57.

[57] Carpenter, *Locality and Polity*, p. 10.

[58] On this point see my 'Bastard Feudalism Revised', pp. 27–64, and the ensuing debate in *Past and Present* 131 (1991).

[59] *Dialogus de Scaccario*, ed. Johnson, p. 84.

to Westminster to discuss taxation, for example, or when it came to the election of members of parliament – there is no reason to doubt that this long remained the crown's essential position.

The gentry tended to feel differently. Central were the issues of appointment and accountability. The case of the sheriff is well known. The crown demanded of sheriffs that they should be, as individuals, personally (and quite literally) accountable; the gentry, by contrast, wished to see them accountable, in the broader sense, to their community.[60] The attitude of the Commons towards the appointment of justices of the peace is also indicative. The Commons first sought their nomination in the counties but then shifted ground to seek parliamentary appointment, most probably because the former system left open the likelihood of magnate intervention.[61]

Their failure here is symptomatic. Full gentry power in the localities was not to be realised. Indeed, it could not be realised without a tamed crown and a higher nobility whose social distance was sufficiently reduced that they constituted, in effect, the highest gradations of the gentry. For a long time to come, English political life, and much else besides, was to be dominated by the interplay of these three forces. This is not to say that there was incessant conflict between three mutually exclusive interests; such a proposition would be patently absurd. When open clashes occurred or clear programmes were articulated they came as a result of specific conjunctures. Nor should it be suggested that individuals held predetermined views in accordance with their position in the social structure. The relationships struck by members of the gentry, magnates and the crown were many and complex, and they naturally influenced attitudes. It would be extremely hazardous to attempt to construct an exclusive gentry mentality. What can be said is that the interests of crown, higher nobility and gentry are at the very least analytically distinct, and were often distinct in practice, and that the views that *were* held were related to the way in which society was structured.

All of this can be put in another way. The gentry can be understood as an ideal type. However, ideal types, although based upon observation of actual

---

[60] On the sheriff see Saul, *Knights and Esquires*, pp. 107–19 and works cited there.

[61] For the protracted debate on these issues between the 1330s and the 1360s and its implications see, in addition to the works noted above (pp. 181–5), Harriss, *King, Parliament and Public Finance*, pp. 401–10; Edward Powell, *Kingship, Law and Society: Criminal Justice in the Reign of Henry V* (Oxford, 1989), pp. 15–19; Saul, *Knights and Esquires*, pp. 128–35 and 'Conflict and Consensus in English Local Society', in John Taylor and Wendy Childs (eds.), *Politics and Crisis in Fourteenth-Century England* (Gloucester, 1990), pp. 38–58. It has recently been argued that there was, in fact, no consistent pattern of Commons petitioning in favour of justices of the peace during the 1320s and 1330s: Anthony Verduyn, 'The Politics of Law and Order during the Early Years of Edward III', *English Historical Review* 108 (1993), pp. 842–67. However, the evidence from these years is comparatively thin and this undoubtedly was the policy of the 1340s. Whilst it may be going too far to say that 'the advocacy of local justice may have been the first conscious policy the Commons had' (Harding, *Law Courts of Medieval England*, p. 95), it certainly corresponded closely to the gentry's interests.

phenomena, are unlikely to be present in reality in a pure, uncontaminated form. The actual configuration is the result of historical circumstance. The English gentry came into being as a social formation in a world dominated by higher social powers, and its form was modified accordingly. Thus, for example, the term esquire was utilised to fulfil a need – to designate a social grade below the knight – but it needed in practice to retain its service connotations to both crown and higher nobility and to encompass the special status of sons of the latter.[62] And, again, the institution of the justice of the peace yielded collective power to the gentry but in a manner which gave the crown overall control and left the magnates with an important stake. Part of the utility of the model approach is precisely that it serves to highlight actual historical limitations.

But whether one thinks in terms of a fully fledged 'ideal type' or only of more exact definition, the results are open to refinement by means of comparative study. Beyond such refinements, however, lies the deeper question of the peculiarity, even the uniqueness, of the English gentry among lesser nobilities. How different was the English experience, and how is this difference to be explained?[63] It is easy enough to point to the precocious strength of the English state. But it would be a restricted view which envisaged the gentry as the creation of the crown, in any unilateral sense. Clearly, it is the *relationship* between the lesser nobility and the central government which is significant. Arguably, this relationship allowed the English gentry to develop in a relatively ordered fashion. A comparative treatment, however, is beyond the scope of the present book. It must be left for another occasion, and perhaps to another historian. In the meantime, I hope I have shown that close definition and attention to the process of formation are vital matters in their own right.

[62] On this point see Sayer, *English Nobility*, pp. 7–11.

[63] The potentiality of this line of inquiry is amply demonstrated by the series of thought-provoking essays in M. Jones (ed.), *Gentry and Lesser Nobility in Late Medieval Europe* (Gloucester, 1986). Their findings argue strongly against the replication of the English situation elsewhere. The focus, however, is rather different from the one adopted here.

Northamptonshire justices of assize and of gaol delivery from the Patent Rolls, 1221–46

1. Novel disseisin, Carlton 3 Aug. 1221:
   Stephen de Segrave, Thomas de Heydon, Maurice de Aundely

2. Nuisance, Charwelton, 22 Nov. 1221:
   Maurice de Aundely, David de Esseby, Walter de Pateshall, Richard Gubiun

3. Novel disseisin, Radstone, 5 Dec. 1222:
   Ralf Hareng, Walter de Pateshall, Robert de Salcey, Walter de Preston

4. Mort d'ancestor, Welton, 17 Feb. 1223:
   Ralf de Bray, Maurice de Aundely, Thomas de Heydon, William de Whiston
   Mandate replaces Thomas de Heydon with Thomas de Haddon

5. Assize d'utrum, Welford, 17 Feb. 1223:
   Justices as no. 4

6. Advowson, Scaldwell, 18 June 1224:
   Walter de Pateshall, Maurice de Aundely, David de Esseby, John de Hulcote

7. Advowson of Bulwick, 2 Oct. 1226:
   Maurice de Aundely, David de Esseby, Robert de Salcey, John de Hulcote

8. Darrein presentment, Irchester, 4 Jan. 1227:
   David de Esseby, Robert de Salcey, Richard Gubiun, John de Hulcote

9. Darrein presentment, Little Harrowden, 9 Jan. 1227:
   Same justices

10. Gaol delivery at Northampton on prisoners appealed by an approver, 10 July 1227:
    Sheriff of Northampton, Maurice de Aundely, William de Insula, Ascelinus de Sidenham, John de Hulcote

11. Novel disseisin, Ashby, 15 Aug. 1228:
    Maurice de Aundely, William de Whiston, Robert de Salcey, Geoffrey de Wandevill

12. Novel disseisin, Wilby, 12 Sept. 1228:
    Ralf Morin, Saer de Wollaston, William de Whiston, John de Hulcote

13. Novel disseisin, Ashby, 9 Dec. 1228:
    Stephen de Segrave, Walter de Preston, William de Insula

14. Novel disseisin, Snorscomb, 9 April 1229:
    Walter de Preston, David de Esseby, Robert de Salcey, John de Hulcote

15. Novel disseisin, Barnack, 5 May 1229:
    Stephen de Segrave and those he will associate with him

16. Novel disseisin, Cold Ashby, Feb.–March 1230:
    David de Esseby, Maurice de Aundely, John de Hulcote, Richard de Bluckevill

17. Novel disseisin, Lilbourne, Feb.–March 1230:
    William de Insula, Robert de Salcey, Walter de Preston, Geoffrey de Armenters

18. Mort d'ancestor, Desborough, 28 June 1230:
    William de Insula and those he will associate with him

19. Gaol delivery at Northampton, 7 May 1231:
    William de Insula, John de Hulcote, Robert de Salcey

20. Mort d'ancestor, Woodcroft, 8 July 1231:
    Stephen de Segrave

21. Mort d'ancestor, Sibberton, 3 June 1233:
    William de Insula, William de Whiston, John de Hulcote, Henry de Raunds

22. Assize d'utrum, Radmore [? *Radenor'*], June–July 1233:
    William de Raleigh, and those he will associate with him as justices of assize

23. Gaol delivery, Northampton, 2 Aug. 1233:
    William de Insula, Henry de Raunds, William de Whiston, John de Hulcote

24. Gaol delivery, Northampton, 29 Aug. 1234:
    William de Insula, Robert de Salcey, Geoffrey de Armenters, John de Hulcote

25. Novel disseisin, Warmington [? *Verninton*], 1234:
    William de Raleigh

26. Novel disseisin, Clapton, 27 June 1235:
    Robert de Salcey, John de Hulcote, Henry de Raunds, Richard de Irchester

27. Gaol delivery at Northampton, and assizes in those parts, to be held 13 Sept. 1235:
    William de Insula, John de Hulcote, Robert Grimbaud, Henry de Raunds

28. Assize d'utrum, Maidwell and Oxendon, 29 Aug. 1235:
    Same justices

29. Novel disseisin, Westpury, to be held 14 Jan. 1236:
    Gilbert de Preston, Robert Grimbaud, John de Hulcote, Henry de Raunds

30. Novel disseisin, Coton, to be held 26 July 1236:
    Geoffrey de Armenters, Gilbert de Preston, Roger de Whelton, Henry de Raunds

31. Novel disseisin, Warmington, to be held 23 Aug. 1236:
    Geoffrey de Armenters, Ralf fitz Reginald, Henry de Raunds, Gilbert de Preston

32. Gaol delivery at Northampton, 15 June 1237:
    William de Insula, Ralf fitz Reginald, Richard de Watervill, Geoffrey de Armenters

33. Gaol delivery at Northampton, 14 May 1238:
    Geoffrey de Armenters, John de Hulcote, Simon de Thorpe, Henry de Raunds

34. Assize, unspecified, Barnwell, to be held 6 July 1238:
    Geoffrey de Armenters, Simon de Thorpe, John de Hulecote, Henry de Raunds

35. Gaol delivery at Northampton, 3 July 1238:
    William de Culworth, Geoffrey de Armenters, Simon de Thorpe, Henry de Raunds

36. Assize, unspecified, Newnham, to be held 13 Oct. 1241:
    Geoffrey de Armenters, Roger de Whelton, Simon de Thorpe, Eustace de Watford

37. Attaint, Northampton, to be held 14 April 1241:
    Geoffrey de Armenters, Peter de Raleigh, Ralf fitz Reginald, Roger de Whelton

38. Assize, unspecified, Brampton, to be held 15 April 1241:
    William de Culworth, Geoffrey de Armenters, Simon de Thorpe, Henry de Raunds

39. Attaint, Addington, 27 June 1241:
    William de Culworth, Ralf fitz Roger, Robert de Pavely, Simon de Thorpe

40. Assize, unspecified, Lowick:
    Same justices

41. Gaol delivery at Northampton, 5 Aug. 1241:
    Geoffrey de Armenters, Henry de Raunds, Ralf fitz Reginald, Peter de Raleigh

42. Assize, unspecified, Brampton, to be held 12 Aug. 1241:
William de Culworth, Geoffrey de Armenters, Simon de Thorpe, Henry de Raunds

43. Assize, unspecified, Sutton, to be held 12 Aug. 1241:
Robert de Lexington

44. Assize, unspecified, Piddington, to be held at next county court after Michaelmas 1241:
Geoffrey de Armenters, Simon de Thorpe, Henry de Raunds, Robert de Pavely

45. Assize, unspecified, Brackley, to be held at next county court after Michaelmas 1241:
Geoffrey de Armenters, Simon de Thorpe, Henry de Raunds, Robert de Pavely

46. Assize, unspecified, Piddington and Denshanger, to be held at next county court after Michaelmas 1241:
Same justices

47. Assize, unspecified, Farthingstone, to be held at next county court after Michaelmas 1241:
William de Culworth, Geoffrey de Armenters, Simon de Thorpe, Robert de Pavely
Postea loco Simonis de Thorp assignatus erat Henricus de Raund'

48. Gaol delivery at Northampton, to be held 30 April 1242:
Henry de Raunds, Geoffrey de Wandevill, Roger de Whelton, Robert de Plumpton

49. Gaol delivery at Northampton, to be held 2 June 1242:
William de Culworth and Gilbert de Preston

50. Gaol delivery at Northampton, 1 Aug. 1242:
Gilbert de Preston, Simon fitz Simon, Geoffrey de Armenters, Simon de Thorpe

51. Mort d'ancestor, Addington, to be held 13 April 1243:
Gilbert de Preston

52. Assize unspecified, Steane, to be held 13 April 1243:
Gilbert de Preston with his fellow justices

53. Gaol delivery at Northampton, to be held 23 Feb. 1243:
Gilbert de Preston, Geoffrey de Armenters, Simon de Thorpe, Philip de Covel

54. Assize unspecified, Harlestone, to be held 2 Aug. 1243:
Gilbert de Preston, justice, with fellows

55. Assize unspecified, Caldecott, to be held 2 Aug. 1243:
    Gilbert de Preston with fellows

56. Novel disseisin, Finedon [*Tyngden'*], day to be arranged 1242:
    Gilbert de Preston with fellows

57. Assize unspecified, Brixworth, to be held 15 Jan. 1244:
    Gilbert de Preston and associates

58. Novel disseisin, Southwick, 27 April 1245:
    Gilbert de Preston

59. Nuisance, Furtho, 27 April 1245:
    Gilbert de Preston

60. Gaol delivery at Northampton, to be held 26 May 1245:
    Nicholas de Bassingbourne, William Brito, Ralf fitz Reginald, John de Hulcote

61. Novel disseisin, Barton, 12 June 1245:
    Robert Passelewe and fellows, justices for pleas of the forest

62. Mort d'ancestor, Barnwell, day and place to be arranged 1245/6:
    Jeremiah de Caxton

63. Gaol delivery at Northampton, to be held 4 June 1246:
    Geoffrey de Armenters, Roger de Whelton, Robert de Pavely, Eustace de Watford

64. Novel disseisin, Slipton, day and place to be arranged 1245/6:
    Gilbert de Preston and fellows

65. Novel disseisin, Badby, day and place to be arranged 1245/6:
    Gilbert de Preston and fellows

66. Novel disseisin, Broughton, to be held 25 Aug. 1246:
    Gilbert de Preston and fellows

67. Novel disseisin, Oxendon, to be held 19 Sept. 1246:
    Gilbert de Preston and fellows

68. Novel disseisin, Yardley, day and place to be arranged:
    Gilbert de Preston and fellows

69. Inquisition, Wollaston, 1246/7:
    Paulinus Piper assigned with Simon de Norwich

70. Novel disseisin, Peterborough, 1246/7:
    Master Simon de Walton

Sources: Dorse of Patent Rolls. Details are taken from the published rolls for the years 1220–32 and from C.A.F. Meekings, *Transcripts from the Dorse of the Patent Rolls*, 3 vols. (PRO unprinted) for the years 1232–46: *Patent Rolls*

1216–25, pp. 311, 342–3, 390, 391, 486; *Patent Rolls 1225–32*, pp. 84, 151–2, 159, 222, 224, 280–1, 288, 290, 354, 355, 365, 446, 449; Meekings vol. I, nos. 80, 99, 100, 224, 263, 317, 370, 372, 430, 529, 566: Meekings vol. II, nos. 654, 863, 894, 909, 961, 1025, 1040, 1088, 1089, 1142, 1234, 1235, 1241, 1265–7, 1320, 1330, 1339; Meekings vol. III, nos. 1370, 1375, 1399, 1407, 1421, 1449, 1468, 1608, 1609, 1628, 1632, 1700, 1704, 1709, 1712, 1720, 1731, 1736, 1737, 1756.

Place-names have been modernised, surnames standardised.

Warwickshire justices of assize and of gaol delivery from the Patent Rolls, 1220–46

1. Novel disseisin, Tamworth and Middleton, 25 Dec. 1220:
   William de Hartshill, William de Arden, Geoffrey Savage, William de Curli

2. Novel disseisin, Stourton, 22 Nov.–11 Feb. 1221–2:
   William de Hartshill, William de Arden, William de Curli, Ralf fitz Ralf
   (The justices were also to deal with an assize of mort d'ancestor between
   the same parties, over property at Stourton)

3. Novel disseisin, Barford, 8 June 1223:
   Prior of Coventry, Robert de Lexington, William de Curli, Master Roger
   de Charlecote

4. Gaol delivery, Warwick and Leicester, 9 March 1220:
   Stephen de Segrave, Thomas de Atley, Reginald Basset, William Picot

5. Assize, advowson, Cherrington, 27 Dec. 1225:
   William de Curli, William de Hartshill, Ralf le Butler, Philip de Kineton

6. Gaol delivery, Warwick and Leicester, 20 June 1227:
   Stephen de Segrave, William de Curli, Walter d'Eyvill, William Basset,
   Henry de Nafford

7. Novel disseisin, three cases, Warwick, 30 Sept. 1227:
   William de Curli, William de Luddington, John d'Abetot, Walter d'Eyvill
   (substituted for Henry de Nafford)

8. Novel disseisin, Harborough, 22 Sept. 1227:
   William de Curli, John Durvassal, William de Luddington, Philip de Esseby

9. Assize of nuisance, Brandon, 29 Sept. 1227:
   Walter d'Eyvill, William de Curli, John Durvassal, William de Wilmcote

10. Assize of novel disseisin, Myton and elsewhere, 9 Oct. 1227:
    William de Bishopton, William Huse, William de Luddington, Philip de
    Esseby

11. Darrein presentment, Alcester, 15 Oct. 1227:
William de Curli, William de Bishopton, William de Luddington, Geoffrey de Charlecote

12. Novel disseisin, Atherstone, 22 Oct. 1227:
Same justices

13. All assizes of novel disseisin at Warwick, 8 Nov. 1228:
Robert de Lexington, Walter d'Eyvill, William de Bishopton, John de Ladbroke

14. Darrein presentment, Wilmcote, 3 April 1228:
Walter d'Eyvill, John de Ladbroke, John Durvassal, Geoffrey de Charlecote

15. Assize, Barford, 13/16 Nov. 1228:
Walter d'Eyvill, John Durvassal, Geoffrey de Charlecote, William de Wilmcote

16. Novel disseisin, Grendon and Whittington, 7 Jan. 1229:
William de Luddington, Philip de Esseby, Roger Foliot, Reginald de Carleolo

17. Novel disseisin, Coleshill, 30 Jan./9 Feb. 1229:
Maurice le Butler, William de Lucy, John de Ladbroke, Geoffrey de Charlecote

18. Novel disseisin, Thurlaston, 5 May 1229:
William de Curli, John de Ladbroke, William de Luddington, Maurice le Butler

19. Novel disseisin, Farnborough, 5 July 1229:
Walter d'Eyvill, William de Bishopton, John de Ladbroke, Richard Peche

20. Novel disseisin, Ryton, 6 July 1229:
Robert de Lexington, John Durvassal, William de Wilmcote, John de Ladbroke

21. Novel disseisin, Thurlaston, 8 Oct. 1229:
William de Crescy, Walter de Estweit, William de Stanton, Thomas Sampson
(The names of the justices reflect the fact that the assize was held at Northampton.)

22. Gaol delivery, Kenilworth, 28 July 1230:
Walter d'Eyvill, John de Ladbroke, Ralf fitz Ralf, Geoffrey de Charlecote

23. Gaol delivery, Kenilworth, 3–7 May 1231:
William Basset, John de Ladbroke, William de Wilmcote

24. Novel disseisin, Marton, 8 July 1231:
[William] de Bishopton, William de Wilmcote, John Durvassal, Robert de Clopton

25. Gaol delivery, Kenilworth and Rothley, Leics., 12 Feb. 1232:
    William Basset, John de Ladbroke

26. Novel disseisin, Willey, 13 June 1233:
    Walter d'Eyvill, John de Ladbroke, William de Bishopton, Robert de Valle

27. Assize common pasture and way, Mancetter, 2 Aug. 1234:
    Robert de Lexington and fellows

28. Novel disseisin, Barford, 2 Aug. 1234:
    Same justices

29. Gaol delivery, Warwick, 9 Sept. 1234:
    William de Camville, John Durvassal, William de Luddington, Philip de Esseby

30. Novel disseisin, Whitnash, 9 Aug. 1235:
    William de Insula, John Durvassal, John de Ladbroke, Philip de Esseby

31. Gaol delivery, Warwick, 16 August 1235:
    William de Luddington, William de Camville, Maurice le Butler

32. Assize d'utrum, Itchington, 30 Aug. 1235:
    Thomas de Clinton [*Chynton'*], Walter d'Eyvill, William de Bracebridge, Alexander de Bickenhill

33. Novel disseisin, Ipsley, 19 Oct. 1235:
    William de Luddington, William de Camville, Maurice le Butler, Robert de Clopton

34. Novel disseisin, Hunningham, 18 Nov. 1235:
    John Durvassal, William de Wilmcote, Robert de Grendon, William de Bishopton

35. Assize, unspecified, Hunningham, 20 Jan. 1236:
    Same justices

36. Novel disseisin, Barford, 6 April 1236:
    Robert de Grendon, John Durvassal, William de Wilmcote, Robert Foliot
    (The same justices were reappointed to this case 13 May except that here the fourth justice is given as Roger Foliot.)

37. Assize, unspecified, Barford, 1236:
    Robert de Grendon, John Durvassal, William de Wilmcote, Robert Foliot

38. Assize of attaint – mort d'ancestor, Warwick, 15 Sept. 1236:
    Stephen de Segrave, John Durvassal, Robert de Grendon, Roger Foliot

39. Assize of nuisance, The Wolds, 9 Sept. 1236:
    William de Bishopton, William de Wilmcote, Robert de Clopton, Robert de Valle

40. Novel disseisin, Stourton and Cherrington, 6 Oct. 1236:
Richard de Amundevill, John Durvassal, William de Wilmcote, Roger Foliot

41. Novel disseisin, Hunningham, 9 Sept. 1236:
John de Ladbroke, John Durvassal, William de Wilmcote, Thomas de Wappenbury

42. Novel disseisin, Compton, 20 Jan. 1237:
Walter de Boyvill, John Durvassal, John de Ladbroke, William de Bishopton

43. Gaol Delivery, Warwick, 26 July 1237:
William de Insula, John de Ladbroke, William de Luddington, William de Bishopton
(Bartholomew Peche is later associated with them and they are described as knights.)

44. Novel disseisin, Sambourn, 22 Sept. 1237:
Maurice le Butler, Hugh de Arden, Richard de Amundevill, Roger Foliot

45. Assize of nuisance, Middleton, 27 Jan. 1237:
Robert de Grendon, Hugh de Mancetter, Richard de Amundevill, Roger Foliot

46. Gaol delivery, Warwick and Kenilworth, 24 Sept. 1238:
Maurice le Butler, Hugh de Arden, Richard de Amundevill, Roger Foliot

47. Novel disseisin, Kenilworth, 16 June 1238:
Richard de Amundevill, William de Curli, John Durvassal, William de Lucy

48. Gaol delivery, Warwick, 21 June 1238:
John Durvassal, Richard de Amundevill, William de Luddington, John de Ladbroke

49. Novel disseisin, Harborough, 23 July 1238:
Richard de Prestcote, John de Ladbroke, Richard Peche, Gerard de Alspath

50. Gaol Delivery, Warwick, 13 Sept. 1238:
Richard de Amundevill, John Durvassal, Roger Foliot, Nicholas de Withybrook
(*Postea* the following were made justices of gaol delivery, 1 Oct.: Maurice le Butler, John Durvassal, Robert de Clopton, William de Luddington)

51. Attaint – novel disseisin, Coventry, 13 Jan. 1240:
William de Culworth and Ralf de Sudeley

52. Novel disseisin, Marton on Dunsmore, 14 Jan. 1240:
Ralf de Sudeley, William de Culworth

53. Gaol delivery, Warwick, 18 Feb. 1241:
William Trussell, Bardolf de Chesterton, Robert de Grendon, Hugh de Arden

54. Assize, unspecified, Packington, morrow of octaves of close of Easter, 1241:
Bardolf de Chesterton, William de Luddington, Philip de Esseby, Nicholas de Withybrook

55. Novel disseisin, morrow of octaves of close of Easter, 1241:
Bardolf de Chesterton, William de Luddington, Philip de Esseby, Nicholas de Withybrook

56. Novel disseisin, Ashow, 27 May 1241:
Bardolf de Chesterton, William de Luddington, William de Curli, Nicholas de Withybrook deleted and John de Ladbroke interlined

57. Assize common pasture, Hardwick, to be taken at next county after St John Baptist 1241:
Thomas de Clinton, William de Curn, William de Luddington, William de Lucy

58. Assize mort d'ancestor, Fullbrook, 2 Aug. 1241:
Ralf de Sudeley, Robert de Grendon, John de Ladbroke, Bardolf de Chesterton

59. Assize, unspecified, at next county, Coventry, 1241:
Robert de Grendon, John de Ladbroke, Thomas de Clinton, William de Lucy

60. Assize common pasture, Brailes, same date and place?:
Same justices

61. Assize common pasture, Stretton, same date and place?:
Same justices

62. Assize, unspecified, Southam, at next county after Michaelmas, 1241:
Same justices

63. Assize, unspecified, Haseley, same date and place?:
Same justices

64. Assize common pasture, Leamington, same date and place?:
Same justices

65. Assize, unspecified, Dosthill, next county after Michaelmas, 1241:
Maurice le Butler, John de Ladbroke, William de Lucy, William de Luddington

66. Gaol delivery, Warwick, 30 July 1241:
Bardolf de Chesterton, William Trussell, Henry Pipard, Robert de Grendon

67. Assize, unspecified, Offord, same date and place?:
Same justices

68. Assize common pasture, Dosthill, next county after Michaelmas, 1241:
Maurice le Butler, Bardolf de Chesterton, Robert Bagod, Philip de Esseby

69. Assize common pasture, Kingsbury, next county after Michaelmas, 1241:
Same justices

70. Assize, unspecified, Ashfurlong, same date and place?:
Same justices

71. Assize, unspecified, Southam, next county after Michaelmas, 1241:
Same justices

72. Assize common pasture, Kingsbury, next county after Martinmas, 1241/2:
Same justices

73. Gaol delivery, Warwick, Monday after mid-Lent, 1242:
Robert de Grendon, William Trussell, Hugh de Arden, Thomas de Astley

74. Gaol delivery, Warwick, 25 Nov. 1242:
William Trussell, Hugh de Arden, Thomas de Astley, Philip de Esseby

75. Gaol delivery, Warwick, 14 Jan. 1243:
John Durvassal, Robert de Grendon, William Trussell, Henry de Ladbroke

76. Assize novel disseisin, Packington, Thursday after close of Easter, 1243:
Gilbert de Preston with fellows

77. Assize novel disseisin, Loxley, Buckley and Weston, 26 July 1243:
Gilbert de Preston with fellows

78. Assize novel disseisin, Barston, 26 July 1243:
Gilbert de Preston with fellows

79. Assize novel disseisin, Sheldon, 26 July 1243:
Gilbert de Preston with fellows

80. Assize, unspecified, date to be arranged, 1243:
Gilbert de Preston with fellows

81. Assize novel disseisin, Packington, 22 August 1243:
Gilbert de Preston with fellows

82. Gaol delivery, Warwick, 1 Sept. 1243:
William Trussell, Richard de Amundevill, Thomas de Astley, William de Curli

83. Gaol delivery, Warwick, 18 July 1244:
John Durvassal, Robert de Grendon, William de Curli, Robert le Megre

84. Novel disseisin, Ettington, 27 July 1244:
Gilbert de Preston and fellows

85. Darrein presentment, Arley, 9 Sept. 1244:
Gilbert de Preston and William de St Edmund

86. Novel disseisin, Chadshunt, date to be arranged, 1244:
Gilbert de Preston and fellows

87. Gaol delivery, Warwick, 12 Dec. 1244:
   John Durvassal, Hugh de Mancetter, William de Luddington, William de Curli

88. Gaol delivery, Warwick, 26 Jan. 1246:
   Maurice le Butler, William de Curli, Hugh de Arden, Hugh de Mancetter

89. Assize common pasture, Evesham, 15 Sept. 1246:
   Gilbert de Preston and fellows

90. Gaol delivery, Warwick, 19 Nov. 1246:
   Hugh de Arden, William de Curli, Henry Pipard, Hugh de Mancetter

Sources: Dorse of Patent Rolls. Details are taken from the published calendars for the years 1220–32 and from C.A.F. Meekings, *Transcripts from the Dorse of the Patent Rolls*, 3 vols. (PRO unprinted) for the years 1232–46: *Patent Rolls 1216–25*, pp. 229, 306–7, 343, 394–5; *Patent Rolls 1225–32*, pp. 70, 158, 161, 165–7, 206, 212, 281–3, 290–1, 296–7, 309, 366, 445, 449, 512; Meekings vol. I, nos. 75, 201, 216, 249, 336, 398–9, 402, 409, 421, 452, 462, 476, 561, 567–9; Meekings vol. II, nos. 605, 710, 754, 811, 831, 877, 880, 905, 946, 996, 1000, 1026–7, 1046, 1078, 1150–1, 1154, 1203, 1214, 1240, 1258–61, 1301; Meekings vol. III, nos. 1357, 1367, 1379, 1394, 1416–17, 1420, 1433, 1435, 1540, 1543, 1548, 1552, 1595, 1674, 1717, 1758.

Place-names have been modernised, surnames standardised.

Deliverers of Warwick gaol, 52 Henry III (1267/8) to 16 Edward I (1287/8)

Name	Regnal year(s) of delivery
1. Amundevill, Richard de	1270/1
2. Appleby, Henry de	1273/4
3. Arundel, Ralf de	1269/70
4. Bagot, William	1275/6
5. Bishopton, Walter de	1271/2, 1272/3
6. Botereus, Reginald de	1269/70
7. Bray, Thomas de	1285/6
8. Burdet, Robert	1282/3 × 4, 1283/4 × 2, 1284/5 × 2, 1285/6 × 5, 1286/7 × 4, 1287/8 × 6
9. Careswell, William de	1275/6 × 2, 1276/7
10. Charlecote, Thomas de (*alias* Thomas de Haseley)	1268/9 × 2, 1271/2, 1272/3 × 2, 1273/4 × 3, 1275/6 × 2, 1276/7 × 2, 1277/8 × 3, 1282/3 × 4, 1283/4 × 2, 1284/5 × 3, 1285/6 × 5, 1286/7 × 4, 1287/8 × 3
11. Charnels, Nicholas de	1273/4, 1274/5, 1276/7 × 2, 1277/8 × 2, 1279/80
12. Clinton, John de	1277/8 × 3, 1278/9, 1284/5, 1287/8 × 4
13. Digby, John de	1282/3 × 4, 1283/4 × 2, 1284/5 × 4, 1285/6 × 5, 1286/7 × 2
14. Farndon, Thomas de	1273/4
15. Foljambe, Thomas de	1280/1
16. Folville, John de	1277/8, 1287/8
17. Fukeram, Richard	1267/8
18. Gras, Nicholas le	1285/6
19. Grendon, Ralf de	1273/4
20. Guy, John fitz	1274/5

21. Hache, Eustace de	1280/1 × 2
22. Handsacre, Robert de	1270/1
23. Harborough, Hugh de	1274/5
24. Hastang, Robert de	1272/3, 1273/4
25. Hodenet, Odo de	1275/6 × 2, 1276/7
26. Hopton, Walter de	1284/5 × 2
27. Huband, Henry	1268/9 × 2, 1269/70, 1271/2, 1272/3 × 3, 1273/4, 1274/5 × 2, 1276/7, 1277/8 × 3, 1278/9
28. Keleby, William	1267/8
29. Ladbroke, John de	1285/6
30. Langley, Walter de	1274/5, 1278/9 × 2, 1279/80
31. Lewknor, Geoffrey de	1272/3, 1278/9
32. Loveday, Roger	1285/6
33. Lucy, Fulk de	1285/6 × 3, 1286/7 × 2
34. Martival, Anketin de	1267/8, 1272/3
35. Maunsel, William	1267/8
36. Murdak, Henry	1271/2, 1272/3
37. Neville, Stephen de	1274/5
38. Neyrunt, John	1279/80
39. Nottingham, Henry de	1269/70, 1274/5 × 2, 1277/8, 1278/9 × 2, 1279/80 × 4, 1280/1 × 10, 1281/2 × 2, 1284/5, 1286/7 × 2, 1287/8
40. Peche, John	1268/9, 1277/8, 1278/9 × 2, 1279/80 × 3, 1280/1 × 2, 1281/2 × 4, 1284/5, 1286/7
41. Pot', Henry de	1281/2 × 2
42. Poter, Peter le	1267/8, 1268/9
43. Roger, Peter fitz	1267/8
44. Russell, Geoffrey	1278/9
45. Sheldon, Henry de	1278/9, 1284/5, 1285/6, 1286/7 × 2, 1287/8 × 5
46. Springhese, Roger	1275/6
47. Vaux, John des	1280/1, 1284/5, 1285/6
48. Verdun, Robert de	1272/3 × 3, 1273/4, 1274/5, 1276/7, 1277/8 × 2, 1279/80 × 3, 1280/1 × 10, 1281/2 × 4, 1282/3 × 4, 1283/4 × 2, 1284/5 × 4, 1285/6 × 3
49. Waleys, Richard le	1281/2 × 2
50. Waleys, Robert le	1278/9 × 2, 1279/80 × 3, 1280/1 × 10, 1281/2 × 2

51. Waleys, William le	1286/7 × 3
52. Waver, William de	1267/8, 1268/9, 1269/70
53. Wheresberg, Adam de	1269/70
54. Whitacre, Jordan de	1267/8, 1268/9
55. Wilnecote, John de	1287/8 × 2
56. Wolverton, Peter de	1278/9

Sources: PRO OBS 1/467 – entries for 52–56 Henry III; Reports of the Deputy Keepers of the Public Records (1881–9), viz. vol. 42 App. 3, p. 682, vol. 43 App. 4, p. 554, vol. 44 App. I, p. 282, vol. 45 App. II no. 3, p. 350, vol. 46 App. II, no. 2, p. 314, vol. 47 App. 7, p. 381, vol. 48 App. I, p. 198, vol. 49 App. I, pp. 182–3, vol. 50 App. I, p. 241; PRO C66/101 mm 3d, 7d, 11d, 15d, C66/102 mm 5d, 6d, 17d, 22d, C66/103 mm 2d, 3d, C66/104 mm 12d, 13d, 15d, 24, C66/105 mm 3, 5, 6d, 8d, 21d, 22d, 24d, 26d, C66/106 mm 2d, 3, 8d, 9d, 15d, C66/107 mm 3, 3d, 5d, 6d, 16d, 17d.

Deliverers of Northampton gaol, 52 Henry III (1267/8) to 16 Edward I (1287/8)

Name	Regnal year(s) of delivery
1. Barry, Robert	1277/8
2. Baud, Robert le	1278/9 × 3, 1279/80 × 9, 1280/1 × 5, 1281/2 × 4, 1282/3 × 4, 1283/4 × 5, 1284/5 × 3, 1285/6 × 5, 1286/7 × 7, 1287/8
3. Beaufeu, John de	1282/3
4. Brus, Peter de	1267/8
5. Cogenhoe, Nicholas de	1277/8
6. Colethorp, William de	1278/9
7. Colevill, Robert de	1283/4
8. Colevill, William de	1280/1 × 3, 1281/2 × 4, 1282/3 × 3, 1283/4 × 3, 1284/5 × 3, 1285/6 × 3, 1286/7 × 7
9. Gatingdon, Nicholas de	1267/8
10. Goldingham, Hugh de	1267/8, 1269/70
11. Goldingham, William de	1283/4
12. Gras, Nicholas le	1285/6
13. Grauntcourt, Walter de	1278/9
14. Graveley, Hugh de	1267/8
15. Hackleton, Roger de	1270/1, 1272/3 × 3
16. Haured, Richard de	1273/4, 1274/5
17. Hay, William	1269/70, 1270/1 × 2, 1271/2, 1273/4, 1274/5 (of Twywell)
18. Hewelton, Thomas de	1278/9
19. Keu, John le	1278/9
20. Lewknor, Geoffrey	1274/5 × 2, 1275/6 × 3, 1277/8 × 2, 1278/9 × 2

21. Lou, John le

> 1272/3 × 3, 1273/4, 1273/4 (of *Esse*), 1274/5, 1277/8, 1278/9 × 3, 1279/80 × 8, 1280/1 × 5, 1281/2 × 4, 1282/3 × 4, 1283/4 × 5, 1284/5 × 3, 1285/6 × 4, 1286/7 × 7, 1287/8

22. Lou, Robert le — 1274/5 × 2
23. Lovet, R. [= Roger Loveday] — 1285/6
24. Mauncel, Robert — 1274/5, 1287/8
25. Morton, Guy de — 1287/8
26. Munceaus, John de — 1277/8, 1278/9
27. Noers, William de — 1283/4
28. Parles, William de — 1274/5, 1277/8
29. Pavely, Robert de — 1271/2, 1272/3, 1273/4, 1274/5 × 2, 1277/8, 1278/9, 1284/5
30. Preston, Gilbert de — 1266/7, 1270/1, 1272/3
31. Quenton, Philip de — 1279/80, 1284/5, 1287/8
32. Robert, Philip fitz — 1267/8, 1269/70, 1270/1 × 2, 1271/2, 1272/3 × 3, 1273/4 × 3, 1274/5 × 5, 1277/8 × 2
33. Russell, Geoffrey — 1275/6 × 3, 1278/9 × 2
34. St Mark, Geoffrey de — 1278/9 × 3, 1279/80 × 9, 1280/1 × 2
35. Seyton, Richard de — 1270/1
36. Skyn, Thomas — 1278/9
37. Stanton, Hervey de — 1278/9
38. Titchmarsh, Ralf de — 1269/70, 1270/1
39. Tingewick, Elias de — 1270/1
40. Trayly, Richard de — 1283/4
41. Turbervill, William de — 1277/8
42. Turvill, William de — 1273/4, 1277/8
43. Vaux, John des — 1285/6
44. Walter, Robert fitz — 1278/9 × 5, 1279/80 × 9, 1280/1 × 5, 1281/2 × 4, 1282/3 × 4, 1283/4 × 3, 1284/5 × 4, 1285/6 × 2, 1286/7 × 7
45. Watford, Eustace de — 1267/8 × 2, 1270/1, 1271/2, 1272/3 × 2, 1273/4 × 3, 1274/5 × 4
46. Welles, Reginald de — 1274/5

Sources: PRO OBS 1/467 – entries for 52, 54–56 Henry III; Reports of the Deputy Keepers of the Public Records (1881–9), viz. vol. 42 App 3, p. 623, vol. 43 App. 4, pp. 503–4, vol. 44 App. I, pp. 199–200, vol. 45 App. II no. 3, p. 262, vol. 46 App. II no. 2, p. 241, vol. 47 App. 7, p. 303, vol. 48 App. I, pp. 136–7, vol. 49 App. I, p. 128, vol. 50 App. I, p. 167; PRO C66/101 mm 5d, 7, 15d, 17d, 19d, C66/102 mm 7, 11d, 18, 22d, C66/103 mm 3d, 4d, 10, 11d, 17, 18d, C66/104 mm 12d, 13d, 23d, 28d, C66/105 mm 2d, 8d, 20d, 22d, 23d, C66/106 mm 3d, 9d, 10d, 13d, 14, C66/107 m 9d.

Holders of Commissions and Major Offices in Warwickshire 1290–1348, compiled by Richard Gorski

FORENAME	DE	SURNAME	OFFICE	COUNTY	YEAR	REFERENCE
ADAM		ABBOT OF STONLE	TAXER	WAR	1341	CPR 1340-3/152
EDMUND	DE	AGMEDESHAM	TAXER	DBY,LEC,NTT,WAR	1304	CPR 1301-07/201
NICHOLAS	DE	ASSHEBY	SHERIFF	WAR&LEC	1326	LIST OF SHERIFFS
THOMAS	DE	ASTELEYE	PEACE	WAR	1308	CPR 1307-13/53
THOMAS	DE	ASTELEY	PEACE	WAR	1332	CPR 1330-34/294
THOMAS	DE	ASTELEYE	ARRAYER	WAR	1335	ROT SCOT I/328
THOMAS	DE	ASTELEYE	PEACE/ARRAY	WAR	1338	CPR 1338-40/136
THOMAS	DE	ASTELE	ARRAYER	LEC,WAR	1339	FOEDERA II/II/1070-2
ROGER	DE	AYLESBURY	ARRAYER	WAR	1322	CPR 1321-24/123
ROGER	DE	AYLESBURY	ARRAYER	WAR	1324	CPR 1324-27/8-11
ROGER	DE	AILLESBURY	KNIGHT OF SHIRE	WAR	1326	LIST OF MPS/61
ROGER	DE	AYLESBURY	SHERIFF	WAR&LEC	1327	LIST OF SHERIFFS
ROGER	DE	AYLESBURY	SHERIFF	WAR&LEC	1330	LIST OF SHERIFFS
ROGER	DE	AYLESBURY	KNIGHT OF SHIRE	WAR	1331	LIST OF MPS/79
ROGER	DE	AYLESBURY	ARRAYER	LEC,WAR	1333	CPR 1330-34/419
ROGER	DE	AILLESBURY	TAXER	WAR	1336	CFR IV/481
ROGER	DE	AYLESBURY	PEACE	LEC,WAR	1336	CPR 1334-38/368
ROGER	DE	AYLLESBURY	TAXER	WAR	1336	CFR IV/504
ROGER	DE	AYLLESBURY	KNIGHT OF SHIRE	WAR	1337	LIST OF MPS/100
ROGER	DE	AYLESBURY	KNIGHT OF SHIRE	WAR	1339	LIST OF MPS/109
RALPH		BASSET	ARRAYER	LEC,STS,WAR	1321	CPR 1321-24/39
RALPH		BASSET OF DRAYTON	PEACE	WAR	1328	CPR 1327-30/220
RALPH		BASSET	PEACE	WAR,WOR	1332	CPR 1330-34/285
THOMAS	DE	BEAUCHAMP, EARL	SHERIFF	WAR&LEC	1344	LIST OF SHERIFFS
THOMAS	DE	BELLO CAMPO, EARL	PEACE	WAR	1345	CPR 1343-45/490
WALTER	DE	BEAUCHAMP	SHERIFF	WAR&LEC	1316	LIST OF SHERIFFS
RALPH		BELER	SHERIFF	WAR&LEC	1318	LIST OF SHERIFFS
RICHARD	DE	BERCHESTON	KNIGHT OF SHIRE	WAR	1322	LIST OF MPS/I9
EDMUND	DE	BERFORD	PEACE/ARRAY	OXF,WAR,WOR	1338	CPR 1338-40/141
ROBERT	DE	BEREFORD	ESCHEATOR	WAR&LEC	1341	LIST ESCHEATORS
ROBERT	DE	BEREFORD	SHERIFF	WAR&LEC	1341	LIST OF SHERIFFS

(cont.)

(cont.)

FORENAME	DE	SURNAME	OFFICE	COUNTY	YEAR	REFERENCE
ROBERT	DE	BERFORD, SHERIFF	TAXER	WAR	1342	CFR V/284
WILLIAM	DE	BERMYNGHAM	ARRAYER	WAR	1324	CPR 1324-27/53
WIL	DE	BERMYNGHAM	ARRAYER	WAR	1325	CPR 1324-27/216-8
WILLIAM	DE	BERMYNGHAM	ARRAYER	WAR	1327	ROT SCOT I/221
WILLIAM	DE	BERMYNGEHAM, ELD.	ARRAYER	WAR	1335	CPR 1334-38/137-9
WILLIAM	DE	BERMYNGHAM, ELD.	PEACE	WAR	1335	CPR 1334-38/209
WILLIAM	DE	BERNYNGHAM	PEACE	WAR	1331	CPR 1330-34/136
JOHN	DE	BYSSHOPESDEN	PEACE	WAR	1325	CPR 1324-27/66
JOHN	DE	BISHOPPESTON	PEACE	WAR	1331	CPR 1330-34/136
JOHN	DE	BISSHOPESTON	KNIGHT OF SHIRE	WAR	1319	LIST OF MPS/56
JOHN	DE	BISSHOPESDON	KNIGHT OF SHIRE	WAR	1326	LIST OF MPS/61
JOHN	DE	BISSHOPESDON	TAXER	WAR	1327	CPR 1327-30/173
JOHN	DE	BISHOPESDON	KNIGHT OF SHIRE	WAR	1330	LIST OF MPS/77
JOHN	DE	BISSHOPESDON	PEACE	WAR	1330	CPR 1327-30/562
THOMAS		BLAUNKFRONT	SHERIFF	WAR&LEC	1328	LIST OF SHERIFFS
THOMAS		BLAUNCFROUNT	KNIGHT OF SHIRE	WAR	1328	LIST OF MPS/69
RALPH	DE	BOLEMERE	TAXER	WAR	1295	CPR 1292-1301/171
JOHN	DE	BOLINGBROK	ESCHEATOR	WAR&LEC&NTT&D	1323	LIST ESCHEATORS
RALPH	LE	BOTILER	KNIGHT OF SHIRE	WAR	1309	LIST OF MPS/29
	DE	BRAY OF COV.	TAXER	WAR	1342	CFR V/284
WILLIAM	DE	BREDON	ESCHEATOR	WAR&LEC&NTT&D	1334	LIST ESCHEATORS
GUIDO		BRETON	KNIGHT OF SHIRE	WAR	1328	LIST OF MPS/66
GUY		BRETOUN	ARRAYER	WAR	1336	ROT SCOT I/469
GUY		BRETON	TAXER	WAR	1340	CPR 1338-40/500
GUY		BRETON	TAXER	WAR	1341	CPR 1340-43/152
GUY		BRITTOUN	TAXER	WAR	1347	CFR VI/5
JOHN	DE	BROUGHTON	SHERIFF	WAR&LEC	1298	LIST OF SHERIFFS
ADAM	DE	BROM	TAXER	DBY,LEC,NTT,WAR	1312	CPR 1307-13/520
ROBERT		BURDET	KNIGHT OF SHIRE	WAR	1320	LIST OF MPS/12

ROBERT		BURDET	KNIGHT OF SHIRE	WAR	1325	LIST OF MPS/59
ROBERT		BURDET	KNIGHT OF SHIRE	WAR	1328	LIST OF MPS/66
ROBERT		BURDET	SHERIFF	WAR&LEC	1328	LIST OF SHERIFFS
JOHN	DE	CANTILUPO	PEACE	WAR	1308	CPR 1307-13/53
JOHN	DE	CANTILUPO	PEACE	WAR	1314	CPR 1313-17/109
JOHN	DE	CANTILUPO	PEACE	WAR	1314	CPR 1313-17/123
JOHN	DE	CANTILUPO	PEACE	WAR	1316	CPR 1313-17/482
JOHN	DE	CARESWELL	PEACE/ARRAY	WAR	1338	CPR 1338-40/137
GEORGE	DE	CASTELLO	ARRAYER	LEC,WAR	1311	ROT SCOT I/97
WILLIAM	DE	CASTELLO	KNIGHT OF SHIRE	WAR	1290	LIST OF MPS/1
WILLIAM	DE	CASTELTON	SHERIFF	WAR&LEC	1293	LIST OF SHERIFFS
WILLIAM	DE	CATEBY	KNIGHT OF SHIRE	WAR	1339	LIST OF MPS/109
WILLIAM	DE	CATESBY	ESCHEATOR	WAR&LEC&NTT&D	1340	LIST ESCHEATORS
WILLIAM	DE	CATEBY	KNIGHT OF SHIRE	WAR	1340	LIST OF MPS/116
GEORGE	DE	CHARNELES	KNIGHT OF SHIRE	WAR	1312	LIST OF MPS/36
GEORGE	DE	CHARNELS	KNIGHT OF SHIRE	WAR	1313	LIST OF MPS/38
NICHOLAS	DE	CHARNELES	ARRAYER	LEC,WAR	1324	CPR 1324-27/77-9
NICHOLAS	DE	CHARNELES	KNIGHT OF SHIRE	WAR	1337	LIST OF MPS/96
NICHOLAS	DE	CHARNELES	KNIGHT OF SHIRE	WAR	1339	LIST OF MPS/107
THOMAS	DE	CHAWORTH	PEACE	LEC,WAR	1336	CPR 1334-38/368
WALTER	DE	CIRENCESTRE	ESCHEATOR	WAR&LEC&NTT&D	1335	LIST ESCHEATORS
JOHN	DE	CLYNTON	ARRAYER	WAR	1297	CPR 1292-1301/309
JOHN	DE	CLYNTON OF COLES.	PEACE	WAR	1300	CPR 1292-1301/515
JOHN	DE	CLYNTONE OF MAX.	KNIGHT OF SHIRE	WAR	1301	LIST OF MPS/13
JOHN	DE	CLYNTON	PEACE(SPECIAL)	LEC,WAR	1314	CPR 1313-17/129
JOHN	DE	CLYNTON OF MAX.	PEACE	WAR	1329	CPR 1327-30/430
JOHN	DE	CLYNTON OF MAX.	PEACE	WAR	1332	CPR 1330-34/296
THOMAS	DE	CLYNTON	KNIGHT OF SHIRE	WAR	1315	LIST OF MPS/48
THOMAS	DE	CLYNTON	KNIGHT OF SHIRE	WAR	1316	LIST OF MPS/49
THOMAS	DE	CLYNTON	ARRAYER	WAR	1316	CPR 1313-17/460
THOMAS	DE	CLYNTON	KNIGHT OF SHIRE	WAR	1316	LIST OF MPS/51
THOMAS	DE	CLYNTON	TAXER	WAR	1316	CPR 1313-17/530
THOMAS	DE	CLYNTON	ARRAYER	LEC,WAR	1317	ROT SCOT I/170
THOMAS	DE	CLYNTON	ARRAYER	LEC,WAR	1317	ROT SCOT I/175

(cont.)

(cont.)

FORENAME	DE	SURNAME	OFFICE	COUNTY	YEAR	REFERENCE
RICHARD	DE	CLODESHALE	TAXER	WAR	1347	CFR VI/5
JOHN	DE	COMPTON	KNIGHT OF SHIRE	WAR	1332	LIST OF MPS/81
JOHN	DE	CUMPTON	KNIGHT OF SHIRE	WAR	1332	LIST OF MPS/83
JOHN		COMYN	KNIGHT OF SHIRE	WAR	1327	LIST OF MPS/63
JOHN		COMYN	KNIGHT OF SHIRE	WAR	1328	LIST OF MPS/72
JOHN		COMYN	ARRAYER	WAR	1337	ROT SCOT I/501
JOHN		COMYN	TAXER	WAR	1338	CFR V/89
JOHN		COMYN OF NEWBOLD	TAXER	WAR	1348	CFR VI/90
JOHN	DE	CONYNGESBY	KNIGHT OF SHIRE	WAR	1344	LIST OF MPS/122
HUGH	DE	CRESCY	TAXER	DBY,LEC,NTT,WAR	1312	CPR 1307-13/520
HUGH	DE	CROFT?	KNIGHT OF SHIRE	WAR	1315	LIST OF MPS/48
JOHN		CROUPES	KNIGHT OF SHIRE	WAR	1328	LIST OF MPS/72
HUGH	DE	CULLY	KNIGHT OF SHIRE	WAR	1314	LIST OF MPS/45
ROGER	DE	CULLY	TAXER	WAR	1340	CPR 1338-40/500
ROGER		CULLY	TAXER	WAR	1341	CPR 1340-43/152
JOHN	DE	DENE	SHERIFF	WAR&LEC	1302	LIST OF SHERIFFS
JOHN	DE	DENE	SHERIFF	WAR&LEC	1305	LIST OF SHERIFFS
JOHN	DE	DENE	SHERIFF	WAR&LEC	1307	LIST OF SHERIFFS
JOHN	DE	DENE	KNIGHT OF SHIRE	WAR	1309	LIST OF MPS/29
JOHN	DE	DENE	SHERIFF	WAR&LEC	1310	LIST OF SHERIFFS
JOHN	DE	DENE	SHERIFF	WAR&LEC	1311	LIST OF SHERIFFS
JOHN	DE	DENE	KNIGHT OF SHIRE	WAR	1311	LIST OF MPS/32
JOHN	DE	DENE	KNIGHT OF SHIRE	WAR	1311	LIST OF MPS/34
JOHN	DE	DENE	KNIGHT OF SHIRE	WAR	1314	LIST OF MPS/45
JOHN	DE	DENE	KNIGHT OF SHIRE	WAR	1318	LIST OF MPS/54
JOHN	DE	DENE	KNIGHT OF SHIRE	WAR	1319	LIST OF MPS/56
JOHN	DE	DENE	KNIGHT OF SHIRE	WAR	1321	LIST OF MPS/14
HUGH	DE	DESPENSER	PEACE/ARRAY	OXF,WAR,WOR	1338	CPR 1338-40/141
JOHN	LE	DUREVASSAL	TAXER	WAR	1347	CFR VI/6

HENRY		EARL OF LANCASTER	ARRAYER	LEC,WAR	1339	FOEDERA II/II/1070-2
		EARL OF LEYCESTRE	ARRAYER	LEC,WAR	1326	CPR 1324-27/220-1
THOMAS		EARL OF WARWICK	PEACE	WAR,WOR	1332	CPR 1330-34/285
THOMAS		EARL OF WARWICK	PEACE	WAR	1332	CPR 1330-34/294
THOMAS		EARL OF WARWICK	PEACE/ARRAY	OXF,WAR,WOR	1338	CPR 1338-40/141
RICHARD	DE	EGEBASTON	TAXER	WAR	1313	CPR 1313-17/50
RICHARD	DE	EGGEBASTON	TAXER	LEC,WAR	1316	CPR 1313-17/474
RICHARD	DE	EGEBASTON	ARRAYER	LEC,WAR	1317	ROT SCOT I/170
RICHARD	DE	EGEBASTON	ARRAYER	LEC,WAR	1317	ROT SCOT I/175
RICHARD	DE	EGGEBASTON	ARRAYER	LEC,WAR	1322	CPR 1321-24/96-7
RICHARD	DE	EGGEBASTON	PEACE	WAR	1327	CPR 1327-30/156
RICHARD	DE	EGGEBASTON	ARRAYER	LEC,WAR	1333	CPR 1330-34/419
HENRY	DE	ERDINTON	TAXER	WAR	1313	CPR 1313-17/50
HENRY	DE	ERDYNGTON	PEACE	WAR	1314	CPR 1313-17/109
HENRY	DE	ERDYNGTON	PEACE	WAR	1314	CPR 1313-17/123
HENRY	DE	ERDYNTON	PEACE(SPECIAL)	LEC,WAR	1314	CPR 1313-17/129
HENRY	DE	ERDYNGTON	ARRAYER	WAR	1315	CPR 1313-17/350
HENRY	DE	ERDYNGTON	PEACE	WAR	1316	CPR 1313-17/482
HENRY	DE	ERDYNGTON	PEACE	WAR	1318	CPR 1317-21/185
HENRY	DE	ERDINGTON	PEACE	WAR	1318	CPR 1317-21/289
WILLIAM		ERNEYS	ESCHEATOR	WAR&LEC&NTT&D	1332	LIST ESCHEATORS
WILLIAM		ERNEYS	ESCHEATOR	WAR&LEC&NTT&D	1333	LIST ESCHEATORS
WILLIAM		ERNEYS	KNIGHT OF SHIRE	WAR	1334	LIST OF MPS/87
WILLIAM		ERNEYS	ESCHEATOR	WAR&LEC&NTT&D	1334	LIST ESCHEATORS
WILLIAM		ERNEYS	KNIGHT OF SHIRE	WAR	1338	LIST OF MPS/102
WILLIAM		ERNEYS	KNIGHT OF SHIRE	WAR	1338	LIST OF MPS/105
WILLIAM		ERNEYS	KNIGHT OF SHIRE	WAR	1340	LIST OF MPS/116
ANDREW	DE	ESTLEYE	ARRAYER	WAR	1297	CPR 1292-1301/309
NICHOLAS	DE	ETON THE YOUNGER	ARRAYER	WAR	1325	CPR 1324-27/127
WILLIAM	DE	FERARIIS	ARRAYER	LEC,NTH,RUT,STS	1322	CPR 1321-24/69
ROBERT		FIL' GUIDON	KNIGHT OF SHIRE	WAR	1307	LIST OF MPS/27
JOHN		FILIUS GWYDONIS	KNIGHT OF SHIRE	WAR	1298	LIST OF MPS/8
RICHARD	DE	FURNEAUX	TAXER	DBY,LEC,NTT,WAR	1304	CPR 1301-07/201
THOMAS	DE	GARSALE	TAXER	WAR	1294	CPR 1292-1301/103

(cont.)

(cont.)

FORENAME	DE	SURNAME	OFFICE	COUNTY	YEAR	REFERENCE
THOMAS	DE	GARSALE	TAXER	WAR	1306	CPR 1301-07/456
THOMAS	DE	GARSALE	TAXER	WAR	1309	CPR 1307-13/185
PHILIP	DE	GAYTONE	KNIGHT OF SHIRE	WAR	1298	LIST OF MPS/8
PHILIP	DE	GAYTON	KNIGHT OF SHIRE	WAR	1300	LIST OF MPS/9
PHILIP	DE	GAYTON	PEACE	WAR	1300	CPR 1292-1301/515
PHILIP	DE	GAYTON	KNIGHT OF SHIRE	WAR	1300	LIST OF MPS/10
PHILIP	DE	GEYTON	SHERIFF	WAR&LEC	1300	LIST OF SHERIFFS
PHILIP	DE	GAYTON	TAXER	WAR	1306	CPR 1301-07/456
PHILIP	DE	GEYTON	PEACE	WAR	1307	CPR 1307-13/30
ROGER	DE	GULDESBURGH	TAXER	WAR	1334	CPR 1334-38/39
WALTER	DE	GOUSELE	TAXER	DBY,LEC,NTT,WAR	1312	CPR 1307-13/520
RALPH	DE	GRENDON	ARRAYER	WAR	1322	CPR 1321-24/45
RALPH	DE	GRENDON	ARRAYER	LEC,NTH,RUT,STS	1322	CPR 1321-24/69
JOHN	DE	HARDESHULL	ARRAYER	WAR	1322	CPR 1321-24/212
JOHN	DE	HARDESHULL	ARRAYER	WAR	1323	CPR 1321-24/261
JOHN	DE	HARINGTON	PEACE(SPECIAL)	LEC,WAR	1314	CPR 1313-17/129
ROBERT	DE	HERLE	PEACE	WAR	1345	CPR 1343-45/397
ROBERT	DE	HERLE	PEACE	WAR	1345	CPR 1343-45/490
JOHN		HASTANG	ARRAYER	LEC,WAR	1311	ROT SCOT I/97
RICHARD	DE	HASTANG	KNIGHT OF SHIRE	WAR	1321	LIST OF MPS/I4
RICHARD	DE	HASTANG'	TAXER	WAR	1347	CFR VI/4
THOMAS	DE	HASTANG'	PEACE	WAR	1328	CPR 1327-30/220
THOMAS	DE	HASTANG	PEACE	WAR	1330	CPR 1327-30/562
THOMAS	DE	HASTANG	PEACE/ARRAY	WAR	1338	CPR 1338-40/136
THOMAS		HASTYNG	ARRAYER	WAR	1324	CPR 1324-27/8-11
HENRY	DE	HERDINGTON	PEACE	WAR	1320	CPR 1317-21/462
RICHARD	DE	HERTHILL	TAXER	WAR	1301	CPR 1292-1301/611
RICHARD	DE	HERTHULL	KNIGHT OF SHIRE	WAR	1302	LIST OF MPS/15
RICHARD	DE	HERTHULL	TAXER	WAR	1302	CPR 1301-07/76
RICHARD	DE	HERTHILL	SHERIFF	WAR&LEC	1304	LIST OF SHERIFFS

Forename	Prefix	Surname	Role	County	Year	Reference
RICHARD	DE	HERTHALL	KNIGHT OF SHIRE	WAR	1306	LIST OF MPS/21
RICHARD	DE	HERTHILL	KNIGHT OF SHIRE	WAR	1307	LIST OF MPS/24
RICHARD	DE	HERTHILL	SHERIFF	WAR&LEC	1308	LIST OF SHERIFFS
RICHARD	DE	HERTHULL	ARRAYER	LEC,WAR	1311	ROT SCOT I/97
RICHARD	DE	HERTHULL	TAXER	WAR	1344	CFR V/392
RICHARD	DE	HERTHILL	TAXER	WAR	1345	CFR V/435
RICHARD	DE	HERTHILL	TAXER	WAR	1346	CFR V/483
RICHARD	DE	HERTHULL	TAXER	WAR	1346	CFR V/492
JOHN	DE	HEYFORD	PEACE	WAR	1332	CPR 1330-34/294
HENRY	DE	HOKKELE	KNIGHT OF SHIRE	WAR	1332	LIST OF MPS/85
HENRY	DE	HOCKELE	SHERIFF	WAR&LEC	1333	LIST OF SHERIFFS
HENRY	DE	HOCLE	TAXER	WAR	1333	CFR IV/354
ADAM		HOLEWEYE	TAXER	WAR	1347	CFR VI/5
JOHN	DE	HOUBY	SHERIFF	WAR&LEC	1314	LIST OF SHERIFFS
JOHN		HUBAUD ELD.	TAXER	WAR	1347	CFR V/493
JOHN		HUBAND	ARRAYER	WAR	1347	FOEDERA III/I/107
HENRY	DE	IDLE	KNIGHT OF SHIRE	WAR	1332	LIST OF MPS/85
GEOFFREY	LE	IRREYS	KNIGHT OF SHIRE	WAR	1302	LIST OF MPS/15
RALPH	DE	KNOLL	PEACE	WAR	1331	CPR 1330-34/136
ROBERT	DE	LALLEFORD	TAXER	WAR	1340	CFR V/158
ROBERT	DE	LALLEFORDE	KNIGHT OF SHIRE	WAR	1340	LIST OF MPS/113
JOHN	DE	LANGELEYE	ARRAYER	WAR	1315*	CPR 1313-17/350
JOHN	DE	LANGELEYE	ARRAYER	WAR	1316	CPR 1313-17/460
JOHN	DE	LANGELEYE	TAXER	WAR	1319	CFR III/10
JOHN	DE	LANGELEYE	TAXER	WAR	1319	CPR 1317-21/348
JOHN	DE	LEE	PEACE/ARRAY	WAR	1338	CPR 1338-40/137
JOHN	DE	LEYE	KNIGHT OF SHIRE	WAR	1343	LIST OF MPS/119
JOHN	DE	LYE OF KINGSTON	TAXER	WAR	1344	CFR V/392
JOHN	DU	LEE	PEACE/ARRAY	WAR	1345	CPR 1343-45/576
JOHN	DE	LYE OF KINGSTON	TAXER	WAR	1345	CFR V/435
JOHN	DE	LYE OF KINGSTON	TAXER	WAR	1346	CFR V/483
JOHN	DE	LYE OF KINGSTON	TAXER	WAR	1347	CFR VI/44
HENRY	DE	LYLE	KNIGHT OF SHIRE	WAR	1324	LIST OF MPS/113
HENRY	DE	INSULA	KNIGHT OF SHIRE	WAR	1331	LIST OF MPS/79

(cont.)

(cont.)

FORENAME	DE	SURNAME	OFFICE	COUNTY	YEAR	REFERENCE
JOHN	DE	LODBROK	KNIGHT OF SHIRE	WAR	1290	LIST OF MPS/1
JOHN	DE	LODBROK	PEACE	WAR	1300	CPR 1292-1301/515
ROGER	DE	LOUNDE	KNIGHT OF SHIRE	WAR	1348	LIST OF MPS/129
WILLIAM	DE	LUCY	KNIGHT OF SHIRE	WAR	1312	LIST OF MPS/36
WILLIAM	DE	LUCY	PEACE	WAR	1320	CPR 1317-21/462
WILLIAM	DE	LUCY	KNIGHT OF SHIRE	WAR	1322	LIST OF MPS/I7
WILLIAM	DE	LUCY	ARRAYER	WAR	1322	CPR 1321-24/123
WILLIAM	DE	LUCY	KNIGHT OF SHIRE	WAR	1323	LIST OF MPS/I11
WILLIAM	DE	LUCY	ARRAYER	LEC,WAR	1323	CPR 1321-24/274
WILLIAM	DE	LUCY	ARRAYER	WAR	1324	CPR 1324-27/53
WILLIAM	DE	LUCY	ARRAYER	WAR	1326	CPR 1324-27/220-1
WILLIAM	DE	LUCY	PEACE	WAR	1327	CPR 1327-30/156
WILLIAM	DE	LUCY	KNIGHT OF SHIRE	WAR	1328	LIST OF MPS/69
WILLIAM	DE	LUCY	KNIGHT OF SHIRE	WAR	1336	LIST OF MPS/94
WILLIAM	DE	LUCY	ARRAYER	WAR	1347	FOEDERA III/I/107
PETER	DE	LYMESEY	KNIGHT OF SHIRE	WAR	1316	LIST OF MPS/49
PETER	DE	LYMESY	ARRAYER	WAR	1316	CPR 1313-17/460
PETER	DE	LYMESY	KNIGHT OF SHIRE	WAR	1316	LIST OF MPS/51
PETER	DE	LYMESY	KNIGHT OF SHIRE	WAR	1320	LIST OF MPS/I2
SIMON	DE	MANECESTR'	KNIGHT OF SHIRE	WAR	1306	LIST OF MPS/21
SIMON	DE	MAINCESTR'	KNIGHT OF SHIRE	WAR	1307	LIST OF MPS/24
SIMON	DE	MANCESTR'	KNIGHT OF SHIRE	WAR	1313	LIST OF MPS/38
SIMON	DE	MANCESTR'	KNIGHT OF SHIRE	WAR	1318	LIST OF MPS/54
RICHARD	DE	MARTON	ESCHEATOR	WAR&LEC& NTT&D	1341	LIST ESCHEATORS
JOHN	DE	MERYNGTON OF COV.	TAXER	WAR	1338	CFR V/97
JOHN	DE	MERYNGTON	TAXER	WAR	1340	CPR 1338-40/500
JOHN	DE	MERYNGTON	TAXER	WAR	1341	CPR 1340-43/152
JOHN	DE	MERYNTON	PEACE	WAR	1345	CPR 1343-45/490
HENRY		MILES	KNIGHT OF SHIRE	WAR	1346	LIST OF MPS/124

HENRY		MILLE	TAXER	WAR	CFR VI/7	1347
PETER	DE	MONTE FORTI	ARRAYER	LEC,STS,WAR	CPR 1321-24/39	1321
PETER	DE	MONTE FORTI	PEACE	WAR	CPR 1343-45/396	1344
PETER	DE	MONTE FORTI	PEACE	WAR	CPR 1343-45/490	1345
PETER	DE	MONTE FORTI	PEACE/ARRAY	WAR	CPR 1343-45/576	1345
PETER	DE	MOUNT FORT	ARRAYER	WAR	FOEDERA III/I/107	1347
ROBERT		MORYN	SHERIFF	WAR&LEC	LIST OF SHERIFFS	1323
JOHN		MURDAK	KNIGHT OF SHIRE	WAR	LIST OF MPS/19	1322
JOHN		MURDAK	ARRAYER	WAR	ROT SCOT I/221	1327
JOHN	DE	MURDAK	ARRAYER	WAR	ROT SCOT I/328	1335
JOHN		MURDAK	ARRAYER	WAR	ROT SCOT I/469	1336
ROBERT	DE	NAPTON	TAXER	LEC,WAR	CPR 1292-1301/611	1301
ROBERT	DE	NAPTON	ARRAYER	WAR	ROT SCOT I/97	1311
ROBERT	DE	NAPTON	TAXER	WAR	CFR III/10	1319
JOHN	DE	NEUBOLT	KNIGHT OF SHIRE	WAR	LIST OF MPS/119	1343
JOHN	DE	NEUBOLD	KNIGHT OF SHIRE	WAR	LIST OF MPS/122	1344
JOHN	DE	NEWEBOLD	TAXER	WAR	CFR VI/4	1347
JOHN	DE	NEVILL	SHERIFF	WAR& LEC	LIST OF SHERIFFS	1311
WILLIAM	DE	NEVILL	SHERIFF	WAR&LEC	LIST OF SHERIFFS	1318
WILLIAM	DE	NEVILL	SHERIFF	WAR&LEC	LIST OF SHERIFFS	1319
HENRY	DE	NOTYNGHAM	SHERIFF	WAR&LEC	LIST OF SHERIFFS	1322
JOHN	DE	OLNEYE	SHERIFF	WAR&LEC	LIST OF SHERIFFS	1312
LAURENCE	DE	PAVELY	TAXER	WAR	CPR 1292-1301/299	1297
JOHN		PECCHE	PEACE	WAR	CPR 1317-21/289	1318
JOHN	DE	PECCHE	PEACE	WAR	CPR 1317-21/462	1320
JOHN		PECCHE	PEACE	WAR	CPR 1317-21/460	1320
JOHN		PECCHE	ARRAYER	LEC,NTH,RUT,STS	CPR 1321-24/69	1322
JOHN		PECCHE	ARRAYER	WAR	CPR 1321-24/212	1322
JOHN		PECCHE	PEACE(SPECIAL)	WAR	CPR 1321-24/215	1322
JOHN		PECCHE	ARRAYER	WAR	CPR 1321-24/261	1323
JOHN		PECCHE	ARRAYER	LEC,WAR	CPR 1324-27/220-1	1326
NICHOLAS		PECCHE	ARRAYER	WAR	C.76/11 m.27	1338
NICHOLAS		PECCHE	TAXER	WAR	CFR VI/92	1348

(cont.)

(cont.)

FORENAME	DE	SURNAME	OFFICE	COUNTY	YEAR	REFERENCE
JOHN		PERCEVAL OF SOM.	KNIGHT OF SHIRE	WAR	1301	LIST OF MPS/13
JOHN		PERSEVAL OF SOM.	KNIGHT OF SHIRE	WAR	1305	LIST OF MPS/18
RALPH	DE	PERHAM	PEACE	WAR	1314	CPR 1313-17/123
RALPH	DE	PERHAM	PEACE	WAR	1329	CPR 1327-30/430
RALPH	DE	PERTON	TAXER	LEC,WAR	1316	CPR 1313-17/474
RALPH	DE	PERTON	TAXER	WAR	1316	CPR 1313-17/530
RICHARD	DE	PESHALE	ESCHEATOR	WAR&LEC& NTT&D	1332	LIST ESCHEATORS
JOHN	DE	PEYTO	PEACE	WAR	1327	CPR 1327-30/156
JOHN	DE	PEYTO	PEACE	WAR	1329	CPR 1327-30/430
JOHN	DE	PEYTO ELD.	KNIGHT OF SHIRE	WAR	1330	LIST OF MPS/77
JOHN	DE	PEYTO ELD.	ARRAYER	WAR	1335	CPR 1334-38/137-9
JOHN	DE	PEYTO ELD.	PEACE	WAR	1335	CPR 1334-38/209
JOHN	DE	PEITO YOUNG.	TAXER	WAR	1336	CFR IV/481
JOHN	DE	PETTO YOUNG.	PEACE	LEC,WAR	1336	CPR 1334-38/368
JOHN	DE	PEITO YOUNG.	TAXER	WAR	1336	CFR IV/504
JOHN	DE	PEYTO YOUNG.	KNIGHT OF SHIRE	WAR	1337	LIST OF MPS/96
JOHN	DE	PEITO ELD.	PEACE/ARRAY	WAR	1338	CPR 1338-40/136
JOHN	DE	PEYTO ELD.	TAXER	WAR	1340	CPR 1338-40/500
JOHN	DE	PEYTO ELD.	TAXER	WAR	1341	CPR 1340-43/152
JOHN	DE	PEYTO ELD.	TAXER	WAR	1342	CFR V/284
JOHN	DE	PETO 'LE FITZ'	PEACE	WAR	1344	CPR 1343-45/396
WILLIAM	DE	PEYTO	ARRAYER	WAR	1335	ROT SCOT I/328
WILLIAM	DE	PEYTO	SHERIFF	WAR&LEC	1340	LIST OF SHERIFFS
WILLIAM		PEYTO	TAXER	WAR	1347	CFR VI/4
JOHN	DE	PEYTON	PEACE	WAR	1318	CPR 1317-21/185
THOMAS	DE	PYPE	ARRAYER	WAR	1325	CPR 1324-27/216-8
HUGH	DE	PRESTWOLD	ARRAYER	LEC,WAR	1323	CPR 1321-24/274
		PRIOR OF KEN.	TAXER	WAR	1334	CPR 1334-38/39
STEPHEN		RABAY OF NORTH.	TAXER	WAR	1297	CPR 1292-1301/299

First Name		Surname	Office	County	Year	Source
STEPHEN	DE	RABAZ	SHERIFF	WAR&LEC	1290	LIST OF SHERIFFS
JOHN	LE	REVEL	PEACE	WAR	1328	CPR 1327-30/220
THOMAS	LE	ROUS	SHERIFF	WAR&LEC	1321	LIST OF SHERIFFS
THOMAS	LE	ROUS	ARRAYER	WAR	1322	CPR 1321-24/45
THOMAS	LE	ROUS	ARRAYER	LEC,WAR	1322	CPR 1321-24/96-7
JOHN		RYVEL	PEACE	WAR	1332	CPR 1330-34/294
JOHN		RYVEL	TAXER	WAR	1333	CFR IV/354
JOHN		RYVEL	ARRAYER	WAR	1336	ROT SCOT I/469
JOHN		RYVEL	KNIGHT OF SHIRE	WAR	1337	LIST OF MPS/100
JOHN		RYVEL	ARRAYER	WAR	1337	ROT SCOT I/501
JOHN		RYVELL	TAXER	WAR	1337	CFR V/51
JOHN		RYVELL	TAXER	WAR	1337	CFR V/53
JOHN		RYVEL	ARRAYER	WAR	1338	C.76/11 m.27
JOHN		RYVEL	ARRAYER	WAR	1338	FOEDERA II/II/1018
JOHN		RYVEL	PEACE	WAR	1344	CPR 1343-45/396
JOHN		RYVEL OF NEWBOLD	PEACE/ARRAY	WAR	1345	CPR 1343-45/576
ROBERT	DE	SADYNGTON	PEACE	LEC,WAR	1336	CPR 1334-38/368
JOHN	DE	SAUNDERESTEDE	KNIGHT OF SHIRE	WAR	1341	LIST OF MPS/118
JOHN	DE	SAUNDERSTEDE	UNDER-SHERIFF	WAR&LEC	1346	LIST OF SHERIFFS
JOHN	DE	SAUNDRESTEDE	KNIGHT OF SHIRE	WAR	1348	LIST OF MPS/126
JOHN	DE	SAUNDRESTON	TAXER	WAR	1342	CFR V/284
GEOFFREY	DE	SEGRAVE	SHERIFF	WAR&LEC	1308	LIST OF SHERIFFS
JOHN	DE	SEGRAVE ELD.	PEACE	WAR	1320	CPR 1317-21/460
JOHN	DE	SEGRAVE ELD.	ARRAYER	LEC,STS,WAR	1321	CPR 1321-24/39
GERARD	DE	SEKYNDON	KNIGHT OF SHIRE	WAR	1334	LIST OF MPS/89
WILLIAM	DE	SHARESHULL	PEACE	WAR,WOR	1332	CPR 1330-34/285
WILLIAM	DE	SHARESHULL	PEACE/ARRAY	OXF,WAR,WOR	1338	CPR 1338-40/141
WILLIAM	DE	SHELDON	KNIGHT OF SHIRE	WAR	1348	LIST OF MPS/126
WILLIAM	DE	SHELDON	KNIGHT OF SHIRE	WAR	1348	LIST OF MPS/129
RALPH	DE	SCHIRLEGH	TAXER	WAR	1294	CPR 1292-1301/103
RALPH	DE	SCHIRLE	KNIGHT OF SHIRE	WAR	1295	LIST OF MPS/4
RALPH	DE	SHIRLEGH	KNIGHT OF SHIRE	WAR	1311	LIST OF MPS/32
RALPH	DE	SHIRLEE	KNIGHT OF SHIRE	WAR	1311	LIST OF MPS/34
RALPH	DE	SHIRLE	TAXER	WAR	1322	CPR 1321-24/224

(cont.)

(cont.)

FORENAME	DE	SURNAME	OFFICE	COUNTY	YEAR	REFERENCE
RALPH	DE	SHIRLEGH	TAXER	WAR	1338	CFR V/64
RALPH	DE	SHERLE	TAXER	WAR	1338	CFR V/97
RALPH	DE	SHIRLE	KNIGHT OF SHIRE	WAR	1340	LIST OF MPS/113
RICHARD	DE	SHYRYNGTON	TAXER	WAR	1347	CFR VI/5
ADAM	DE	SOMERVILL	KNIGHT OF SHIRE	WAR	1327	LIST OF MPS/63
JOHN	DE	SOMERVILL	KNIGHT OF SHIRE	WAR	1295	LIST OF MPS/4
JOHN	DE	SOMERVILL	TAXER	WAR	1295	CPR 1292-1301/171
JOHN	DE	SOMERVILL	TAXER	WAR	1301	CPR 1292-1301/611
JOHN	DE	SUMERY	KNIGHT OF SHIRE	WAR	1300	LIST OF MPS/9
JOHN	DE	SOMERY	ARRAYER	LEC,STS,WAR	1321	CPR 1321-24/39
JOHN	DE	SOMERY	ARRAYER	LEC,NTH,RUT,STS	1322	CPR 1321-24/69
JOHN	DE	SOTEMAY	KNIGHT OF SHIRE	WAR	1330	LIST OF MPS/74
WILLIAM	DE	SPYNEYE OF COUG.	TAXER	WAR	1345	CFR V/436
WILLIAM		SPYNEYE	TAXER	WAR	1348	CFR VI/90
ADAM	DE	STVVYNTON	KNIGHT OF SHIRE	WAR	1332	LIST OF MPS/83
ADAM	DE	STYVYNGTON	KNIGHT OF SHIRE	WAR	1334	LIST OF MPS/89
ADAM	DE	STIVYNTON	KNIGHT OF SHIRE	WAR	1335	LIST OF MPS/92
ADAM	DE	STYVYNGTON	KNIGHT OF SHIRE	WAR	1339	LIST OF MPS/107
ROBERT	DE	STOKES	TAXER	WAR	1308	CPR 1307-13/34
ROBERT	DE	STOKES	TAXER	WAR	1309	CPR 1307-13/185
ROBERT	DE	STOKES	PEACE(SPECIAL)	LEC,WAR	1314	CPR 1313-17/129
ROBERT	DE	STOKE	TAXER	LEC,WAR	1316	CPR 1313-17/474
ROBERT	DE	STOK	PEACE	WAR	1318	CPR 1317-21/185
ROBERT	DE	STOKE	PEACE	WAR	1318	CPR 1317-21/289
ROBERT	DE	STOKE	TAXER	WAR	1319	CPR 1317-21/348
ROBERT	DE	STOKE	PEACE	WAR	1320	CPR 1317-21/462
RICHARD	DE	STONLEYE	KNIGHT OF SHIRE	WAR	1341	LIST OF MPS/118
RICHARD	DE	STONLE	TAXER	WAR	1342	CFR V/284
RICHARD	DE	STONLEYE	UNDER-SHERIFF	WAR&LEC	1344	LIST OF SHERIFFS
RICHARD	DE	STONLEGH	PEACE	WAR	1345	CPR 1343-45/490

First name		Surname	Role	County	Year	Reference
NICHOLAS	DE	STRATFORD	KNIGHT OF SHIRE	WAR	1332	LIST OF MPS/81
NICHOLAS	DE	STRETFORD	KNIGHT OF SHIRE	WAR	1334	LIST OF MPS/87
NICHOLAS	DE	STRATFORD	KNIGHT OF SHIRE	WAR	1335	LIST OF MPS/92
NICHOLAS	DE	STRATFORD	KNIGHT OF SHIRE	WAR	1336	LIST OF MPS/94
NICHOLAS	DE	STRETFORD	KNIGHT OF SHIRE	WAR	1336	LIST OF MPS/95B
NICHOLAS	DE	STRETFORD	KNIGHT OF SHIRE	WAR	1338	LIST OF MPS/102
HENRY	DE	SUTTON	TAXER	DBY,LEC,NTT,WAR	1304	CPR 1301-07/201
WILLIAM	DE	SUTTON	KNIGHT OF SHIRE	WAR	1322	LIST OF MPS/I7
WILLIAM	DE	SUTTON	TAXER	WAR	1322	CPR 1321-24/224
WILLIAM	DE	SUTTON	KNIGHT OF SHIRE	WAR	1324	LIST OF MPS/113
WILLIAM	DE	SUTTON	KNIGHT OF SHIRE	WAR	1325	LIST OF MPS/59
WILLIAM	DE	SUTTON	TAXER	WAR	1337	CFR V/4
WILLIAM	DE	SUTTON	TAXER	WAR	1337	CFR V/51
WILLIAM	DE	SUTTON	TAXER	WAR	1337	CFR V/53
WILLIAM	DE	SUTTON	KNIGHT OF SHIRE	WAR	1338	LIST OF MPS/105
JOHN	DE	TORVILE	TAXER	WAR	1347	CFR VI/4
WILLIAM		TRUSSEL	SHERIFF	WAR&LEC	1314	LIST OF SHERIFFS
WILLIAM		TRUSSEL ELD.	PEACE	LEC,WAR	1336	CPR 1334-38/368
WILLIAM		TRUSSEL	PEACE/ARRAY	OXF,WAR,WOR	1338	CPR 1338-40/141
WILLIAM		TRUSSEL	ARRAYER	LEC,WAR	1339	FOEDERA II/II/1070-2
WILLIAM		TRUSSEL ELD.	PEACE/ARRAY	WAR	1345	CPR 1343-45/576
JOHN		TRYMENEL	ARRAYER	WAR	1337	ROT SCOT I/501
JOHN		TRYMENEL	ARRAYER	WAR	1338	C.76/11 m.27
JOHN		TRYMENEL	ARRAYER	WAR	1338	FOEDERA II/II/1018
RICHARD	DE	TURVILLE	KNIGHT OF SHIRE	WAR	1313	LIST OF MPS/43
JOHN	DE	UPTON	TAXER	WAR	1347	CFR VI/5
ROBERT	DU	VAAL	TAXER	WAR	1309	CPR 1307-13/185
ROBERT	DE	VAAL	PEACE	WAR	1325	CPR 1324-27/66
ROBERT	DE	VALE	TAXER	WAR	1327	CPR 1327-30/173
ROBERT	DE	VERDON	KNIGHT OF SHIRE	WAR	1297	LIST OF MPS/5
ROBERT	DE	VERDON	KNIGHT OF SHIRE	WAR	1307	LIST OF MPS/27
ROBERT	DE	VERDUN	PEACE	WAR	1307	CPR 1307-13/30
ROBERT	DE	VERDON	KNIGHT OF SHIRE	WAR	1313	LIST OF MPS/43
JOHN		WALEYS	SHERIFF	WAR&LEC	1343	LIST OF SHERIFFS

(cont.)

(cont.)

FORENAME	DE	SURNAME	OFFICE	COUNTY	YEAR	REFERENCE
JOHN		WALEYS	ESCHEATOR	WAR&LEC	1343	LIST ESCHEATORS
JOHN	LE	WALEYS	UNDER-SHERIFF	WAR&LEC	1344	LIST OF SHERIFFS
OLIVER	LE	WALEYS	SHERIFF	WAR&LEC	1324	LIST OF SHERIFFS
ROBERT	DE	WARDON	PEACE	WAR	1308	CPR 1307-13/53
ROBERT	DE	WARDON	PEACE	WAR	1314	CPR 1313-17/109
ROBERT	DE	WARDON	PEACE	WAR	1314	CPR 1313-17/123
NICHOLAS	DE	WAREWIK	TAXER	LEC,WAR	1301	CPR 1301-07/2
ROBERT	DE	WAREWIK	KNIGHT OF SHIRE	WAR	1330	LIST OF MPS/74
THOMAS		WEST	KNIGHT OF SHIRE	WAR	1323	LIST OF MPS/11
RICHARD	DE	WHITAKRE	KNIGHT OF SHIRE	WAR	1297	LIST OF MPS/5
RICHARD	DE	WHITACRE	SHERIFF	WAR&LEC	1305	LIST OF SHERIFFS
RICHARD	DE	WHITACRE	ARRAYER	WAR	1338	C.76/11 m.27
RICHARD	DE	WHITACRE	PEACE/ARRAY	WAR	1338	CPR 1338-40/136
RICHARD	DE	WHITACRE	PEACE	WAR	1344	CPR 1343-45/396
RICHARD	DE	WHITACRE YOUNG.	PEACE	WAR	1344	CPR 1343-45/396
RICHARD		S. SIMON DE WHIT.	TAXER	WAR	1346	CFR V/492
RICHARD		WHITACRE OF ARD.	TAXER	WAR	1347	CFR VI/4
RICHARD	DE	WHYTACRE	TAXER	WAR	1347	CFR VI/44
PETER	DE	WOLVARDINGTON	KNIGHT OF SHIRE	WAR	1305	LIST OF MPS/18
JOHN		WORTHYN	KNIGHT OF SHIRE	WAR	1346	LIST OF MPS/124
JOHN		WORTHIN	TAXER	WAR	1347	CFR VI/4
JOHN	DE	WYNDESORE	ESCHEATOR	WAR&LEC	1344	LIST ESCHEATORS
ROGER	LA	ZUSCHE	ARRAYER	LEC,WAR	1324	CPR 1324-27/77-9
ROGER	LA	ZOUSCHE	SHERIFF	WAR&LEC	1329	LIST OF SHERIFFS
ROGER	DE	ZOUSCHE	SHERIFF	WAR&LEC	1334	LIST OF SHERIFFS

Key: ELD. = The Elder; YOUNG. = The Younger; ARD. = Arden; COLES. = Coleshill; COUG. = Coughton; COV. = Coventry; KEN. = Kenilworth; MAX. = Maxstoke; NORTH. = Northamptonshire; SOM. = Somery; WHIT. = Whitacre.

References: *Cal. Pat. Rolls*; *Cal. Fine Rolls*; *Foedera, conventiones, litterae* etc., ed. T. Rymer, revised edn. A. Clarke *et al.*, 4 vols. in 7 parts, Record Commission, 1816–69; *Rotuli Scotiae*, ed. D. Macpherson *et al.*, 2 vols. Record Commission, 1814; *PRO List and Indexes* no. ix (List of Sheriffs), pp. 44–5; *PRO List and Index Society*, vol. 72 (List of Escheators), p. 172; PRO C.76/11; *Official Return of Members of Parliament*.

Bibliography

MANUSCRIPT SOURCES

British Library, London

Cotton MSS:
  Caligula A.XVIII
  Claudius C.II
Harley 1192

Public Record Office, London

Chancery

C47 (Chancery Miscellanea)
C66 (Patent Rolls)

Exchequer

E32 (Forest Proceedings)
E101 (King's Remembrancer, Accounts Various)
E164/21 (Coventry Priory Register)
E179 (Poll Tax Returns)
E213 (Ancient Deeds, Series RS)

Judicial records

Just 1 (Eyre Rolls)

Special collections

SC1 (Ancient Correspondence)

C.A.F. Meekings, *Transcripts from the Dorse of the Patent Rolls 1232–46*

OBS 1/432–8 (Manuscript Indexes to Patent Rolls 10–16 Edward I)
OBS 1/465–7 (Manuscript Calendars to Patent Rolls 31–57 Henry III)

Shakespeare Birthplace Trust, Stratford-upon-Avon

Archer Deeds
Baddesley Clinton MSS
Gregory Hood Deeds

PRINTED SOURCES

Anglo-Saxon Charters, ed. A.J. Robertson (Cambridge, 1956)
Annales Monastici, ed. H.R. Luard, Rolls Series (London, 1864–9)
Aspilogia II: Rolls of Arms of Henry III, ed. A.R. Wagner (London, 1967)
Aspilogia III: The Rolls of Arms of Edward I, 2 vols., ed. G.J. Brault (Woodbridge, 1997)
The Book of Fees, Commonly Called Testa de Nevill, 1198–1293, 3 vols. (London, 1920–31)
Bracton's Notebook, ed. F.W. Maitland, 3 vols. (London, 1887)
Calendar of Ancient Deeds, 6 vols. (London, 1890–1915)
Calendar of Chancery Rolls, Various, 1277–1326 (London, 1912)
Calendar of Close Rolls (London, 1900–)
Calendar of Fine Rolls (London, 1911–)
Calendar of Inquisitions Miscellaneous (London, 1916–)
Calendar of Inquisitions Post Mortem (London, 1904–)
Calendar of Patent Rolls (London, 1906–)
Close Rolls, Henry III, 14 vols. (London, 1902–38)
Complete Peerage of England, Scotland, Ireland, Great Britain and the United Kingdom, 13 vols. in 14, ed. Vicary Gibbs *et al.* (London, 1910–59)
Crook, D., *Records of the General Eyre*, Public Record Office Handbook no. 20 (London, 1982)
Crown Pleas of the Wiltshire Eyre, ed. C.A.F. Meekings, Wiltshire Archaeological and Natural History Society 16 (Devizes, 1961)
Curia Regis Rolls (London, 1922–)
Dialogus de Scaccario: The Course of the Exchequer, ed. C. Johnson (Oxford, 1983)
Documents of the Baronial Movement of Reform and Rebellion 1258–67, ed. R.F. Treharne and I.J. Sanders (Oxford, 1973)
The Earliest English Law Reports, 2 vols., ed. P.A. Brand, Selden Society 112 (London, 1996)
The Earliest Northamptonshire Assize Rolls, A.D. 1202 and 1203, ed. Doris M. Stenton, Northamptonshire Record Society 5 (s.l., 1930)
The Early Records of Medieval Coventry, ed. P.R. Coss, British Academy Records of Social and Economic History, new series, 11 (Oxford, 1986)
English Historical Documents, vol. I, ed. D. Whitelock (London, 1955)
The Estate Book of Henry de Bray, ed. D. Willis, Camden Society, 3rd series, 27 (London, 1916)
Estate Records of the Hotot Family, ed. E. King, in *A Northamptonshsire Miscellany*, Northamptonshire Record Society 32 (s.l., 1983)
The Eyre of Northamptonshire, 1329–30, ed. D.W. Sutherland, Seldon Society 97 (London, 1983)
Eyton, R.W., *The Antiquities of Shropshire*, 12 vols. (London, 1854–60)
Foedera, Conventiones, Litterae et Acta Publica 1101–1654, ed. T. Rymer: new edn, ed. A. Clarke *et al.* (London, 1816–69)
Feudal Aids, 6 vols. (London, 1899–1920)

Die Gesetze der Angelsachsen, 3 vols., ed. F. Liebermann (Halle, 1903–16)

Household Accounts from Medieval England, ed. C.M. Woolgar, British Academy Records of Social and Economic History, new series, 17–18 (Oxford, 1992–3)

John of Gaunt's Register, 1372–6, 2 vols., ed. S. Armitage-Smith, Camden Society, 3rd series, 20–21 (1911)

Jurkowski, M., Smith, C.L. and Crook, D., *Lay Taxes in England and Wales 1188–1688*, Public Record Office Handbook 31 (London, 1998)

The Knights Hospitallers in England; Being the Report of Prior Philip de Thame to the Grand Master Elyan de Villanova for A.D. 1338, ed. L.B. Larking with an historical introduction by J.M. Kemble, Camden Society, old series, 65 (London, 1857)

The Langley Cartulary, ed. P.R. Coss, Dugdale Society Main Series 32 (Oxford, 1980)

The Lay Subsidy Roll for 1327, Supplement to the Transactions of the Midland Record Society 6 (s.l., 1902)

The Lay Subsidy Roll for Warwickshire of 6 Edward III (1332), ed. W.F. Carter, Dugdale Society Main Series 6 (London, 1926)

Lists and Indexes, Public Record Office, vol. IX (List of Sheriffs for England and Wales) (London, 1898)

Lists and Index Society, Public Record Office, vol. LXXII (List of Escheators) (London, 1932)

Matthew Paris, *Chronica Majora*, ed. H.R. Luard, 7 vols., Rolls Series (London, 1872–3)

Middle English Dictionary, ed. H. Kurath *et al.* (Ann Arbor, 1954–)

Oxford English Dictionary (1st edn, Oxford, 1884–1928; 2nd edn, Oxford, 1989)

Parliamentary Writs, ed. F. Palgrave, 2 vols. in 4 (London, 1827–34)

Patent Rolls, 1216–32, 2 vols. (London, 1901–3)

Pipe Rolls of the Reigns of Henry II, Richard, John and Henry III, Pipe Roll Society (London, 1884–)

Placita de Quo Warranto, Record Commission (London, 1818)

Thomas Wright's Political Songs of England, ed. Peter Coss, Royal Historical Society (Cambridge, 1996)

The Poll Taxes of 1377, 1379 and 1381, Part 2, ed. Carolyn C. Fenwick, British Academy Records of Social and Economic History, new series, 29 (Oxford, 2001)

Private Indentures for Life Service in Peace and War 1278–1476, ed. M. Jones and S. Walker, Camden Society Miscellany XXXII, 5th series, 3, Royal Historical Society (London, 1994)

Proceedings before the Justices of the Peace in the Fourteenth and Fifteenth Centuries: Edward III to Richard III, ed. B.H. Putman, Ames Foundation (London, 1938)

Raoul de Hodenc, Le Roman des Eles: The Anonymous 'Ordene de chevalrie', ed. K. Busby (Amsterdam, 1983)

The Red Book of the Exchequer, ed. H. Hall, 3 vols. (London, 1896)

Register of Edward the Black Prince, ed. M.C.B. Davies, 4 vols. (London, 1930–33)

Report of the Deputy Keeper of the Public Records, vols. 42–50 (London, 1881–9)

Return of Members of Parliament, vol. I (London, 1978)

Rolls of the Fifteenth... and Rolls of the Fortieth, ed. F.A. Cazel and A.P. Cazel, Pipe Roll Society, new series, 45 (London, 1976–7)

Rotuli Curiae Regis, ed. F. Palgrave, 2 vols., Record Commission (London, 1835)

Rotuli Hundredorum, 2 vols., Record Commission (London, 1812–18)

Rotuli Litterarum Clausarum, ed. T.D. Hardy, 2 vols., Record Commission (London, 1833–4)

Rotuli Litterarum Patentium, ed. T.D. Hardy, Record Commission (London, 1835)

Rotuli Scotiae, ed. D. Macpherson *et al.*, 2 vols., Record Commission (London, 1814)

Royal and Other Historical Letters Illustrative of the Reign of Henry III, ed. W.W. Shirley, Rolls Series (London, 1866)

Select Cases in the Court of King's Bench, ed. G.O. Sayles, vol. V, Selden Society (London, 1957)

Select Charters, ed. W. Stubbs (9th edn, Oxford, 1913)

Select Pleas of the Forest, ed. G.J. Turner, Selden Society 13 (London, 1889)

Sir Thomas Smith, *De Republica Anglorum: A Discourse on the Commonwealth of England*, ed. L. Alston (Cambridge, 1906)

The Stoneleigh Leger Book, ed. R.H. Hilton, Dugdale Society Main Series 25 (Oxford, 1960)

The Treatise on the Laws and Customs of the Realm of England Commonly called Glanvill, ed. G.D.G. Hall (Oxford, 1965)

Wagner, A.R., *Aspilogia I: A Catalogue of English Medieval Rolls of Arms* (London, 1950)

Walter Map, *De Nugis Curialium*, trans. M.R. James (revised edn, Oxford, 1983)

Walter of Henley and Other Treatises on Estate Management and Accounting, ed. D. Oschinsky (Oxford, 1971)

Warwickshire Feet of Fines, vol. II, ed. Ethel Stokes and Lucy Drucker, Dugdale Society Main Series 15 (London, 1939)

The Warwickshire Hundred Rolls of 1279–80, ed. Trevor John, British Academy Records of Social and Economic History, new series, 19 (Oxford, 1992)

Woodbine, G.E. (ed.), trans. (with revision and notes) Samuel E. Thorne, 'Bracton' (*Bracton de legibus et consuetudinibus Angliae: Bracton on the Laws and Customs of England*), 4 vols. (Oxford, 1968–77)

SECONDARY SOURCES

Abels, R.P., 'An Introduction to the Bedfordshire Domesday', in *The Bedfordshire Domesday* (Alecto Historical Editions, London, 1991)

   Lordship and Military Obligation in Anglo-Saxon England (London, 1988)

Acheson, E., *A Gentry Community: Leicestershire in the Fifteenth Century c.1422–c.1485* (Cambridge, 1992)

Ailes, A., 'Heraldic Marshalling in Medieval England', in *Proceedings of the VIII Colloquium at Canterbury: Académie Internationale d'Héraldique* (Canterbury, 1995)

   'Up in Arms: The Rise of the Armigerous *Valettus*', in A. Curry (ed.), *Thirty Years of Medieval Studies at the University of Reading: A Celebration* (Reading, 1996)

Alcock, N.W., 'The Catesbys in Coventry: A Medieval Estate and Its Archives', *Midland History* 15 (1990)

Alexander, J. and Binski, P., *Age of Chivalry: Art in Plantagenet England 1200–1400*, exhib. cat., Royal Academy of Arts (London, 1987)

Astill, G.G., 'Social Advancement through Seignorial Service? The Case of Simon Pakeman', *Transactions of the Leicestershire Archaeological Society* 54 (1978–9)

Aston, T.H. (ed.), *Landlords, Peasants and Politics in Medieval England* (Cambridge, 1987)

Ault, W.O., 'Open Field Husbandry', *Transactions of the American Philosophical Society*, new series, 55 (1965)

   'Some Early Village By-laws', *English Historical Review* 45 (1930)

Ayton, A., 'Edward III and the English Aristocracy at the Beginning of the Hundred Years War', in M. Strickland (ed.), *Armies, Chivalry and Warfare in Britain and France* (Stamford, 1998)

'English Armies in the Fourteenth Century', in A. Curry and M. Hughes (eds.), *Arms, Armies and Fortifications in the Hundred Years War* (Woodbridge, 1994)

'Knights, Esquires and Military Service: The Evidence of the Armorial Cases before the Court of Chivalry', in A. Ayton and J.L. Price (eds.), *The Medieval Military Revolution* (New York, 1995)

'Sir Thomas Ughtred and the Edwardian Military Revolution', in J.S. Boswell (ed.), *The Age of Edward III* (Woodbridge, 2001)

Baldwin, J.F., 'The Household Administration of Henry Lacy and Thomas of Lancaster', *English Historical Review* 42 (1927)

Barker, J.R.V., *The Tournament in England, 1100–1400* (Woodbridge, 1986)

Barratt, N., 'The Revenues of John and Philip Augustus Revisited', in S.D. Church (ed.), *King John: New Interpretations* (Woodbridge, 1999)

Bartlett, R., *England under the Angevin and Norman Kings, 1075–1225* (Oxford, 2000)

Basset, M., *Knights of the Shire for Bedfordshire during the Middle Ages*, Bedfordshire Record Society 29 (Bedford, 1929)

Bean, J.M.W., *From Lord to Patron: Lordship in Late Medieval England* (Manchester, 1989)

'Landlords', in E. Miller (ed.), *The Agrarian History of England and Wales*, III: *1348–1500* (Cambridge, 1991)

Beckerman, John S., 'Procedural Innovation and Institutional Change in Medieval English Manorial Courts', *Law and History Review* 10, no. 2 (1992)

Becket, J.C., *The Aristocracy in England 1660–1914* (Oxford, 1986)

Bennett, Matthew, 'The Status of the Squire: The Northern Evidence', in C. Harper-Bill and R. Harvey (eds.), *The Ideals and Practice of Medieval Knighthood, I* (Woodbridge, 1986)

Beresford, G., *Goltho: The Development of an Early Medieval Manor, c.850–1150*, Historical Buildings and Manuscript Commission for England (London, 1987)

Biancalana, J., 'For Want of Justice: Legal Reforms of Henry II', *Columbia Law Review* 88 (1988)

Biddick, K., *The Other Economy: Pastoral Husbandry on a Medieval Estate* (Berkeley, 1989)

Binski, P., 'The Stylistic Sequence of London Figure Brasses', in J. Coales (ed.), *The Earliest English Brasses: Patronage, Style and Workshops 1270–1350* (London, 1987)

Birrell, J., 'A Great Thirteenth-Century Hunter: John Giffard of Brimpsfield', *Medieval Prosopography* 3 (1994)

'The Status Maneriorum of John Catesby, 1385 and 1386', in *Miscellany I*, Dugdale Society Publications (Oxford, 1977)

'Who Poached the King's Deer?', *Midland History* 7 (1982)

Blair, J., *Anglo-Saxon Oxfordshire* (Stroud, 1994)

Early Medieval Surrey: Landholding, Church and Settlement before 1300 (Stroud, 1991)

'Hall and Chamber: English Domestic Planning 1000–1250', in G. Meirion-Jones and M. Jones (eds.), *Manorial Domestic Building in England and Northern France*, Society of Antiquaries of London, Occasional Papers 15 (London, 1993)

'Local Churches in Domesday Book and Before', in J.C. Holt (ed.), *Domesday Studies* (Woodbridge, 1987)

Blair, J. (ed.), *Minsters and Parish Churches: The Local Church in Transition 950–1200* (Oxford, 1988)

Bolton, J.L., 'The English Economy in the Early Thirteenth Century', in S.D. Church (ed.), *King John: New Interpretations* (Woodbridge, 1999)

Brand, P.A., 'Courtroom and Schoolroom: The Education of Lawyers in England prior to 1400', *Historical Research* 60 (1992); reprinted in his *The Making of the Common Law* (London, 1992)

'The Drafting of Legislation in Mid Thirteenth-Century England', *Parliamentary History* 9 (1990); reprinted in his *The Making of the Common Law* (London, 1992)

' "Multis Vigiliis Excogitatam et Inventam", Henry II and the Creation of the English Common Law', reprinted in his *The Making of the Common Law* (London, 1992)

'Oldcotes v. d'Arcy', in R.F. Hunnisett and J.B. Post (eds.), *Medieval Legal Records Edited in Memory of C.A.F. Meekings* (London, 1978)

'The Origins of the English Legal Profession', *Law and History Review* 5, no. 1 (1987); reprinted in his *The Making of the Common Law* (London, 1992)

The Origins of the English Legal Profession (Oxford, 1992)

Brault, G.J., *Early Blazon* (2nd edn, Woodbridge, 1997)

Britnell, R.H., *The Commercialisation of English Society 1000–1500* (Cambridge, 1993)

Britnell, R.H. and Campbell, B.M.S. (eds.), *A Commercialising Economy: England 1086–c.1300* (Manchester, 1985)

Brooks, N.P., 'Arms, Status and Warfare in Late Saxon England', in D. Hill (ed.), *Ethelred the Unready*, BAR British Series 59 (Oxford, 1978)

Bullock-Davies, C., *Menestrellorum Multitudo: Minstrels at a Royal Feast* (Cardiff, 1978)

Burton, J., *The Monastic Order in Yorkshire 1069–1215* (Cambridge, 1999)

Monastic and Religious Orders in Britain 1000–1300 (Cambridge, 1994)

Bush, M.L., *The English Aristocracy: A Comparative Synthesis* (Manchester, 1984)

Noble Privilege (Manchester, 1983)

Cadman, G. and Foard, G., 'Raunds, Manorial and Village Origins', in M.L. Faull (ed.), *Studies in Anglo-Saxon Settlement* (Oxford, 1984)

Cam, H., 'The Community of the Shire and the Payment of Its Representatives in Parliament', in her *Liberties and Communities in Medieval England* (Cambridge, 1944; reprinted London, 1963)

'Some Early Inquests before "Custodes Pacis" ', *English Historical Review* 40 (1925)

Camille, M., *Mirror in Parchment: The Luttrell Psalter and the Making of Medieval England* (London, 1998)

Campbell, J., *The Anglo-Saxons* (Oxford, 1982)

The Anglo-Saxon State (London, 1998)

'England c. 991', in J. Cooper (ed.), *The Battle of Maldon: Fact and Fiction* (London, 1983); reprinted in J. Campbell, *The Anglo-Saxon State* (London, 1998)

'The Late Anglo-Saxon State: A Maximum View', *Proceedings of the British Academy* 87 (1994); reprinted in *The Anglo-Saxon State* (London, 1998)

'Some Agents and Agencies of the Late Anglo-Saxon State', in J.C. Holt (ed.), *Domesday Studies* (Woodbridge, 1987); reprinted in *The Anglo-Saxon State* (London, 1998)

'Stubbs and the English State', Stenton Lecture, University of Reading (1989); reprinted in *The Anglo-Saxon State* (London, 1998)

'Was It Infancy in England? Some Questions of Comparison', in M. Jones and M. Vale (eds.), *England and Her Neighbours, 1066–1453: Essays in Honour of Pierre Chaplais* (London, 1989); reprinted in *The Anglo-Saxon State* (London, 1998)

Carpenter, C., 'Gentry and Community in Medieval England', *Journal of British Studies* 33 (1994)

Lordship and Polity: A Study of Warwickshire Landed Society, 1401–1499 (Cambridge, 1992)

Carpenter, D.A., 'The Decline of the Curial Sheriff in England, 1194–1258', *English Historical Review* 101 (1976); reprinted in his *The Reign of Henry III* (London, 1996)

'The Fall of Hubert de Burgh', *Journal of British Studies* 19 (1980); reprinted in his *The Reign of Henry III* (London, 1996)

'King, Magnates and Society: The Personal Rule of King Henry III, 1234–1258', *Speculum* 60 (1985); reprinted in his *The Reign of Henry III* (London, 1996)

The Minority of Henry III (London, 1990)

'The Plantagenet Kings', in D. Abulafia (ed.), *The New Cambridge Medieval History*, V: *c.1198–1300* (Cambridge, 1999)

The Reign of Henry III (London, 1996)

'The Second Century of English Feudalism', *Past and Present* 168 (2000)

'Was There a Crisis of the Knightly Class in the Thirteenth Century? The Oxfordshire Evidence', *English Historical Review* 377 (1980); reprinted in his *The Reign of Henry III* (London, 1996)

'What Happened in 1258?', in J. Gillingham and J.C. Holt (eds.), *War and Government in the Middle Ages: Essays in Honour of J.O. Prestwich* (Woodbridge, 1984); reprinted in his *The Reign of Henry III* (London, 1996)

Cave-Brown, Rev. J., 'Knights of the Shire of Kent from A.D. 1275 to A.D. 1831', *Archæologia Cantiana* 21 (1985)

Cazel, F., 'The Fifteenth of 1225', *Bulletin of the Institute of Historical Research* 34 (1961)

Cherry, J., 'Heraldry as Decoration in the Thirteenth Century', in W.M. Ormrod (ed.), *England in the Thirteenth Century* (Stamford, 1991)

Chibnall, A.C., *Sherington: Fiefs and Fields of a Buckinghamshire Village* (Cambridge, 1965)

Church, S.D., *The Household Knights of King John* (Cambridge, 1999)

Clanchy, M.T., *From Memory to Written Record: England 1066–1307* (2nd edn, Oxford, 1993)

Clark, E., 'Medieval Labor Laws and the English Local Courts', *American Journal of Legal History* 27 (1983)

Clark, P., *English Provincial Society from the Reformation to the Revolution: Religion, Politics and Society in Kent, 1500–1640* (Hassocks, 1977)

Clarke, P.A., *The English Nobility under Edward the Confessor* (Oxford, 1994)

Cliffe, J.T., *The Yorkshire Gentry from the Reformation to the Civil War* (London, 1969)

Cooper, J.P., 'Ideas of Gentility in Early Modern England', in G.E. Aylmer and J.S. Morrill (eds.), *Land, Men and Beliefs: Studies in Early Modern History* (London, 1983)

Cooper, J. (ed.), *The Battle of Maldon: Fact and Fiction* (London, 1993)

Coss, P.R., 'Bastard Feudalism Revised', *Past and Present* 125 (1989)

'The Formation of the English Gentry', *Past and Present* 147 (1995)

'Heraldry and Monumental Effigies in the North East', in T.E. Faulkner (ed.), *Northumbrian Panorama: Studies in the History and Culture of North East England* (London, 1996)

The Knight in Medieval England 1000–1400 (Stroud, 1993)

'Knighthood and the Early Thirteenth-Century County Court', in P.R. Coss and S.D. Lloyd (eds.), *Thirteenth Century England II* (Woodbridge, 1988)

'Knighthood, Heraldry and Social Exclusion in Edwardian England', in P. Coss and M. Keen (eds.), *Heraldry, Pageantry and Social Display in Medieval England* (Woodbridge, 2002)

The Lady in Medieval England 1000–1500 (Stroud, 1998)

The Langley Family and Its Cartulary: A Study in Late Medieval 'Gentry', Dugdale Society Occasional Papers 22 (Oxford, 1974)

'Literature and Social Terminology: The Vavasour in England', in T.H. Aston *et al.* (eds.), *Social Relations and Ideas: Essays in Honour of R.H. Hilton* (Cambridge, 1983)

Lordship, Knighthood and Locality: A Study in English Society c.1180–c.1280 (Cambridge, 1991)

'Sir Geoffrey de Langley and the Crisis of the Knightly Class in Thirteenth-Century England', *Past and Present* 68 (1975); reprinted in T.H. Aston (ed.), *Landlords, Peasants and Politics in Medieval England* (Cambridge, 1987)

Cressy, D., 'Describing the Social Order of Elizabethan and Stuart England', *Literature and History* 3 (1976)

Crook, D., 'The "Petition of the Barons" and Charters of Free Warren, 1227–1258', in M. Prestwich *et al.* (eds.), *Thirteenth Century England VIII* (Woodbridge, 2001)

Crouch, D., 'Bastard Feudalism Revised', *Past and Present* 131 (1991)

The Image of Aristocracy in Britain 1000–1300 (London and New York, 1992)

'The Local Influence of the Earls of Warwick, 1088–1242: A Study in Decline and Resourcefulness', *Midland History* 21 (1996)

'From Stenton to McFarlane: Models of Societies of the Twelfth and Thirteenth Centuries', *Transactions of the Royal Historical Society*, 6th ser., 5 (1995)

Dalton, P., *Conquest, Anarchy and Lordship: Yorkshire 1066–1154* (Cambridge, 1994)

Davidson, B., 'Excavations at Sulgrave, Northamptonshire, 1960–76', *Archaeological Journal* 125 (1968)

Davies, R.G. and Denton, J.H. (eds.), *The English Parliament in the Middle Ages* (Manchester, 1981)

Davies, W., *Small Worlds: The Village Community in Early Medieval Brittany* (London, 1988)

Davis, R.H.C., *The Medieval Warhorse* (London, 1989)

Denholm-Young, N., *Country Gentry in the Fourteenth Century* (reprinted Oxford, 1969)

'Feudal Society in the Thirteenth Century: The Knights', *History* 29 (1924); reprinted in his *Collected Papers on Medieval Subjects* (Cardiff, 1969)

Seignorial Administration in England (Oxford, 1937)

'The Song of Carlaverock, the Parliamentary Roll of Arms and the Galloway Roll', in *Collected Papers on Medieval Subjects* (Cardiff, 1969)

Duby, G., 'The Transformation of the Aristocracy', reprinted in *The Chivalrous Society*, trans. C. Postan (London, 1977)

Dugdale, W., *The Antiquities of Warwickshire* (London, 1656), rev. W. Thomas (London, 1730)

Düll, S., Luttrell, A. and Keen, M., 'Faithful unto Death: The Tomb Slab of Sir William Neville and Sir John Clanvowe', *Antiquaries Journal* 71 (1991)

Dyer, C., *Standards of Living in the Later Middle Ages: Social Change in England c.1200–1520* (Cambridge, 1989)

Edwards, J.G., 'The Personnel of the Commons in Parliament under Edward I and Edward II', in *Essays in Medieval History Presented to Thomas Frederick Tout*

(Manchester, 1925); reprinted in E.B. Fryde and E. Miller (eds.), *Historical Studies of the English Parliament*, I: *Origins to 1399* (Cambridge, 1970)

Everson, P., 'What's in a Name? Goltho, "Goltho" and Bullington', *Lincolnshire History and Archaeology* 23 (1988)

Faith, R., 'Demesne Resources and Labour Rent on the Manors of St Paul's Cathedral, 1066–1222', *Economic History Review*, 2nd ser., 47 (1994)

    The English Peasantry and the Growth of Lordship (Leicester, 1997)

Faulkner, K., 'The Knights in the Magna Carta Civil War', in M. Prestwich *et al.* (eds.), *Thirteenth Century England VIII* (Woodbridge, 2001)

    'The Transformation of Knighthood in Early Thirteenth-Century England', *English Historical Review* 111 (1996)

Fleming, D.F., 'Milites as Attestors to Charters in England, 1000–1300', *Albion* 22 (1990)

Fleming, R., *Kings and Lords in Conquest England* (Cambridge, 1991)

    'Rural Elites and Urban Communities in Late-Saxon England', *Past and Present* 141 (1993)

Flori, J., 'Pour une histoire de la chevalerie: l'adoubement dans les romans de Chrétien de Troyes', *Romania* 100 (1979)

Flower, C.T., *Introduction to the Curia Regis Rolls*, Seldon Society 62 (London, 1944)

Foulet, L., 'Sir, messire', *Romania* 71 (1950)

Gem, R., 'The English Parish Church in the Eleventh and Early Twelfth Centuries: A Great Rebuilding?', in J. Blair (ed.), *Minsters and Parish Churches: The Local Church in Transition 950–1200* (Oxford, 1988)

Génicot, L., 'Recent Research on the Medieval Nobility', in T. Reuter (ed. and trans.), *The Medieval Nobility: Studies on the Ruling Class of France and Germany from the Sixth to the Twelfth Century* (Amsterdam, 1979)

Gillingham, J., '1066 and the Introduction of Chivalry into England', in G. Garnett and J. Hudson (eds.), *Law and Government in Medieval England and Normandy* (Cambridge, 1994)

    'Kingship, Chivalry and Love. Political and Cultural Values in the Earliest History Written in French: Gaimer's *Estoire des Engleis*', in W.W. Hollister (ed.), *Anglo-Norman Political Culture and the Twelfth Century Renaissance* (Woodbridge, 1997)

    'Thegns and Knights in Eleventh-Century England: Who Was Then the Gentleman?', *Transactions of the Royal Historical Society*, 6th ser., 5 (1995)

Given-Wilson, C., *The English Nobility in the Later Middle Ages* (London and New York, 1987)

Gooder, A. and Gooder, E., 'Coventry before 1355: Unity or Division?', *Midland History* 6 (1981)

Green, J., *The Aristocracy of Norman England* (Cambridge, 1997)

Hadley, D.M., *The Northern Danelaw: Its Social Structure, c.800–1100* (London, 2000)

Harding, A., *England in the Thirteenth Century* (Cambridge, 1993)

    The Law Courts of Medieval England (London, 1973)

    'The Origins and Early History of the Keeper of the Peace', *Transactions of the Royal Historical Society*, 5th ser., 10 (1960)

Harmer, F.E., *Anglo-Saxon Writs* (Manchester, 1952)

Harriss, G.L., 'The Formation of Parliament, 1272–1377', in R.G. Davies and J.H. Denton (eds.), *The English Parliament in the Middle Ages* (London, 1998)

    King, Parliament and Public Finance in Medieval England to 1369 (Oxford, 1975)

    'Political Society and the Growth of Government in Late Medieval England', *Past and Present* 138 (1993)

Hartshorne, A., 'The Cogenhoe Family and Cogenhoe Church, Northamptonshire', *Proceedings of the Society of Antiquaries*, 2nd ser., 19 (London, for 1901–3)

Harvey, B., 'The Aristocratic Consumer in England in the Long Thirteenth Century', in M. Prestwich *et al*. (eds.), *Thirteenth Century England VI* (Woodbridge, 1997)

Harvey, P.D.A., *Cuxham: A Medieval Oxfordshire Village* (Oxford, 1965)

'Personal Seals in Thirteenth-Century England', in I. Wood and G.A. Loud (eds.), *Church and Chronicle in the Middle Ages: Essays Presented to John Taylor* (London, 1991)

Harvey, P.D.A. and McGuinness, A.F., *A Guide to British Medieval Seals* (London, 1995)

Hassell Smith, A., *County and Court: Government and Politics in Norfolk, 1558–1603* (Oxford, 1974)

Hilton, R.H., *A Medieval Society: The West Midlands at the End of the Thirteenth Century* (London, 1966)

'Peasant Movements in England before 1381', *Economic History Review*, 2nd ser., 2 (1949)

Hollister, C.W., 'The Aristocracy', in E. King (ed.), *The Anarchy of Stephen's Reign* (Oxford, 1994)

Holmes, G.A., *The Estates of the Higher Nobility in Fourteenth-Century England* (Cambridge, 1957)

Holt, J.C., *Magna Carta* (Cambridge, 1965; 2nd edn Cambridge, 1992)

The Northeners: A Study in the Reign of King John (Oxford, 1961; reprinted 1992)

'The Prehistory of Parliament', in R.G. Davies and J.H. Denton (eds.), *The English Parliament in the Middle Ages* (Manchester, 1981)

Horrox, R., 'The Urban Gentry in the Fifteenth Century', in J.A.F. Thomson (ed.), *Towns and Townspeople in the Fifteenth Century* (Gloucester, 1988)

Howell, M., *Eleanor of Provence: Queenship in Thirteenth-Century England* (London, 1998)

Hudson, J., *The Formation of the English Common Law: Law and Society in England from the Norman Conquest to Magna Carta* (London, 1996)

Land, Law and Lordship in Anglo-Norman England (Oxford, 1994)

Hunnisett, R.F., *The Medieval Coroner* (Cambridge, 1961)

'Sussex Coroners in the Middle Ages', *Sussex Archaeological Collections* 95 (1957), 96 (1958), 98 (1960)

Hunt, J., 'Families at War: Royalists and Montfortians in the West Midlands', *Midland History* 22 (1997)

Lordship and Landscape: A Documentary and Archaeological Study of the Honor of Dudley c.1066–1322, BAR British Series 264 (Oxford, 1997)

Hunter Blair, C.H., 'Members of Parliament for Northumberland (October 1258–January 1327)', in *Archæologia Æliana*, 4th ser., 10 (1933)

'Northern Knights at Falkirk, 1298', *Archæologia Æliana*, 4th ser., 25 (1947)

Hurnard, N., *The King's Pardon for Homicide Before AD 1307* (Oxford, 1969)

Hyams, P.R., 'Warranty and Good Lordship in Twelfth Century England', *Law and History Review* 5 (1987)

Illsley, J.S., 'Parliamentary Elections in the Reign of Edward I', *Bulletin of the Institute of Historical Research* 49 (1976)

Jacob, E.F., *Studies in the Period of Baronial Reform and Rebellion, 1258–67*, Oxford Studies in Social and Legal History 8 (Oxford, 1925)

Jaeger, C.S., *The Origins of Courtliness: Civilizing Trends and the Formation of Courtly Ideas 939–1210* (Philadelphia, 1985)

Jones, M. (ed.), *Gentry and Lesser Nobility in Late Medieval Europe* (Gloucester, 1986)

Kaeuper, R.W., 'Law and Order in Fourteenth-Century England: The Evidence of Special Commissions of Oyer and Terminer', *Speculum* 54 (1979)

Violence and Chivalry in Medieval Europe (Oxford, 1999)

War, Justice and Public Order: England and France in the Later Middle Ages (Oxford, 1988)

Keefe, T.K., *Feudal Assessments and the Political Community under Henry II and His Sons* (Berkeley, 1987)

'Proffers for Heirs and Heiresses in the Pipe Rolls: Some Observations on Indebtedness in the Years before Magna Carta (1180–1212)', *Haskins Society Journal* 5 (Woodbridge, 1993)

Keen, M., 'Brotherhood-in-Arms', *History* 47 (1964); reprinted in M. Keen, *Nobles, Knights and Men-at-Arms in the Middle Ages* (London, 1996)

Chivalry (Yale, 1984)

'Heraldry and Hierarchy: Esquires and Gentlemen', in J. Denton (ed.), *Orders and Hierarchies in Late Medieval Europe* (Manchester, 1999)

The Origins of the English Gentleman (Stroud, 2002)

Kemp, B., 'English Church Monuments during the Period of the Hundred Years War', in A. Curry and M. Hughes (eds.), *Arms, Armies and Fortifications in the Hundred Years War* (Woodbridge, 1994)

King, E., 'Economic Development in the Early Twelfth Century', in R.H. Britnell and J. Hatcher (eds.), *Progress and Problems in Medieval England* (Cambridge, 1996)

'Large and Small Landowners in Thirteenth-Century England', *Past and Present* 47 (1970)

King, E.J., *The Seals of the Knights of St. John of Jerusalem* (London, 1932)

Knowles, C., 'The Resettlement of England after the Barons' War, 1264–7', *Transactions of the Royal Historical Society*, 5th ser., 32 (1982)

Kosminsky, E.A., *Studies in the Agrarian History of England in the Thirteenth Century*, ed. R.H. Hilton (Oxford, 1956)

Lack, W., Stuchfield, M. and Whittemore, P., *The Monumental Brasses of Wiltshire*, Monumental Brass Society (London, 1993)

Lapsley, G.T., 'Buzones', *English Historical Review* 47 (1932)

Latimer, P., 'Early Thirteenth-Century Prices', in S.D. Church (ed.), *King John: New Interpretations* (Woodbridge, 1999)

'The English Inflation of 1180–1220 Reconsidered', *Past and Present* 171 (2001)

Lawrance, H., *Heraldry from Military Monuments before 1350 in England and Wales*, Harleian Society 98 (London, 1946)

Lewis, C., Mitchell-Fox, P. and Dyer, C., *Village, Hamlet and Field: Changing Medieval Settlements in Central England* (Manchester, 1997)

Lewis, C.P. 'The Domesday Jurors', *Haskins Society Journal* 5 (1993)

Leyser, K., 'Early Medieval Canon Law and the Beginnings of Knighthood', in L. Fenske, W. Rösener and T. Zotz (eds.), *Institutionen, Kultur and Gesellschaft im Mittelalter: Festschrift für J. Fleckenstein* (Sigmaringen, 1984); reprinted in his *Communications and Power in Medieval Europe: The Carolingian and Ottonian Centuries*, ed. T. Reuter (London, 1994)

Loyn, H., *Anglo-Saxon England and the Norman Conquest* (London, 1962)

'Gesiths and Thegns in Anglo-Saxon England from the Seventh to the Tenth Century', *English Historical Review* 70 (1955)

The Governance of Anglo-Saxon England 500–1087 (London, 1984)

'The Hundred in England during the Tenth and Early Eleventh Centuries', in H. Hearder and H.R. Loyn (eds.), *British Government and Administration:*

Studies Presented to S.B. Chrimes (Cardiff, 1974); reprinted in H. Loyn, *Society and Peoples: Studies in the History of England and Wales, c.600–1200* (London, 1992)

'Thegns', in P.E. Szarmach, M.T. Tavormina and J.T. Rosenthal (eds.), *Medieval England: An Encyclopedia* (New York and London, 1998)

Macfarlane, A., *The Culture of Capitalism* (Oxford, 1987), ch. 1 reprinted from D. Green *et al.* (eds.), *Social Organisation and Settlement*, BAR International Series (Supplementary) 47 (ii) (Oxford, 1978)

McFarlane, K.B., *The Nobility of Later Medieval England* (Oxford, 1973)

Maddicott, J.R., 'The Birth and Setting of the Ballads of Robin Hood', *English Historical Review* 93 (1978)

'The County Community and the Making of Public Opinion in Fourteenth-Century England', *Transactions of the Royal Historical Society*, 5th ser., 28 (1978)

'The Crusade Taxation of 1268–70 and the Development of Parliament', in P.R. Coss and S.D. Lloyd (eds.), *Thirteenth Century England II* (Woodbridge, 1988)

'The Earliest Known Knights of the Shire: New Light on the Parliament of April 1254', *Parliamentary History* 18, no. 2 (1999)

'Edward I and the Lessons of Baronial Reform: Local Government, 1258–80', in P.R. Coss and S.D. Lloyd (eds.), *Thirteenth Century England I* (Woodbridge, 1986)

' "An Infinite Multitude of Nobles": Quality, Quantity and Politics in the Pre-Reform Parliaments of Henry III', in M. Prestwich *et al.*, *Thirteenth Century England VII* (Woodbridge, 1999)

'Magna Carta and the Local Community, 1215–1259', *Past and Present* 102 (1984)

'Parliament and the Constituencies, 1272–1377', in R.G. Davies and J.H. Denton (eds.), *The English Parliament in the Middle Ages* (Manchester, 1981)

Simon de Montfort (Cambridge, 1994)

Thomas of Lancaster 1307–22: A Study in the Reign of Edward II (Oxford, 1970)

Marks, R., 'Sir Geoffrey Luttrell and Some Companions: Images of Chivalry c.1320–50', *Wiener Jahrbuch für Kunstgeschichte*, Band 46–7 (Cologne, 1993–4)

Stained Glass in England during the Middle Ages (London, 1993)

Meekings, C.A.F., 'Martin Pateshull and William Raleigh', *Bulletin of the Institute of Historical Research* 26 (1953); reprinted in his *Studies in 13th Century Justice and Administration* (London, 1981)

The 1235 Surrey Eyre, vol. I, Surrey Record Society 31 (Guildford, 1979)

Mertes, K., *The English Noble Household* (Oxford, 1988)

Michel, P., 'Sir Philip d'Arcy and the Financial Plight of the Military Knight in 13th-Century England', *Lincolnshire History and Archaeology* 19 (1984)

Mingay, G.E., *The Gentry: The Rise and Fall of a Ruling Class* (London, 1976)

Mitchell, S.K., *Taxation in Medieval England* (New Haven and London, 1951)

Moor, C., *Knights of Edward I*, 5 vols., Publications of the Harleian Society 80–4 (London, 1929–32)

Moreton, C., 'A Social Gulf? The Upper and Lesser Gentry of Later Medieval England', *Journal of Medieval History* 17, no. 3 (1991)

Morgan, D.A.L., 'The Individual Style of the English Gentleman', in M. Jones (ed.), *Gentry and Lesser Nobility in Late Medieval Europe* (Gloucester, 1986)

Morgan, P., 'Making the English Gentry', in P.R. Coss and S.D. Lloyd (eds.), *Thirteenth Century England V* (Woodbridge, 1995)

War and Society in Medieval Cheshire 1277–1403 (Manchester, 1987)

Musson, A., *Medieval Law in Context: The Growth of Legal Consciousness from Magna Carta to the Peasants' Revolt* (Manchester, 2001)

'New Labour Laws, New Remedies? Legal Reaction to the Black Death "Crisis" ', in N. Saul (ed.), *Fourteenth Century Studies* (Woodbridge, 2000)

Public Order and Law Enforcement: The Local Administration of Criminal Justice, 1294–1350 (Woodbridge, 1996)

Musson, A. and Ormrod, W.M., *The Evolution of English Justice: Law, Politics and Society in the Fourteenth Century* (London, 1999)

Naughton, K.S., *The Gentry of Bedfordshire in the Thirteenth and Fourteenth Centuries* (Leicester, 1976)

Nelson, J.L., 'Ninth-Century Knighthood: The Evidence of Nithard', in her *The Frankish World 750–900* (London, 1996)

Newman, J.E., 'Greater and Lesser Landowners and Parochial Patronage: Yorkshire in the Thirteenth Century', *English Historical Review* 92 (1977)

Newton, P.A., *The County of Oxford: A Catalogue of Medieval Stained Glass* (London, 1979)

Norris, M., *Monumental Brasses: The Craft* (London, 1978)

Monumental Brasses: The Memorials, 2 vols. (London, 1977)

Norton, R., 'The Arms of Eustace de Hatch and Others', *Coat of Arms*, new ser. 5, no. 121 (1982)

'The Arms of Robert fitz Roger and Others', *Coat of Arms*, new ser. 3, no. 110 (1979)

Ormrod, W.M., 'Agenda for Legislation, 1322–c.1340', *English Historical Review* 105 (1990)

The Reign of Edward III: Crown and Political Society in England 1327–1377 (New Haven and London, 1990)

Page, M., 'Cornwall, Earl Richard and the Barons' War', *English Historical Review* 115 (2000)

Palmer, R.C., *The County Courts of Medieval England, 1150–1350* (Princeton, 1982)

'County Year Book Reports: The Professional Lawyer in the Medieval County Court', *English Historical Review* 91 (1971)

English Law in the Age of the Black Death, 1348–1381: A Transformation of Governance and Law (Chapel Hill and London, 1993)

'The Origins of the Legal Profession in England', *The Irish Jurist*, new ser., 11 (1976)

Parsons, J. Carmi, *Eleanor of Castile: Queen and Society in Thirteenth-Century England* (New York, 1995)

Payling, S.J., *Political Society in Lancastrian England: The Greater Gentry of Nottinghamshire* (Oxford, 1991)

'The Widening Franchise – Parliamentary Elections in Lancastrian Nottinghamshire', in D. Williams (ed.), *England in the Fifteenth Century: Proceedings of the 1986 Harlaxton Symposium* (Woodbridge, 1987)

Pelham, R.A., 'The Early Wool Trade in Warwickshire and the Rise of the Merchant Middle Class', *Transactions of the Birmingham Archaeological Society* 63 (1944)

Polden, A., 'A Crisis of the Knightly Class? Inheritance and Office among the Gentry of Thirteenth-Century Buckinghamshire', in P. Fleming, A. Gross and J.R. Lander (eds.), *Regionalism and Revision: The Crown and Its Provinces in England 1200–1650* (London, 1998)

Pollock, F. and Maitland, F.W., *The History of English Law before the Time of Edward I*, 2 vols. (2nd edn, Cambridge, 1968)

Post, J.B., 'Courts, Councils and Arbitrators in the Ladbroke Manor Dispute, 1382–1400', in R.F. Hunnisett and J.B. Post (eds.), *Medieval Legal Records* (London, 1978)

Postan, M.M., *The Medieval Economy and Society* (London, 1972)

Postles, D., *The Surnames of Leicestershire and Rutland* (Leicester, 1998)

Powell, E., *Kingship, Law and Society: Criminal Justice in the Reign of Henry V* (Oxford, 1989)

Powell, J.E. and Wallis, K., *The House of Lords in the Middle Ages* (London, 1968)

Powicke, M., 'Distraint of Knighthood and Military Obligation under Henry III', *Speculum* 25 (1950)

> *Military Obligation in Medieval England: A Study in Liberty and Duty* (Oxford, 1962; rev. edn Westport, CT, 1975)

Powys, J., *Aristocracy* (Oxford, 1984)

Prestwich, M.C., *Armies and Warfare in the Middle Ages: The English Experience* (London, 1996)

> 'Cavalry Service in Early Fourteenth-Century England', in J. Gillingham and J.C. Holt (eds.), *War and Government in the Middle Ages: Essays in Honour of J.O. Prestwich* (Woodbridge, 1984)

> *Edward I* (London, 1988)

> *English Politics in the Thirteenth Century* (London, 1990)

> 'An Indenture between Ralph, lord Basset of Drayton, and Philip de Chetwynd, 4 March 1319', *Stafford Historical and Civic Society, Transactions* (1971–3)

> 'Parliament and the Community of the Realm in Fourteenth Century England', in A. Cosgrove and J.I. McGuire (eds.), *Parliament and Community* (Belfast, 1983)

> *The Three Edwards: War and State in England 1272–1377* (London, 1980)

> *War, Politics and Finance under Edward I* (London, 1972)

Pugh, T.B., 'The Magnates, Knights and Gentry', in S.B. Chrimes, C.D. Ross and R.A. Griffiths (eds.), *Fifteenth-Century England* (Manchester, 1972)

Putnam, B.H., 'The Transformation of the Keepers of the Peace into the Justices of the Peace, 1327–80', *Transactions of the Royal Historical Society* 4th ser., 12 (1929)

Quick, J., 'The Number and Distribution of Knights in Thirteenth-Century England: The Evidence of the Grand Assize Lists', in P.R. Coss and S.D. Lloyd (eds.), *Thirteenth Century England II* (Woodbridge, 1988)

Raban, S., 'The Church in the 1279 Hundred Rolls', in M.J. Franklin and C. Harper-Bill (eds.), *Medieval Ecclesiastical Studies in Honour of Dorothy M. Owen* (Woodbridge, 1995)

> 'The Land Market and the Aristocracy in the Thirteenth Century', in D. Greenway, C. Holdsworth and J. Sayers (eds.), *Tradition and Change: Essays in Honour of Marjorie Chibnall* (Cambridge, 1985)

Razi, Z. and Smith, R.M., 'The Origins of the English Manorial Court Rolls as a Written Record: A Puzzle', in Razi and Smith (eds.), *Medieval Society and the Manor Court* (Oxford, 1996)

Reid, R.R., 'Barony and Thanage', *English Historical Review* 35 (1920)

Richardson, H.G., 'Business Training in Medieval Oxford', *American History Review* 46 (1941)

> *The English Jewry under the Angevin Kings* (London, 1960)

Richmond, C., 'The Rise of the English Gentry 1150–1350', *The Historian* 26 (1990)

Ridgeway, H.W., 'The Lord Edward and the Provisions of Oxford (1258): A Study in Faction', in P.R. Coss and S.D. Lloyd (eds.), *Thirteenth Century England I* (Woodbridge, 1986)

> 'Mid Thirteenth-Century Reformers and the Localities: The Sheriffs of the Baronial Regime, 1258–1261', in P. Fleming, A. Gross and J.R. Lander (eds.), *Regionalism*

and Revision: The Crown and Its Provinces in England 1250–1650 (London and Rio Grande, 1998)

Roberts, J., 'The Old English Vocabulary of Nobility', in A. Duggan (ed.), *Nobles and Nobility in Medieval Europe: Concepts, Origins, Transformations* (Woodbridge, 2000)

Roffe, D., 'From Thegnage to Barony: Sake and Soke, Title, and Tenants-in-Chief', in M. Chibnall (ed.), *Anglo-Saxon Studies*, XII: *Proceedings of the Battle Conference 1989* (Woodbridge, 1990)

Saul, N., 'Conflict and Consensus in English Local Society', in J. Taylor and W. Childs (eds.), *Politics and Crisis in Fourteenth-Century England* (Gloucester, 1990)

Death, Art and Memory in Medieval England: The Cobham Family and Their Monuments 1300–1500 (Oxford, 2001)

Knights and Esquires: The Gloucestershire Gentry in the Fourteenth Century (Oxford, 1981)

Scenes from Provincial Life: Knightly Families in Sussex, 1280–1400 (Oxford, 1986)

Sayer, M.J., *English Nobility: The Gentry, the Heralds and the Continental Context* (Norwich, 1979)

Scammell, J., 'The Formation of the English Social Structure: Freedom, Knights, and Gentry, 1066–1300', *Speculum* 68, no. 3 (1993)

Scragg, D. (ed.), *The Battle of Maldon AD 991* (Oxford, 1991)

Searle, E., *Lordship and Community: Battle Abbey and Its Banlieu 1066–1538* (Toronto, 1974)

Shanin, T. (ed.), *Peasants and Peasant Societies* (Harmondsworth and New York, 1971)

Short, I., 'Gaimer's Epilogue and Geoffrey of Monmouth's *Liber Vetustissimus*', *Speculum* 69 (1994)

Simpson, G.G., 'The *Familia* of Roger de Quincy, Earl of Winchester and Constable of Scotland', in J.K. Stringer (ed.), *Essays on the Nobility of Scotland* (Glasgow, 1985)

Spring, E., *Law, Land and Family: Aristocratic Inheritance in England, 1300–1800* (Chapel Hill, 1993)

Stacey, C., 'Jewish Lending and the Medieval English Economy', in R.H. Britnell and B.M.S. Campbell (eds.), *A Commercialising Economy: England 1086 to c.1300* (Manchester, 1995)

'Parliamentary Negotiation and the Expulsion of the Jews from England', in M. Prestwich *et al.* (eds.), *Thirteenth Century England VI* (Woodbridge, 1997)

Politics, Policy and Finance under Henry III, 1216–1245 (Oxford, 1987)

Stafford, P., *The East Midlands in the Early Middle Ages* (Leicester, 1985)

Unification and Conquest: A Political and Social History of England in the Tenth and Eleventh Centuries (London and New York, 1989)

Stenton, F.M., 'The Thriving of the Anglo-Saxon Ceorl', in D.M. Stenton (ed.), *Preparatory to Anglo-Saxon England: Being the Collected Papers of Frank Merry Stenton* (Oxford, 1970)

Stevenson, E.R., 'The Escheator', in J.F. Willard, W.A. Morris *et al.* (eds.), *The English Government at Work 1327–1336* (Cambridge, MA, 1947)

Strickland, M., *War and Chivalry: The Conduct and Perception of War in England and Normandy, 1066–1217* (Cambridge, 1996)

Stringer, K.J., *Earl David of Huntingdon 1152–1219: A Study in Anglo-Scottish History* (Edinburgh, 1985)

Stone, L., 'Social Mobility in England', *Past and Present* 33 (1966)

Stone, L. and Stone, J.C. Fawtier, *An Open Elite? England 1540–1880* (Oxford, 1984)

Storey, R. L., 'Gentlemen Bureaucrats', in C.H. Clough (ed.), *Profession, Vocation and Culture in Later Medieval England* (Liverpool, 1982)

Summerson, H., 'The Enforcement of the Statute of Westminster, 1285–1327', *Journal of Legal History* 13, no. 3 (1992)

Sutherland, D.W., *Quo Warranto Proceedings in the Reign of Edward I, 1278–1294* (Oxford, 1963)

Swabey, ff., *Medieval Gentlewoman: Life in a Widow's Household in the Later Middle Ages* (Stroud, 1999)

Taylor, M.M., 'Parliamentary Elections in Cambridgeshire, 1332–8', *Bulletin of the Institute of Historical Research* 18 (1940–1)

Templeman, G., *The Sheriffs of Warwickshire in the Thirteenth Century*, Dugdale Society Occasional Papers 7 (Oxford, 1948)

Thomas, Hugh M., *Vassals, Heiresses, Crusaders and Thugs: The Gentry of Angevin Yorkshire, 1154–1216* (Philadelphia, 1993)

Thorne, S.E., 'English Feudalism and Estates in Land', *Cambridge Law Journal* 17 (1959)

Titterton, J., 'The Valence Casket and Its Original Owner', *Coat of Arms*, new ser., 10 (1993)

Tomkinson, A., 'Retinues at the Tournament of Dunstable, 1309', *English Historical Review* 84 (1959)

Treharne, R.F., 'The Knights in the Period of Reform and Rebellion, 1258–67: A Critical Phase in the Rise of a New Social Class', *Bulletin of the Institute of Historical Research* 21 (1946–8)

Tummers, H.A., *Early Secular Effigies in England in the Thirteenth Century* (Leiden, 1980)

Turner, R.V., *The English Judiciary in the Age of Glanvill and Bracton c.1176–1239* (Cambridge, 1985)

Verduyn, A., 'The Politics of Law and Order during the Early Years of Edward III', *English Historical Review* 108 (1993)

'The Selection and Appointment of Justices of the Peace in 1338', *Historical Research* 68 (1995)

Victoria County Histories: Bedfordshire, Berkshire, Leicestershire, Oxfordshire, Rutland, Warwickshire, Worcestershire

Vincent, N., 'The Earliest Nottinghamshire Will (1257): Robert of Wichford Counts His Debts', *Transactions of the Thoroton Society of Nottinghamshire* 102 (1998)

The Lucys of Charlecote: The Invention of a Warwickshire Family, 1170–1302, Dugdale Society Occasional Papers 42 (Stratford-upon-Avon, 2002).

Walker, S., 'Sir Richard Abberbury (c.1330–1399) and His Kinsmen: The Rise and Fall of a Gentry Family', *Nottingham Medieval Studies* 34 (1990)

Watkins, W., 'The Monuments in Pitchford Church', *Transactions of the Shropshire Archaeological Society* 53 (1949–50)

Waugh, S.L., 'Reluctant Knights and Jurors: Respites, Exemptions, and Public Obligations in the Reign of Henry III', *Speculum* 58 (1983)

'Tenure to Contract: Lordship and Clientage in Thirteenth-Century England', *English Historical Review* 401 (1986)

White, A.B., *Self-Government at the King's Command* (Minneapolis, 1933; reprinted Westport, CT, 1974)

White, G.J., *Restoration and Reform 1153–1165: Recovery from Civil War in England* (Cambridge, 2000)

Willard, J.F., *Parliamentary Taxes on Personal Property 1290–1334: A Study in Medi-aeval English Financial Administration* (Cambridge, MA, 1934)

Williams, A., 'A Bell-House and a Burh-Geat: Lordly Residences in England before the Norman Conquest', in C. Harper-Bill and R. Harvey (eds.), *Medieval Knighthood IV* (Woodbridge, 1992)

    The English and the Norman Conquest (Woodbridge, 1995)

    'Land, Power and Politics: The Family and Career of Odda of Deerhurst' (published by The Friends of Deerhurst Church, 1997)

    'Lost Worlds: Kentish Society in the Eleventh Century', *Medieval Prosopography* 20 (1999)

    '*Princeps Merciorum Gentis*: The Family, Career and Connections of Ælfhere, Ealderman of Mercia', *Anglo-Saxon England* 10 (1981)

    'A West-Country Magnate of the Eleventh Century: The Family, Estates and Patronage of Beorhtric son of Ælfgar', in K.S.B. Keats-Rohan (ed.), *Family Trees and the Roots of Politics* (Woodbridge, 1997)

Wood-Leigh, K.L., 'The Knights' Attendance in the Parliaments of Edward III', *English Historical Review* 47 (1932)

    'Sheriffs, Lawyers and Belted Knights in the Parliaments of Edward III', *English Historical Review* 46 (1931)

Woolgar, C., 'Diet and Consumption in Gentry and Noble Households: A Case Study from around the Wash', in R.E. Archer and S. Walker (eds.), *Rulers and Ruled in Late Medieval England: Essays Presented to Gerald Harriss* (London, 1995)

Wormald, P., 'Charters, Law and the Settlement of Disputes in Anglo-Saxon England', in W. Davies and P. Fouracre (eds.), *The Settlement of Disputes in Early Medieval Europe* (Cambridge, 1986)

    'Lordship and Justice in the Early English Kingdom: Oswaldslow Revisited', in W. Davies and P. Fouracre (eds.), *Property and Power in the Early Middle Ages* (Cambridge, 1995)

    The Making of English Law: King Alfred to the Twelfth Century, I: *Legislation and Its Limits* (London, 1999)

Wright, S.M., *The Derbyshire Gentry in the Fifteenth Century* (Chesterfield, 1983)

Wrottesley, G., 'An Account of the Military Service Performed by Staffordshire Ten-ants in the Thirteenth and Fourteenth Centuries', in *Collections for a History of Staffordshire*, William Salt Archaeological Society 8 part 1 (1887)

Young, C.R., *The Royal Forests of Medieval England* (Leicester, 1979)

Zell, M.L., 'Early Tudor JPs at Work', *Archaeologia Cantiana* 93 (1977)

UNPUBLISHED THESES

Fernandes, M.J., 'The Role of the Midland Knights in the Period of Reform and Rebellion 1258–67' (Univ. of London PhD thesis, 2000)

Gorski, R.C., 'The Fourteenth-Century Sheriff: English Local Administration in the Late Middle Ages' (Univ. of Hull PhD thesis, 1999)

Illsley, J.S., 'The Essex Gentry in the Reign of Edward I' (Univ. of Cambridge MLitt thesis, 1971–2)

Knowles, C.H., 'The Disinherited 1265–80' (Univ. of Wales PhD thesis, 1959)

MacIver, T.E., 'Aspects of the Gentry of 13th-Century Hampshire' (Univ. of Oxford MLitt thesis, 1984)

Mullan, J.D., 'Landed Society and Locality in Gloucestershire, *c.*1240–80' (Univ. of Cardiff PhD thesis, 1999)

Quick, J.A., 'Government and Society in Kent 1232–1280' (Univ. of Oxford DPhil thesis, 1986)

Ridgeway, H.W., 'The Politics of the English Royal Court, 1247–65: With Special Reference to the Role of the Aliens' (Univ. of Oxford DPhil thesis, 1983)

Wales, C., 'The Knight in Twelfth Century Lincolnshire' (Univ. of Cambridge PhD thesis, 1983)

Woolgar, C.M., 'The Development of Accounts for Private Households in England to c.1500 AD' (Univ. of Durham PhD thesis, 1986)

Index

Aaron of Lincoln, Jew 84
Abberbury family 73
    Richard de 221
abbey or priory 63
abbots 32, 64, 114, 191, 217
Abels, Richard 20, 31
Abingdon, abbot and communities of 32
Acheson, E. 7
Acle, Robert de 50
Addington, Northamptonshire 56
administrators 17, 188, 245, 246, 248
    professional 67, 131, 135
administrators/men of law 199, 200, 244, 247
advowsons 80, 103
Ælfgyth, wife of Azur Swart 27
Æthelred, King 33
    Æthelred's laws 33
affinity 47, 134, 140, 170, 208
    magnate 17, 41, 42
Agillun, Hugh de 150
Agnes, daughter of Geoffrey de Charlecote 85
aids 99, 120
    of 1235–6 41
        collection of, in Northamptonshire 57
        collection of, in Warwickshire 60
Alcester, Warwickshire 179
Allesley, manor of, Warwickshire 93
Alneto, Henry de (of Maidford) 48
Alneto, Henry de (of Cornwall) 48
Alspath, Gerard de 65
Alstoe Hundred, Rutland 224
Amundevill
    Richard de (several) 60, 61, 153, 171
    Robert de 61
Andrew the Chaplain, French writer on love 37
Angevin
    legal processes 39, 45–51, 91, 92, 94–5
    legal reforms 12, 22, 38, 39, 42, 109, 110, 135, 202

legal system 45–51
    polity 12
Anglo-Norman literature 162
Anglo-Saxon Chronicle 32
Anglo-Saxon state, the late 11
Ansty, north of Coventry 196
approver 117, 118
Aquitaine 175
arbitration 8
archbishoprics 211
archbishops 32, 64, 114
Archer family, of Tanworth in Arden 233, 234, 236; pedigree 233
    John le (several) 233, 234
    Nicholas le 233
    Robert the archer 233
        William, his son 233, 234
    Brother Thomas le, prior of the hospital of St John of Jerusalem 233–4, 236
    Thomas le 236, 237
archers 226
d'Arcy
    Norman 81
    Sir Philip 81, 82, 83, 85
d'Arcy, Roger 137
Arden, Forest of 97
Arden
    Hugh de 67
    Robert de 192
    Thomas de 171
Ardens, of Radbourne 77
Ardens, of Ratley 77
aristocracy 7–8, 9, 29, 103, 108; service 29
Armenters
    Geoffrey de 55, 56, 57, 61
    Henry de 48
armies, of Edward III 242–3
armigers (*armigeri*) 217–29, 236, 242
arms, armour 81, 104, 219, 226

Past and Present Publications

General Editors: LYNDAL ROPER, *University of Oxford,* and
CHRIS WICKHAM, *University of Birmingham*

East-Central Europe in Transition: From the Fourteenth to the Seventeenth Century, edited by Antoni Mączak, Henryk Samsonowicz and Peter Burke*

Small Books and Pleasant Histories: Popular Fiction and Its Readership in Seventeenth-Century England, Margaret Spufford*

Society, Politics and Culture: Studies in Early Modern England, Mervyn James*

Horses, Oxen and Technological Innovation: The Use of Draught Animals in English Farming 1066–1500, John Langdon*

Nationalism and Popular Protest in Ireland, edited by C.H.E. Philpin*

Rituals of Royalty: Power and Ceremonial in Traditional Societies, edited by David Cannadine and Simon Price*

The Margins of Society in Late Medieval Paris, Bronislaw Geremek†

Landlords, Peasants and Politics in Medieval England, edited by T.H. Aston

Geography, Technology, and War: Studies in the Maritime History of the Mediterranean, 649–1571, John H. Pryor*

Church Courts, Sex and Marriage in England, 1570–1640, Martin Ingram*

Searches for an Imaginary Kingdom: The Legend of the Kingdom of Prester John, L.N. Gumilev

Crowds and History: Mass Phenomena in English Towns, 1790–1835, Mark Harrison*

Concepts of Cleanliness: Changing Attitudes in France since the Middle Ages, Georges Vigarello†

The First Modern Society: Essays in English History in Honour of Lawrence Stone, edited by A.L. Beier, David Cannadine and James M. Rosenheim

The Europe of the Devout: The Catholic Reformation and the Formation of a New Society, Louis Châtellier†

English Rural Society, 1500–1800: Essays in Honour of Joan Thirsk, edited by John Charters and David Hey

From Slavery to Feudalism in South-Western Europe, Pierre Bonnassie†

Lordship, Knighthood and Locality: A Study in English Society c. 1180–c. 1280, P.R. Coss

English and French Towns in Feudal Society: A Comparative Study, R.H. Hilton*

An Island for Itself: Economic Development and Social Change in Late Medieval Sicily, Stephan R. Epstein

Epidemics and Ideas: Essays on the Historical Perception of Pestilence, edited by Terence Ranger and Paul Slack*

The Political Economy of Shopkeeping in Milan, 1886–1922, Jonathan Morris*

After Chartism: Class and Nation in English Radical Politics, 1848–1874, Margot C. Finn

Commoners: Common Right, Enclosure and Social Change in England, 1700–1820, J.M. Neeson

Land and Popular Politics in Ireland: County Mayo from the Plantation to the Land War, Donald E. Jordan Jr.*

The Castilian Crisis of the Seventeenth Century: New Perspectives on the Economic and Social History of Seventeenth Century Spain, I.A.A. Thompson and Bartolomé Yun Casalilla

The Culture of Clothing: Dress and Fashion in the Ancien Régime, Daniel Roche†*

The Sense of the People: Politics, Culture and Imperialism in England, 1715–1785, Kathleen Wilson*

Witchcraft in Early Modern Europe: Studies in Culture and Belief, edited by Jonathan Barry, Marianne Hester and Gareth Roberts*

Fair Shares for All: Jacobin Egalitarianism in Practice, Jean-Pierre Gross

The Wild and the Sown: Botany and Agriculture in Western Europe, 1350–1850, Mauro Ambrosoli

* Also published in paperback
† Co-published with the Maison des Sciences de l'Homme, Paris